THE ROUTLEDGE COMPANION TO ASIAN AMERICAN MEDIA

The Routledge Companion to Asian American Media offers readers a comprehensive examination of the way that Asian Americans have engaged with media, from the long history of Asian American actors and stories that have been featured in mainstream film and television, to the birth and development of a distinctly Asian American cinema, to the ever-shifting frontiers of Asian American digital media. Contributor essays focus on new approaches to the study of Asian American media, including explorations of transnational and diasporic media, studies of intersectional identities encompassed by queer or mixed race Asian Americans, and examinations of new media practices that challenge notions of representation, participation, and community. Expertly organized to represent work across disciplines, this companion is an essential reference for the study of Asian American media and cultural studies.

Contributors: Vanessa Au, Shilpa Davé, Brian Hu, Elaine H. Kim, L. S. Kim, Rachel Kuo, Lori Kido Lopez, Ming-Yuen S. Ma, Kimberly D. McKee, Leilani Nishime, David C. Oh, Eve Oishi, Jun Okada, Vincent N. Pham, Takeo Rivera, Valerie Soe, Tony Tran, Cecilia S. Uy-Tioco, Grace Wang, and Myra Washington.

Lori Kido Lopez is an Assistant Professor of Media and Cultural Studies in the Communication Arts Department at the University of Wisconsin–Madison, where she is also affiliate faculty in the Asian American Studies Program and the Department of Gender and Women's Studies. She is the author of *Asian American Media Activism: Fighting for Cultural Citizenship* (NYU Press, 2016).

Vincent N. Pham is an Assistant Professor of Civic Communication and Media at Willamette University, where he is also affiliate faculty in the American Ethnic Studies program. He is the co-author of *Asian Americans and the Media* with Kent A. Ono (Polity, 2009).

THE ROUTLEDGE COMPANION TO ASIAN AMERICAN MEDIA

Edited by
Lori Kido Lopez
and Vincent N. Pham

Routledge
Taylor & Francis Group
NEW YORK AND LONDON

First published 2017
by Routledge
711 Third Avenue, New York, NY 10017

and by Routledge
2 Park Square, Milton Park, Abingdon, Oxon OX14 4RN

Routledge is an imprint of the Taylor & Francis Group, an Informa business

Library of Congress Cataloging in Publication Data
A catalog record for this book has been requested

ISBN: 978-1-138-84601-2 (hbk)
ISBN: 978-1-315-72774-5 (ebk)

Typeset in Bembo
by Deanta Global Publishing Services, Chennai, India

CONTENTS

CONTRIBUTORS

Vanessa Au is an event content manager at Tableau. She is also the co-founder and co-director of the Seattle Asian American Film Festival. Vanessa earned a PhD in Communication from the University of Washington. Her dissertation was titled *Contemporary Popular Culture and the Politics of Asian American Representation, Resistance, and Cultural Production*.

Shilpa Davé is Assistant Dean of the College of Arts and Sciences and Assistant Professor of Media Studies and American Studies at the University of Virginia. She is the author of *Indian Accents: Brown Voice and Racial Performance in American Television and Film* (2013) and co-editor of *Global Asian American Popular Cultures* (2016) and *East Main Street: Asian American Popular Culture* (2005).

Brian Hu is the artistic director of Pacific Arts Movement, presenters of the San Diego Asian Film Festival. He received his PhD in Cinema and Media Studies from UCLA and has published in *Screen*, *Velvet Light Trap*, *Film Quarterly*, and other journals. He teaches at the University of San Diego.

Elaine H. Kim is Professor of the Graduate School and Professor Emerita of Asian and Asian Diaspora Studies at UC Berkeley. She wrote, co-wrote, and co-edited ten books and co-produced and directed several films and videos on Asian American literature and culture. She is a recipient of the Association for Asian American Studies Lifetime Achievement Award.

L. S. Kim researches and teaches in television studies, Asian American cultural production, racial discourse analysis, feminist film theory and criticism, media, and social change. She is Associate Professor and Director of Graduate Studies in the Department of Film and Digital Media at the University of California, Santa Cruz.

Rachel Kuo is a doctoral student at New York University in the Department of Media, Culture, and Communication studying digital media organizing and racial justice activism.

Lori Kido Lopez is an Assistant Professor of Media and Cultural Studies in the Communication Arts Department at the University of Wisconsin–Madison, where she is also affiliate faculty in the Asian American Studies Program and the Department of Women's, Gender, and Sexuality Studies. She is the author of *Asian American Media Activism: Fighting for Cultural Citizenship* (2016).

Ming-Yuen S. Ma is Professor of Media Studies at Pitzer College, and the Co-Chair of Intercollegiate Media Studies at the Claremont Colleges. He is the co-editor of *Resolutions 3: Global Networks of Video* (2012), which won SCMS's Best Edited Volume Award in 2014. He is working on a new book, *There Is No Soundtrack: Theorizing Sound Culture through Experimental Media.*

Kimberly D. McKee is the director of the Kutsche Office of Local History and assistant professor in the Liberal Studies Department at Grand Valley State University. She also serves as the assistant director/secretary for KAAN (the Korean American Adoptee Adoptive Family Network).

Leilani Nishime is an Associate Professor of Communication and an Adjunct Professor of Gender, Women and Sexuality Studies at the University of Washington. She is the author of *Undercover Asians: Multiracial Asian Americans in Visual Culture* and the co-editor of *Global Asian American Media* and *East Main Street*, and has published articles in numerous journals and collections.

David C. Oh received his PhD from Syracuse University. He is an Assistant Professor of Communication Arts at Ramapo College of New Jersey. He researches Asian/American representations in U.S. media, Korean American diasporas and mediated identities, and multiculturalism in Korean media.

Eve Oishi is Associate Professor of Cultural Studies at Claremont Graduate University. Her research is on Asian American, queer, and experimental film and video. Her work has appeared in anthologies and journals including *Signs*; *Women's Studies Quarterly*; *Camera Obscura*; and *Aztlan*. She is also an independent film and video curator.

Jun Okada is associate professor in the Department of English at State University of New York, where she teaches film studies and writing. Her book *Making Asian American Film and Video: History, Institutions, Movements* was published by Rutgers University Press in 2015. She has published essays and reviews in such journals as *Cinema Journal*, *Film Quarterly*, *The Velvet Light Trap*, and *Screen*.

Vincent N. Pham is an Assistant Professor of Civic Communication and Media at Willamette University. He is the co-author of *Asian Americans and the Media* with Kent Ono.

Takeo Rivera is a PhD candidate in Performance Studies at UC Berkeley whose work focuses on masochism, techno-orientalism, and masculinity in Asian American cultural politics. He is also a playwright whose work has been staged in New York City, Los Angeles, and the San Francisco Bay Area.

Valerie Soe is Associate Professor of Asian American Studies at San Francisco State University. Her award-winning experimental videos, documentaries, and installations have exhibited worldwide. She has published extensively on Asian and Asian American art, film, culture, social media, and activism, and she is the author of the blog *beyondasiaphilia.com*.

Tony Tran is a PhD candidate at the University of Wisconsin-Madison. His research explores online and offline Vietnamese diasporic cultures in urban spaces.

Cecilia S. Uy-Tioco is an assistant professor in the Department of Communication at California State University San Marcos and holds a PhD in Cultural Studies from George Mason University. Her research focuses on the Philippine mobile phone industry and the reproduction of power and new media and transnational migration.

Grace Wang is Associate Professor of American Studies at University of California, Davis and the author of *Soundtracks of Asian America: Navigating Race through Musical Performance* (2015).

Myra Washington is an Assistant Professor at the University of New Mexico specializing in critical cultural and media studies. Her research focuses primarily on race, non-White racially mixed people, and popular culture. She connects mediated representations to cultural formations, and looks for possibilities in those relationships. Myra enjoys ocean expanses, everything yellow, and Nutella.

ACKNOWLEDGMENTS

We extend our warmest thanks to all of our contributors, whose work inspires and excites us. The Asian American media studies community is small but mighty, and we are thrilled to have played a role in creating a bigger and more public space for your work—may the conversations started here extend long into the future. Thanks to Erica Wetter at Routledge for agreeing that this collection was a good idea and supporting us throughout the process, always with such kindness. Thanks also to our reviewers for strengthening this collection with their advice. Lori would like to thank her colleagues in the University of Wisconsin–Madison Communication Arts Department and Asian American Studies Program, her parents Doug and Sharlene, her dog Boba, and her life partner Jason Kido Lopez. Vincent would like to thank his old colleagues at California State University San Marcos and his new ones at Willamette University's Department of Civic Communication and Media, his mother Phuong Pham, and siblings in the Midwest, his dog Kopi, his life partner Yaejoon Kwon, and wonderfully cute-yet-occasionally grumpy child Jovin MinHo Pham-Kwon.

1

INTRODUCTION

Why Asian American Media Matters

Lori Kido Lopez and Vincent N. Pham

2015 marked a banner year for Asian Americans in the media. In early 2015, ABC premiered *Fresh Off the Boat*—the first Asian American sitcom since the legendary failure of Margaret Cho's *All American Girl* in 1994. The adaptation of celebrity chef Eddie Huang's memoir was met with excitement from both audiences and critics, and was eventually renewed for additional seasons. In late 2015, ABC did the unthinkable and released a second Asian American sitcom. *Dr Ken* starred Ken Jeong of *The Hangover* fame, and was loosely based on Jeong's life as a doctor. Along with the prominence of Asian American actors like Aziz Ansari, John Cho, Mindy Kaling, Kal Penn, Ming-Na Wen, Sandra Oh, and many others, it seemed that Asian Americans had finally arrived, particularly within the television landscape.

Yet there was barely time to celebrate these victories before Asian Americans were cut back down to size. At the 2016 Academy Awards, comedian Chris Rock slammed Asian Americans in a distasteful joke featuring three Asian child actors. Rock described the kids as accountants from the firm PricewaterhouseCoopers, stating: "They sent us their most dedicated, accurate, and hard-working representatives. Please welcome Ming Zhu, Bao Ling, and David Moskowitz. If anybody's upset about that joke, just tweet about it on your phone that was also made by these kids." The anti-Asian sentiment felt particularly out of place at an event where Hollywood's racism problem was already on full display. Prior to the event, the Academy had been roundly condemned for failing to nominate people of color in the acting categories. On social media, commenters used the hashtag #OscarsSoWhite, originally created by writer April Reign, to call attention to the obvious inequalities. While the ceremony was flooded with Black presenters and Rock addressed the controversy in multiple jokes, it was clear that race was only understood as a Black/White issue. As usual, Asian Americans were left out of the picture.

Although the recent visibility of Asian American concerns with regard to media issues seems novel, it most certainly is not new. For the last 50 years, Asian American artists and storytellers have utilized moving images to share their cultures, histories, and traditions both inside and outside their own communities. Their continued passion for doing so reminds us why Asian American media matters—it gives Asian Americans the ability to document and create representations of themselves, and in doing so, sustain community identities and develop a sense of belonging in the United States, where over 19 million Asian Americans continue to struggle against racism and cultural exclusion. In the last decade we have begun to see shifts in the symbolic landscape, as a growing number of Asian Americans are being featured as actors, writers, and directors for television and film. From becoming bona fide Hollywood blockbuster directors like Justin Lin (the *Fast and Furious* franchise) and Jennifer Yuh Nelson (*Kung Fu Panda*) to dominating the YouTube scene, Asian Americans have become more prominent in mainstream and niche media and across various media platforms. But this move toward the mainstream does not even begin to describe the complicated pathways that Asian American scholars are now charting as they investigate the meaning behind these shifts. What do Asian Americans bring to mainstream media that reshapes public culture and ideas of race? How does Asian American participation in online and digital media shift notions of media representation? How can we revisit a history of Asian American media in ways that reinvigorate our understanding of the present and future?

Past explorations have yielded a small but important body of work that laid the foundation for understanding Asian American media. An edited anthology called *Moving the Image: Independent Asian Pacific American Media Arts* (Leong 1992) was one of the first collections to explore some of these themes, mixing essays from academics, artists, and filmmakers in their exploration of the early days of Asian American cinema. *Countervisions: Asian American Film Criticism* (Hamamoto and Liu 2000) and *Screening Asian Americans* (2002) discuss early Asian American film and video with essays on the specific films that shaped the direction of the field in its infancy, while *Identities in Motion* (2002) by Peter X Feng focuses on Asian American filmmakers and their representations of Asian American identity. These seminal texts have been integral in charting the development of Asian American cinema and the contours of its representations. Yet, the category of "Asian American media" expands far beyond film, including a wide range of media, such as television, music, advertising, and mobile and digital media. There is also a need to examine the complex media industries and institutions in which Asian Americans are now playing a key role.

Some of these issues have been taken up within Kent Ono and Vincent Pham's *Asian Americans in the Media* (2009) and two edited collections: *East Main Street: Asian American Popular Culture* (2005) and the follow-up *Global Asian American Popular Cultures* (2016), co-edited by Shilpa Davé, Leilani Nishime, and Tasha Oren. Yet the landscape of Asian America is always changing beneath us, and there is an urgent need for producing original scholarship that examines Asian American media issues specifically from a media studies or communication perspective, shedding the constraints of literary theory or sociology that have long provided interdisciplinary lenses of analysis in the field. In this collection we have assembled a wide diversity of scholars who approach the study of Asian American media on its own terms, rigorously historicizing their work from the scholarship that has come before while charting new pathways and innovative approaches. Although we recognize that we cannot possibly explore all the aspects of Asian American media, this book attempts to probe the breadth and depth of its contours—examining both historical and contemporary texts, considering all facets of media production and consumption, and including the often marginalized voices of queer, mixed race, transnational, and diasporic Asian Americans.

Postracial Media Environments, Industries, and the Relocation of Asian America

In posing a response to the contemporary challenges of Asian American media in an evolving mediasphere, a number of common themes began to organically emerge across the contributions from our authors. First, scholars must contend with the "postracial" context that has come to influence so many conversations about racialized communities, identities, and cultural products. It has become widely accepted that race is a social construction, constituting an insoluble way of living and being in the world. Yet, the postracial context assumes that race is no longer an issue and that treating it as such serves to divide and constrain U.S. society. As a result, media and media makers have responded accordingly to survive in a postracial (and capitalist) media environment by choosing to remain silent on racial issues, avoiding explicit assertions of racial identification, or to highlight race only in terms of ethnic flavor and difference. Across the different chapters in this collection, postraciality emerges as an unavoidable aspect of contemporary life that scholars must account for in understanding how Asian American media attends to this new environment. Responses to postraciality are seen taking place through sounds, accents, coded ways of dealing with identity, commercialization, and more. Yet the evidence of postraciality and the ways Asian American media reify or oppose it remains a challenge to Asian American media going forth.

As the postracial context becomes the norm, another recurring theme for Asian American media scholars is a grappling with contemporary relationships to media industries—including negotiating relations between mainstream and independent, "new" and "old" media forms, and physical versus online spaces. Foundational scholarship on Asian American media often focused within the confines of a single setting—most commonly, film or television. Yet such boundaries and borders have become increasingly porous in response to media convergence, with media makers, organizers, and consumers easily traversing different media platforms in search of content. Asian American media no longer operates as an independent silo or community-driven endeavor, but now additionally helps provide exposure and training for those who are involved. Asian American film festivals utilize digital and social media tools to connect with new audiences or to drive conversations, while online producers call attention to independent films and mainstream media. These complex engagements enrich the scope and impacts of media representations through their interactive and participatory modes, and demand sensitivity in accounting for their possibilities and limitations.

Finally, as we consider the question of why Asian American media matters, we posit relocation as an important theme that reminds us to continually ask where Asian America resides. The concept of relocation operates both physically and metaphorically, particularly in examining relocations via transnational and diasporic flows of bodies, ideas, and technologies. Whether it is through ethnic media, documentary film, or mobile platforms, Asian American media's purview of the local is no longer confined to the United States, but instead shifts in relation to the locations of its users and their interconnected networks. In the chapters that follow, we can begin to relocate the margins and move participating voices to the center in efforts to show the possibilities for Asian American media in moving forward. Overlooked forms of media and previously unheard stories can then come to the forefront and blaze new paths for the study of Asian American media.

Outline of Chapters

This book is organized into five parts, although there is significant thematic overlap between and among them. The first section, "Theorizing Representation: Visions and Voices of Asian America," contains chapters that lay a theoretical groundwork for the analysis of Asian Americans and media. They ask: how has Asian American media been studied in the past, and what kind of research has been missing? What belongs to the category of "Asian American media," and more importantly, what is its social and political significance? The collection opens with two pieces exploring the important role of sound, which is often overlooked in favor of focusing on visuality and representation in Asian American media. Ming-Yuen S. Ma takes us back to the early days of Asian American cinema and examines the relationship between mediated sound and the much-heralded creation of an "Asian American voice." Ma asks whose voices are audible and whose are silenced in early Asian American independent films, positing the power of what he calls the "negative voice" to more accurately represent the struggles and experiences of Asian American communities. Grace Wang continues this investigation of sound in "Diasporic Soundscapes of Belonging: Mediating Chineseness with Shanghai Restoration Project." Her analysis moves into our current era, where she argues that one way of addressing questions about Asian America and its global relationship to Asia is through music. She particularly focuses on David Liang's Shanghai Restoration Project, whose blending of Chinese traditional instruments and electronic hip-hop beats creates a sonic landscape that reflects the transnational sensibilities and search for belonging that are familiar to many Asian Americans today.

These questions about what constitutes fluid and shifting categories such as "Asian American music" are also at the heart of Jun Okada's chapter, which examines who belongs to the category of the "Asian American artist." In her exploration of the biracial artist and filmmaker Laurel Nakadate, Okada asks if it is possible for an Asian American to disavow race when collective identification has so long defined Asian American politics. Her examination of the way that Nakadate's media works express feelings of loneliness and alienation helps to explode these categories and make room for a new and politically productive form of postraciality. While the categories of Asian American music, sound, and art are shifting, so is the role of Asian American media organizations that attempt to coordinate these media. In Vincent N. Pham's chapter, he returns to the Center for Asian American Media, one of the oldest and most recognizable Asian American media organizations in the nation, and examines the discourse at its Present/Future Summit event, which sought to assess the state of Asian American media. His analysis of the public discussion reveals the particular anxieties and concerns of Asian American media makers and organizations as they deal with the paradigm-shifting presence of digital media, examining both its complications and potential for creating a financially stable yet apolitical system of storytelling.

Many scholars who are interested in the field of Asian American media studies are also drawn to the artistic and professional media world, where their hands-on participation as practitioners can result in a very different kind of intervention than in traditional academia. Ma, Okada, and Pham remind us in their chapters that Asian American media has always been a deeply political practice, premised on the ability of media to promote social justice and impact communities on the ground. As such, it is not uncommon to see Asian American media studies professors and graduate students taking up parallel careers as directors of film festivals, filmmakers, or media arts organizers. We are excited to highlight the writing and unique perspectives of four "scholar-practitioners" in this collection. Their insights are grounded in a productive blend of academic literature and personal experience, as each has spent significant time immersed in the world of Asian American filmmaking and film festivals. Brian Hu is the artistic director of Pacific Arts Movement and the presenter of the San Diego Asian Film Festival, while Vanessa Au is the director of the Seattle Asian American Film Festival. Both are interested in the evolution of the Asian American film festival from its earliest iterations to today. Hu examines the contentious rise of the feature film and the way that Asian American film festivals have both celebrated and maligned this particular form. While some believe that the feature film represents mainstream acceptance and financial viability, others see it as capitulating to market forces that negate the political impact of alternative media. Au similarly recognizes the difficulties of programming Asian American content in an increasingly diversified media landscape and worries about the continued relevance of Asian American film festivals. Yet in drawing on her own experiences, she is able to put forward a powerful set of strategies for adapting to the digital environment so that Asian American film festivals can continue to survive and thrive.

Elaine H. Kim and Valerie Soe both explore what they believe must be recognized as important contributions to the Asian American film canon—Kim examines feature films made by women directors, while Soe examines contemporary documentary films and their political messages. Kim is the co-founder of Asian Women United of California and director of documentaries such as *Slaying the Dragon: Asian Women in U.S. Television and Film* (1988) and *Slaying the Dragon: Reloaded* (2010). Her chapter calls attention to the works of Asian American female filmmakers, assessing films by Bertha Bay-Sa Pan, Alice Wu, and Jennifer Phang. Her analysis is based on interpretations of the way that their films deal with issues of race, gender, and culture, alongside observations based on her own conversations with the filmmakers themselves. Soe is an award-winning experimental videomaker whose productions include *The Chinese Gardens*, *The Oak Park Story*, *"All Orientals Look The Same," Mixed Blood*, *Picturing Oriental Girls: A (Re) Educational Videotape*, and many others. Her examination of recent documentary films reminds us that there are still important nonfiction stories being told about Asian Americans today, but points out that their focus has shifted from examining community struggles to focusing on the rise of individual Asian American celebrities.

The borders of what constitutes "Asian America" itself are always in need of revising. In our third section, "Hybrid Asian Americans: Media at the Margins," four authors examine populations whose experiences are often marginalized or even negated: queer, transracially adopted, and mixed race Asian Americans. Eve Oishi looks at the doubly marginalized category of queer experimental Asian American film, a category that she argues needs new methodological approaches in order to make sense of its development. Kimberly D. McKee's exploration of documentaries made by Korean adoptees reminds us that when we open our lens to include such perspectives, the works that emerge have the potential to shatter previous discourses and mythologies about adoption. The adoptee-authored documentaries *In the Matter of Cha Jung Hee* (2010) and *Resilience* (2009) recast adoption and family reunification as lifelong processes that impact birth families, not just adoptees and the families who "save" them.

Leilani Nishime and Myra Washington both examine mediated representations of mixed race Asian Americans—a population that has long been thrust into the spotlight as an object of visual fixation. Nishime analyzes the ideologies espoused within the supposedly celebratory *Mixed Blood* photographic exhibition and compares it to a collaborative digital project called *We Are the 15%*. She argues that the genre of the family portrait offers a productive lens for interrogating the relationship between mixed race families and narratives of nation, globalization, and the idealized national family. Washington similarly asks about the way that global racial politics intersect with the bodies of mixed race individuals in her analysis of Blasian performers on reality television. Her analysis of *The Voice* performers Tessanne Chin and Judith Hill broadens the analysis of Asian American identities beyond serving to disrupt the Black/White binary; mixed race Black and Asian individuals stem from a long history of global relations and are interpreted in multiple ways by viewers and themselves. As a result, Washington sees representations of Blasians as a productive site for challenging essentialist notions of identity and racial paradigms altogether.

As Nishime's work reminds us, the digital landscape itself deserves examination for its unique affordances as an interactive, participatory way for Asian Americans to directly engage with media. Chapters from the fourth section, "Asian American New Media: Digital Artifacts,

Networks, and Lives," focus specifically on Asian American engagements with new media technologies and the possibilities that they open up. Lori Kido Lopez sets the stage by pointing to the highly visible successes of Asian Americans on YouTube, where a small set of videographers have dominated for so long that digitally native youth are growing up in a world where Asian American representations have always been accessible. She asks how "the next generation" of Asian American YouTubers are now building from these successes by opening up spaces for ethnically specific forms of discourse that heavily rely upon the communicative properties of memes. L. S. Kim builds on the strengths of Asian Americans in the online arena to ask how we can use digital media to intervene in larger conversations about race and representation, like those that have long centered around Asian Americans on television. She posits her theorization of the "matrix stage" as one possibility, arguing that the space between the margin and the mainstream and its interrelated elements is where Asian Americans are gaining power. Her example of the interplay between television's *Fresh Off the Boat* and YouTube's *Fresh Off the Show* demonstrates the way that Asian Americans are using multiple forms of media and multiple forms of participation to voice their demands. In her chapter "Reflections on #Solidarity: Intersectional Movements in AAPI Communities," Rachel Kuo moves beyond entertainment media to explore the political potential for Asian American activists who are using online media. She is able to historicize recent hashtag campaigns by comparing their rhetoric to the arguments deployed by Asian American activists in the 1970s and 1980s, including Asian Women United (AWU), the Asian American Legal Defense Fund, and Asian Cinevision. Her deep dive into these archival materials reminds us that digital discourses may open new possibilities for participation, but that the fight for intersectional solidarity is both longstanding and ongoing.

The interactivity and potential for engagement via new media technologies are intensified in Takeo Rivera's exploration of the video game *World of Warcraft*—the world's highest-grossing video game, played by millions of people every day. While there are countless video games that problematically rely upon negative stereotypes and characterizations of racial minorities, Rivera is interested in what it means when *World of Warcraft* adds an expansion with a distinctly Oriental twist—it takes place on "Pandaria" and is inhabited by panda people. He analyzes its gameplay through the Foucauldian lens of biopower, asking how its racial logics are connected to the need to control populations, and what it means to "play" with racial identification in this way.

In the final section, scholars work to relocate and expand the borders of "Asian America" in their examinations of diasporic and transnational communities. The history of Asian American community formations has long had a troubled relationship with the global. While there have been many attempts to emphasize national citizenship and belonging in the United States, the reality is that many who identify as Asian American are immigrants themselves, possess dual citizenship, or otherwise maintain vital pathways between Asia and the United States. These chapters examine the role that media play in reifying the complicated connections between Asia and the United States, examining film, television, print magazines, websites, and mobile phone technologies. It opens with Tony Tran's investigation of two films made in the Vietnamese diaspora, *Owl and the Sparrow* [*Cú và Chim Se Sẻ*] and *The Rebel* [*Dòng Máu Anh Hùng*]. He conducts two different readings of the films with regard to themes of family, considering the potentially different audiences in Vietnam and the United States. In doing so, he points to the consequences of hybridity in shaping reception, particularly for films that are transnational in both production and distribution. David C. Oh looks at the now-defunct magazine *KoreAm Journal* and its website as an example of media targeted to a second-generation diasporic audience. Like Tran, he sees hybridity as a key analytic framework for making sense of the way that the transnational diasporas are addressed and constituted. Oh puts forward a hybrid diasporic approach as a way of making sense of the complex dynamics of ethnicity, race, nation, and cultural identities that shape discourses in ethnic media outlets such as *KoreAm Journal*.

Shilpa Davé specifically focuses on the issue of accent in negotiating diasporic identities, assessing the depiction of call center workers on NBC's 2010–2011 series *Outsourced*. Like Ma's and Wang's chapters early in the collection, Davé emphasizes aural analysis over the visual mode that often dominates in media studies. She finds that even in a show set in India, the Indian accent is still homogenized and marked as less desirable. Yet, the show also uses its nuanced, multiple characterizations to challenge these hierarchies and the way that they uphold the dominance of the United States and its cultural values. In the final chapter, Cecilia S. Uy-Tioco moves beyond the way that Asian Americans are represented by media producers to examine the polymedia environment in which professional, "elite" Filipino immigrants exist. She asks what communication platforms are used and why, looking in particular at the social media sites, digital apps, and Voice over Internet Protocols that facilitate connections between transnational Filipino families. Beyond considering the impact of emotion on which technologies are used to communicate with loved ones, she also considers the role that communication technologies play in facilitating emotional relationships and connections to the homeland for those who live overseas. This kind of scholarship reminds us that media provide a vessel not only for sounds and images, but also for the production and maintenance of emotions, identities, political affiliations, cultures and values, and so much more. In centering scholarly inquiries on Asian Americans and their specific relationships to media, this collection more broadly serves to widen our understanding of how the ever-changing media landscape continues to impact the lives of Asian American communities.

References

Davé, Shilpa, Leilani Nishime, and Tasha Oren (eds). 2005. *East Main Street: Asian American Popular Culture*. New York: NYU Press.

Davé, Shilpa, Leilani Nishime, and Tasha Oren (eds). 2016. *Global Asian American Popular Cultures*. New York: NYU Press.

Feng, Peter X. (ed). 2002. *Screening Asian Americans*. New Brunswick: Rutgers University Press.

Feng, Peter X. 2002. *Identities in Motion: Asian American Film and Video*. Durham: Duke University Press.

Hamamoto, Darrell Y. and Sandra Liu (eds). 2000. *Countervisions: Asian American Film Criticism*. Philadelphia: Temple University Press.

Leong, Russell. 1991. *Moving the Image: Independent Asian Pacific American Media Arts*. Los Angeles: UCLA Asian American Studies Center and Visual Communications, Southern California Asian American Studies Central.

Ono, Kent A. and Vincent N. Pham. 2009. *Asian Americans and the Media*. Cambridge: Polity Press.

Part I

THEORIZING REPRESENTATION

VISIONS AND VOICES OF ASIAN AMERICA

2

CLAIMING A VOICE

Speech, Self-Expression, and Subjectivity in Early Asian American Independent Media

Ming-Yuen S. Ma

The work of Asian American media arts centers is often said to be historically significant because of its role in giving Asian Americans "a voice." This narrative is particularly dominant in Arthur Dong's *Claiming a Voice: The Visual Communications Story* (1990), a documentary that chronicles "the twenty-year history of the first arts group dedicated to productions by and about Asian Pacific Americans" (Dong n.d.). In interviews with the founding members of Visual Communications (VC), we learn about what was at stake in creating a center for producing and exhibiting Asian American independent media in the late 1960s and early 1970s. However, despite the documentary's title, there is very little discussion in it actually focusing on the Asian American voice. Rather, the voice in the documentary's title refers to self-representation in predominantly visual terms. This includes media images and narratives from film, video, photography, print-based media such as cartoons and comics, mass-distributed texts including novels, plays, newspapers, advertisement, and other forms—things to watch and read. Linda Mabalot, longtime executive director of VC, articulates its mission as being "a part of this whole movement of seeing how we can utilize media as a form to empower our communities. So in terms of the arts, that meant creating our own images that counter the stereotypical images that were in the media, that were really racist."[1] Mabalot's statement highlights visuality as central to the struggle for Asian American self-representation. The voice that is claimed here is primarily seen first, and then heard.

Yet, *Claiming a Voice* is full of Asian American voices. The documentary is built around a series of interviews with VC's founders and staff, as well as the group of Asian American artists, writers, and musicians who have been featured in or have collaborated with VC in their media productions. These interviews are shot in what is commonly called the "talking head" format, in which the subject directly addresses the camera (and by extension, the audience) in a synchronized audio-visual representation. This representational strategy accentuates the fact that we are seeing Asian Americans as themselves, and listening to them speak in their own voices. Films made at and through VC are excerpted throughout the documentary, and collectively they speak as a larger representational "voice" that is then put in dialogue with the voice interviews discussing VC's history. Eddie Wong, one of VC's founders and a filmmaker, makes the connection between speaking, voice, and representation particularly clear in the discussion of his film *Wong Sinsaang* (1971):

> At the time, I had just finished reading the autobiography of Malcolm X, and I began to understand a little bit more about what was discussed as "colonial relations," where people who are colonized relate to their parents in a very ... Well, in a very stilted manner. They see them through the eyes of their oppressors. And in this case, with my father, I saw him as someone who was subservient most of his life, having to deal with these white customers, who would often be verbally abusive. And so I really saw the film as someone re-examining his relationship with his own father, and trying to explain this person with a whole other life, beyond the stereotype was a whole other life that most people would never see.[2]

Here, the lack of a voice—Wong relating to his father in a stilted manner and his father's verbal abuse by White customers—is connected to his father's silence and hidden "voice," a subjectivity that Wong seeks to represent in the film. Other voices are also heard on *Claiming a Voice*'s soundtrack, and these Asian American voices sing, recite poetry, recall oral history, talk story, swear, joke, laugh, and otherwise vocalize in a variety of accents and often more than one language.

In this chapter, I examine a representative program of early Asian American independent media to further explore the complex and sometimes contradictory relationships between the claiming of an Asian American "voice" and the many voices heard on the soundtracks of early Asian American films. I argue that the conceptual ocularcentrism in *Claiming a Voice* and its celebration of a multivocal and syncretic Asian American voice is reflected in the larger discourse of Asian American media scholarship and cultural criticism. Further, multivocality and syncretism are defining characteristics of this Asian American "voice", and are key to discussions of Asian American identity and subjectivity. The audio-visual relationships constructed in these early Asian American films often de-emphasize the realist tropes of a visible and clearly identified speaker: one whose voice is tightly synchronized to its visual image. Instead, there is a predominance of disembodied speakers and loosely or non-synchronized audio-visual relationships in these germinal media representations of Asian American subjectivity. Additionally, the bi- or multilingual Asian American communities formed through immigration and migration, colonial relationships, racist discrimination, and cultural protectionism further complicate any attempt to define a singular Asian American voice.

I also explore the way that the male-dominated roster of early Asian American filmmakers directly or indirectly resulted in the silencing of women's voices in these early films. In turning to a group of more recent experimental videos produced by Asian American women artists, we can see the deployment of opaque and "negative voices"—absent or barely articulated words as well as the nonverbal qualities of the voice—as their primary conveyors of meaning. These videos are also focused on exploring the experiences of historical trauma by Asian and Asian American women and men. My critique of the ocularcentrism in Asian American independent media production and scholarship is thus accompanied by a questioning of whether our voices must be translated, comprehensible, or even audible to articulate Asian American experiences. What I found through listening to and watching these videos is that we must listen to what is not said: that when it comes to the subjective experiences of memory, migration, exile, and trauma, the materiality of Asian American voices can speak volumes without uttering a single word.

Voice, Subjectivity, and Asian American Identity

What are the stakes for Asian Americans in the broader discourse on voice and subjectivity? And is there, as the VC documentary's title suggests, a uniquely Asian American voice that can be claimed? Scholars of the voice have explored the significance of spoken language and what it can communicate to the self and others. Jonathan Sterne writes: "Voices are among the most personalized and most naturalized forms of subjective self-expression; speakers and auditors routinely treat them as the stuff of consciousness" (Sterne 2012: 491). Ferdinand de Saussure (1983) examines both spoken language and its "deep structure" from the perspectives of structuralism and semiotics, while Marshall McLuhan (1962) and Walter Ong (1982) both privilege a voice-centered, universal orality over writing in their respective theories of communication. Edmund Husserl (1962) and Don Ihde (1976) have also emphasized voice and listening in their phenomenological investigation. Interestingly, Jacques Derrida (1973) is equally focused on the experience of listening to one's voice in his critique of Husserl's model of phenomenology. This critique is centered on what Derrida calls the "metaphysics of presence." He argues that speaking—long considered to be a fundamental act of human subjective communication—is, in fact, an act of "pure auto-affection" that is built on a set of differences. He writes:

> To speak to someone is doubtless to hear oneself speak, to be heard by oneself; but, at the same time, if one is heard by another, to speak is to make him *repeat immediately* in himself the hearing-oneself-speak in the very form in which I effectuated it. This immediate repetition is a reproduction of pure auto-affection without the help of anything external.

For Derrida, this auto-affection, enabled by hearing one's own voice while speaking, is also fundamental to any assertions of subjecthood: "This auto-affection is no doubt the possibility for what is called *subjectivity* or the *for-itself*, but, without it, no world *as such* would appear" (Derrida 1973: 79–80).

Within cinema and media studies, the voice has been a specialized area of study; although, as Michel Chion asserts, "there are voices, and then everything else" (Chion 1999: 5). He reminds us that the human voice speaking dialogue is likely the most important sound heard in the majority of commercially released films today.[3] He traces the origins of what he considers the most uniquely cinematic voice—the *acousmêtre*, a disembodied vocal subject—back to the primal experience of the infant hearing its mother's voice while still in the "uterine darkness" of her womb (Chion 1999: 61–62). Kaja Silverman has critiqued Chion's dystopic origin myth of the powerful and malevolent *acousmêtre* as a patriarchal fantasy exhibiting a fear of entrapment that is symptomatic of "an ambivalence that attests to the divided nature of subjectivity" (Silverman 1988: 72). Indeed, Freudian and Lacanian psychoanalysis has played a pivotal role in the theorizing of voice in cinema, especially in the work of feminist film theorists, including Silverman (1991), Mary Ann Doane (1985), and others. A parallel body of scholarship centering on female vocality in music also developed around this time. Pioneered by feminist musicologists, these studies of female voice and subjectivity in diverse musical forms ranging from opera to the blues soon expanded into the examination of other forms, including Shakespearean plays and classical mythology. They also joined with the aforementioned work in feminist film theory, marking the 1990s and early 2000s as an important time in the interdisciplinary scholarship on voice among U.S. feminists.[4] These theories and criticisms, centered on female voices and built around the psychoanalytical emphasis on the subconscious, drives, fantasies, and trauma, have informed our understanding of the complexities and contradictions in the process of subject formation.

As the title of Dong's documentary suggests, the symbolism of the voice and its accompanying discourse are also key to the discussion of race and subjectivity. The slogans and speeches from racial civil rights movements are peppered with terms such as "breaking the silence" and "reclaiming our voices." Liberationist writing, poetry, and songs are often collected in volumes titled "The Voice of …" It is also a common moniker for activist media projects, including radio and documentaries, which seek to represent a marginalized community or speak from a minoritarian perspective. Postcolonial discourse, such as in the work of Frantz Fanon, explores the importance of how speech and language are deployed as tools of domination in colonial as well as other oppressive regimes (Fanon 1963, 1967). It follows, then, that decolonization and other liberationist movements often highlight the unlearning of the colonizer's imposed language and resistance to its linguistically embedded cultural values, which are accompanied by the rediscovery and cultivation of native language, culture, and beliefs—the reclaiming of the "mother tongue." Poetry and oratorical performance by voices as diverse as Martin Luther King, Jr, Malcolm X, Langston Hughes, Amir Baraka/LeRoi Jones, Alice Walker, Maya Angelou, and many others have been vital testimonials to the African American Civil Rights Movement, while more contemporary iterations by Audre Lorde, June Jordan, Sapphire, Essex Hempill, Donald Wood, Assoto Saint, and others articulate more complex experiences incorporating race along with the issues of gender and sexuality. Chicana poets Cherríe Moraga and Glora Anzaldúa, in turn, explore the bilingual articulation of identity and subjecthood through the cultivation of *mestizaje* voices that speak and write in "Spanglish"—a hybrid of Spanish and English. The bi- and multilingual voice is similarly central to the work of Asian American writers and poets, including Maxine Hong Kingston, Frank Chin, Lawson Inada, and others.[5] It is no accident that the title of a seminal collection of Asian American writing, published in 1974, is itself a vocalization: *Aiiieeeee!*[6]

At around the same time as defining articulations of the Asian American "voice" in literature were being compiled and published in collections including *Aiiieeeee!*, young, predominantly male Asian American filmmakers including Wong, Duane Kubo, Robert Nakamura, Alan Ohashi, Steven Tatsukawa and others were producing their first filmic representations of Asian American experiences in UCLA's Ethno-Communications program. Ethno-Communications was an alternative film school founded at UCLA "as a response to the Watts Rebellion in Los Angeles in 1965 and the civil rights movement and in 'immediate response to student complaints about racial exclusivity' of the UCLA School of Film and Television, renowned for graduating white, male directors" (Okada 2015: 15). Ethno-Communications was ground zero for independent cinema by filmmakers of color in the late 1960s and early 1970s, and its participants, including Charles Burnett, Ben Caldwell, Moctezuma Esparza, Barbara McCullough, Sylvia Morales, Sandra and Yasu Osawa, Jose Luis Ruiz, and Richard Wells, in addition to the Asian American filmmakers named above, became some of the most important independent filmmakers of color and media activists in the 1970s and 1980s.[7] Its ethos was influenced by Third Cinema and other liberationist media movements, and especially by the films and writing of Latin American filmmakers, including Glauber Rocha, Fernando Solanas, Octavio Getino, and Julio Garcia Espinosa (Leong 1991: xx). Many of these first-generation Asian American graduates of Ethno-Communications went on to form VC, serving as the first staff members of the oldest Asian American media arts center in the U.S.

Voice and "Voice" in Early Asian American Independent Films

I now turn my attention to a body of work produced by the first generation of self-identified Asian American filmmakers to explore, through in-depth analyses of selected films, how voice is deployed in them as well as whose "voices" are claimed in these films. "Asian American Ethnos: A Twentieth Anniversary Retrospective" is a program of six short films curated by Abraham Ferrer, exhibitions director at VC, for the 1990 Los Angeles Asian Pacific American Film Festival.[8] It included works by students in Ethno-Communications' first and second classes, with most of the films completed between 1970 and 1973. Their origins in Ethno-Communications and the date of their production make the films in "Asian American Ethnos" comparable to the Asian American writing collected in *Aiiieeeee!* While there were certainly Asian media makers and artists working in the United States prior to the 1970s, most of them were associated with the visual arts, including Theresa Hak Kyung Cha, Nam June Paik, Shigeko Kubota, and Yoko Ono; or avant-garde and underground film, including Fu-Ding Cheng and Arne Wong.

I argue that the Ethno-Communications filmmakers are uniquely Asian American in three ways: one, they have a critical mass at UCLA and later at VC; two, they have a direct connection to social protest movements of the 1960s and 1970s, especially to grassroots political and cultural organizing among Asian Americans; and three, the profound influence of the graduates, such as in the founding of VC.[9] It is clear when viewing "Asian American Ethnos" that these filmmakers made conscious efforts to reflect upon and actively engage with the Asian American Movement in their films. The films in this retrospective also reflect the "anti-slick" stance of early filmmakers, who rejected the values and standards of the dominant media industries of Hollywood and network television in the form, budget, and content of their films. This "anti-slick" stance was particularly dominant in the early collective VC productions.[10] In the following analyses, I closely examine the audio-visual relationships in the films collected in "Asian American Ethnos," including *Wong Sinsaang*, *Manzanar*, *Homecoming Game*, *Yellow Brotherhood*, *I Don't Think I Said Much*, and *Sleepwalker*. In these formational "claimings" of the Asian American voice on film, I ask what voices are heard, and what do they say or remain silent on? If, as Sterne suggests, voice is among the most personal forms of subjective self-expression, what can these early Asian American filmic "voices" tell us about Asian American subjectivity?

Eddie Wong's film *Wong Sinsaang* is one of the films in "Asian American Ethnos." *Wong Sinsaang* is a filmic portrait of Franklin Wong, the filmmaker's father, who operated a dry-cleaning and laundry shop in Hollywood, CA. As Eddie Wong explains in his interview in *Claiming a Voice*, he was influenced by Malcolm X's critique of intergenerational dynamics among colonized subjects, and sought to re-examine his relationship with his father. He also sought to challenge the stereotype of the subservient Chinese laundryman by portraying Franklin as a person with "a whole other life that most people would never see" in this film.[11] We can note that *Wong Sinsaang* features almost no synchronous voices. The first time Franklin Wong's voice is heard is when he sings a Chinese lullaby or folk song over images of him working in his shop. Later in the film, he is heard bantering with his customers, while related non-synchronous images of him serving them are shown. These sound and image pairings do not follow the conventions of a realist audio-visual relationship. Nevertheless, selected sound bites from seemingly prosaic conversations between Wong and his customers are looped on the film's soundtrack to highlight the underlying power dynamics in their interactions. Here, the impressionistic and ethnographic effect of the non-synchronized dialogue is pierced through by the sharp political critique in Eddie Wong's use of the looped voices. Repeated exchanges such as: "Nice shirt ..." "Yeah, let's keep it that way, okay? Bye bye!" between Wong and his predominantly White customers cumulatively accentuate their condescension and Wong's subservience. In a voiceover narration that follows this sequence, Eddie Wong further points out that his father's "laundryman mask"—his daily performance of the stereotype of the "docile, quiet, courteous little Chinaman"—hides a secret world "shaped by poetry, painting, scholarly essays."[12] We are offered one more glimpse of Franklin Wong's unspoken (to an English-only audience) subjectivity in the film, when he answers two brief questions from the filmmaker:

> Eddie Wong (EW): "How long have you been in the laundry business?"
> Franklin Wong (FW): "Oh … for twenty-one years."
> EW: "What do you … what do you think about it?"
> FW: "Can't think about it, just make living."[13]

Wong's succinct and pragmatic answers to his son's questions about his experience as a Chinese laundryman show just how little his verbalized subjectivity corresponds to Eddie Wong's liberationist position. Indeed, the comprehensible subject position in *Wong Sinsaang* is expressed in Eddie Wong's Asian American voice. At the end of the film, Franklin Wong's hidden subjectivity is shown more fully in a sequence that shows him writing Chinese poetry and practicing martial arts, while traditional Chinese music plays on the soundtrack.[14] However, whether his culturally specific activities here are fully transparent to a non-Chinese and non-Chinese-speaking audience, or even to his Asian American son, is questionable.

Manzanar (1970), directed by Robert Nakamura, another film by a VC founding member included in "Asian American Ethnos," shares some of *Wong Sinsaang*'s tactics in using culturally specific "voices" to impressionistically and emotively convey the experience of Japanese American internment during World War II. The filmic images alternate between location shots at the site of the internment camp of the film's title, and archival images: camp photographs, newsreel and propaganda images, President Roosevelt's Executive Order 9066, anti-Japanese signage, and documents from that period in U.S. history. Traditional Japanese music, parts of which include vocal singing, infuses the soundtrack of the film.[15] When paired with archival images of Japanese American camp life, the music evokes a sense of pathos and loss. The music becomes more active in some places, such as when it is synchronized to the image in the contemporary shots in which a moving, handheld camera travels through the ruins of the former internment camp accompanied by the rapid plucking of shamisens (Malm 1963: 58). The point-of-view (POV) shot in these sequences conveys a subjective sense of haunting, as if we were seeing through the eyes of a ghost who has returned to its past life in search of something … perhaps its own history?

The music in *Manzanar* functions as a "voice," linking the past generation's historical trauma to the present generation's search for an identity that is marked by that trauma. Nakamura's own voiceover narration, in which he reminisces about his experience as a six-year-old living in the camp with his parents, also connects the past and the present. However, the voices of the adults who lived through this experience remain silent in the conventional sense, only evoked in the film using the sound of water over a desert landscape, and sounds of children playing over shots of the empty ruins of the camp's grounds, thus emphasizing their absence and loss. Nakamura and Wong both accentuate silences and the failure or lack of cultural understanding as important expressive audio and linguistic qualities in the Asian American voice, which may seem counterproductive in the collective cultural and political project of claiming that voice. Here, I argue that these vocal opacities are key to the representation of the Asian American voice as subjectivity. Namely, gaps in understanding and miscommunication, in terms of language as well as cultural meaning, are important facets within the immigrant experience—not just for Asian Americans, but also for most migratory and diasporic communities.

Syncretism, Asynchronicity, Voiceovers

While the previously discussed films emphasize the Asian American subject's inarticulate silence and culturally specific knowledge—often nonverbal—to assert their Asian American voice, other films from "Asian American Ethnos" are multivocal in their experimental construction of collectivity and intercultural relationships within Asian American communities. Danny Kwan's film *Homecoming Game* (1970), a filmic portrait of a contemporary Asian American community of recovering drug users, predominantly features scenes with synchronous sound. In vignettes, Asian American young men and women talk, argue, flirt, joke, dance, laugh, chant political slogans, and are interviewed about their drug use and experience in gangs. We watch and listen to these young Asian Americans in a variety of settings, ranging from a happening at Stanford University, to swimming outdoors and lifting weights, to playing a verbosely contentious game of Scrabble. For the most part, they interact in informal and spontaneous ways, and their speech exemplifies the vernacular "hip" or "jive" talk honed through an urban upbringing. These Asian Americans are bi- or multilingual, like the older generation portrayed in *Wong Sinsaang* and *Manzanar*, but they speak a multicultural tongue. In *Homecoming Game*, it is perfectly natural to hear an East LA Chicano accent coming out of a Japanese American mouth, or an Asian woman freely peppering her speech with African American street slang.

The vernacular and hybrid voices in *Homecoming Game* indicate an Asian American "voice" that is streetwise and unapologetic. It is a syncretic "voice" that is created out of American popular culture, multicultural and multilingual urban communities, as well as the rebellion and militancy of 1960s social protest movements and counterculture. In the film, synch-sound sequences are punctuated by ones in which filmic images are played over popular music or voiceover narration. Popular songs by The Angels and Classics IV play over handheld panning shots of the neighborhood (similar to the subjective POV shots in *Manzanar*).[16] Interviews start off in the "talking heads" direct address mode, then veer off into disembodied voiceovers paired with images of construction sites and vacant lots. There is a particularly powerful sequence in which a young Asian woman talks about trying to look White by taping her eyelids in high school. Her recollection of trying to conform to hegemonic standards of beauty is tempered by her realization that such cosmetic alterations of her racialized features make her look "cheap … like a low person."[17] Her voiceover narration is played over a slow motion image of an Asian woman with taped eyelids and heavy make-up. We do not see or hear from this woman again in the rest of the film, so we never find out whether the woman on film is the same person speaking on the soundtrack. This uncoupling of the image and sound disrupts the conventions of documentary verisimilitude that her testimonial voice leads one to expect. However, the effect here is that her specific experience becomes one that many can (and do) share. While echoing Derrida's description of "hearing oneself speak," this effect opens her voice up and into a "voice" that signifies collective utterance. The song "Something about Me Today," composed and performed by Asian American folk musicians Chris Iijima, Nobuko Miyamoto, and Charlie Chin, plays on the soundtrack while the woman speaks, underscoring this opening up of the individual voice into a collective experience. "Something about Me Today" reinforces the powerful effect of a multivocal utterance in this audio-visual image, in which many voices resonate in a communal political awakening (Iijima and Miyamoto 1973).

Other films in the program, including *Yellow Brotherhood* (1970), directed by Brian Tadashi Maeda, *I Don't Think I Said Much* (1973), directed by Jeff Furumura, and *Sleepwalker* (1971–1972), directed by Laura Ho, similarly de-emphasize synchronous sound in their representation of Asian American subjectivity. *Yellow Brotherhood* features shots of an all-male Asian

American motorcycle gang played over sounds of engine revving and 1960s countercultural rock anthems by Jethro Tull and Steppenwolf, placing this film within the tropes of countercultural representation, à la *Easy Rider* (1969), albeit with an Asian American twist.[18] A male voiceover alternates with the rock songs on the soundtrack, riffing on issues ranging from Asian American identity politics to gang life. Again, it is a voice that is not synchronized to a specific speaker or person in the film. Nonetheless, its rough quality and barely comprehensible speech—filled with expletives and street slang—make it a fitting "voice" for the Asian American gang members.[19] *I Don't Think I Said Much* also de-emphasizes synchronous voices in its portrayal of Japanese American gardeners. In a shot where one of the gardeners is shown digging in the earth while synchronous location sound can be heard, Furumura chose to mix in a voiceover narration from the subject. The circumstances of the shot leads us to believe voice and image should be synchronized, yet we can clearly see that the subject's mouth is not moving even though his voice is speaking on the soundtrack. The film juxtaposes the voices of the gardeners, their employers, passers-by, and family members to create a complex multigenerational portrait of the Japanese American gardener that juxtaposes his outer image and inner thoughts. The film's title ironically refers to the interracial dynamics exposed by the multiple voices on the soundtrack. In particular, the racist assumption of the employer that "there must be something in the Japanese nature or character that allows them to do this kind of hard work without complaint" rings dissonantly against the more internalized reflections of the gardener, who recalls his life growing up in internment camps and his love of Suiseki, the Japanese art of rock gardening and stone appreciation.[20] While the subject's visual silence (we never see the gardeners speak on camera) is accentuated by the predominant use of voiceover, the partially translated Japanese voiceover of his mother further positions speech as a culturally specific act that is only entirely comprehensible to a Japanese-speaking audience.

The de-emphasis of synchronized speech and sound in this collection of early Asian American independent film finds its most radical expression in Laura Ho's *Sleepwalker*, which does not feature any speech at all. The film, shot in black and white 16 mm film, shows an Asian female protagonist wandering in the urban setting of 1970s Los Angeles. She remains silent throughout the film. Its initially realist soundtrack of urban street noise gradually mixes with sounds of sea gulls, wind, and then an electronic drone, similar to whale calls, which drowns out the more realist location sounds. This sonic departure from realism is accompanied by increasingly expressive cinematography, surreal scenarios, superimposed images, and symbolic objects that recall the avant-garde filmic language of Maya Deren's *Meshes in the Afternoon* (1943).

There are most likely practical reasons for the predominance of non-synchronized sound in these early Asian American independent films. First, they were all shot in 16 mm or 8 mm film, a format in which image and sound are recorded separately, if at all. To shoot images with synchronous sound would have required the relative luxury of additional equipment, tape stock, and crew members, which these independent filmmakers could not afford, or chose not to. Second, synchronizing sound and image in post-production also requires additional processes, equipment, and expertise for the filmmaker or editor; thus bigger budgets, more work prints, and access to more expensive post-production facilities. Third, these films all embraced an experimental approach to filmmaking, following the examples of Third Cinema as well as avant-garde and underground films rather than Hollywood features, traditional documentaries, or network television. The de-emphasis of conventionally synchronous audio-visual relationships is as much a result of these rough-and-tumble low-budget student films as it is an "anti-slick" aesthetic choice.

When we do hear Asian American voices in these films, they are predominantly in voiceover narrations that are not necessarily attributed to a visual image of a speaker. These disembodied voices are what Michel Chion calls *acousmêtres*: disembodied voices that "belong to the cinema and to it alone" (Chion 1999: 4). In Chion's theorization of the *acousmêtre*, he imbues its voice (and sometimes it is only a voice) with an almost supernatural power, which he attributes to its possible biological and religious origin.[21] More relevant to our discussion here is the figure of the *montreur d'images*, the off-screen narrator and vocal performer who accompanied proto-cinematic media presentations such as magic lantern shows and slide lectures, as well as silent film screenings. The *montreurs d'images* provide context, narrate stories, as well as impersonate characters and provide sound effects for these early and proto-cinematic media forms.[22] Their voices variously enhance, prescribe, and suggest meaning for the images that the audiences at the time were watching. Although Chion's theorization of the *acousmêtre* is primarily concerned with narrative films, his discussion is also relevant to other filmic forms, including documentary, in which the "voice of god" narrator is often deployed to provide meaning for the images seen.

While their approaches to documenting Asian American experiences are more experimental than in traditional documentary, the Ethno-Communications filmmakers examined here nonetheless utilize voiceover narration as their primary device to represent Asian American subjecthood. When heard, these voices enhance and often significantly complicate the meaning of the images seen, resulting in the creation of complex audio-visual representations. Eddie Wong's narration politicizes the mundane shots of his father tending shop and serving customers. Robert Nakamura's childhood recollection in *Manzanar* infuses an otherwise barren desert landscape with the erased history of Japanese American internment, which is further evoked by the traditional Japanese vocal music and absent sounds. The vernacular and streetwise voiceover in *Yellow Brotherhood* enhances and livens the syncretic images of Asian American bikers and inflects them further with a distinct but unexpected "ethnic" accent. The juxtaposition between the different voices in *I Don't Think I Said Much* contrasts the complex lived experiences of the Japanese American gardeners with the simplistic stereotype assumed of them, and gives "voice" to an otherwise muted image of the model minority. The taped eyelid scene in *Homecoming Game* challenges White hegemonic beauty standards, again through a personal recollection that broadens into a collective "voice" for Asian American women. On the other hand, Laura Ho's completely silent female protagonist stands out even among the plethora of filmic experiments in unconventional audio-visual relationships in "Asian American Ethnos." It is hard not to read her silence as a metaphor for Asian American women's lack of a voice in both commercial and independent media. In addition to Deren, whose female protagonist in *Meshes in the Afternoon* also remains silent throughout the film, we see a general distrust of language and voice in experimental media produced by women. I next turn to a group of experimental videos produced by Asian American women in the 1980s and 1990s that also exhibit this distrust of voice and language in their representation of female subjectivity. I conclude my discussion of early Asian American "claiming" of "voice" and voice through media by focusing on this group of contemporary practitioners, who use what I call the "negative voice" to represent the experiences and subjecthood of Asian and Asian American women and men.

Hearing the Negative Voice: Absence and Materiality

Heard as a collective Asian American "voice," the voices in "Asian American Ethnos" are multigenerational, multilingual, and syncretic. They are vernacular, streetwise, unapologetic, anti-slick, and often ironic. They are multicultural, reflecting the influence of both their native tongues and U.S. popular culture, and they hybridize and emulate other racialized countercultural voices of the 1960s and 1970s. These voices are also predominantly male. Although Asian American women's voices are included in *Homecoming Game* and *I Don't Think I Said Much,* I already noted that in *Sleepwalker,* the only work in "Asian American Ethnos" that is directed by a woman, the Asian American female protagonist is silent. Whether intentionally or not, Ho's protagonist is an apt symbol for Asian American women's "voices" during this period. Although one could argue that the earliest known Asian American film was directed by a woman, and that women have played pivotal roles in the establishment of Asian American media art centers, most of the first generation of Asian American independent films were, when credited, directed by men. It is not until the second and third generations of Asian American independent media production that we see women playing directorial roles.[23]

In an interview with Laleen Jayamane and Anne Rutherford, Vietnamese American filmmaker and cultural theorist Trinh T. Minh-ha discusses the potential and the pitfalls she perceives in the act of claiming a feminist voice within the context of her film *Surname Viet Given Name Nam* (1989):

> The question of empowering women through speech is highly problematic, because women's relationship with language and speech has always been an uncomfortable one. Language, of course, is never neutral. It is the site where power relationships are most complex and pernicious; yet it is also a place of liberation.
>
> (Trinh 1992: 169–170)

Trinh's ambivalence toward "empowering women through speech" is echoed in a number of powerful moments in the herstory of Asian American independent media. For instance, in an excerpt in *Claiming a Voice* from Renee Tajima-Peña and Christine Choy's 1988 documentary *Who Killed Vincent Chin?* we see Chin's mother struggling to speak at a press conference. Distraught at the death of her son, her presence is powerful in its abject inarticulateness. Laura Ho's silent female protagonist is another such "negative voice" that articulates the marginalization of Asian American women by not speaking at all. Indeed, moments of inarticulateness and the breakdown of verbal communication abound in experimental media produced by Asian American women in the 1980s and 1990s. What is fascinating about these moments and breakdowns is that they are powerfully expressive of the subjectivity of Asian American women and men; and that this expressivity rejects or moves beyond speech and verbal communication. In these works, vocal expressivity is "claimed" without relying on speech and language.

Rea Tajiri's experimental video *History and Memory: For Akiko and Takashige* (1991) documents her family's experience with Japanese American internment by weaving together a plethora of "voices," including newsreel footage; propaganda films made by both U.S. and Japanese governments; Hollywood films that re-present events from World War II as popular entertainment; as well as letters from and conversations with her family members.[24] However, these "voices" are structured around a central absence in *History and Memory*—the refusal of Tajiri's mother to speak about her internment experiences. A sense of absence and incomprehension, similar to that in *Manzanar,* is structured in the video around her mother's claim that she does not remember life in the camps. This haunted subjectivity is further represented in *History and Memory* by the ghost of Tajiri's grandfather, whose scenes are shown as textual descriptions scrolling over a black background. The ghostly presence of her grandfather bearing silent witness is a "negative voice" in the video, which, along with the lost memories of Tajiri's mother, are silences that all the other "voices" in *History and Memory* gravitate around. They are, to quote Fredric Jameson, the "spectrality [that] makes the present waver."[25]

In *Who's Going to Pay for These Donuts, Anyway?* (1992), another experimental documentary on the effects of Japanese American internment, video artist Janice Tanaka searches for her father, whom she has not seen since age three. When she finds him in a convalescent home for the mentally ill, ravaged by his internment experience and ineffective treatments for his schizophrenia, their conversations are characterized by inarticulateness, memory loss, and misrecognition. Even his ability to speak is compromised by his ordeal, as his illness is primarily represented on video through his difficulty with coherent speech and in the involuntary movements of his mouth. Speech, these works seem to suggest, is inadequate when it comes to articulating the experiences of historical trauma such as Japanese American internment. For many Asian Americans, the limitation of language is further compounded by the fact that we inhabit cross-cultural, immigrant, and diasporic communities that speak in more than one tongue.

In the opening sequence of Soo Jim Kim's *Comfort Me* (1993), partially voiced words, fragments of syllables, and visual text on screen together form the title of the video, which the audience has to literally piece back together using the fragmented sounds and images, along with in-articulated gaps of silence. In the video's layered soundtrack, the most expressive "voice" is not the verbally communicative voiceover narrating the history of Korean comfort women in World War II, but, rather, the monotonous counting and the exaggerated scrubbing sound that play over close-up images of an Asian woman repeatedly and obsessively washing herself. Here, these vocal and sound devices function in a manner that is similar to what Michel Chion calls the "anempathetic effect," in which the "indifferent and automatic unwinding" of a sound is in and of itself expressive (Chion 1994: 8–9). In *Comfort Me*, the monotonous counting on the soundtrack bespeaks the repetitive and unending sexual violence the comfort women had to endure, until they were "simply left to die, or shot."[26] Additionally, the loud and exaggerated scrubbing sound can be understood in relation to what Roland Barthes calls the "grain of the voice." In Barthes' theorization, which is primarily focused on singing, the grain of the voice is "not what it says, but the voluptuousness of its sound-signifiers, of its letters—where melody explores how the language works and identifies with that work. It is, in a very simple word but which must be taken seriously, the *diction* of the language" (Barthes 2000: 294–295). In my adaptation here, the scrubbing sound, as the grain of the video's "voice," voluptuously engenders a sense of discomfort in the auditor. Listening to this difficult and grating sound while watching the close-up images of the woman washing herself, the audience may feel in their own bodies a sensorial embodiment of the trauma the comfort women had to endure.

I have previously argued in studying Tran T. Kim-Trang's experimental video *Blindness Series* (1992–2006) that the materiality of a voice, and not its content, can become the primary conveyor of meaning. In Tran's *Ekleipsis* (1998), the trauma endured by a group of Cambodian women refugees might have been so horrific that it caused them to become hysterically blind. Or rather, these women—the largest group of hysterically blind people in the world—chose blindness over the "eye-searing horrors" they witnessed on a daily basis in the Khmer Rouge labor camps. The subjectivity of these women is represented by a voiceover narration in the video. Yet, the sound of this voiceover is so processed and distorted that the words are practically incomprehensible. I wrote: "Tran is able to create a voice in which its grain, corporeally implicated deep inside our bodies, can both give us a sense of the horrors these women experienced and impinge upon us the impossible struggle of articulating their experience in rational speech and language" (Ma 2012: 75). In other words, the materiality of this voice, not its content, is the primary conveyor of its meaning. This emphasis on the materiality of the voice as subjective expression both affirms and expands upon the possible interpretations of Derrida's theory of auto-affection, in which "To speak to someone is doubtless to hear oneself speak, to be heard by oneself; but, at the same time, if one is heard by another, to speak is to make him *repeat immediately* in himself the hearing-oneself-speak ..." (Derrida 1973: 80). In these experimental videos by Asian American women, the "voice" that one hears oneself speak is not speech but the materiality of the voice, its grain. Juxtaposed with the "pure auto-affective" speech of Asian American "voices" speaking to and about ourselves (self-representation) in the early Ethno-Communications films, these experimental videos by Asian American women ask important questions about whether efforts such as claiming a voice are themselves limiting and, in turn, marginalizing to a sub-population (in this case women) in a historically marginalized group (Asian Americans).

This chapter has shown that there is certainly an ironic ocularcentrism in our ongoing efforts to "claim a voice" through the production and study of Asian American independent media, and that this effort has always been a complex experimental process. This is highlighted by the above-mentioned videos, produced by Asian American women in the 1980s and 1990s during the height of the culture wars and identity politics in the United States, which show a conceptual skepticism and critical resistance to this very paradigm of empowerment through language and speech. Instead, these videos collectively show that the extra-linguistic elements in the voice—what I called the "negative voice"—can be extremely powerful conveyors of meaning. The questions raised by these experimental videos are echoed in larger debates and discussions on the relationship between voice, speech, and subjectivity within philosophy and linguistics. Adriana Cavarero writes: "The voice is sound, not speech. But speech constitutes its essential destination. What is therefore at stake in any inquiry into the ontology of the voice—where uniqueness and relationality come to the fore—is a rethinking, without metaphysical prejudices, of this destination" (Cavarero 2005: 12). In our continual exploration and definition of Asian American subjecthood, it is certainly important to continue to listen to the syncretic, multilingual, multigenerational, vernacular, unapologetic, and anti-slick voices recorded in our independent media. But it is equally important that we also listen for the "negative" voice—that which is inarticulate, difficult, or impossible to translate; the nonverbal sounds we make; our refusal to speak; the spaces in between the words; the silences.

Notes

1 Linda Mabalot interview from *Claiming a Voice*. Also see Mabalot's obituary in *LA Times Online*, http://articles.latimes.com/2003/may/29/local/me-mabalot29.

2 Eddie Wong interview from *Claiming a Voice*.

3 Chion's concepts of "vococentrism" and "verbocentrism" also highlight the centrality of the human voice in film sound (1994, p. 6, 1999, pp. 5–6). It is important to note that Chion's theories of film sound are derived from his study of predominantly feature narrative films from the U.S., Europe, and Japan.

4 Anthologies that collected the interdisciplinary and feminist musicology scholarship on voice from this period include Dunn and Jones (1994) and Smart (2000).

5 Lawson Inada is himself the subject of Alan Kondo's 1974 film *I Told You So*, produced at Visual Communications. The film featured reading of his poetry on its soundtrack.

6 The connection between voice and Asian American identity is articulated in the Preface of *Aiiieeeee!* (Chin et al. 1974, vii–viii).

7 While most were students making their first films through the Ethno-Communications program, some, including Burnett and Sylvia Morales, were already film students at UCLA, and joined Ethno-Communications as teaching assistants (Tajima 1985, pp. 38–39).

8 Ferrer also curated different versions of this program for several other venues: he incorporated the Asian American Ethno-Communications films with works by other graduates of the program from African American, Chicano/a, and Native American communities and presented a program titled "Ethnovisions: The Roots of Diversity for Community-Based Media in Los Angeles" for the 1990 Los Angeles Festival. In 1999, he re-presented the six films from the 1990 Los Angeles Asian Pacific Film Festival (LAAPAFF) as "In the Beginning: A 30th Anniversary Salute to Asian American Ethno" for Japanese American National Museum's Welcome Weekend.

9 Nakamura returned to UCLA and taught in Asian American Studies and motion picture/television for 33 years. He founded the UCLA Center for Ethnocommunications in 1996, a re-vamping of sorts of the original Ethno-Communications film school, now housed in UCLA's Asian American Studies Center. He retired from UCLA in 2012 (*Rafu Shimpo* 2012).

10 Tajima discusses the aesthetics and production conditions for the ideology of "anti-slick" as well as its contradictions for first- and second-generation Asian American independent filmmakers (1991, pp. 20–21). Jun Okada also explored the mix of aesthetics and politics in this early period in Asian American independent cinema. In a chapter that focused on the institutions of VC and Asian CineVision (ACV) in New York, Okada compared how the anti-slick stance of VC influenced its early collective institutional authorship and ACV, and its residential programmer and critic Daryl Chin's emphasis on formal intervention and avant-garde experimentation (Okada 2015, 12–38).

11 Eddie Wong interview from *Claiming a Voice*.

12 Eddie Wong's voiceover narration in *Wong Sinsaang*.

13 Dialogue between Eddie Wong and Franklin Wong from *Wong Sinsaang*.

14 The music is the classical Chinese composition "Fisherman's Song at Dusk" (漁舟唱晚).

15 The music is from the album *Azuma Kabuki Musicians* (1954), and is excerpted from "Ocho" (Ancient Court Days), "O-Matsuribayashi" (Festival Music), "Nagare" (Water Images), and other tracks.

16 The tracks include The Angels' "My Boyfriend's Back" (1963) and "Traces" by Classics IV (1968).

17 Voiceover narration in *Homecoming Game*, un-credited.

18 Songs used in the film's soundtrack include "Dharma for One" by Jethro Tull (1969) as well as "Magic Carpet Ride" (1968) and "Born to Be Wild" (1967) by Steppenwolf. "Born to Be Wild" is played over the opening credits of *Easy Rider* (1969, dir. Dennis Hopper).

19 Since what the voice describes, including social protest, the Black Panthers, and—toward the end of a film—a staged fight in a pool hall, is shown as images in the film, we are led to assume that the voiceover is an interview with one of the men in the motorcycle gang.

20 Voiceover narration in *I Don't Think I Said Much*, un-credited.

21 Chion has attributed the possible origins of the *acousmêtre* to "a Pythagorean sect whose followers would listen to their Master speak behind a curtain" as well as to an infant's hearing of the first voice—its mother's—while still in her womb. See Chion 1999, pp. 18–23, 61–62.

22 See Chion 1999, p. 49. For a discussion of film lecture practices in the U.S. from the 1890s to the 1950s, see Altman 2004, pp. 133–155.

23 *The Curse of Quon Gwon* (1916–1917) was directed by Marion Wong, who was also its writer and producer. I was only able to identify two Asian American women who participated in Ethno-Communications: Marie Kodani and Ho. There were certainly other, non-Asian American women in the program, including Morales, McCullough, Alile Sharon Larkin, Julie Dash, and Sandra Osawa, who was Native American and took her husband's Japanese last name. Women including Mabalot, Amy Kato, and Janice D. Tanaka were either long-time staff members or volunteers at VC. Mabalot joined VC as a staff member in 1977, and served as VC's executive director from 1985 to 2003. While Asian women media artists, including Shigeko Kubota and Yoko Ono, have been making avant-garde and experimental media in the U.S. since the 1960s, self-identified Asian American women filmmakers, including Tajima-Peña herself, Christine Choy, J. T. Takagi, Loni Ding, Trinh T. Minh-ha, Valerie Soe, Janice Tanaka, and others did not start making documentary and experimental media (films and videos) until the 1980s. In the late 1980s and 1990s, a younger generation including Rea Tajiri, Freida Lee Mock, Tran T. Kim-Trang, Angel Velasco Shaw, Mari Keiko Gonzales, Grace Lee, Meena Nanji, Kayo Hatta, and others produced media ranging from feature narratives to video art.

24 World War II films quoted in *History and Memory* include *From Here to Eternity* (1953, dir. Fred Zinnemann), *Bad Day at Black Rock* (1955, dir. John Sturges), *Come See the Paradise* (1990, dir. Alan Parker), and others, as well as non-World War II-specific films with "patriotic messages" such as *Yankee Doodle Dandy* (1942, dir. Michael Curtiz).

25 The Jameson quote is from "Marx's Purloined Letter" in the *New Left Review* (Jan/Feb 1995, 209). I came across it in Gordon 1997, p. 168.

26 Voiceover narration in *Comfort Me*.

References

Altman, Rick. 2004. *Silent Film Sound.* New York: Columbia University Press.

The Angels. 1963. "My Boyfriend's Back." Smash Records. 7″ single.

"Asian American Studies Professor Nakamura Retiring from UCLA." 2012. Rafu Shimpo Online, January 27. http://www.rafu.com/2012/01/asian-american-studies-professor-nakamura-retiring-from-ucla/.

Azuma Kabuki Musicians. 1954. Azuma Kabuki Musicians. Columbia Masterworks. LP.

Barthes, Roland. 2000. "The Grain of the Voice." In *On Record: Rock, Pop, and the Written Word*, Simon Firth and Andrew Goodwin (eds), 293–300. London: Routledge.

Cavarero, Adriana. 2005. *For More Than One Voice: Toward a Philosophy of Vocal Expression.* Stanford: Stanford University Press.

Chin, Frank, Jeffrey Paul Chan, Lawson Fusao Inada, and Shawn Wong (eds). 1974. *Aiiieeeee! An Anthology of Asian-American Writers.* Washington DC: Howard University Press.

Chion, Michel. 1994. *Audio-Vision: Sound on Screen.* New York: Columbia University Press.

Chion, Michel. 1999. *The Voice in Cinema.* New York: Columbia University Press.

Classics IV. 1968. "Traces." Imperial Records. 7″ single.

Curtiz, Michael (director). 1942. *Yankee Doodle Dandy.*

Derrida, Jacques. 1973. "The Voice That Keeps Silence." In *Speech and Phenomena and Other Essays on Husserl's Theory of Signs*, 70–87. Chicago: Northwestern University Press.

Doane, Mary Ann. 1985. "The Voice in the Cinema: The Articulation of Body and Space." In *Film Sound: Theory and Practice*, Elisabeth Weis and John Belton (eds), 162–176. New York: Columbia University Press.

Dong, Arthur. 1990. *Claiming a Voice: The Visual Communications Story.* DVD.

Dong, Arthur. n.d. "*Claiming a Voice Synopsis*." Deep Focus Productions website, www.deepfocusproductions.com/claiming_a_voice.php.

Dunn, Leslie C. and Nancy C. Jones (eds). 1994. *Embodied Voices: Representing Female Vocality in Western Culture.* Cambridge: Cambridge University Press.

Fanon, Frantz. 1963. *The Wretched of The Earth.* New York: Grove Press.

Fanon, Frantz. 1967. *Black Skin, White Masks.* New York: Grove Press.

Furumura, Jeff (director). 1973. *I Don't Think I Said Much.*

Gordon, Avery. 1997. *Ghostly Matters: Haunting and the Sociological Imagination.* Minneapolis, MN: University of Minnesota Press.

Hopper, Dennis (director). 1969. *Easy Rider.*

Husserl, Edmund. 1962. *Ideas: General Introduction to Pure Phenomenology.* New York: Collier Books.

Ihde, Don. 1976. *Listening and Voice: Phenomenologies of Sound.* Albany, NY: State University of New York Press.

Iijima, Chris, and Nobuko Miyamoto. 1973. "Something about Me Today" (words and music). In *A Grain of Sand: Music for the Struggle by Asians in America* by Chris Kando Iijima, Joanne Nobuko Miyamoto, and "Charlie" Chin. Paredon Records. Side 1, Band 4 (3:35).

Jethro Tull. 1969. *This Was.* Island Records. LP.

Kim, Soo Jin (director). 1993. *Comfort Me.*

Kondo, Alan (director). 1974. *I Told You So.*

Kwan, Danny (director). 1970. *Homecoming Game.*

Leong, Russell. 1991. "Introduction: To Open the Future." In *Moving the Image: Independent Asian Pacific American Media Arts*, Russell Leong (ed), xi–xxi. Los Angeles: UCLA Asian American Studies Center and Visual Communications.

Lou, Shuhua. 1936. "Night Song of the Fisherman," (漁舟唱晚).

Ma, Ming-Yuen S. 2012. "The Voice of Blindness: On the Sound Tactics of Tran T. Kim-Trang's Blindness Series." In *Resolutions 3: Global Networks of Video*, Ming-Yuen S. Ma and Erika Suderburg (eds), 65–80. Minneapolis, MN: University of Minnesota Press.

McLuhan, Marshall. 1962. *The Guttenberg Galaxy: The Making of Typographic Man.* Toronto: University of Toronto Press.

Malm, William P. 1963. "The Azuma Kabuki Musicians, Nihon no ongaku, and Nihon no gakki." *Ethnomusicology* 7(1) (January): 58–60.

Okada, Jun. 2015. *Making Asian American Film and Video: Histories, Institutions, Movements.* New Brunswick, NJ: Rutgers University Press.

Ong, Walter J. 1982. *Orality and Literacy: The Technologizing of the Word.* London: Methuen & Co./Routledge.

Parker, Alan (director). 1990. *Come See the Paradise.*

Saussure, Ferdinand de. 1983. *Course in General Linguistics.* London: Duckworth.

Silverman, Kaja. 1988. *The Acoustic Mirror: The Female Voice in Psychoanalysis and Cinema.* Bloomington, IN: Indiana University Press.

Smart, Mary Ann (ed). 2000. *Siren Songs: Representations of Gender and Sexuality in Opera.* Princeton, NJ: Princeton University Press.

Steppenwolf. 1968. "The Second." ABC Dunhill Records. LP.

Steppenwolf. 1967. "Born to Be Wild." Dunhill RCA Records. 45-single.

Sterne, Jonathan. 2012. "Introduction to Part VI: Voices." In *The Sound Studies Reader,* Jonathan Sterne (ed.), 491–494. New York: Routledge.

Sturges, John (director). 1955. *Bad Day at Black Rock.*

Tajima, Renee. 1985. "Ethno-Communications: The Film School Program That Changed the Color of Independent Filmmaking." In *The Anthology of Asian Pacific Film and Video, 38–45.* New York: Third World Newsreel.

Tajima, Renee. 1991. "Moving the Image: Asian American Independent Filmmaking 1970–1990." In *Moving the Image: Independent Asian Pacific American Media Arts,* Russell Leong (ed), 10–33. Los Angeles: UCLA Asian American Studies Center and Visual Communications.

Tajiri, Rea (director). 1991. *History and Memory: For Akiko and Takashige.*

Trinh, Minh-ha T. 1992. *Framer Framed.* New York: Routledge.

Wong, Eddie (director). 1971. *Wong Sinsaang.*

Woo, Elaine. 2003. "Linda Mabalot, 49; Nurtured Asian American Filmmakers." In *Los Angeles Times Online,* May 29. http://articles.latimes.com/2003/may/29/local/me-mabalot29/.

Zinnemann, Fred (director). 1953. *From Here to Eternity.*

3

DIASPORIC SOUNDSCAPES OF BELONGING

Mediating Chineseness with Shanghai Restoration Project

Grace Wang

I was returning to my seat during the intermission break of David Henry Hwang's play *Chinglish* at East West Players—the venerable Asian American theater group located in Los Angeles—when "The Bund," an instrumental track from Shanghai Restoration Project, began filling the theater. A reference to Shanghai's famed riverfront and the legendary nightclubs and dance halls that flourished there during the city's swinging jazz era in the 1930s, the song channels the spirit of that time and place through a heady mix of musical referents. Chinese traditional instruments layer onto hip-hop beats that weave into synthesizers and jazz piano riffs. Listening to the song in the context of *Chinglish*—a play that explores the manifold mistranslations that impede cultural understanding between China and the United States—it struck me how well it serves as a musical counterpart to the play. While Hwang plays with the chasm between meanings and words, using the sometimes humorous gaffes found in mistranslated "Chinglish" signs as a springboard to meditate on the limits of cross-cultural understanding, Dave Liang, the artist and producer who records as Shanghai Restoration Project, remixes bits and samples of Chinese traditional instruments onto beat-driven, electronic soundscapes that create new contexts for hearing those sounds. In so doing, both artists invite reflection on the place of China in the U.S. public imaginary, negotiating the fears, projections, and fantasies that structure U.S. narratives of China's ascent as a global superpower as well as their own attachments and identifications to China and Chineseness within these changing global relationships.

How do we hear and imagine China in the United States, where longstanding Orientalist and Yellow Peril paradigms of structuring Asian difference collide with and become ambivalently incorporated into newer narratives of "China on the rise"? The accelerated pace of change in China specifically and the Asia/Pacific region generally have unsettled the coordinates of power and privilege that historically marked the relationship between the United States and China and the frameworks of distance and otherness typically used to represent Asia. As global interest in understanding China intensifies, Chinese American artists have begun situating themselves as cultural brokers uniquely positioned to mediate this critical relationship. Reflecting, for instance, on the shift away from themes of multiculturalism to what Hwang terms internationalism in his work, the playwright marvels at the "sheer coincidence" of being Chinese and interested in U.S.–China relations at a moment when that topic has, somewhat unexpectedly, emerged as "one of the big subjects of the rest of the century" (Polkow 2011). In related fashion, Liang ties his interest in experimenting with music that combines "traditional Chinese instruments with hip-hop and electronica" to the lag in cultural productions that truly reflect the dynamism of modern China and his desire to update the soundtrack of China for U.S./Western listeners ("Shanghai Restoration Project: Hybrid Backbeats" 2008). For both artists, their subject position as Chinese Americans is not incidental to their investment in exploring changing perceptions of China and Chineseness, given both their diasporic connections and their awareness of how closely tied the fates of Chinese Americans in the United States are to such understandings.

While this increased attention to China has created some openings for Chinese Americans to engage anew with questions of diaspora and to participate in ongoing conversations about shifting meanings of China, narratives in the United States about China's rise are inevitably intertwined with a complex mix of feelings, from admiration to angst, and, sometimes, outright racism. For Chinese American artists, toeing this line between personal interest, fascination, and racialized projection can thus be fraught. There are, on the one hand, market opportunities for tapping into growing interest in China through remixed sounds and images of Chineseness that complicate essentialized understandings while still appealing to U.S./Western sensibilities. On the other hand, the context in which cultural work such as music circulates digitally and globally, particularly when repackaged as fun and upbeat "world music," sample embodiments of "Chinese culture," and/or hip, stylized blends of sonic Orientalism, are often linked to economic imperatives outside an artist's control and the material realities of making a living as a musician. Moreover, in mining questions of diasporic identification, Chinese Americans can be equally complicit in reproducing class-inflected, romanticized visions of Chineseness, rendering global cities like Shanghai as cosmopolitan wonderlands of East/West hybridity set to an ambient soundtrack of techno-cool.

How do the economic and cultural transformations of China over the past quarter century prompt a reassessment of existing narratives about the place of China in the U.S. imaginary? And how can music lead listeners to challenge longstanding, inherited categories used to organize understanding about U.S.–China relations?[1] This chapter explores these related questions through the case study of Shanghai Restoration Project, asking how Liang navigates transpacific affiliations to create, as he describes on the band's website, "high-energy electronic music rooted in modern day Chinese culture." Music, as the musician argues, represents a particularly powerful medium to tap into listeners' subconscious—to reach them at a more intuitive level of feeling and knowing that challenges them to "think beyond the categorizations that [they] are comfortable with."[2]

In what follows, I provide background about Liang and his musical development, connecting his impulse to create Shanghai Restoration Project to questions of diasporic attachment and Asian American musical belonging. I analyze the particular inspiration he finds in 1930s Shanghai jazz, a musical form rooted in colonial entanglement and interracial admixture, arguing that it captures Liang's desire to find rootedness in places of flux, discrepant fluencies, and creativity. And finally, I examine how an understanding of Shanghai Restoration Project as "Asian American music" allows us to consider this category less as fixed—bounded by questions of racial descent or musical elements—and more as a mode of inquiry that allows us to pose certain questions about the idea of China in the U.S. imaginary, the afterlife of Orientalism, and the imprint of details from elsewhere onto racialized experiences in the United States.

Creating Shanghai Restoration Project

While musicians like Liang tend to speak of their musical projects in terms of personal and musical goals, it is useful to contextualize Shanghai Restoration Project within broader questions about conflicts that Asian Americans encounter with musical belonging. Music, in this sense, helps amplify the broader tensions that Asian Americans face in finding belonging in national and transnational spaces. For, while Asian Americans make music of every kind, to further scrutiny about their place within particular music traditions. Kevin Fellezs (2007) observes, for instance, how in both scholarly and popular jazz discourse, Asian American musicians are "seen as 'coming into' a jazz tradition from an external place," viewed as lacking a rich jazz tradition of their own from which to draw (77). We hear strains of that sentiment echoed by acclaimed jazz pianist Vijay Iyer, who muses how, as an Asian American entering an African American expressive culture and "striving for some place within it," his status has "been called into question." He observes how critics used to place him "outside the history of jazz," filtering their listening through racialized beliefs about Asian Americans that led to assessments of his music as rigorous, cerebral, mathematical, and intellectual (Wilkinson 2016). We see how this racialized imagination extends to other music genres as well. Writing on hip-hop, scholars such as Nitasha Sharma, Antonio Tiongson, Oliver Wang, and Deborah Wong analyze the complex range of positions that Asian American musicians mobilize to authenticate their place within musical cultures not typically viewed as their own, from framing hip-hop as rooted in global, multicultural sensibilities to depicting the music as a vehicle to explore the particularities of the racialized experiences of Asian Americans in national and diasporic contexts (Sharma 2010; Tiongson 2013; Wang 2007; Wong 2004). Positioned at the boundary of music traditions—an othering that mirrors more broadly the racialization of this pan-ethnic group in the United States—Asian American musicians have adopted a variety of musical and narrative strategies for navigating their place and presence in different musical cultures.

For Liang, creating Shanghai Restoration Project grew out of a desire to explore questions of musical belonging and to make music that reflected the full range of his musical and familial inheritances. Growing up in upstate New York, he participated in a wide range of music-making activities: classical music, jazz and improvisation, musical theater, and choral and *a cappella* music. Other types of music filled his home as well. His mother, trained in Chinese opera in Taiwan, sang and played the *guzheng* (a traditional Chinese stringed instrument), while his grandfather played the *dizi* (a Chinese flute). As the child of immigrants from Taiwan who came to the United States to pursue graduate degrees in math and science, the experience of living in a new language and culture led his mother to enroll Liang in music and other artistic activities. As he put it, his mother saw the arts as a means to nurture the expressive elements of self, a priority she placed on her children given the cultural exclusions that she encountered as a racialized immigrant in the United States:

> She was like, 'the more you're in tune with different emotional components within yourself, the easier it is going to be to navigate America,' was her theory. My mom felt that one of the big ways to succeed in America was to express yourself … As an Asian American and a woman, my mom definitely heard her share of racist comments from her co-workers and when you encounter that, your instinct is probably that you want to fight back. But as an immigrant you don't necessarily have the words or the expression to do it necessarily at the time.

Liang understood how inclusion in the professional middle class did not necessarily signal full societal acceptance.

While Liang connected his parents' musical nurturance to broader dynamics of race and immigration in the United States, such issues did not feel particularly relevant to him when it came to his own music making while growing up. As he commented, "I would just find friends who were musicians and musicians don't care about the other person's race, they just care about if you're good or not, or if you like to jam." It was his immersion into the commercial music industry that heightened his understanding of the business aspects of making music, and the role that race played in selling music, from creating boundaries around music genres to the commodification of ethnicity and the segmentation of markets.

In Liang's retelling, his path toward making music professionally seems both a deliberate and a fortuitous path. He was working in consulting while still performing music on the side, when he heard from a former classmate who was then working as a producer at Bad Boy Records. He began apprenticing for his friend in 2003, eventually leaving behind his consulting work to delve full time into hip-hop music and production. It was his work as a music producer that led him to begin considering creating his own group, one that would challenge the music industry impulses toward categorization and explore a musical vocabulary that spoke to the full complexity of his experience as a Chinese American. In this sense, Shanghai Restoration Project can be interpreted as a journey back to the goals that his mother had in mind when she enrolled Liang in music training: to express yourself.

There is a certain irony in that the genre of electronic music and the use of a pseudonym, in some ways, run counter to ideas about self-expression. Liang mused: "I think compared to other genres, electronic music tends to be more detached from the biographical background of the artist and as a result, race does not play as much of a role on the listening front." His decision not to make music under his own name further redirected focus away from the particularities of his own background. Ethnomusicologist Timothy Taylor (2010) observes how electronic bands that involve only one person (like Liang's) tend "to draw attention to themselves not as individuals, but as hidden, mysterious creators" (140). While Liang explains his choice to use the name Shanghai Restoration Project in more pragmatic terms (as he notes, many electronic groups use pseudonyms to feature different vocalists and instrumentalists without confusing the audience too much), it also shifts attention away from the personal background of the artist.

At the same time, "electronic music" is an inadequate descriptor for Liang's music. As he readily admits, despite using that term, "there's a lot of other stuff going on. Shanghai Restoration Project was a way I could combine everything I like into one thing." For what Liang aspired to achieve was a sound that captured the full range of his musical inheritances. As he explains, performing and listening to jazz, classical, choral music, and hip-hop, he began to sense an inchoate longing:

> I never felt completely myself in terms of musical identity … It was not until one day, somebody gave me a suggestion, well, if you want to be true to yourself, why don't you use some of these instruments that you grew up with and grew up listening to. So that's when I started to fuse the Chinese instrumentation with all the musical experiences I had leading up until that point. ("Shanghai Restoration Project: Hybrid Backbeats" 2008)

More than just a fusion of different sounds, Liang aimed to capture the sense of hybridity—the assemblage of past and present, foreign and local—that recombined in the 1930s Shanghai jazz that he fell in love after visiting the Peace Hotel in Shanghai and encountering some old Chinese jazz bands during college. "In my mind," he recalls, "it was the perfect blend of Chinese and Western musical styles from that era." This "perfect blend" resonated with his own sense of self, someone who was at once "a combination of Chinese culture and American culture."

While Liang's description might, at first glance, appear to depict Chinese American subjectivity as the melding of two distinct cultures, it is worth emphasizing that the musical inspiration he finds in 1930s Shanghai jazz is more than an "East–West" mixture, but, rather, a hybrid popular form rooted in colonial entanglement and interracial exchange between Chinese and African American musicians. Colonized by multiple Western powers as well as Japan, the port city of Shanghai—famously dubbed the "Paris of the East"—was the thriving jazz capital of Asia. 1930s Shanghai jazz reflected this history of colonial encounters, merging together American big band, Tin Pan Alley, Hollywood film music, and Chinese folk melodies and instruments. The music, later deemed "yellow" or "pornographic" for its colonial influences when the Chinese communist government came to power in 1949, forced musicians to go underground, many of them not emerging again until the end of the Cultural Revolution.[3] In his interpretation of Shanghai as a mediating point of cultures colliding and coming together, Liang thus taps into what Chinese scholar Leo Lee (1999) calls "Shanghai modern": "If cosmopolitanism means an abiding curiosity in 'looking out'—locating oneself as cultural mediator at the intersection between China and other parts of the world—then Shanghai in the 1930s was the cosmopolitan city par excellence" (19). Lee's evocation of 1930s Shanghai as an embodiment of cosmopolitanism that allows an engagement with questions of Chinese modernity finds parallels in the inspiration that Liang finds in Shanghai jazz as a touchstone for interpreting the hybridity of Chinese diasporic subjectivities. Rather than find diasporic attachment to what we might view as "authentic" vestiges of Chinese culture—classical poetry and art or the musical forms of Beijing opera and *kunqu*—Liang chooses "impure" sites of contestation, collision, and colonial incursion.

Unfixing Categories

How can the remnants of the sounds of Shanghai jazz, remixed for the present, represent the sonic pulse of China in the U.S. imaginary? This question, specific in its details and references, invites us to consider how Liang's music provides a model for understanding China that moves us away from totalizing visions—what Ien Ang aptly describes as the "larger-than-life phantom China in the global imagination, a China that is at once mighty and scary, far too large and powerful for its own good" (Ang 2013: 19). Liang himself expresses wariness about the fear-mongering tactics of mainstream U.S. media and its monolithic depictions of China:

> It's almost like everything is bad about China and the government is always bad. There are no humanizing individual stories. The individual stories are always about suffering, usually at the hands of the government or Chinese behaving badly … If you're reading the news constantly and all you see about China is this, your entire perception of anybody who's Chinese that you meet is informed by these mainstream publications.

As he observes that such blanket coverage can be dangerous, creating distortions lead to misunderstandings, conflicts, and violence. Having grown up in the United States, Liang concedes that he will "never have full understanding" regardless of his travel, research, interpersonal relationships (his wife is a Chinese visual artist), and professional collaborations. At the same time, he cautions against the desire to gain or claim "full understanding." In this sense, rather than see discrepant fluencies as a shortcoming, these provide a template for approaching cultural interpretation. Such a view is in keeping with Liang's aim to challenge the desire for categorization, whether about genres, groups, ethnicity, or culture: "I don't want people to think in terms of the broad categories, I think it's ultimately unhealthy for society in the long run … Music is one of the ways you can actually get through to people's subconscious … to challenge them to think a little bit differently."

We can interpret Liang's desire to contest received categories and totalizing views of China—a place for which he feels both intimacy and distance—as part of his inheritance as the child of immigrants. Here, I draw from Alexandra Vazquez's evocation of the assemblage of fragmented, puzzling, cherished, and often elusive details that the children of Cuban immigrants cull from to forge diasporic attachments. Writing about the idea of Cuba and Cuban music for the generation raised in the United States, she observes:

> for children of immigrants, details from their parents' other lived locations are precarious things. They are openings that can be sought out, avoided, honored, rejected, and loved. The details are often all that is left behind from a near past. They remind us that that place is always partial, that we will never have a fullness of a past picture or sound. Details are things that we learn to live on, imagine off, and use to find other kinds of relationships to our parents' natal locations.

Such an intricate piecing together allows, as Vazquez suggests, for the emergence of something "that is both foreign and somehow familiar into something new" (Vazquez 2013: 7–8). That is, more than what is sometimes referred to glibly as a second generation's "search for roots," these fragments and details offer new ways of listening and understanding. Such a view resonates with Liang's musical goals of unsettling the categories we use to fix and assign meaning. Reframing 1930s Shanghai jazz, traditional Chinese instruments, and children's songs onto hip-hop beats and electronic vistas, his projects evoke and confound fixed definitions of China or Chinese culture that invite closer listening.

This attention to slips of memory and local, everyday contexts extends to Liang's many collaborative projects, helping listeners make links between the displacements wrought by immigration with processes of colonialism, migration, urbanization, and social/natural disasters. For instance, in the 2009 album *Afterquake*, a project that Liang undertakes with American folk singer Abigail Washburn and the humanitarian nonprofit Sichuan Quake Relief, he gathers field recordings of the continuing impact of the 2008 earthquake that killed more than 88,000 people and displaced more than five million people. *Afterquake*, as described on its website, "remixes voices and sounds from the Chinese earthquake zone to raise awareness for victims still in need." Songs sung in straightforward and moving simplicity by children attending relocation schools (for children displaced outside of the disaster zone and separated from their families) are placed onto electronic beats along with fragments of ambient sounds found in the local environment, from cement mixers to ping pong balls. In the multimedia website that accompanies the album, listeners gain a glimpse into the process of gathering research and materials for the album. Interview transcripts with the children featured on the album, raw video footage of field recordings, and photos of places and people visited allow listeners to gain a sense of how these tracks were compiled, descriptions of contexts for choosing and recording songs, and the individual stories and emotions behind the songs, allowing listeners a glimpse into their process of interpreting the soundscape of post-earthquake Sichuan—the rebuilding, the feelings of longing and loss, the resilience of children, the redemptive power of music.

Repackaging Chineseness

Still, while Liang aims to destabilize categories through his music, the ways in which listeners engage with his music speak to their own interests and desires. He concedes as much, noting: "people gravitate towards a certain type of music because it speaks to them. It's a product. It's doing something for them." This should not suggest that musicians do not have certain goals in mind or pathways toward which they want to lead listeners. But it does mean that the contexts in which their music is consumed and understood can sometimes lie in contradiction to the artists' intentions. Deborah Wong (2004) aptly cautions artists who draw on traditional Asian instruments and sounds, as they run a heightened risk of having their music consumed through frameworks of Orientalism and exoticism (215). While Liang acknowledges that a certain amount of "otherizing" might be inevitable, particularly for listeners who are hearing particular instruments for the first time, he also accepts responsibility as an artist for guiding listeners. Reflecting on his earlier albums, which often included more overt and decontextualized Chinese sounds, he notes: "I was a little bit more irresponsible in not sort of leading folks to the right places, but now I'm hoping to do that less." We can, in part, interpret Liang's remarks as stemming from his desire to work against reductive views of Chineseness—views that he may have even partially held himself earlier in his career. His comments reflect an understanding of the ease with which Chinese music/sounds can be slotted into an Orientalist framework, particularly when presented without a great deal of contextual knowledge or research into the musical traditions being cited.

Liang's intentions and sense of responsibility notwithstanding, it is worth questioning how Shanghai Restoration Project taps into longstanding desires for Asian difference, whether packaged as sonic Orientalism or rebranded through cosmopolitan visions of "Asian cool" aimed in the United States at global-minded National Public Radio (NPR)/ film festival/museum crowds (among the market segments that the group circulates within in the United States). This is particularly true with regard to the secondary circulation of Shanghai Restoration Project in commercials and albums such as Starbucks' *World Is China* and Putamayo's children's album *Asian Playgrounds*, which traffic more explicitly in romanticized visions of China/Asia.[4] Putamayo's *Asian Playgrounds*, for instance, invites listeners on "magical and educational journeys to the rich diverse lands of Asia," while Starbucks' *World Is China* (which follows the albums *World Is Africa* and *World Is India*) aims to "display the diversity of China. Encompassing classic Chinese pop, Beijing opera, hip-hop and electronica, these East-meets-West selections reveal the span of China's sound and how it colors and is colored by music from around the globe." Listening to these albums, one has the sense of being on a fun, curated adventure, engaging in what Georgina Born and David Hesmondhalgh describe as a type of "psychic tourism through music" (Born and Hesmondhalgh 2000: 35). Such compilations provide a window onto the cultural strategies by which China is packaged and commodified in the U.S. cultural imagination—resembling less a threatening global hegemon than a source of cultural richness that enhances our global diversity.

Rethinking Asian American Music

If the analytics of "world music" can foreclose understanding, it is worth asking whether the category "Asian American" in relation to Shanghai Restoration Project can open up inquiry, even though the group is not typically placed within an Asian American framework. Here, it may be productive to shift attention to the ways that Asian American cinema studies scholars have analyzed how the label "Asian American" film and video depends not only on unsettled criteria regarding race, politics, and aesthetics, but also on questions of commerce, distribution, and resources. Jun Okada, for example, traces the inextricable role that state and public institutions—in particular PBS (Public Broadcasting Service)—played in the development of Asian American film and video. Arguing against the idea of an "authentic, organic, or autonomous 'Asian American film and video,'" Okada emphasizes how the category itself arose out of marketplace politics: "It is a concept invented by the network of grassroots, local, and national institutions that emerged following the civil rights and student movements of the 1960s and 1970s" (Okada 2013: 5). Broader debates around the shifting boundaries of the label "Asian American" thus inform, as well as arise out of, the often material contexts for making and distributing films.[5]

Okada's capacious understanding of Asian American film and video as dynamic and shifting echoes Glen Mimura's proposition to view the lack of definitive answers to the question "What is Asian American film?" not as a shortcoming but rather, as an open-ended and ever-unfolding "gift": "Its meaning is no longer something we must anxiously seek to define, free in its tracks, conquer; it is no longer an answer at the end of a well-traveled question, but the beginning of our journey into other stories, problems, question" (Mimura 2009: xxii). For Mimura, analyzing Asian American cinema within the anticolonial, international movement called Third Cinema that emerged in the 1960s productively opens up lines of inquiry about Asian American racialization, queer sexuality, and globalization. In this sense, both Okada and Mimura allow for an open-ended understanding of Asian American film and video as engaged in a mode of social, political, and historical critique.

We can understand the category "Asian American music" as similarly enabling particular forms of critique—encompassing what Joseph Lam describes as a "flexible heuristic device" rather than a codified set of race-based expectations and criteria (Lam 1999: 44). To think of Shanghai Restoration Project as making "Asian American music" can thus prompt us to ask how the music engages with a set of questions about, for instance, U.S.–China relations, the critical afterlives of Orientalism, and/or the racializing distortions that render certain groups as "other" within the U.S. imaginary. Such a conception allows us to apprehend how race continues to matter in music such as Shanghai Restoration Project, even it might not, at first glance, seem centrally engaged with questions of Asian American identity or representation.

When I asked Liang about his impressions of the category "Asian American" in relation to his music, he expressed hesitation, noting that while he understood race to be important and expressed support for Asian American activism, what is most significant to him is the work—the music itself: "I'm an artist first and foremost, and I'm an individual artist. ... 'If you hear my music on Pandora, it shouldn't matter to you what my race is, what my ethnicity is. What should matter to you is, do you like the music?" On the one hand, Liang's measured response speaks to the suffocating ways that ethnicity can be tethered to cultural productions, limiting and calcifying how listeners consume them and what their work might encompass. On the other hand, the belief that music can ever speak for itself is debatable.

Everything from the packaging and marketing of the music/musician to the construction of music genres and the history of intertextual references and beliefs that the listener brings to the music impacts the "pure" experience of listening. Still, when I hear musicians like Liang emphasize individual artistry and the "work, first and foremost," I place their comments within an understanding of the vexed place that Asian Americans occupy in the musical cultures in which they participate. Elsewhere, I have written about young Asian American singer-songwriters on YouTube who often eschew race as central to their project of music making while mobilizing visibility around its category. In such instances, gestures toward the universalism of their art and an emergent sense of ethnic pride are not mutually exclusive positions (Wang 2015). While the contexts and audiences for whom they make music differ greatly, what emerges for both Liang and these young YouTube musicians is a desire for race and ethnicity not to lead listeners down a singular path that confirms existing conceptions, but to open up new ways of listening, dislodge existing categories, and perhaps, in the process, create more capacious imaginations of what the category "Asian American" might entail.

Conclusion

There is an album by Shanghai Restoration Project that is on constant replay in my household, a compilation of Chinese children's songs called *Little Dragon Tales*. I blame my preschooler for this compulsive listening and the delight she finds in familiarity and repetition. It could be worse. Liang notes that that he had in mind "children's songs that parents could stand listening to again and again" while working on the album and, in fact, made the album to fill a perceived gap in the U.S. market for Chinese children's songs. "A few years back," he recalled, "I had a lot of [parent] friends ask me for recommendations for Chinese children's music and I couldn't find any that I felt were produced well. But during my search, I rediscovered some songs I had learned as a child and found others that I hadn't been exposed to but enjoyed. So I decided to make a children's record of my own." Liang's album notwithstanding, my own search for compilations of Chinese children's songs continues to yield few albums that are not overladen with traditional sounds and cadences, a somewhat surprising fact given the growing interest in China and Chinese language learning among youth in the United States, the latter increasingly seen as imperative in order to compete globally.[6]

In my repeated listening to *Little Dragon Tales*, I have struggled to puzzle out what makes this album feel distinct from the collections by Starbucks and Putamayo—what makes it feel, in short, like a Chinese American interpretation of these children's songs. It may be the context I bring to my listening, my understanding of the research Liang conducted into these songs, and his intentions and goals for the project. It may be from watching the video of Yip's Children's Choir of Canada (the choral group featured on this album), which provides a glimpse into the process of making the album and the giddiness and exuberant sense of play these children bring to their singing. And it may be in the rawness of the kids' voices, the imperfections that Liang retains, the vocal improvisations he adds, and the mix of electronica and hip-hop that gives the music an extra layer of familiarity. I have come to the conclusion that the difference lies in the fact that the accretion of these details does not tally up to a whole—the sense that one is entering into another world, that of China or Asia more broadly—but rather, an invitation to listen with the openness and imagination of a child. As my preschooler sings along to the tracks and claps along to the syncopated rhythms, I wonder what soundtracks she will inherit about Chineseness, about being Asian American, about the stories she inherits about the United States and China, and whether projects like this can help her listen differently.

Notes

1 For an exploration of cultural strategies adopted by Chinese diasporic groups in the past two decades, see, for instance, Kuehn et al. (eds.), *Diasporic Chineseness after the Rise of China* (Vancouver: University of British Columbia Press, 2013).

2 Unless otherwise noted, quotes from Liang are from interviews conducted with the author, including a phone interview conducted on September 1, 2015 and various email correspondences.

3 For more on Shanghai jazz see Andrew Jones, *Yellow Music: Media Culture and Colonial Modernity in the Chinese Jazz Age* (Durham, NC: Duke University Press, 2001).

4 Putamayo is a world music label that had its origins as a clothing company.

5 Here, too, it is useful to turn our attention to how Asian American literary critics engage the problematics of the label "Asian American literature." For instance, Stephen Sohn reveals the tension between a literary marketplace that "continues to aggressively promote a form of racial authenticity" and Asian American writers who do not feel bound in their fictional worlds to necessarily write about recognizably Asian American characters and experiences. See Stephen Sohn, *Racial Asymmetries: Asian American Fictional Worlds* (New York: NYU Press, 2014), 14.

6 See, for instance, Audrey Cleo Yap, "The Changing Face of America's Chinese Schools," *The Atlantic*, November 30, 2015 and Nancy Lofhom, "Mandarin Chinese Becoming First Choice as a Second Language," *The Denver Post*, October 22, 2012.

References

Ang, Ien. 2013. "No Longer Rising? Residual Chineseness after the Rise of China." In *Diasporic Chineseness after the Rise of China*, Julia Kuehn, Kam Louie, and David M. Pomfret (eds), 17–31. Vancouver: University of British Columbia Press.

Born, Georgina and David Hesmondhalgh (eds). 2000. *Western Music and Its Others: Difference, Representation, and Appropriation in Music.* Berkeley: University of California Press.

Fellezs, Kevin. 2007. "Silenced but Not Silent: Asian Americans and Jazz." In *Alien Encounters: Popular Culture in Asian America*, Mimi Thi Nguyen and Thuy Linh Nguyen Tu (eds), 69–110. Durham, NC: Duke University Press.

Jones, Andrew. 2001. *Yellow Music: Media Culture and Colonial Modernity in the Chinese Jazz Age.* Durham, NC: Duke University Press.

Kuehn, Julia, Kam Louie, and David M. Pomfret (eds). 2013. *Diasporic Chineseness after the Rise of China: Communities and Cultural Production.* Vancouver: University of British Columbia Press.

Lam, Joseph. 1999. "Asian-American Music: Issues of an Heuristic Device." *Journal of Asian American Studies* 2(1): 29–60.

Lee, Leo Ou-fan. 1999. *Shanghai Modern: The Flowering of a New Urban Culture in China, 1930–1945.* Cambridge, MA: Harvard University Press.

Lofhom, Nancy. 2012. "Mandarin Chinese Becoming First Choice as a Second Language," *The Denver Post*, October 22.

Mimura, Glen. 2009. *Ghostlife of Third Cinema: Asian American Film and Video.* Minneapolis, MN: University of Minnesota Press.

Okada, Jun. 2013. *Making Asian American Film and Video: History, Institutions, Movements.* New Brunswick, NJ: Rutgers University Press.

Polkow, Dennis. 2011. "Chinglish Lessons: The Playwright on the Chicago Summer of David Henry Hwang," *Newcity Stage*, June 15. http://www.newcitystage.com/2011/06/15/chinglish-lessons-the-playwright-on-the-chicago-summer-of-david-henry-hwang/.

"Shanghai Restoration Project: Hybrid Backbeats." 2008. NPR Music, August 5. http://www.npr.org/templates/story/story.php?storyId=93298228.

Sharma, Nitasha. 2010. *Hip Hop Desis: South Asian Americans, Blackness, and a Global Race Consciousness.* Durham, NC: Duke University Press.

Sohn, Stephen. 2014. *Racial Asymmetries: Asian American Fictional Worlds.* New York: New York University Press.

Taylor, Timothy. 2010. *Strange Sounds: Music, Technology, and Culture.* New York: Routledge.

Tiongson, Jr, Antonio T. 2013. *Filipinos Represent: DJs, Authenticity, and the Hip Hop Nation.* Minneapolis: University of Minnesota Press.

Vazquez, Alexandra. 2013. *Listening in Detail: Performances of Cuban Music.* Durham, NC: Duke University Press.

Wang, Grace. 2015. *Soundtracks of Asian America: Navigating Race through Musical Performance.* Durham, NC: Duke University Press.

Wang, Oliver. 2007. "Rapping and Repping Asian: Race, Authenticity, and the Asian American MC." In *Alien Encounters: Popular Culture in Asian America*, Mimi Thi Nguyen and Thuy Linh Nguyen Tu (eds), 35–68. Durham, NC: Duke University Press.

Wilkinson, Alec. 2016. "Time Is a Ghost," *The New Yorker*, February 1.

Wong, Deborah. 2004. *Speak It Louder: Asian Americans Making Music.* New York: Routledge.

Yap, Audrey Cleo. 2015. "The Changing Face of America's Chinese Schools," *The Atlantic*, November 30.

4

COLLECTIVITY AND LONELINESS IN LAUREL NAKADATE'S POSTRACIAL IDENTITY AESTHETICS

Jun Okada

The concept of the postracial exists in great tension with Asian American film and video's history of collectivity, where racial solidarity has been formed through material, institutional, discursive, and aesthetic connections. Postraciality more generally came into vogue during Barack Obama's first term in office, when celebrations for the first Black U.S. president masked what sociologist Eduardo Bonilla-Silva (2010) has critiqued as evidence, instead, of an insidiously "colorblind racism." Although many reject postraciality due to the inaccurate implication that racial inequality has ended, there is a case to be made for a productive postraciality. Such a postraciality would not necessarily align with the familiar group identity politics that have formed the basis for Ethnic Studies, but with what I call an Asian American identity aesthetics. Although identity politics and, by implication, group identity have been the cornerstone of Asian American studies as established by scholars David Palumbo-Liu, Lisa Lowe, Sau-ling Cynthia Wong, and others, the notion of postraciality, whether real or imagined, problematizes the politics of racial collectivity. In this chapter, I posit the term "identity aesthetics" as an alternative to "identity politics" for describing the existence of critical, abstract or oblique references to racial identity that are beyond the usual (literal and political) investments in race by texts and authors, particularly as the former term refers to groups or collectivity. [1]

I specifically examine how the work of mixed race filmmaker and photographer Laurel Nakadate illustrates such an Asian American postracial discourse. Nakadate's work both supports and critiques postraciality in its paradoxical textual and contextual meanings. In order to come to terms with this paradox, I focus on her video installations: *Happy Birthday* (2000), *Lessons 1–10* (2001), *I Want to Be the One to Walk in the Sun* (2006), *Trouble Ahead Trouble Behind* (2005), *Love Hotel* (2005), and others. These videos feature Nakadate, scantily clad and provocatively posed, either alone or with an older White man playacting a variety of clichéd gender role scenarios. I explore how in this work, race is ignored, resisted, left out, and denied, despite its recalcitrant presence made visible through the vectors of critical discourse, hypersexuality, spectatorship, and relationality.

Key to contextualizing Nakadate's work within Asian American identity aesthetics is considering its concern with connection and relationality—concepts that come close to collectivity. And yet, as moving images, Nakadate's works ironically put forward the possibility of connection through the employment of its opposite: objectification, spectacle, and alienation. Nakadate holds the possibility of connection, either between herself and the audience or between herself and the White, older men in her films, in the balance, by incorporating the very codes that engage the spectator in an economy of power and desire. What is being desired and is ultimately out of reach is neither sex or power, but connection and community. I argue that, rather than simply distancing the viewer from the interaction depicted in the artwork, the videos engage in the mechanisms of scopophilia—not to illustrate the gendered powers of the gaze, but to illustrate the loss of connection and community in a so-called postracial world. Moreover, Nakadate's simultaneous engagement with and disavowal of race suggest the absence of any kind of solidarity in the act of making films, while reinforcing the longing for community, a conundrum that suggests how this work can be essential to the discourse of racialized identities while standing outside of its communal formation. In other words, racial collectivity as a concept raises the question of its opposite: apartness, isolation, and solitude. Specifically, the preoccupation with solitude in Nakadate's work reminds us that the nature of cinema—looking without being looked at and without being vulnerable to the look—fundamentally keeps us apart from one another.

While Nakadate's work has been most commonly understood as a feminist critique of the representation of gender, I tease out the less talked-about aspect of race in her work. I do so by historicizing her work within Asian American film and video production, in which Nakadate is nominally included. Asian American film and video has primarily built its reputation on collectivity, for reasons of material necessity as well as political intention against the institutional racism of Hollywood and network television. Before the explosion of widespread independent film production, collectivity was essential to Asian American film and video. The first films considered to have initiated Asian American film and video as a genre were produced by students in the EthnoCommunications program at UCLA in the early 1970s.

The Rise of EthnoCommunications and Asian American Collectivity

EthnoCommunications emerged as a film school forged by a collective mutiny of sorts, made up of students of color in reaction to the overwhelming Whiteness and maleness of the UCLA School of Film and Television's student body. These filmmakers of color—Black, Latino, Asian, and Native American—emerged in the wake of the Third World Peoples' Liberation movement, Civil Rights, and the state-wide Ethnic Studies movement, which established the nation's first of such programs at San Francisco State University and UC Berkeley. Subsequently, Asian American graduates of EthnoCommunications and other Asian American filmmakers established themselves, not by knocking on the doors of White, male Hollywood, but by creating grassroots media collectives like Visual Communications in LA, Asian CineVision in New York, and the National Asian American Telecommunications Association (NAATA) in San Francisco.

Collectivity was an economically necessary and politically sound philosophy that supported Asian American media production, distribution, exhibition, and reception. The first Visual Communications films were funded through various state and local grant programs. Importantly, they were credited not to a single director, writer, or producer, but to Visual Communications as an organization. This crediting served to emphasize the egalitarian and Marxist values of the group. In 1979–1980, larger shifts in public media enabled Asian American grassroots film production to move to a national and international platform. At this time, the Minority Consortia, a group representing the concerns of Native American, Black, Latino, Asian American, and Pacific Islander media, formed to help rededicate PBS's commitment to racial and ethnic diversity in public media. The Asian American consortium, NAATA, continued reinforcing the importance of the collective by working as a group to make programming decisions for films airing on PBS. Indeed, a strong ethos of collectivity undergirds much of the history of Asian American film and video up to the early 2000s. The first scholarly explorations of Asian American film and video (Leung 1992; Hamamoto and Liu 2000) foreground collectivity as the hallmark of the genre, even in the collaborative writing and editing processes that led to the publication of scholarship on Asian American media. Glen Mimura (2009) has argued that Asian American film and video is a descendent of the strongly communal ethos of Third Cinema, while Peter Feng (2002) traces the collectivity of Asian American filmmaking back to the notion of spectatorship. All of these works say in one way or another that what is unique to Asian American media production has been collectivity—that is, the community of filmmakers and their supporters working together to make films. Yet, this does not mean that notions of collectivity with regard to Asian American media are unproblematic, as we can see in the case of Laurel Nakadate.

Racializing Laurel Nakadate through Identity Aesthetics

My definition of an "identity aesthetics" comes out of a concern with art that is problematically centered on "identity politics"—in other words, art that prioritizes social change above "pure" creativity, or perhaps one that posits a binary between the two. Many have criticized and even dismissed Asian American film and video because it seemingly emphasizes the importance of racial identity, politics, and history in its creation over the more basic aspects of art making: form. And yet, for much of the history of the moving image, American Orientalism, in which notions of beauty masked the racist ways in which Asian people, places, and things were represented, troubled notions of "aesthetics" for Asian Americans trying to forge a new, historically accurate perspective in film and video. In between these critical positions lies an impasse, as neither allows the possibility for growth in a productive Asian American studies perspective on art: specifically, film and video. Nakadate's work presents the possibility to peer productively into this impasse, because her work concerns itself with the form of the video apparatus as well as registering the significance of racial difference represented by it. This complicates her work's concerns with connections and disconnections between male and female desires vis-à-vis filmmaking and the video image. In other words, despite the reception of her work in the mainstream press as a discourse on gender and power, what is not as commonly discussed is the obvious racial difference between Nakadate and her White male subjects as a part of that exchange.

One way that literary studies has arrived at a solution to the Asian American political/aesthetic impasse is in the idea of racial form, outlined as a significant turn in Asian American literary studies in Colleen Lye's *America's Asia: Racial Form and American Literature (1893–1945)*. Recent examples of this approach include Joseph Jeon's *Racial Things, Racial Forms* (2012) and Stephen Sohn's *Racial Asymmetries* (2014), which explore avant-garde and narrative texts from a postracial perspective. They focus on a need to find new ways of thinking about literary formalism beyond the historical struggle for racial equality and identity that marked so much of Asian American literature of the twentieth century. In his explanation of looking beyond racial identity concerns in his study of Asian American avant-garde literature, Jeon says:

> Eschewing many of the conventions of minority writing, these poets investigate the nexus of issues that I have grouped under the rubric of *things*, instead of rehearsing the traditional claims of resistant subjectivity that characterizes more recent iterations of identity politics, which tend to challenge political marginalization without contesting a priori assumptions about how race is fundamentally visualized.
>
> (Jeon 2012: xxxvi)

Like Jeon's study of "things" over identities, my study of Laurel Nakadate's video installations focuses on an aesthetics that is untethered to the usual methods of tracing meaning in Asian American art, and by necessity, as Nakadate's work *does* indeed interrogate formal aspects of the moving image—frame, point of view, mise-en-scène, cinematography—as pointed questions about the way both race and gender are "fundamentally visualized." Race is necessarily a part of her work's meaning without needing to fly the well-worn flag of Asian American identity politics. Instead, what we find is a fine-tuned, sharp, and open exploration into what film/video is, and who we are in it: identity aesthetics.

Although Laurel Nakadate does not self-identify as an Asian American artist or filmmaker, she has nonetheless been recognized within criticism and academic scholarship on Asian American media arts production. This recognition has created a certain ambivalence about the role of race in her work,[2] despite the fact that the obvious racial difference between Nakadate and her White male subjects is crucial to its interpretation. On the one hand, Nakadate understands the racial power of her work and sometimes acknowledges the fact that race is being read in her work. As she says in a *New York Magazine* interview, "After hundreds of years of art history, a young half-Asian girl meets older white men, and *she's* the predator? Suddenly no one can take it?" (Siegel 2015). On the other, Nakadate has also minimized the role that race plays in her work. For instance, in an interview with Laura Kina and Way Ming Dariotis (2013), she denies the relevance of her Japanese American heritage and her appearance as central to her work, admitting that she feels more "Midwestern" than Asian American. Kent Ono and Sarah Projansky (2003) argue that the race of an author does enter into meaning and interpretation through what they term the "discursive auteur" who "produces discourse about her or his film, is often seen as the origin of textual meaning by members of the press, and by the audience, is a subject positioned in particular ways in relation to the larger culture, and is a laborer within a global capitalist economy" (Projansky and Ono 2003: 264).

Thus, despite the disavowal of an explicit racialization of the image in her work, Nakadate as an Asian American/mixed race artist inevitably becomes a part of the production of meaning. In 2006, when her work appeared in the major group show of Asian American art organized by the Asia Society, "One Way or Another," the exhibition's co-curator, Melissa Chiu, stated:

> For a lot of these artists, there's a comfort level, almost an innocence about being Asian. Compared to previous ones, they have less of a conflicted sense of self .... I take [video artist] Laurel Nakadate as an example. When we invited her to participate in this show, she said: "Oh, yeah, that sounds kinda fun. I've never been in a show like that before."
>
> (Chiu et al. 2006: 227)

Regardless of the "innocence about being Asian," the simultaneous centrality and disavowal of race in the work creates a dissonance. Ultimately, it is Nakadate's choice to use herself in her work and connect it to the concerns of Asian American film and video culture.

In order to understand the way that Laurel Nakadate's work stands outside of Asian American film and video's preoccupation with collectivity, let us explore the identity aesthetics of her work. In doing so, we can see the way that Nakadate's works can be (and are inevitably) understood through a racial lens, but that she disavows an easy form of collectivity and community formation simply because of her racial identity. In contrast, she often deploys a racial aesthetic in order to depict the loss of connection, or the establishment of new, sometimes troubling, power dynamics. For instance, her visual presence can often be seen to elevate the gendered power games through her harnessing of a racialized hypersexuality that has become inextricably linked to the Asian American female body (Parreñas Shimizu 2007).

The performance of a specifically racialized hypersexuality is underscored within one of Nakadate's first video installations, *Lessons 1–10*. The videos document the artist turning the tables on a collection of awkward, middle-aged, White male strangers whom she met on the internet or on the street. In one video from *Lessons 1–10*, Nakadate parodies the male artist/female model cliché by becoming "a model for a middle-aged artist of uncertain talent" (Chiu et al. 2006: 92). She sits in the foreground of a static shot, staring relentlessly and knowingly at the camera, while the man is ordered to produce drawings of her semi-nude or nude body. *Lessons 1–10* is a joke on the man playing the artist, because Nakadate, who plays the model in the piece, is actually the artist, and she makes sure you know it by looking repeatedly into her camera. As the girl with the camera, Nakadate's character quite literally looms large in her playfully tacky, girl-power lace skivvies, compared with her much smaller male counterpart in the background. Ultimately, the spectatorial position is one of being somehow uncomfortably stared down by the over-confident gaze of post-feminism, with Nakadate intensely aware of her "to-be-looked-at-ness." As a by-product, it is the enfeebled, shy men who take the place of women as scopophilic objects.

Critics picked up on this reversal, but failed to point out how race plays out in Nakadate's table-turning power play. Nakadate is seen as "a kind of aggressive 'Olympia' presence," a scandal-causing nineteenth-century painting of a prostitute of the pre-Impressionist Paris Salons (Saltz 2005). The sex and gender dynamic is framed through the tradition of European painting, disregarding the context of the racial strategies of American popular cinema. Though it is obvious that she "returns the gaze" onto her bewildered co-stars, what was not problematized in the work's critical discourse was the role of racialized sexuality. Hypersexuality gives this work an important representational texture related to ways in which racial difference "involves an inherently different sexuality essentialized to race and culture" (Parreñas Shimizu 2007: 65). Not only does Nakadate reconfigure the gaze economy to confront the voyeurism and fetishism inherent in Hollywood cinema, but she does so in a way that references one of the key films of postwar Hollywood Orientalism, *The World of Suzie Wong* (Richard Quine, 1960). In this classic film, an ex-pat painter (William Holden) goes to Hong Kong to find himself by falling in love with his "Eurasian" model, Suzie (Nancy Kwan), a woman who turns out to be a prostitute. What is more, as the men in Nakadate's videos are exclusively White, a racialized gaze is crucial to their meaning. The critical discourse surrounding Nakadate's work, therefore, demonstrates the ways in which the "high art" context of Nakadate's video installations gets connected to the history of continental art, but not to popular forms of Hollywood genre cinema and media in general. This points out the dearth of a politicized discourse of race in contemporary art criticism and the importance of the role of race, wherever it be, in art. What the history of Asian American media collectives does not address is the need for an inclusive discursive practice that considers all Asian American artists, regardless of the political nature of their work.

Relationality and Scopophilia

Nakadate's deployment of identity aesthetics in order to question Asian American collectivity can also be seen within the specifically "relational" (and racial) interaction between the artist and her subjects. By capturing encounters with strangers on video, Nakadate practices the open, interactive, stripped-down nature of a mode of interactive, participatory art known as "relational art." Yet, the intervention of the video camera changes it irrevocably, taking the work back to a space of control and a unidirectional relationship between the viewer and the viewed. Relationality or relational aesthetics appeared as an art trend in the late 1990s, which Nicholas Bourriaud (1998) defined as "a set of artistic practices which take as their theoretical and practical point of departure the whole of human relations and their social context, rather than an independent and private space" (113). Relational art distinguished itself by displacing the traditional object in art with relations between participants, suggesting that participation, connection, and interaction in real time might themselves become art. For example, Bourriaud describes: "Rirkrit Tiravanija organizes a dinner in a collector's home, and leaves him all the ingredients required to make a Thai soup. Philippe Parreno invites a few people to pursue their favorite hobbies on May Day, on a factory assembly line" (7). The dinner party as artwork reveals relational aesthetics as "the moment of shared communication in the realization of the artwork" (7). Relational art came of age at the dawn of the internet, when the status of social networks began to be transformed by the digital and the virtual. It tries to break ties with heavy conceptualizations of postwar art and art theory and focuses on the relationship between the art and the viewer or participant, envisaging the audience as a community. Rather than the artwork being an encounter between a viewer and an object, relational art produces intersubjective encounters. Through these encounters, meaning is elaborated *collectively*, rather than in the space of individual consumption. This kind of participatory art emerged during a Utopian moment in the 1990s when links to a more egalitarian past and the connectedness promised by the digital future hung in the balance. This is crucial in contextualizing the evolution of Nakadate's work from pure participation to the hybrid participation/spectacle, which appears as a kind of elegy for the community created by that earlier trend in art—and by extension, collectivity of any order, including Asian American collectivities.

Within this historical context, rather than fetishizing body parts, Nakadate's videos fetishize lost connection and friendship through the ruse of "resisting the male gaze." Nakadate's videos long for the possibility of connection between two disparate people—a connection that must be created and revived under false pretenses by putting it into the service of a classic gaze economy. It is this so-called "relationality" that is being objectified and held at a distance. By bottling up possible scenarios of social connection for us to watch, Nakadate's videos create a sense of nostalgia for friendship, which may at first be obscured through her superficial evocation of Lolita, Olympia, and Suzie Wong. Indeed, in many ways, it is the apocryphal stories of how Nakadate found these sad-looking men in real life that create the videos' aura of authenticity, danger, pathos, and relationality.

In Nakadate's earliest video series in this vein, *Happy Birthday* (2000), she has a fake birthday party with a series of middle-aged, poverty-stricken bachelors who live in a single room occupancy hotel. This offers another example of how the loss of community and connection haunts all of her work. In this series, Nakadate and one of her subjects sing "Happy Birthday," blow out birthday candles, and have cake. The videos suggest a milieu of solitary individuals living under difficult and spare circumstances, and yet, in choosing to film a childlike birthday party for two, Nakadate diverts the lascivious gaze onto a solemn vision of humble connection between two unlikely acquaintances taking place in an unlikely location. Nakadate is clearly pointing out the absurdity of hyperobjectification as an antidote to connection and community.

Another painful example of the problem of hyperobjectification is a video from her series *I Want to Be the One to Walk in the Sun* (2006). Nakadate sits on the counter in a convenience store with multiple trophies of buck heads hanging on the wall. She and an older, overweight White man, perhaps the store's proprietor, take turns removing items of clothing in an awkward game of strip poker. Laurel wears a white cowboy hat, a midriff-baring Superman baby t-shirt, and a hot pink mini skirt. Sitting, half straddled, on the counter that separates the two, Laurel first takes off her cowboy hat; then, her co-star takes off his trucker cap. Laurel gazes intently, giddily, into the camera and takes off her shrunken superman t-shirt, revealing a Hawaiian printed bikini top. They exchange words and the man takes off his denim shirt, revealing a fat, untoned, pale, hairy torso. Laurel keeps looking defiantly outside the store and into the camera as she takes off her mini skirt and stands up on the counter as the man quickly puts his shirt back on. In this exchange, it is clear from the man's affect that he is uncomfortable with taking his clothes off. Rather than a seductive collaborative striptease, it becomes a taunting competition between a beautiful, fit young body in full possession of itself and one that is overweight, unsightly, and therefore vulnerable. Nakadate invites looking, but instead of the classic pleasure of looking at an attractive young female body, the pleasure of witnessing the squirming discomfort of the unattractive older man becomes part of the pleasure/displeasure of the viewing experience, hence bringing to fore the sadism inherent in objectification.

In these videos, Nakadate is successful in diverting the so-called male gaze—not by challenging the position and identity of the spectator, but by bringing the gaze under the contemporary scrutiny of judgment of personal appearance or to-be-looked-at-ness, which, under extreme forms of capitalism, has become equal territory for men as well as women. In her videos, the men are lacking. To instill ridicule and embarrassment as the cause of pleasure in looking has caused some to call her work cruel and raises the issue of whether the structure of scopophilia ultimately objectifies whoever is the one with less power. So, although Nakadate has discovered how to redirect the male gaze back onto the men, the mechanism is inherently still that of disempowerment. Yet, there is something else going on that may free her work from this predicament, which is born precisely out of the pathos that viewers and critics may experience on witnessing the shaming of the men in Nakadate's videos. Ultimately, she wields the power of looking relations, but shifts attention from who wields this power to focus on absence, loneliness, and the possibility for connection in a disconnected world. Viewed as a clever spectacle, her videos are art in the classical, pictorial, objective sense. But viewed as an exercise in participation or relationality, her videos exceed objectification, spectacle, and the power relations they manipulate. By interweaving the process of participation and relational aesthetics, they confound the simplistic effect of looking relations. It is through participation that the work speaks to the sense of isolation and yearning for connection that is just out of reach.

What Nakadate's videos demonstrate is the binary imposed between relationality/collectivity/interactivity and solipsism/alienation/passivity in art. If the premise of Nakadate's work is to suggest that marginalized, older, blue-collar White men connect to a privileged, upper-middle-class, Ivy League-educated biracial young woman through the commonality of loneliness, what does it mean for this relationship to be captured on video, to be viewed from a single perspective under the classical, narrowly defined, non-interactive, visual codes of cinema? Claire Bishop says:

> [T]he dominant narrative of the history of socially engaged, participatory art across the twentieth century is one in which the activation of the audience is positioned against its mythic counterpart, passive spectatorial consumption. Participation thus forms part of a larger narrative that traverses modernity: art must be directed against contemplation, against spectatorship, against the passivity of the masses paralyzed by the spectacle of modern life.
>
> (Bishop 2012: 275)

In delving beneath the shock value of Nakadate's videos, we can see the possibility of social change through a longing for connection that is denied through classical spectatorship. Even more, reading racial difference as part of the discourse in her videos heightens the works' reference to the visual language of objectification. Again, it raises the issue of Nakadate's authorial persona as Asian American, and hence, her association with the collective politics of Asian American film and video. Nakadate's work exemplifies what Celine Parreñas Shimizu (2007) has called a hypersexual strategy of productive perversity, which she describes as "identifying with 'bad' images" in order to lay claim to a sense of ownership over these images (Parreñas Shimizu 2007: 21). Though this racial discourse is not made explicit, Nakadate's videos critique and poke fun at "normative scripts for sexually and racially marginalized subjects" by referencing and ironically treating conventions of classically sexist genres of visual culture—classical Western oil painting, Hollywood cinema, music videos, and pornography.

Loneliness as a Counter to Collectivity

The explosion of Asian American collective digital video production on YouTube, including those discussed by Vanessa Au and Lori Lopez in this collection, can make it seem that Asian American film and video have enjoyed a continued history of collectivity and community. And yet, Asian American film and video artists such as Nakadate seem to haunt this history at the edges. In fact, Nakadate's work even seems aggressively antithetical to this collectivity in fetishizing the aesthetics of loneliness. If sexual possession is the goal of desire, friendship is the goal of loneliness. My focus on the fetish of friendship/community/collectivity in Nakadate's work speaks to the lack, decay, or decline of "Asian American solidarity." In an oblique way, I read her work as a commentary on the solitary non-White artist working in a still very White art establishment that deems itself a part of a mythical postracial world.

Nakadate's work troubles the narrative of an unbroken, historically rooted Asian American media production that grew out of a sense of racial resistance and racial solidarity. Though some Asian American media producers have taken to YouTube and the digital world to continue to seek mainstream relevancy, there are others who work alone and who uphold a notion of racial form and identity aesthetics that expands the notion of Asian American moving image art. Nakadate's videos, therefore, offer a productive critique of the myth of collectivity as the preferred path to resistance against racism, sexism, and other forms of alienation. I agree with Claire Bishop when she says that "the most striking projects … unseat all of the polarities on which this discourse [of participatory art] is founded—individual vs. collective, author vs. spectator, active vs. passive, real life vs. art—but not with the goal of collapsing them" (278). Particularly as artists are turning away from racial and ethnic communal identification, the relationship of Nakadate's work to Asian American film and video is worthy of discussion.

The videos Nakadate has made by herself, with no participants, and which focus on solitude, absence, and loneliness, drive the point home even more. For example, her video *Trouble*

Ahead Trouble Behind presents a scenario of Nakadate in a train car by herself, baring her breasts at the window toward a barren landscape devoid of people. The train passes, and she lifts her shirt repeatedly and randomly, with a look of accomplishment on her face toward the camera. As a defiant and humorous mimicry of the *Girls Gone Wild* pornographic video franchise that was popular in the 1990s, *Trouble Ahead* reveals the absurdity of the bizarre combination of narcissism, abuse, and profit that this phenomenon produced. In *Love Hotel*, Nakadate films herself in flamboyant lingerie mimicking the movements of sexual intercourse with an invisible partner in various love hotels, which are Japanese hotel rooms rented by the hour, usually by couples. Both of these examples offer versions of classical scenes of female objectification. Yet, a crucial element is subtracted from these scenes. In classical examples of the male gaze, the viewer of the photograph or moving image is triangulated with that of a male spectator. In *Trouble Ahead*, the video triangulates the viewer into its gaze economy, but the necessary second gaze, of the spectator in the image, is missing. By subtracting the male gaze within the text, the viewer shares his/her spectatorship with no one, with an empty space where male spectatorship should be. As Nakadate looks at both the empty landscape devoid of human eyes and the camera, or the viewer, we are left to share the spectacle with no one. Similarly, in *Love Hotel*, the hollowness and awkwardness of Nakadate going through the motions of sex with an invisible partner are just that—hollow and awkward, made even more so with the addition of her festive underwear, bought, as she notes, in a Walmart. There, again, the participant spectator is missing, and we are left alone.

In the same way as relational art in the 1990s reflected the optimism of that time, Nakadate's work exudes a sense of unforeseen isolation. Nakadate's early work revolves around the concept of loneliness as an effect of contemporary life that levels everything else, even the battle of the sexes. Despite the violence and power struggles that continue to exist between men and women, she finds a point of connection in identifying with the loneliness and isolation she sees in her White male participants. She says: "I am obsessed with men who live alone with no one to care for them. I am always watching them, because they are invisible people in our culture. They don't have wives or children; they don't have anyone to go home to. I think about the desire to be saved from loneliness, the way one life can change another" (Nakadate 2006). It can be assumed that these men are alone due to lack of family, jobs, or capital of any sort, or to any number of unsupported physical, mental, or emotional disabilities. Ultimately, the act of containing relationality and participation through video seems to deny the possibility of art making social change, or celebrating connectedness as some sort of ideal. It exposes the problematic utopianism that attended the rhetoric around participatory art and its potential to change society. By watching these men participate in her art from afar, one continues to be distant from others, not connected.

Conclusion

While Nakadate's complex negotiations of collectivity and individuality are important to untangle, ultimately we must consider what her work means within the framework of Asian American media art. As mentioned previously by Ono and Projansky, an artist of color will be identified as such regardless of the topic or discourse of the text that has been produced. Although collectivity in Asian American media production has historically been a political response to marginalization, elitism, and racism, it itself marginalizes those who work alone and whose work thematizes aloneness apart from the collective, despite being inevitably categorized as part of an Asian American collectivity. Despite Nakadate's self-imposed isolation and lack of awareness, she will always be identified as an Asian American artist. In 2014, poet and art critic John Yau showed how this occurs in his discussion of the Whitney Biennial:

> Now that the Whitney Biennial is finally over, did anyone notice that Patty Chang, Nikki S. Lee, and Laurel Nakadate weren't included, just to mention three mid-career, Asian-American women artists who were conspicuously absent? Forget about younger Asian-American women artists like Jiha Moon and Chie Fueki—they don't seem to stand a chance. And of course Mel Chin wasn't in the Biennial, because what's he ever done for you lately? What's up with that?
>
> When the ubiquitous term "people of color" is used, does the speaker or writer also mean Asian Americans—itself a complicated category? Or do yellow and red get tossed out, like dirty bathwater?
>
> Or should Asian Americans simply check the box labeled "Other" and quietly and politely go—like all well-behaved Asian Americans—into the room marked INVISIBLE.
>
> (Yau 2014)

As Yau points out, it doesn't matter if an Asian American artist disavows race—she will be grouped as such because of an inherent institutional marginalization. Despite the well-documented continuation of institutional racism and gender marginalization in the art world, Nakadate and others refute the need to address this either in their work or outside of it.

In *Strangers and Relations* (2014), Nakadate eschews her racial identity in two ways—first, by not appearing in the images herself; second, by including photographs of her relatives from her White mother's side of the family, which she found using a DNA testing service. Nakadate bases this series of images exclusively on her White (or at least non-Asian) lineage, completely bypassing the so-called genetics of her father's Japanese American lineage. She describes the exhibit in a press release:

> In my early videos, I physically appeared in the work. In these new portraits, I am allowing my body, my DNA, to navigate my direction; where I will travel and whom I will meet. These strangers, who are also distant cousins, share bits of DNA with me—in some ways, these images become modern day self-portraits. I see these strangers, who are also relatives, as little glimmers of the ancestors who connected us hundreds of years ago.

By creating a lineage of her own that starts with herself, she "physically appeared in the work." Yet, these images of her distant American relatives seem to suggest a celebration of White America by subtly sweeping the complications of her "DNA" under the rug. This work also points to Nakadate's own determination of her identity as mostly "Midwestern," as she was born and raised in Iowa. She disavows any significant racial or ethnic label, taking up a pos-tracial identity for herself. So, despite her marginalization as an Asian American, which is a racial issue, her work at once deliberately eschews race while at the same time, it strangely and powerfully invokes it.

While one may regard this work as Nakadate passing for White, or further denying her Asian Americanness, what is clear is that she resists the established path toward recognition from the art world. John Yau asks:

> Is it true that if you are a person of color (black, brown, yellow or red), the only way to get into the Biennial is to make work that deals with racial identity in a way that is acceptable? Who determines that agenda? If you go by the Whitney's curatorial choices, the answer is obvious. You have to do what white curators want or you are going to remain invisible. So while everyone was applauding the number of mid-career abstract women artists who were in this year's Biennial, no one gave a hoot that they were all white.
>
> (Yau 2014)

While one may critique Nakadate's choice to avoid race, she also avoids falling into the trap dictating that in order to be recognized by the White establishment, you have to make race explicit. This requirement reminds us that the trends of postracism and resisting racial community and collectivity are both necessary and problematic. Nakadate's work reflects a post-Asian American aesthetic, which paradoxically centers on the way that Asian Americans can attempt to dispel the notion that race matters, but will be ignored as a result. It seems that in order for artists of color to transcend this institutional racism, they must continue making art that doesn't reference race. If this is the case, collectives like Asian American film and video must continue to support this choice.

Notes

1 Asian American literary studies is strongly informative for Asian American media studies; for example, Joseph Jeon's *Racial Things, Racial Forms* (2012) and Stephen Sohn's *Racial Asymmetries* (2014) explore avant-garde and narrative literatures from a postracial perspective, an approach that I try to emulate here.

2 A Yale MFA-trained photographer who has made video installations for galleries, as well as the independent feature films *Stay the Same Never Change* (2009), *The Wolf Knife* (2010), and *The Miraculous* (2012), Nakadate's films do not explicitly reference Asian American themes. Her video art and photography has been the focus of numerous awards and honors, including a one-woman retrospective, *Laurel Nakadate: Only the Lonely* at Museum of Modern Art: PS 1, in 2011.

References

Bishop, Claire. 2012. *Artificial Hells: Participatory Art and the Politics of Spectatorship*. New York: Verso Books.

Bonilla-Silva, Eduardo. 2010. *Racism without Racists: Color-blind Racism and the Persistence of Racial Inequality in the United States*. Lanham: Rowman & Littlefield Publishers.

Bourriaud, Nicolas. 1998. *Relational Aesthetics*. Paris: Les Presses Du Reel.

Chiu, Melissa, Karen Higa, and Susette Min (eds). 2006. *One Way or Another: Asian American Art Now*. New Haven, CT: Asia Society with Yale University Press.

Feng, Peter. 2002. *Identities in Motion: Asian American Film and Video*. Durham: Duke University Press.

Hamamoto, Darrell Y. and Sandra Liu (eds). 2000. *Countervisions: Asian American Film Criticism*. Philadelphia: Temple University Press.

Jeon, Joseph Jonghyun. 2012. *Racial Things, Racial Forms: Objecthood in Avant-garde Asian American Poetry*. Iowa City: University of Iowa Press.

Kina, Laura and Way Ming Dariotis (eds). 2013. "Gravity Always Wins: An Interview with Laurel Nakadate." In *War Baby/Love Child: Mixed Race Asian American Art*. Seattle: University of Washington Press.

Leong, Russell (ed). 1992. *Moving the Image: Independent Asian Pacific American Media Arts*. Los Angeles: UCLA Asian American Studies Center Press.

Lye, Colleen. 2005. *America's Asia: Racial Form and American Literature (1893–1945)*. Princeton, NJ: Princeton University Press.

Mimura, Glen M. 2009. *Ghostlife of Third Cinema Asian American Film and Video*. Minneapolis: University of Minnesota Press.

Nakadate, Laurel. 2006. *I Want to Be the One Who Walks in the Sun*. Artist's Statement.

Nakadate, Laurel (director). 2009. *Stay the Same Never Change.*

Nakadate, Laurel (director). 2010. *The Wolf Knife.*

Nakadate, Laurel (director). 2014. *The Miraculous.*

Parreñas-Shimizu, Celine. 2007. *The Hypersexuality of Race: Performing Asian/American Women on Screen and Scene.* Durham: Duke University Press.

Projansky, Sarah and Kent A. Ono. 2003. "Making Films Asian American: *Shopping for Fangs* and the Discursive Auteur." In *Authorship and Film*, David A. Gerstner and Janet Staiger (eds), New York: Routledge Chapman and Hall.

Saltz, Jerry. 2005. "Whatever Laurel Wants," *Village Voice*, April 26. http://www.villagevoice.com/arts/whatever-laurel-wants-7137871.

Siegel, Miranda. 2011. "The Provocateur: Laurel Nakadate," *New York Magazine*, December 4. http://nymag.com/arts/cultureawards/2011/laurel-nakadate/.

Sohn, Stephen Hong. 2014. *Racial Asymmetries: Asian American Fictional Worlds.* New York City: New York University Press.

Yau, John. 2014. "Postscript to the Whitney Biennial: An Asian American Perspective," hyperallergic.com, June 29. http://hyperallergic.com/135205/postscript-to-the-whitney-biennial-an-asian-american-perspective/.

5

ASIAN AMERICAN MEDIA PUBLIC VERNACULARS

Debating the State of Asian American Media

Vincent N. Pham

In 1980, a small group of Asian American media activists convened on the campus of University of California, Berkeley and created the National Asian American Telecommunications Association (NAATA), currently known as the Center for Asian American Media (CAAM). Since its inception, CAAM's influence regarding independent Asian American media is arguably unparalleled. Its annual film festival, started in 1982, helped launch the careers of filmmakers like Wayne Wang, Justin Lin, and Jennifer Phang. CAAM's partnership with the Public Broadcasting Service (PBS) provided selected documentaries with inroads to distribution and exhibition with mainstream audiences. In addition, CAAM's institutional relationship with PBS's funding and programming system shaped Asian American self-representation by cultivating a vibrant yet limited documentary film culture (Okada 2005, 2015). And as part of the National Minority Consortia, which is funded by the Corporation for Public Broadcasting, CAAM and other minority groups help diversify public television, as a whole, with minority (self-)representations and stories. Their distribution arm helped bring Asian American documentaries into college and community center classrooms across the nation.

CAAM's support helped institutionalize Asian American media through distributing Asian American film and cultivating young filmmakers via production grants and exhibitions at Asian American-themed film festivals. Yet with the establishment of Asian American media infrastructures, contemporary Asian American media culture, community, production, and consumption began shifting to online settings, such as YouTube and Twitter. As a result, audience members can now spend their time sifting through online forums or streaming on-demand video; audience members can get their taste of Asian American media in their homes and on their computers or phones instead of venturing to organizations and festivals where such Asian American-focused media previously resided. This shift poses challenges and potential opportunities for the development of Asian American media and the goals of media organizations like CAAM.

Cognizant of these changes in contemporary media culture, CAAM sponsored the "Present/Future Summit" (hereafter known as the Summit) during its 2012 annual film festival. On March 11, 2012, Asian American media makers, their supporters, internet celebrities, academics, students, and network associates filled a small conference hall in the Hotel Kabuki in San Francisco's Japantown to have a public conversation. While the 1980 meeting of Asian American media activists sought to address the dearth of Asian American representation and the prevalence of negative Asian American images in mainstream media, the 2012 Summit sought to make sense of a quickly shifting media environment that dialectically threatens and assists the very mission of CAAM—"to confront and challenge negative images of Asians within mainstream media" (Wang n.d.).

Taken alongside CAAM's work, the Summit provides an opportunity to engage with Asian American rhetoric in its multiplicity of forms for a community invested in questions about Asian American media. In this chapter, I examine the 2012 Present/Future Summit and how participants implicitly and explicitly make sense of an "Asian American media" within the often unspoken historical background of CAAM and its mission. While "Asian American media" can be defined by its content (movies, television shows, YouTube videos, and film festivals), this chapter focuses on the discussions and debates about its past, current, and future possibilities. This discourse-oriented approach emphasizes how participants construct meaning and place values on arguments about "Asian American media," as opposed to leaving such meaning making to content creators and media makers. Importantly, this recognizes the flexibility of the term "Asian American" and how it can be, as Ono (1995) asserts, "re/signed"; that is, simultaneously retired and/or refigured for contemporary purposes. I start with a description of the Summit and contextualize its history within the larger mission of the organization and its previous events. I suggest analyzing organized events that address Asian American media makers and organizations through public sphere theory, which emphasizes attending to the circulation of ideas via debate and discussion (Habermas 1964, 1989). I briefly draw upon public sphere, particularly public modality, and rhetorical theory to situate the Summit as a persuasive event about the direction and mission of Asian American media. Then I turn my attention to the "Summit" as a meaning-making event—one meant to revisit and reconsider the "state of Asian American media." In doing so, I recognize that an event like the Summit enacts a vernacular discourse about Asian American media, reflecting the needs of the community while challenging and reifying mainstream conceptions of such a community.

By drawing on my own presence at the Summit as well as publicly available YouTube videos of the speakers, I dive into the specific discourse itself, attending to the micro-level arguments, dialogues, and discussions present at the Summit and the various rhetorical strategies that articulate and disarticulate the political project of Asian American media.[1] I elucidate the themes that revolve around storytelling and the politics of Asian America, arguing that the Summit situates itself within the market logic of cultural production where film, television, and media can communicate the possibilities of "Asian American" identity devoid of political action. Thus, it problematically absolves Asian American media of having a political goal and individuates media makers from a community and history of activism while allowing the freedom to complicate/adapt a notion of Asian American media to suit contemporary times.

Private Discussions to the Public Forum

Held on a Sunday afternoon at 1 pm, the Summit filled a large conference room with an audience of over 100 people—well beyond the expected attendance, and requiring more chairs to be brought in to accommodate the standing crowd. The 2012 Summit is a self-described "fast-paced, provocative dialogue engaging today's most interesting thinkers and creators" under a "one-part TED Talk, one-part Town Hall" style of engagement (Marky 2012). Stephen Gong, the executive director of CAAM, described the setting as a "mini-conference" of sorts, uniting the creative minds present at the film festival to have a public conversation about Asian American media. The Summit was structured with five speakers, and corresponding respondents followed with an audience question and answer section. Spanning five topics and in 30-minute time blocks, the Summit expanded upon a strictly lecture format—where a speaker stands in front of an audience—to include audience members on the sides and a projection screen behind the speakers, not only for their presentations but also to display live tweets under the #pfsummit identifier after the speaker/respondent section and during their question and answer sessions. In addition, physically present audiences could ask questions through two wireless microphones and two microphone stands near their seating.

Whereas rhetorical scholars often direct their attention to political conventions and the speeches within them, media scholars often overlook these types of events and the organizations that hold them. Comic Con has received recent attention from media scholars, since it serves an intersecting site of fandom and media industry (Hanna 2013a,b; Jenkins 2012; Kohnen 2014; Perin 2010). Although Shankar (2015) and Lopez (2016) have analyzed Asian American marketing agencies and their physical conventions, they were primarily concerned with the cultivation of an Asian American consumer. Rhetorical theory provides a useful entrée into understanding the public discourse at the Summit, since it is well equipped to look at discourse with instrumental and constitutive purposes while being cognizant of cultural, social, and political constraints. Although rhetoric can be understood as a functional *techne* to persuade via the "available means of persuasion" (Aristotle 1991: 36), rhetoric can also be seen in its constitutive fashion and as the primary process by which social conduct is coordinated and social knowledge is constructed (Farrell 1976). Asian American rhetoric is concerned specifically with, as Mao and Young (2008) state, the "rhetoric of becoming" or the constant process of negotiating with and adapting to the identity of being Asian American. In this case, what is Asian American media (be)coming in this moment, and what social knowledge is created in this process of becoming? While this rhetoric is discernable via textual analysis of the speeches and videos, I also draw on my experience of being present at the event, where the tenor and tone of discussion, as well as the energy of conversation, are relevant. The event was set in a large conference room, lending it an air of importance by the programmers. Yet the enthusiasm and interest in the topic and speakers exceeded expectations, resulting in standing room only for attendees and going over the scheduled three-hour time slot into a solid four-hour event. Being in the audience and festival space organized by CAAM provides access to and insight into the discussions that are occurring in the presence of established media makers, producers, and influencers that are often lost when mediated through recorded videos.

Even though artists and media makers construct the very content that encompasses the category of "Asian American media," CAAM maintains an important role as the preeminent Asian American media organization with institutional connections to the PBS. In this role, CAAM inhabits the "middle-zone" of cultural production: the space where not necessarily artists and consumers but, rather, gatekeepers, proponents, and administrators of culture work reside (English 2005). Thus, CAAM acts a representative of the Asian American community in places from which they have been excluded historically, mainly in public television and high culture spaces such as cinema. Most of the organizational decisions—from festival programming to distribution—are made internally and privately. In this instance, this conversation is made into a public one, providing a formalized avenue to interrogate Asian American media practices and media environment and to cultivate a discussion between experts, organizations, and audience. Such discourse can shape "Asian American media" itself: how the festival is curated, which films are marketed, which filmmakers will be supported with production grants, what topics are discussed, and what types of content are featured, to name a few.

Importantly, *how* they come to such a response can dictate whose voices are heard, what perspectives are taken into account, and which perspectives and approaches are foregrounded while others are overlooked or ignored. The 2012 Present/Future Summit was one of the rare moments when such an organization facilitated a public conversation between media makers, institutional funders, and audience members caught in between.

It's important to note that the Summit is not a unique event. As stated earlier, CAAM was founded in a similar type of Summit in 1980, and a follow-up event to the 2012 CAAM Summit was held at the 2012 San Diego Asian Film Festival. In recent years, a version of "the Summit" was held at the festival known as the Film Festival Programmers' Meeting. However, the Programmers' Meeting was held in private, privy only to those involved with Asian Pacific Islander American APIA film festivals across the nation. These meetings were often held on the Friday afternoon of the film festival, when few films are screened and the general audience of the festival might be at work but out-of-town guests would easily be able to attend. I attended these meetings from 2009 to 2011 and in 2013, when as many as 13 APIA film festival programmers—those who are at the forefront of Asian American independent media exhibition—convened in a conference room to privately discuss their trials, tribulations, and successes among a group of like-minded individuals.

The 2012 Summit was unique is its publicness, the very mode it sought to engage via its TED-townhall-Twitter style. The Summit provided an opportunity to unite interested parties in a place where the social conduct pertaining to "Asian American media" could be debated, discussed, and negotiated. It resembled a public sphere in its emphasis on public discussion via the large conference room, where many people could discuss the trials and tribulations of Asian American media, but also a counterpublic one due to the shared experience of being historically marginalized by the (mainstream) media (Asen and Brouwer 2001, Felski 1989, Fraser 1990, Squires 2001). Members of the Asian American community sought to affirm their relationship and commitment to some form of "Asian American media" in the process of discussing its state, despite the relative lack of inclusion in more mainstream spaces and the general avoidance of any meaningful discussion of Asian American media representation.

Although other scholars, such as Wong (2016), Okada (2005), and Au (this collection), have discussed the public/counterpublic roles that film festivals inhabit, this chapter emphasizes the Summit's public modality, or rather, how publics and publicity are constituted via activity, movement, and process (Brouwer and Asen 2010). Moreover, the Summit's discourses and the genre of Asian American film festival discourses are inherently vernacular discourses. Theorized by Ono and Sloop (1995), vernacular discourses are those that resonate within localized and often marginalized communities. They do not privilege the "good men speaking well" model of rhetoric, but shift attention to the everyday talk and conversations that happen within overlooked communities. They simultaneously affirm community that may or may not be counter-hegemonic and often borrows from other forms. Ono and Pham (2009) have argued that Asian American independent media serves as a vernacular discourse for the Asian American community, interacting with dominant media via pastiche while serving as a form of media subculture for the Asian Americans. Such places, like the film festival, can also serve as generative spaces for Asian American vernacular discourses about media and its constantly shifting relationship with the Asian American community—a changing relationship brought about by changing demographics and evolving technologies. In the space of the film festival, the Present/Future Summit serves an example of vernacular discourses, focusing attention toward the community discussion about the state of Asian American media, in all its facets and environments, instead of a private discussion about the state of Asian American film festivals. The concerns of Asian American media no longer rested on the shoulders of a dedicated media organization or a recurring film festival, but rather, for better or for worse, the audience, community, and corporate or financial sponsors.

The Summit's presence in public/counterpublic spheres and its public modality via conference/Twitter/townhall serve as an ideal place for examining Asian American vernacular discourses and rhetorics of media. Now moved from the private organizational discourses and into the public forum for festival attendees and interested parties, the Summit's speakers, invited respondents, audience question and answer, and tweets lay out a cacophony of arguments, theses, predictions, condemnations, and anecdotes about the state of Asian American media. This upcoming section elucidates the structure, introduces the speakers of the Summit, and summarizes the contents of the speeches and respondents. In doing so, I lay out the major themes of the Summit and its various articulations and disarticulations.

Asian American Media as Storytelling: Making the Private Public

The Summit began with an introduction by Stephen Gong, who referenced the founding of CAAM (then NAATA) as similar to this Summit but "with a fewer number of people than are here." In doing so, he established what he described as a "context for the conversation" or, more appropriately, CAAM's historical relationship with the project of Asian American media within a larger U.S.-located democratic project. He described the important work of media makers in telling the stories of community and family and asked Summit attendees to consider "who we do this work for and whose stories have not been told and who is not at this table and to keep them in our thoughts." In doing so, he established CAAM's role as an Asian American media organization: to foreground community and the often-untold stories that lie buried within the lives of Asians in America. Karin Chien, an independent media producer, founder of dGenerate films, and one of the organizers of the Summit, provided the exigence for the Summit in that the "Media landscape has been transformed" both for the producer and for the consumer and "across the landscape" of arts and politics. This Summit, for her, is "an attempt to make sense of what's going on … and how are you dealing with this? … How do I pay the rent? … How do I survive and do what we love?" Whereas Gong emphasized history and a connection to community, she foregrounded the media makers and focused the audience's attention on the impending future that may jeopardize or catalyze media makers' careers if they're able to survive the day-to-day. In addition, Chien's comments pointed to both the public and the private lives of the media makers. She draws attention to the changing landscape of media—a public and sharable experience—while unearthing the private and often constant concerns of media makers; is this career sustainable and is this passion worth pursuing at the cost of one's own financial and emotional survival? Although it easy to understand and view media makers as separate from communities in a YouTube age, releasing their "art" for us to consume for subscribers and an online virtual community, Gong's comments connected the audience to a history of physical community reception and reflection. Yet as Chien reminded us, the current market economics shift media consumption and survival onto individual choices and responsibilities. This forum (and at various moments in the festival) serves as a place where the private lives of media makers and the process of media making are made public as part of a larger conversation around a community-oriented media practice.

After this introduction, the Summit proceeded in two separate halves with an intermission. The first half dealt primarily with technological change—particularly how social networks and new media technologies have changed the production and reception of media. Introduced by former San Francisco International Asian American Film Festival director Chi-Hui Yang, the second half was concerned with funding and distribution and the politics involved that sheds light on "who controls power and who controls what we are able to see and how we see it." The Summit concluded with a summary note by then University of California-Santa Barbara professor and filmmaker, Celine Parrenas Shimizu.

Given the length of the Summit and the number of speakers, this chapter does not allow the space to give each speech due diligence and a close reading, as is often done in rhetorical studies. Instead, I turn my attention to two themes that arose from the discourse of the Summit. While issues of technological innovation, dispersed networks, and innovative ways of storytelling through newly accessible digital tools and forums are relevant and interesting, I focus my attention on the tropes of "paradigm shifts" and "stories/storytelling" that arise, both implicitly and explicitly, in the discourse of the Summit, in the speeches and the live tweets. What becomes clear is that "storytelling" becomes a vernacular discourse that stands in for "community stories," but that it also serves to (dis)articulate the commitments of media makers.

A Present/Future Paradigm Shift

The title "Present/Future Summit" alludes to the tension underlying the Asian American media environment—one that pits mainstream/independent contemporary practices against the new digital ones. This title and its allusion could be seen in the organization of the speakers, but also in a discourse of "paradigm shift" that was constructed throughout the event. The speakers in the first session represented each side through their professional status and their expertise. On the "new" media digital side were Kenyatta Cheese, the founder of "Know your meme"; former venture capitalist manager Gary Chou; and the Taiwanese American YouTube stars Wong Fu Productions. Paired with these speakers were people who might have represented the "old" side, such as Quan Phung, executive producer for NBC's now defunct "Whitney" show, and Sundance Institute media advisor Wendy Levy. Thus, the speakers in the first session were organized in a way that pitted "old" against "new"; mainstream representatives and independent media icons against the internet enthusiast, YouTube stars, and venture capitalists.

Yet the term "paradigm shift" was used to illustrate the tension, pitting hierarchies against networks and the structural and cultural changes wrought by new media technologies in the social network, and to describe Gary Chou's talk for the Summit. Citing technologies like YouTube and Reddit, Chou highlights the uncertainty ushered into the relatively stable space of filmmaking, particularly the practices of distribution. Indeed, the Present/Future Summit served as an example of dealing with the "paradigm shift" while simultaneously naming it as such. The tension that the "paradigm shift" sought to alleviate through its nomenclature was upheaval in the previously established rules about funding and financial success. While the paradigm shift directly addresses how we produce, consume, and share media, it also draws attention to the (financial) states disrupted by it.

Thus, the subtext of this tension was the concern over survival and monetization by the media maker or media organization in this new environment. These are linked together, as monetization refers to the ability to generate income from a previously public or personal good—in this case, the media that one creates and shares. Sustainability becomes the key word to highlight the private struggles of media makers by alluding to an image of a burnt-out and overworked artist. Yet, the discourse of sustainability that was deployed masks the market logic that underpins attempts at monetization. Sustainability, resonating with environmental discourses is not the only method that masks market logic in an attempt to survive it. In addition, discourses around "stories" and "storytelling" are key.

The discourse surrounding the practice "storytelling" became the primary trope and tool to resolve the tension created by the paradigm shifting effect of social networks and sharing on mainstream/traditional media distribution. While the paradigm shifting networks argument took hold, speakers countered it via a commitment to a variety of stories/storytelling. Wong Fu Productions, one of the most popular Asian American YouTube stars and "the Holy Trinity," represented the potential (market) success of new media artists. Asserting the viability of YouTube as an artistic endeavor, they strategically started their session with their reel in order to dispel the idea of YouTube as only a place for "cat videos" and highlighted the market power of digital spaces.

The presence and possibility of networked stories and their dedicated audiences drew on the power of the network but foregrounded the importance of stories. One exchange between executive producer Quan Phung and internet enthusiast Kenyatta Cheese displayed the commitments to traditional versus internet, and also exposed the market logics dictating the cultivation and distribution of Asian American media. Phung dismissed internet stories for lacking the ability to "stick" and thus hold longstanding cultural weight and relevance; a cultural relevance still beholden to successful television sitcoms such as *Friends* or *Seinfeld*. Yet, Cheese countered Phung's defense and praise of traditional media, describing the attempts to get into such spaces, like primetime sitcoms, as playing the "content-lottery," and beckoned the audience (but specifically media makers) to "stop gambling." Instead, he'd rather gamble and monetize our own authenticity in the digital and networked realm. Cheese's metaphor of the "lottery" frames mainstream media industry as a risky game to play, repositioning the skills and audiences of social networks as more bankable. In both cases, "stories" are what serve as currency.

The first half of the Summit revealed the contours and tensions within the Asian American media maker community at this moment—networked vs hierarchical, and mainstream television vs digital spaces such as YouTube. In bringing up such topics, CAAM's Summit simultaneously voiced the concerns of the community while framing them under outside experts, who provided the vocabulary for such concerns. The opening speakers exposed the concerns about the changing media environment away from the well-established independent film scene and traditional mainstream media spots, while explaining what this new networked and self-produced structure allows—"authenticity" and a do-it-yourself way of media production and circulation that is often easier and cheaper than going through the mainstream channels. "Stories" and the capacity for "storytelling" within each become the trope that assuages the tensions between mainstream and digital media by becoming the solution to surviving in both spaces. Yet, which stories matter and are valued? In this next section, I elucidate how "authenticity" is linked to successful stories in ways that individuate media makers from larger community concerns.

(A)politicizing Asian American Stories and Storytelling

Stories and storytelling have always been central to the Asian American media project. CAAM and other Asian American media organizations have focused on sharing stories about the community, individual experiences, untold histories, and newly created stories. CAAM's tagline is "Stories to light," which references a story's general ability to light the way. This nod to the apparatus of cinema projection creating the illusion of life as a shadow delivered through film centers CAAM's role in bringing stories to the open public via funding, production, and distribution. CAAM recognizes the impact of stories and the influence media makers as storytellers can have, particularly in affirming a sense of Asian American culture while recognizing the uniqueness of those who identify as "Asian American." As Wendy Levy stated in a line that echoed CAAM's mission, "When we want to learn about a culture, we listen to storytellers. Culture is made of stories. To change culture, change stories."

Internet stars like Wong Fu Productions bring stories to light via computer screens and smartphones, changing culture through a medium that is still in its nascent stage. Wong Fu Productions emphasize their use of and practice of YouTube as a mode of telling transparent and "authentic" stories while organically capitalizing on their own fan economy. While traditional media like cinema or television also tell and share stories, YouTube is seen as a new tool for constructing and distributing "authentic" stories. That traditional media is not as authentic as YouTube reinforces what Banet-Weiser (2015) describes as the authentic/commercial divide, whereby YouTube's amateur-ness and do-it-yourself perception are contrasted against the slickly produced and profit-driven goals of mainstream media. Although differences between media platforms exist, the currency in this age of storytelling becomes an ephemeral notion of "authenticity" and being "authentic."

This trope of "authenticity" or "authentic" storytelling often elides a political edge that is at odds with the activist history of CAAM, whose founding grew out of the Asian American movements of the 1970s. In the vein of Stuart Hall, CAAM engages in "articulation," symbolically linking CAAM to a larger political aim of activism and movement politics through framing its story and mission with an activist history (Fiske & Watts 1986; Slack 1996). In viewing CAAM through a lens of articulation, we can see that CAAM deploys a mechanism and strategy for the organization to see itself in relation to its cultural products and politics in ways that shape the "intervention within a particular social formation, conjuncture or context." It also allows, as Laclau and Mouffe (1985) describe, a chain of equivalence to be drawn from Asian American movements to Asian American media organizations to minority media movements and independent filmmaking practice.

Increasingly, however, the chain of equivalence with the history of Asian American movements has been disarticulated from "authenticity," resulting in the disarticulation of activism from Asian American media. In disarticulation, McRobbie (2009) states that "a force which devalues, or negates and makes unthinkable the very basis of coming-together" works as "a dispersal strategy," thus defusing the likelihood of cross-border solidarity. Making "authentic" stories also means that it should lack politics, particularly since political goals are perceived to contradict what it means to be "authentic."

Not all of the Summit's speakers agreed on the disarticulation of politics through "authentic" storytelling. In her response to Wong Fu Production's talk, Ana Serrano, from the Canadian Film Centre Media Lab, highlighted the perils of Wong Fu's digital nativity by questioning the "inherent apoliticalness" of networked storytelling. She recognizes that for media makers like Wong Fu, telling and sharing authentic stories is part of one's being, and that the network is just the tool to facilitate this craft. However, she challenges the audience and Wong Fu to consider the values promoted when producing engaged networked stories for the audience who inevitably consume and share them. She points to other examples where YouTubers have used deception to raise money that goes into their own pockets, rather than toward social change. While she does not say that Wong Fu are literally engaging in such deceptive practices, she implies that they most certainly have the power to do so, and thus questions whether or not we should see their work as apolitical.

The (dis)articulation of community responsibility from individual creators through the claim of individual authenticity was further debated in an exchange between Kenyatta Cheese and the final speaker, then University of California Santa Barbara professor and renowned film scholar Celine Parrenas Shimizu. Shimizu advocates for "ethical responsibility" when creating stories; hence, she argues that Asian American media makers are obliged to account for the possibilities and constraints of their representations. This was a call to Wong Fu Productions, whose trademark of authenticity was questioned by Shimizu's critique that authenticity is an illusion since "all representations are mediated." Kenyatta tweeted: "disagree with Shimizu's point of imposing 'ethical obligation' on Wong Fu. They are nodes. Responsibility comes from within." Kenyatta foregrounds the individual and avoids the issue of responsibility and obligation. Importantly, he is attempting to establish ethical obligations with the disarticulated storyteller, one that exists primarily on YouTube and whose only connection with others is through the platform of the internet and not the larger community and organization that served as its previous infrastructure. Here, we see the tension regarding stories throughout the discussion—between something that is networked and can contribute to change, and something that is individual, or even marketable.

Within the Summit, it would be unlikely that participants would define themselves as "activists" or as doing political work through media. Not only can this term deflect and divide, but it can also reinvigorate the false binary of "politics" versus "aesthetics" when it comes to artistic and creative projects. While the speakers all recognized the history of organizations like CAAM and Visual Communication as activist, they also realized that doing so can conflict with CAAM's position within the cultural marketplace, which prizes individual artistic vision over collective actions. In the age of corporate sponsorship and decreased public funding, organizations founded in the spirit of social and cultural change that are equipped with the goals of diversifying public media, cultivating media makers and storytellers, and exhibiting stories for and by the community become defanged in the process of disarticulating from any sense of political action via the notion of individual "authentic" stories that dominate the networked landscape.

What Kind of Storytellers Are We?

In this chapter, I assert the value of conceptualizing Asian American media organizations and their events as sites of Asian American public vernacular discourses. Beyond the speakers and Q & A portions, the concurrent use of Twitter to live-tweet and then display such tweets behind the speakers created another discussion forum that existed during the Summit, while the Tumblr site and blogs by CAAM Fellows continued the discussion after the Summit officially ended. Each of these served as a space where vernacular discourses about Asian American media existed for public consumption.

Asian American vernacular discourses about media and the "state of Asian American media" illustrate a community in tension between old and new forms of media, and their respective ways of building a community of viewers, makers, and the infrastructure for these sides to meet. Whereas the annual film festival was a prime meeting ground to connect viewers and makers and help with distribution and exhibition, new media technologies at that moment rendered such well-established roles optional at best, or marginal and unnecessary at worst. A common thread through these two sessions was the community—a community engaged in media that was connected to a larger goal beyond cultural products for a wider audience. Yet the question remains as to what responsibility, if any, media makers have to a larger community versus the media maker's individual aspirations. Although this question may seem irrelevant to most (White) media makers, it clearly remains important for those involved with CAAM, whose very goals and mission statement were up for public debate and discussion. It is also surprising that such a key part of CAAM's history and mission must be made explicit, as if the ideals of "community" had become lost within the development of Asian American media.

I conclude with two questions that point to the *telos* of this chapter, as well as one last anecdote. First, is this the fate that organizations like CAAM are destined for, in order to survive in the harsh world of nonprofits? Second, whose responsibility is it to continue this conversation, and what motivates them to do so? Interestingly, CAAM's presence became eerily quiet after kicking off the event. And although Asian American media came out of struggle and political movement, any current conception of such a movement is now couched within the cultural logics of markets. While the Summit focused on the state of Asian American media, it also reflected larger anxieties and concerns about Asian American media organizations. I suggest that Asian American media organizations assume ethical responsibility in their curation and gatekeeping in order to play a larger role in constructing the discursive environment for how the community, both Asian American and otherwise, connects with Asian American media. Indeed, this way of situating the political discussion of Asian America could be the evolving role of organizations like CAAM. Here, curation can be seen as a mode of argumentation that makes particular statements about the Asian American condition, instead of a purely aesthetically driven decision process. Distribution can be seen as a means of audience-building, signaling a media organization's particular commitments, as opposed to a purely market-driven apolitical process.

As the conversation shifted to history and the political origins of Asian American media organizations, the audience thinned out, with particularly the young people leaving the room. This could have been for a variety of reasons—Wong Fu Productions had finished their stint, the day was dragging on outside of the schedule, or the conversation no longer interested them. Yet, Philip Lorenzo tweeted: "I am concerned that the younger crowd is leaving while we are talking history and preservation." One of the invited speakers, Nā'ālehu Anthony from Paliku Documentary Films and 'Ōiwi TV, recognized that tweet publicly as he began to answer a question about the grander vision of his projects and validation. He recognized that we need to support content creators and have platforms that allow people to live off their art. But for validation, he says:

> How do we get validated? I don't know. For me, it's like the little old lady who comes to me in the Star Market and says 'Thank you for what you're doing' and talks to me in Hawaiian. That's my validation. That's it. Do I want to go to Sundance? Hell yeah! Am I gonna go yet? No. But that's okay. That's another thing we want to work towards but the validation has to come from within your community if you're going to have long term lasting effects. Because you can go to Sundance and you still don't get your film sold. Right? You still don't make a dollar. You have to come back to the core of what your motivation is.

Events like the Summit and organizations like CAAM beckon us to revisit our motivations for Asian American media and to debate, discuss, and engage with others in ways that promote being held accountable to communities outside the ones we see on our screens.

Note

1 The videos for all the speakers and sessions analyzed in this chapter are available on YouTube under the channel and playlist: CAAMCHANNEL. "Present/Future Summit 2012."

References

Aristotle. 1991. *On Rhetoric: A Theory of Civic Discourse.* New York: Oxford University Press.

Asen, Robert and Daniel C. Brouwer (eds). 2001. *Counterpublics and the State.* Albany, NY: SUNY Press.

Au, Vanessa. 2017. "Using the Tools of the YouTube Generation: How to Serve Communities through Asian American Film Festivals." In *Routledge Companion to Asian American Media*, Lori Kido Lopez and Vincent N Pham (eds). New York: Taylor and Francis.

Banet-Weiser, Sarah. 2012. *Authentic™: The Politics of Ambivalence in a Brand Culture.* New York: New York University Press.

Brouwer, Daniel and Robert Asen (eds). 2010. *Public Modalities: Rhetoric, Culture, Media, and the Shape of Public Life.* Tuscaloosa: University of Alabama.

CAAMCHANNEL. "Present/Future Summit 2012." Filmed [March 2013]. YouTube playlist. Post [April 2013]. www.youtube.com/playlist?list=PLF641A805CD1988BC.

English, James F. 2005. *The Economy of Prestige: Prizes, Awards, and the Circulation of Cultural Value.* Cambridge, MA: Harvard University Press.

Farrell, Thomas B. 1976. "Knowledge, consensus, and rhetorical theory." *The Quarterly Journal of Speech* 62(1): 1–14.

Felski, Rita. 1989. "Politics, Aesthetics, and the Feminist Public Sphere." In *Beyond Feminist Aesthetics: Feminist Literature and Social Change*, 154–182. Cambridge, MA: Harvard University Press.

Fiske, John and Jon Watts. 1986. "An Articulating Culture—Hall, Meaning and Power." *Journal of Communication Inquiry* 10(2): 104–107.

Fraser, Nancy. 1990. "Rethinking the Public Sphere: A Contribution to the Critique of Actually Existing Democracy." *Social Text*, 25/26: 56–80.

Habermas, Jurgen. 1964. "The Public Sphere: An Encyclopedia Article". Translated by Sara Lennox and Frank Lennox. *New German Critique* 3 (Autumn): 49-55.

Habermas, Jurgen. 1989. *The Structural Transformation of the Public Sphere: An Inquiry into a Category of Bourgeois Society.* Cambridge, MA: MIT Press.

Hanna, Erin. 2013a. "Comic-Con 2013: The Fan Convention as Industry Space." *Antenna: Responses to Media Culture.* July 19. http://blog.commarts.wisc.edu/2013/07/19/comic-con-2013-the-fanconvention-as-industry-space/.

Hanna, Erin. 2013b. "Comic-Con 2013: The Fan Convention as Industry Space, Part 2." *Antenna: Responses to Media Culture*, July 22. http://blog.commarts.wisc.edu/2013/07/22/comic-con-the-fanconvention-as-industry-space-part-2/.

Jenkins, Henry. 2012. "Superpowered fans: The many worlds of San Diego's Comic-Con." *Boom: A Journal of California* 2(2): 22–36.

Kohnen, Melanie. 2014. "'The Power of Geek': Fandom as Gendered Commodity at Comic-Con." *Creative Industries Journal* 7(1): 75–78. doi:10.1080/17510694.2014.892295.

Laclau, Ernesto, and Chantal Mouffe. 1985. *Hegemony and Socialist Strategy: Towards a Radical Democratic Politics.* London: Verso Books.

Lopez, Lori Kido. 2016. *Asian American Media Activism: Fighting for Cultural Citizenship.* New York: New York University Press.

McRobbie, Angela. 2009. *The Aftermath of Feminism: Gender, Culture, and Social Change.* Thousand Oaks: SAGE Publications.

Mao, LuMing, and Morris Young (eds). 2008. *Representations: Doing Asian American Rhetoric.* Logan, UT: Utah State University Press.

Marky. 2012. "Present/Future: A Community Conversation on Asian American Media (FREE)." http://caamedia.org/blog/2012/03/10/presentfuture-a-community-conversation-on-asian-american-media/. Center for Asian American Media, last modified March 10, 2012.

Okada, Jun. 2005. "The PBS and NAATA Connection: Comparing the Public Spheres of Asian American Film and Video." *The Velvet Light Trap* 55(Spring): 39–51.

Okada, Jun. 2015. *Making Asian American Film and Video: Histories, Institutions, Movements.* New Brunswick, NJ: Rutgers Press.

Ono, Kent A. 1995. "Re/signing 'Asian American': Rhetorical Problematics of Nation." *Amerasia Journal* 21(1 and 2): 67–78.

Ono, Kent A. and John M. Sloop. 1995. "The Critique of Vernacular Discourse." *Communication Monographs* 62:19–46.

Ono, Kent A. and Vincent N. Pham. 2009. *Asian Americans and the Media.* Malden, MA: Polity Press.

Perin, Alisa. 2010. "Highs and Lows of Comic-Con 2010." *Antenna: Responses to Media Culture.* July 29, 2010. http://blog.commarts.wisc.edu/2010/07/29/highs-and-lows-of-comic-con-2010/.

Shankar, Shalini. 2015. *Advertising Diversity: Ad Agencies and the Creation of Asian American Consumers.* Durham, NC: Duke University Press.

Slack, Jennifer Daryl. 1996. "The Theory and Method of Articulation in Cultural Studies." In *Stuart Hall: Critical Dialogues in Cultural Studies*, David Morley and Kuan-Hsing Chen (eds), 112–127. New York: Routledge.

Squires, Catherine. 2001. "The Black Press and the State: Attracting Unwanted (?) Attention." In *Counterpublics and the State*, Robert Asen and Daniel C. Brouwer (eds), 111–136. Albany, NY: SUNY.

Wang, Oliver. n.d. "About CAAM: History." Center for Asian American Media, http://caamedia.org/about-caam/.

Wong, Cindy H.-Y. 2016. "Publics and Counterpublics: Rethinking Film Festivals as public Spheres." In *Film Festivals:* History, Theory, *Method, Practice*, Marjike de Valck, Brendan Kredell, and Skadi Loist (eds), 83–99. New York: Routledge.

Part II

ASIAN AMERICAN MEDIA PRODUCTION

PERSPECTIVES FROM SCHOLAR-PRACTITIONERS

6

THE COIN OF THE REALM

Valuing the Asian American Feature-Length Film

Brian Hu

What happened to Asian American cinema? It's a reasonable question, considering the momentum built by the first wave of scholarship on Asian American cinema in publications such as *Moving the Image* (1991) and Peter X Feng's *Identities in Motion* (2002). These books discussed Asian American cinema in the present tense and theorized identity formation, minority filmmaking practices, and gender and sexuality in the narrative, experimental, and documentary films made by Asian Americans in the 1980s and 1990s. More than just documenting and acknowledging the existence of contemporaneous Asian American films and videos, this scholarship was often in dialogue with filmmakers themselves in collectively theorizing Asian American identity, representation, and history. But if one looks to current academic literature for signs of new Asian American independent filmmaking, one would wonder whether Asian American cinema still exists at all. With the exception of a surge of interest in Justin Lin's 2002 feature *Better Luck Tomorrow* and the chapters written for this collection, there has been very little academic writing on films directed by Asian Americans since 2000.[1]

Perhaps it is too easy to simply blame the academy, which is subject to its own trends, particularly in a marginalized field such as Asian American cinema and media studies. Perhaps Asian American filmmaking has disappeared too. The cinematic output of the past 15 years suggests a kind of crisis on the scene, whereby what made Asian American film studies so vibrant in the 1980s and early 1990s—namely, a lively corpus of films that self-imagined and articulated the meaning of Asian America on screen—was simply not being made anymore. Commentators, film festivals, funding bodies, and media arts organizations have had to adjust to an environment in which the category of "Asian American film" was being emptied out by its own artists. As an academic, the artistic director of Pacific Arts Movement, and the presenter of the San Diego Asian Film Festival, I have seen these shifts up close. In recent years, there has been a surge in films directed by Asian Americans but not about Asian subjects, as in the work of M. Night Shyamalan, Cary Fukunaga, and others ("~~Asian~~ American film"). There is also a trend of Asian American filmmakers like Victor Vu, Arvin Chen, and others who make films in Asia ("Asian diasporic film"). Finally, there is the substantial wave of moving image storytellers who have turned to internet genres such as vlogs and web series ("Asian American media"). Of course, Asian American independent films and videos that validate and explore the category of "Asian American film" continue to be made; in fact, with the proliferation of digital production, editing, and distribution, there is certainly more of it than ever before. But with the critical category of "Asian American film" becoming drowned out by these three potentially more "mainstream" phenomena, Asian American films are becoming increasingly invisible and are not eliciting conversation as they did in the past. With the dearth of distribution, the ephemerality of the digital, and the absence of archives, we might then ask—if nobody is aware of these films, do they really exist?

The question "What happened to Asian American cinema?" is a historical one that can be distinguished into two separate lines of inquiry: "What discourses, as well as institutions that shaped and disseminated such discourses, led to Asian American cinema becoming largely unrecognizable today?" and "What forces led to Asian American cinema's self-erasure?" We can begin with the fact that this form of cinema traces its roots to Third Cinema theory and method, Asian American community organizing, and student movements for affirmative action and Asian American studies. Its pioneers proudly flaunted their anticapitalist and anticolonial stances, and explored important issues such as the politics of memory surrounding Japanese incarceration and the injustices of anti-Asian violence. Yet, the dominant discourse surrounding Asian American filmmaking in the twenty-first century is a postracial one: filmmakers seek to make films with assimilated characters who "just happen to be Asian," which is a popular mantra among filmmakers. Some dispense with Asian characters altogether in an attempt to prove that an Asian American filmmaker can make films about people of any race (just as White filmmakers have historically proven that prowess through the Western, colonial gaze). In these cases, the effacing of Asianness buys into a myth of success and "making it" that accords with mainstream respectability politics but sits uneasily with the politics of protest that made Asian American cinema viable to begin with. Perhaps the inability of Asian American cinema's critics, scholars, and observers to acknowledge the output of this new phase is a testament to their unwillingness to reconcile Asian American cinema's neoliberal forces within.

In this chapter I trace a shift from the race-conscious discourses of Asian American filmmaking, which are contemptuous of the mainstream, to an assimilationist discourse that de-emphasizes race and prioritizes conversations about financial success and interfacing with Hollywood. I present a history of Asian American cinema through focusing in particular on the feature-length film—a format that rejuvenated Asian American cinema in the second half of the 1990s, and that would come to dominate the conversation about its national impact and future directions. I contextualize the rise of the feature film in Asian American film festivals by describing the impact of the so-called "Class of 1997," when an unprecedented number of features made a splash on the festival circuit. In presenting this history, I look at the changing ways that stakeholders in Asian American cinema discuss, or fail to discuss, race, while addressing the growing prominence of feature films. This format has vitally promoted filmmaker professionalization and cross-over potential, but has also shied away from direct interrogations with race and racism in the United States, Given the large costs associated with feature films, as well as their potential for vaulting filmmakers into the mainstream, the narrative feature became what Alvin Lu calls the "coin of the realm" of Asian American filmmaking.[2] The feature film became the currency by which Asian American filmmakers are legitimized as auteurs, by which Asian American filmmaking institutions are deemed to be serving the filmmaker community, and by which Asian American cinema is measured to have achieved its potential as a cultural, social, and economic commodity.

This conversation has largely taken place on the Asian American film festival circuit, which has not only been the primary site for the exhibition of Asian American cinema, but has also played major roles in production, distribution, and publicity. Furthermore, with the absence of any central critical journal or forum for Asian American cinema, "the most significant exchanges of ideas among filmmakers and critics take place on those occasions and those venues" of the film festival (Xing 1998: 178). These exchanges exemplify the ways that film festivals can play the role of a counterpublic sphere (Ono and Pham 2009; Wong 2011), setting the parameters of conversation in order to set agendas, carve boundaries, and define what Asian American cinema is allowed to be. To track the historical development of today's de-racialized Asian American cinema, I look at festival discourse from the major Asian American film festivals from the early 1980s to the early 2000s. These include the Asian American International Film Festival (presented by the New York-based Asian CineVision since 1978), the San Francisco International Asian American Film Festival (presented by the National Asian American Telecommunications Association (NAATA) since 1982), the Los Angeles Asian Pacific Film Festival (presented by Visual Communications since 1983), and to a lesser extent Washington DC's Asian American Film Festival (presented by Asian American Arts and Media from 1983 to 1996). Specifically, I examine industry self-knowledge and the normative arguments made in the festival program booklets; in particular, their essays, program notes, lineups, and topics for workshops and panel discussions. I assess the way these materials served to accommodate and motivate filmmakers' professional needs in the shift to feature-length filmmaking, and lent legitimacy and social capital to a cinema described increasingly in relation to crossing over into the mainstream. As I will show, these archival materials and the industrial culture they represent reveal festivals' anxieties over the deracinated narrative feature, even as they attempt to co-opt the narrative feature into their own missions of promoting Asian American voices and counter the mainstream media's negligence and distortion of Asian American characters and subjects.

Feature Films in Alternative Contexts

Film festivals are some of the few remaining spaces where the distinction between short- and feature-length films has much significance. From a creative perspective, the distinction between a film that is under or over 40 minutes (by Academy of Motion Pictures Arts and Sciences rules) is an arbitrary one, but from a commercial perspective, the boundary is significant. Historically, the feature is a film that can sell an entire night's entertainment, which during the height of the Hollywood studio era might also include short subjects, newsreels, and trailers. In other words, this is the title that is the "featured" film in advertising (Thompson 2007). As we can see in this description, the feature film is first and foremost a format designed to sell. At film festivals, too, feature-length film programs are distinguished from short film programs, whose contents are not listed on the ticket or marquee. By industry convention, the only films whose name and stature can sell a program at a festival are feature-length ones. Because of their length, feature-length films are significantly more expensive and resource intensive to produce than short films, but because of their marquee value, they promise greater returns in box office, sales, or publicity.

The first decade of the Asian American film festival following Asian CineVision's inaugural Asian American International Film Festival (AAIFF) in 1978 saw very few feature films by domestic directors.[3] The total number of feature films produced is unknown, given the difficulty of tracking the features that were rejected by festivals. Meanwhile, the known output is sporadic. After two experimental features by Shusaku Arakawa in the late 1960s and early 1970s (*Why Not: A Serenade of Eschatological Ecology* and *For Example: A Critique of Never*) and the Yonemoto brothers' *Garage Sale* (1976), prominent features included Visual

Communication's *Hito-Hata: Raise the Banner* (1980), the work of Wayne Wang, including *Chan Is Missing* (1982), *Dim Sum: A Little Bit of Heart* (1985), *Eat a Bowl of Tea* (1989), and *Life Is Cheap... But Toilet Paper Is Expensive* (1989), Peter Wang's *A Great Wall* (1986), Mira Nair's *Mississippi Masala* (1991), and Ang Lee's *Pushing Hands* (1992) and *The Wedding Banquet* (1993). Many of these features achieved considerable financial success, which could not be said about other works of Asian American cinema. *Chan Is Missing* put Asian American cinema on the art house map, while *The Wedding Banquet* famously beat *Jurassic Park* by having the highest financial rate of return of any film in 1993 (Klady 1994). However, most features (premiering at around one or two titles per festival per year) were financially less fortunate and today survive only as titles listed in festival catalogues.

Most of the successful features in this early era did not premiere at one of the Asian American film festivals, such as the San Francisco International Asian American Film Festival (SFIAAFF), the Los Angeles Asian Pacific Film Festival (LAAPFF), or New York's AAIFF. Ang Lee's films were Taiwanese co-productions, and *The Wedding Banquet* had its world premiere at the prestigious Berlin Film Festival, where it won the top prize. Off the heels of her hit *Salaam Bombay!*, Mira Nair was able to showcase *Mississippi Masala* at the Venice Film Festival and the São Paolo International Film Festival before hitting stateside. Kayo Hatta's *The Picture Bride* played the Cannes Film Festival in 1994 and the Sundance Film Festival in early 1995 before entering the Asian American film festival circuit. In other words, feature films at festivals like SFIAAFF and LAAPFF were productions initiated in the mainstream and adopted by the Asian American film community. This was a way of giving prestige to the smaller scene and showcasing the growth and diversity of productions by Asian American artists. They were the notable exceptions at Asian American film festivals, which were otherwise filled with shorts, documentaries, and experimental film and video—the kinds of low-budget, often amateur work that exemplified the festivals' activist spirit of community storytelling and showcasing unique perspectives.

But the second half of the 1990s saw an increase in narrative feature films homegrown within the Asian American film network. Jun Okada (2015) attributes this rise to the growing prominence of Asian international cinema at these increasingly diasporic film festivals. The prestige bestowed on filmmakers like Wong Kar-wai at SFIAAFF (and elsewhere) gave Asian American filmmakers a model for widespread critical and market success with the feature-length film. Yet, the growing number of feature-length films is attributable to more than the rise of transnational Asian cinephilia. Okada makes the important point that the aspiration toward mainstream marketability was shaped by festivals that were moving away from a social change model to one focused on accumulating Asian American filmmaker capital (99).

This dramatic shift went hand-in-hand with a change in how festivals discussed racism in relation to production and film form. In the early decades of the Asian American film festival, essays in the festivals' catalogues were explicit about the tie between Asian American cinema and its political imperatives. For instance, the published introduction to the 1992 LAAPFF (then called the Los Angeles Asian Pacific Film & Video Festival) states that the festival exists "as a forum to engage both filmmaker and audience in dialogue on issues aesthetic and political."[4] The politics of these festivals centered on resistance to the mainstream, which was seen as fundamentally racist. Years before the explosion of the feature film, Daryl Chin wrote in New York's AAIFF program:

> As minority artists, we can expect nothing but the most difficult course to run if we expect to create art ... Majority rule has not always allowed for minority access. We should never accept this fact (for injustice should never be accepted), but we should

> be aware of this fact. We have, in the seven years of the Asian American Film Festival, attempted to provide a continual forum and a sustained encouragement for Asian American filmmakers: we have attempted to develop an audience, to publicize, to provide the beginnings of patronage for Asian American film.[5]

For Chin, racism in the mainstream meant that Asian American filmmaking and exhibition could only be an alternative creative and industrial practice, which the film festival must support. Lori Tsang, writing in the program of the 1992 edition of the Asian American Film Festival of Washington DC, made a similar claim: "Obviously, the limited opportunities for Asian Pacific Americans to produce feature-length commercial films reflect our (lack of) status as 'minorities' in America."[6] Tsang's certitude ("obviously") shows how fundamental anti-racism was to festival organizing, and by connecting racial discrimination to the feature film in particular, she makes a distinction between film forms appropriate to Asian American cinema (shorts, documentaries) and those appropriate to the commercial, discriminatory realm (features). To these festival organizers of the 1980s and early 1990s, there was doubt that feature-length films by Asian Americans could exist except as outliers or as international co-productions, as Tsang also noted. In this period, not only was the idea of Asian American feature production unthinkable, but it ran counter to the way the festivals came to understand their own politics as anti-racist media organizations seeking alternative forms and exhibition spaces.

The "Class of 1997" and Reprogramming Festivals

Given this environment of doubt and suspicion, it is easy to see why the so-called "Class of 1997"—a whopping four feature films by Asian Americans at SFIAAFF—was seen as so seminal.[7] The organizers of SFIAAFF played up the moment, dedicating a special panel to discussing the feature film, and claiming the works represented a "new wave."[8] Film movements and "new waves" are as much commercial designations as they are cultural or aesthetic ones, and by naming these four films a "new wave," the festival was also building Asian American filmmaker capital through the commercial value of feature-length films. After all, nobody was celebrating the achievements of short-form and experimental filmmaking, which thrived. Given the fact that stakeholders in Asian American cinema had previously cast doubt on the political appropriateness of feature-length filmmaking, SFIAAFF's 1997 statements were also seminal, because they collapsed the long-held distinctions between grassroots/alternative and high-budget/commercial in an unprecedented way.

Not surprisingly, this shift did not come without resistance and qualification. After all, if "obviously" Asian American feature films could not be made because of racism, then is a celebration of a "new wave" of Asian American feature filmmaking an indication that racism is over? Essays in festival programs weighed in on the subject, riding the excitement of the "Class of 1997" and the features they inspired while recontextualizing the moment in terms of race and activism. In the wake of the "Class of 1997," as well as other feature films of national visibility like *The Debut* (Gene Cajayon, 2001), *American Desi* (Piyush Dinker Pandya, 2001), *Long Life, Happiness & Prosperity* (Mina Shum, 2002), and *Better Luck Tomorrow* (2002), Asian American film festivals found another way to counteract the commercial impulses of Asian American cinema: by actively reminding their audiences and filmmakers that their presenting media organizations have long roots in anti-racist, anti-commercial activism. As early as 1998, Abraham Ferrer, a lead organizer of LAAPFF, responded to the excitement over features during the previous year, writing:

> What gets me so riled up these days is this nagging sense that while our communities' artists are taking the next step and producing features and pushing them into the mainstream market, the significance of the "alternative screen" is becoming less important as a newer generation of makers are establishing a beach-head in the mainstream entertainment industry.[9]

Ferrer then grounds the festival's work back in the activist spirit of its founding, celebrating those filmmakers who resist mainstream temptations and the feature film:

> Notwithstanding the sentiments of a select few, Asian American cinema today reflects a continuum from the good ol' days, when telling honest and accurate stories about Asian American peoples, culture and heritage was inseparable from the movement for social justice and enfranchisement, a movement that, in many ways, continues today.[10]

In fact, challenging the trend toward market-defined respectability became practically an annual tradition for Ferrer in the pages of the LAAPFF booklets. "Why are many of us Asian American cinema artists today so obsessed with 'mainstream' success?" he asks in 2000, and then calls out other Asian American organizations for giving awards to Hollywood for " 'including us' in high-profile entertainment."[11] Similarly, a short essay in 2002 by Gita Reddy, a former AAIFF programmer, argues that the success of Justin Lin's *Better Luck Tomorrow* was, like all good things for Asian Americans in the mainstream, simply a "fluke," and she contextualizes the film's success within the larger mechanisms of the mainstream's cultural appropriation and exotification. She then encourages filmmakers to "cash in" on this opportunity, but stick to "a personal vision."[12] Here, Reddy does warn against feature filmmaking, as was the case in earlier festival essays, but promotes a model of Asian American independent filmmaking that is, as Ono and Pham have described, "not truly 'independent' of dominant media but are in relationship with them, through pastiche and through the economics of media production and distribution" (Ono and Pham 2009, 123).

The two other major Asian American film festivals of the time, SFIAAFF in San Francisco and AAIFF in New York City, also felt the need to emphasize their institutions' political foundations—at least in essay form. On the occasion of the twentieth anniversary of NAATA, the presenter of the SFIAAFF festival invited scholar Darrell Hamamoto to contribute an essay. He wrote: "It is worth recalling that the art of independent Asian American film evolved from the political struggles and countercultural practices that attended the new social movements of the 1960 and 70s."[13] At AAIFF, Daryl Chin echoed these sentiments, writing that the trend toward commercial work "would have surprised the founders of ACV," and that "at no point in its history was ACV ever a liaison with the motion picture industry." He warns that "with this, there is a cost"—namely, that the promotion of a commercially viable feature film would result in a turn against challenging programs that have no box-office appeal.[14] We can note that these essays were exceptions to the general tone of their respective festival booklets, which otherwise catalogued a sea tide against Ferrer's, Hamamoto's, and Chin's warnings and memories. But their publication gave the festivals a last-gasp way to plead their case and see what might transpire.

Another way that festivals attempted to recontextualize the opening floodgates for features was to politicize them as alternative, rather than complicit with the mainstream market. The description for a 1998 roundtable at SFIAAFF noted that making a feature film is a sure-fire way to become "flat broke," thus repositioning features in the guerrilla traditions of impoverished independent filmmaking.[15] In 2002, SFIAAFF put together a seminar about how feature films like *The Debut* and *American Desi* achieved "high visibility and commercial viability without Hollywood distributors." The seminar participants would then "explore potential strategies that can offer an alternative for achieving success without Hollywood."[16] In both of these panels, SFIAAFF emphasizes how feature filmmaking can have alternative, even anti-establishment, potential, perhaps not at odds with the traditions of countercultural struggle that Hamamoto celebrated in the festival's own pages. In 2005 and 2008, SFIAAFF would also convene panel discussions about the financing and market opportunities for Asian American feature filmmakers wanting to "cross over" to Asia. Here, festivals reminded feature filmmakers that taking advantage of overseas markets represents another strategy for remaining "alternative" to Hollywood. Panelists included Victor Vu (*Spirits*), who found success making features in Vietnam, and Gina Kim, whose feature *Never Forever* was made in conjunction with South Korean powerhouse CJ Entertainment.

The programming of these feature film production panels, which grew in number in all three of the major festivals in the late 1990s and 2000s, speaks also to the professionalization of Asian American cinema and the festivals' roles in promoting best practices and industrial knowledge. The festivals thus provided not just exhibition spaces and audiences, but professional services as well. Chin attributes this shift to festivals acknowledging filmmakers' desires to follow in the footsteps of commercially successful feature films like *The Debut* and *Better Luck Tomorrow*. He observes that "in order to continue as a vital media organization, ACV and its programs must address the concerns of the current generation of filmmakers, attain information so that these filmmakers can learn how to navigate within the waters of the commercial industry and interest itself in the situation for artists in the present tense."[17] Chin expresses urgency and desperation. For him, it's not simply a matter of adding value for filmmakers. These kinds of services are the only way festivals can address the new demands of commercially minded filmmakers. Thus, the idea that feature films are the "coin of the realm" of Asian American cinema can be extended to the film festival circuit too: the promotion of feature films is now what gives these festivals their value. Festivals were quick to seize this opportunity to cater to and help shape the feature filmmaker, in effect giving their assent and acknowledging that features can and should be part of how Asian American cinema will now be defined. Between 1997 and 1999, the LAAPFF programmed a special workshop, sponsored by NAATA, called the "Asian American Independent Feature Workshop." Spearheaded in part by "Class of 1997" alum Quentin Lee, the multi-session event directly addressed the needs of aspiring feature filmmakers, discussing the challenges of financing, distribution, promotion, working with studios, and pitching, which the 1999 catalogue called "a key ingredient for insuring the realization of any mainstream feature production."[18] That the workshop continued for three consecutive years speaks precisely to its value; that a new media-oriented iteration of it was developed 12 years later as Visual Communications' "C3: The Conference for Creative Content" speaks to mainstream filmmaker services becoming a vital part of how Visual Communications builds capital for itself and for its filmmakers.

Locating Race in Asian American Cinema: Dual Trajectories and Beyond

In a humorous piece for the 2000 SFIAAFF booklet, filmmakers Kayo and Mari Hatta lampoon pitching workshops by narrating a fictional pitch meeting that reveals the limits of professionalization. In it, their fictional filmmaker pitches to a studio that balks at the idea of Asian American leads, and only perks up at the mention of tired tropes of Asian exoticism.[19]

Written simply to galvanize Asian American makers into seeing the importance of alternative organizations like NAATA, the piece also writes race back into a conversation that was increasingly becoming dominated by myths of meritocracy, postraciality, and playing by the color-blind rules of the mainstream. For instance, the 2012 brochure for Visual Communications' C3 Conference only mentions Asian Americans to note that they exist in leadership roles in Hollywood, without mention of glass ceilings or industry racism. In contrast, with a similar panel in 1994 called "In the Biz," LAAPFF organizers responded to the growing place of Asian Americans in the mainstream by asking: "What are the particular challenges and rewards of being Asian American in the nation's preeminent culture industry? Does race matter? In front of the camera? Behind the camera? How should films or television about Asian Americans be marketed?"[20] Such questions were absent from any descriptions in the 1997–1999 workshops or the later C3 Conference, whose discourse on race changed from one of caution and strategy in light of a larger struggle, to one that celebrates simply having a seat at the table.

As a result, we are left with the question: does race matter for Asian American film festivals in the feature-film era? Surely, race is still present, as "Asian" is in the name of many festivals. There continue to be filmmakers, audiences, sponsors, and other participants repelled by the idea of entering this racialized space, as well as others who feel comforted and encouraged by its existence. Behind the scenes, race also becomes foregrounded when film festivals program features directed by Asian Americans, but which do not contain any Asian characters. Examples include mixed-race director Mora Stephens' *Conventioneers* (2003) or Ernie Park's *Late Summer* (2012). These are films programmed to showcase the diversity of subject matter that interests Asian Americans; these two films show the fluency of Asian American directors in producing content focusing on White and Black communities. LAAPFF made the bold decision to open its 2011 film festival with Justin Lin's Hollywood production *Fast Five*—a film that includes only one minor Asian American role. For this film to receive such a high-profile slot underscores Asian American cinema's reinvention from racialized content to racialized authorship. This is not the authorship of classic models of auteurism that explore content such as authorial signatures or pet themes. Instead, it's authorship based on the industrial idea of a "directed by" credit or "above-the-line" status. Programming *Fast Five* was a celebration less of Justin Lin's art than of "his place as a power player in the Hollywood blockbuster machine."[21] Furthermore, Lin's status as a long-time friend of VC—a relationship made known in the first line of LAAPFF's program notes of the film—reminds audiences of their commitment to developing and investing in successful feature filmmakers like Lin. Opening their 2011 festival with *Fast Five* was thus not just a strategy to pack an opening night screening, and it was certainly not a way to explore how Asian American perspectives can be injected into a Hollywood film. Rather, it was a way to reassert LAAPFF's value as an organization dedicated to the promotion of Asian American feature filmmakers all the way to the mainstream.

The way race is here grafted onto mainstream capital, and the way "Asian American cinema" is valued by its commercial potential, is exemplary of other discourses of money, race, and democracy prevalent on the Asian American film festival circuit during this period. The idea that buying power has become conflated with racial politics is reflected in a truism repeated by a SFIAAFF program co-director: "Going to the box office in the film world is equivalent to casting a ballot at the polling booth."[22] This statement echoes the well-trodden idea that "the only color Hollywood sees is green," which pervades the Asian American film festival circuit. Between 2003 and 2006, while I was a journalist covering Asian American arts and culture, this line was repeated to me by individuals as diverse as director Justin Lin, actor Sung Kang, and producer Mia Riverton—all alums of Asian American festivals in this period of professionalizing filmmakers. Asian American commentators like Phil Yu[23] and Keith Chow[24] have also made similar arguments in discussing ethnic casting and Asian American cinema. The downplaying of mainstream racism and community activism in favor of a fundamental faith in market forces is in concert with festival discourses that have shifted, however uncomfortably, to emphasizing commercially viable feature films over films that take Hollywood as their target or that have no clear market value.

On the 30th anniversary of AAIFF, ACV's acting executive director John C. Woo led his festival essay with an epigraph attributed to George Bernard Shaw: "If at age 20 you are not a Communist then you have no heart. If at age 30 you are not a Capitalist then you have no brains." Later in his essay, he writes that in 2007, Asian Pacific American filmmakers have achieved "transcendence of racial politics."[25] These statements should perfectly encapsulate Asian American cinema's embrace of neoliberalism as its oldest festival enters its third decade. Yet, Woo closes his essay with a nod to "a return to activism," the "use of media for advocating our concerns," and the "responsibility to fight the good fight." Of course, that "fight" could be for programs that only see green. The nod could also simply be an empty rallying call delivered to lend AAIFF greater grassroots legitimacy. Most likely, though, this confusion between embracing cross-over product and reasserting Asian American cinema's activist roots reflects the opportunities and challenges festivals have had for two decades with regard to feature films. These dual trajectories are also seen in the way that LAAPFF responded in 1999 to its own Asian American Independent Feature Workshop by counter-programming a panel at the Japanese American National Museum that directly questioned what mainstream success was doing to the Asian American audience and to non-commercial filmmakers.

Today, all three festivals continue under this dual model, serving the professionalization of commercially oriented filmmakers while programming films that are personal, unusual, critical, or community-building. These include *In the Family* (Patrick Wang), *Grave Goods* (Leslie Tai), *Johnnie Loves Dolores* (Clarissa De Los Reyes), *Punching at the Sun* (Tanuj Chopra), *To Weave a Name* (Christen Hepuakoa Marquez), and many others. Such films have generally been ignored by critics, mainstream audiences, and academics, though they continue to flourish at festivals. They have been particularly successful at a newer generation of Asian American festivals in Boston, Chicago, Philadelphia, San Diego, Seattle, and Washington DC, whose staff have learned from LAAPFF, AAIFF, and SFIAAFF how to cultivate sponsors, filmmakers, and audiences. Yet, they continue to sidestep industry support and dedicate their resources primarily to the presentation of films that best illuminate the spirit and vitality of Asian American cinema. In these alternative festivals, the feature-length narrative film can and should draw audiences, as features have long been designed to do. But festivals in non-industry cities can propose other ways of thinking about the mainstreaming of Asian American cinema through the feature film. They do not have to remain focused on simply serving as grassroots marketing for the films' later theatrical releases or bestowing laurels upon filmmakers for their resumes. A challenge facing the independent Asian American film festival is to harness the appeal of features to develop an "Asian American mainstream" that is not governed by the aesthetic and cultural rules of the Hollywood or "indie" mainstreams. To sustain themselves and build audiences, film festivals need tentpole, "four-quadrant," star-driven, hype-worthy, and crowd-pleasing films too. But in the alternative public space of the Asian American film festival, the content of such films and the demand for them can be shaped by the nuances of local demographics, the needs of community action, and, indeed, by how "Asian American" is racialized locally by parameters other than the perils of "crossing over."

Notes

1 An exception that proves the rule is the final chapter of Jun Okada's *Making Asian American Film and Video*, which discusses Justin Lin's *Finishing the Game* (2007) and Grace Lee's *American Zombie* (2007) only to cite them as examples of Asian American cinema's post-life.

2 Alvin Lu, "Feature Films – Fast and Furious," *San Francisco International Asian American Film Festival* booklet (San Francisco: National Asian American Telecommunications Association, 2002), 14.

3 For the sake of argument, in this article, "feature length-film" refers primarily to feature-length narrative films and not feature-length documentaries, which have their own history within Asian American cinema. Most significantly, because of the central role of public television in Asian American cinema, feature-length documentaries are produced, sold, and exhibited by institutional and market forces different from those of the narrative features in the period I discuss. See Okada (2015).

4 *Los Angeles Asian Pacific Film & Video Festival* booklet (Los Angeles: Visual Communications, 1992), 1.

5 Daryl Chin, "The 1984 Asian American International Film Festival," *Asian American International Film Festival* booklet (New York: Asian CineVision, 1984), 19.

6 Lori Tsang, "Asian and Pacific Islander Cinema: Beyond Borders," *11th Asian American Film Festival* booklet (Washington: Asian American Arts and Media, 1992), 13.

7 These features were *Shopping for Fangs* (directed by Quentin Lee and Justin Lin), *Strawberry Fields* (directed by Rea Tajiri), *Sunsets* (Michael Idemoto and Eric Nakamura), and *Yellow* (directed by Chris Chan Lee).

8 Paul Yi, "A New Wave: Asian American Films," *San Francisco International Asian American Film Festival* booklet (San Francisco: National Asian American Telecommunications Association, 1997), 6.

9 Abraham Ferrer, "Notes from an Observer," *Los Angeles Asian Pacific Film & Video Festival* booklet (Los Angeles: Visual Communications, 1998), 7.

10 Ibid.

11 Abraham Ferrer, "Where We Are, Where We Gotta Go," *Los Angeles Asian Pacific Film & Video Festival* booklet (Los Angeles: Visual Communications, 2000), 9.

12 Gita Reddy, "You Go! Tell 'Them' Who 'We' Are," *Asian American International Film Festival* booklet (New York: Asian CineVision, 2002), 69.

13 Darrell Y. Hamamoto, "Coming into Focus: Thirty Years of Asian American Independent Filmmaking," *San Francisco International Asian American Film Festival* booklet (San Francisco: National Asian American Telecommunications Association, 2000), 6.

14 Daryl Chin, "A Place at the Table," *Cinevue: Asian American International Film Festival* booklet (New York: Asian CineVision, 2004), 22–23.

15 "Dramatic Roundtable," *San Francisco International Asian American Film Festival* booklet (San Francisco: National Asian American Telecommunications Association, 1998), 26.

16 "Seminar One – Better Look Tomorrow: Strategies for Asian American Feature Film Success," *San Francisco International Asian American Film Festival* booklet (San Francisco: National Asian American Telecommunications Association, 2002) 22.

17 Chin, "A Place at the Table," 23.

18 *Los Angeles Asian Pacific Film & Video Festival* booklet (Los Angeles: Visual Communications, 1999), 16.

19 Kayo and Mari Hatta, "Pitching Lessons," *San Francisco International Asian American Film Festival* booklet (San Francisco: National Asian American Telecommunications Association, 2000), 23.

20 "Panel Discussion: In the Biz," *Los Angeles Asian Pacific Film & Video Festival* booklet (Los Angeles: Visual Communications, 1994), 27.

21 Abraham Ferrer, "Fast Five," *Los Angeles Asian Pacific Film Festival* booklet (Los Angeles: Visual Communications, 2011), 61.

22 Kayo Hatta, "Festival Letter," *San Francisco International Asian American Film Festival* booklet (San Francisco: National Asian American Telecommunications Association, 1998), 10.

23 Phil Yu, "There Is No Market for Asian American Films," *Angry Asian Man* (September 2, 2009), http://blog.angryasianman.com/2009/09/there-is-no-market-for-asian-american.html.

24 Keith Chow, "Asian Americans and Mainstream Hollywood: 21, Forbidden Kingdom, and Harold & Kumar," *Got This Blog on Lok* (April 18, 2008), http://lokblogging.blogspot.com/2008/04/asian-americans-and-mainstream.html.

25 John C.Woo, "ACV & AAIFF: Some Thoughts on Turning 30," *Asian American International Film Festival* booklet (New York: Asian CineVision, 2007), 7.

References

Chin, Daryl. 2004. "A Place at the Table," *Cinevue: Asian American International Film Festival* booklet. New York: Asian CineVision.

Chin Daryl, "The 1984 Asian American International Film Festival," *Asian American International Film Festival* booklet (New York: Asian CineVision, 1984) 19.

Chow, Keith. 2008. "Asian Americans and Mainstream Hollywood: 21, Forbidden Kingdom, and Harold & Kumar," *Got this Blog on Lok*, (April 18). http://lokblogging.blogspot.com/2008/04/asian-americans-and-mainstream.html

"Dramatic Roundtable." 1998. *San Francisco International Asian American Film Festival* booklet. San Francisco: National Asian American Telecommunications Association.

Ferrer, Abraham. 1998. "Notes from an Observer," *Los Angeles Asian Pacific Film & Video Festival* booklet. Los Angeles: Visual Communications.

Ferrer, Abraham Ferrer. 2000. "Where We Are, Where We Gotta Go," *Los Angeles Asian Pacific Film & Video Festival* booklet. Los Angeles: Visual Communications.

Ferrer, Abraham Ferrer. 2011. "Fast Five," *Los Angeles Asian Pacific Film Festival* booklet. Los Angeles: Visual Communications.

Hamamoto, Darrell Y. 2000. "Coming into Focus: Thirty Years of Asian American Independent Filmmaking," *San Francisco International Asian American Film Festival* booklet. San Francisco: National Asian American Telecommunications Association.

Hatta, Kayo. 1998. "Festival Letter," *San Francisco International Asian American Film Festival* booklet. San Francisco: National Asian American Telecommunications Association.

Hatta, Kayo and Mari Hatta. 2000. "Pitching Lessons," *San Francisco International Asian American Film Festival* booklet. San Francisco: National Asian American Telecommunications Association.

Idemoto, Michael and Eric Nakamura. 1997. *Sunsets*

Klady, Leonard. 1994. "Dimos are 'Wedding' Bridesmaid," *Variety*, January 11. http://variety.com/1994/film/news/dinos-are-wedding-bridesmaid-117353.

Lee, Chris Chan (director). 1998. *Yellow*.

Lee, Quentin and Justin Lin (directors). 1997. *Shopping for Fangs*

Los Angeles Asian Pacific Film & Video Festival booklet. 1992. Los Angeles: Visual Communications, 1.

Los Angeles Asian Pacific Film & Video Festival booklet. 1999. Los Angeles: Visual Communications.

Lu, Alvin. 2002. "Feature Films – Fast and Furious," *San Francisco International Asian American Film Festival* booklet. San Francisco: National Asian American Telecommunications Association).

Okada, Jun. 2015. *Making Asian American Film and Video: History, Institutions, Movements*. New Brunswick: Rutgers University Press.

Ono, Kent A. and Vincent N. Pham. 2009. *Asian Americans and the Media*. Cambridge: Polity Press.

Reddy, Gita. 2002. "You Go! Tell 'Them' Who 'We' Are," *Asian American International Film Festival* booklet. New York: Asian CineVision.

"Seminar One – Better Look Tomorrow: Strategies for Asian American Feature Film Success." 2002. *San Francisco International Asian American Film Festival* booklet. San Francisco: National Asian American Telecommunications Association.

Tajiri, Rea. 1997. *Strawberry Fields*

Thompson, Kristen. 2007. "What Is a Film?" *Rogerebert.com*, August 29. http://www.rogerebert.com/rogers-journal/what-is-a-film.

Tsang, Lori. 1992. "Asian and Pacific Islander Cinema: Beyond Borders," *11th Asian American Film Festival* booklet. Washington: Asian American Arts and Media, 13.

Wong, Cindy H. 2011. *Film Festivals: Culture, People, and Power on the Global Screen*. New Brunswick: Rutgers University Press.

Woo, John C. 2007. "ACV & AAIFF: Some Thoughts on Turning 30," *Asian American International Film Festival* booklet. New York: Asian CineVision.

Xing, Jun. 1998. *Asian American through the Lens: History, Representations, and Identity*. Lanham MD: Alta Mira Press.

Yi, Paul. 1997. "A New Wave: Asian American Films," *San Francisco International Asian American Film Festival* booklet. San Francisco: National Asian American Telecommunications Association.

Yu, Phil. 2009. "There Is No Market for Asian American Films," *Angry Asian Man*, September 2. http://blog.angryasianman.com/2009/09/there-is-no-market-for-asian-american.html.

7

USING THE TOOLS OF THE YOUTUBE GENERATION

How to Serve Communities through Asian American Film Festivals

Vanessa Au

Introduction: The New Media Landscape

The independent Asian American media landscape has undergone significant changes in the past decade. With video capture and editing technologies becoming increasingly affordable and easy for novices to learn, the creation of short videos has become a commonplace pastime among the digital natives who make up today's "YouTube generation." While film festivals once served as the only vehicle for minority filmmakers to find an audience for their work, now social media platforms like YouTube let anyone publish videos for the world to see. This has helped filmmakers to share their videos quickly and gain large audiences with minimal investment in time or money. In this new media landscape, traditional film festivals can seem entirely irrelevant. This chapter, however, presents an alternative model of film festival organizing that negotiates this online–offline divide. Drawing on my experiences reviving an Asian American film festival in Seattle over the last five years, I illustrate how taking the best practices from traditional offline festivals and online video sharing through social channels can enable the production of an event that is not only relevant, but critical to serving the needs of local Asian Pacific American (APA) communities. In particular, I focus on bringing film festivals back to the activist roots that once drove the creation and distribution of independent media.

Traditional film festivals like the Northwest Asian American Film Festival and previous iterations of the Seattle Asian American Film Festival have existed in fits and starts across the United States for decades. Boston, DC, Eugene, San Francisco, San Diego, Philadelphia, New York, Los Angeles, and Seattle have all been home to such events, which last anywhere from a few days to a few weeks. One of the biggest challenges in operating a film festival is the months of planning and volunteer hours that are needed well in advance of the first screening. Organizing committees write grants, find sponsors, promote the call for film submissions, view the submissions, program and market the festival, and plan event logistics. Once the operations and logistics are in place, there is the hurdle of competing with other local events for attendees. Given the amount of labor for an event that might sell a few thousand tickets at most, it's no wonder traditional film festivals have struggled and often fizzled out, while the popularity of sharing and watching online digital video has skyrocketed.

Another problem facing traditional film festivals is that decades-old groups may have developed the skills for putting on successful traditional film events, but they are struggling to accommodate new media technologies. Vincent Pham (2011) observes that the proverbial "elephant in the room" among festival organizers is how to best deploy new media and capitalize on their potential, while addressing the competition that they provide. Despite the challenges of operating a film festival in this new media landscape, the reasons to do so are both abundant and important. In line with Jurgen Habermas's (1989) theory of the public sphere, film festivals can provide a space for private people to come together face-to-face and discuss matters of common concern. Asian American film festivals in particular can be seen to create what Nancy Fraser (1990) calls a counterpublic sphere. Films provide commentary on the experiences of Asian Americans, discuss issues that concern them, and allow viewers to meet others with common experiences or ideas that are outside of dominant media discourses. Cindy Wong (2016) has pointed out that ethnic film festivals can serve as counterpublic spheres because they screen films that "articulate different experiences and expressions" and provide a space for the exchange of ideas that are ignored in the larger mainstream (160). Traditional Asian American film festivals can serve the communities that comprise this APA counterpublic sphere, but such an undertaking adds more work to the already laborious logistics of event planning. With sparse resources and a volunteer workforce, it is hard enough to do what is generally considered the bare minimum for a film festival: screening films, facilitating Q&A with directors, and hosting receptions or parties. Outreach to community groups, social activists, community leaders, and scholars is generally considered an afterthought or a nonessential add-on.

In my experience, I have found that new media tools can be productively used to assist in a number of ways to sustain traditional film festivals and maintain this important counterpublic space. But successfully operating and attracting an audience for a live in-person event in this new media landscape requires two things: first, an understanding of the tools, channels, and strategies that the YouTube generation has used to build a following; and second, an event that offers more than just film screenings, because viewers are now able to view digital media at home on their personal devices. This is why, in 2012, while I was employed as a senior analyst and strategist at a marketing agency, I decided to revive the Seattle Asian American Film Festival (SAAFF). Its predecessor, the Northwest Asian American Film Festival, had fizzled out in 2007 after a five-year run—just before the use of social media to plan and promote events became commonplace. Determined to use my expertise in social media marketing, I was excited to revive an annual event for the Seattle-area Asian American community, and was even more excited by the prospect of using it to serve as a counterpublic sphere for local APA community leaders, nonprofit groups, artists, academics, activists, students, and, of course, film enthusiasts.

Negotiating the Online-Offline Divide: An Operating Model for Film Festivals

In the sections that follow, I map out the key components that comprise a film festival—the audience, programming, and operations. In my discussion of each, I share insights from SAAFF's operating model, which draws from both on- and offline engagements in order to serve the APA community. Our goals are to continue bringing people together in a counterpublic space to watch films by and about them.

Audiences

Even in a city known for hosting one of the largest film festivals in the nation (the Seattle International Film Festival), it is a challenge to attract attendees out of their homes to attend a film festival. But it is particularly difficult to lure millennials away from their mobile devices to watch unknown independent films collectively on the big screen at a festival. People of all ages watch videos online, but millennials (18–29-year-olds) comprise the largest age group among YouTube subscribers (Anderson 2015). Film festival attendees, on the other hand, tend to represent a broader age range, and the average age runs higher. SAAFF, for example, has quite a high turnout among seniors, both at the annual festival (12% of survey takers) and at our summer film series in Seattle's Chinatown-International District (CID), where they make up at least half the audience.

One way we've succeeded in attracting our audiences is by inviting popular filmmakers to attend events. At our 2015 festival, we invited Chris Dinh to attend the screening of his film *Crush the Skull*. Dinh, a YouTube celebrity who is part of Wong Fu Productions and has over 24,000 followers on Twitter, is not a frequent visitor to Seattle. Like many popular YouTubers, he hails from southern California and couldn't possibly interact face-to-face with even a small fraction of his many young fans. Inviting these online celebrities to our festival can cause quite a stir, particularly when coupled with appearances by local area musicians and celebrities at the opening night party.

Another effective strategy for targeting younger audiences is showcasing the work of young filmmakers from the community. Since 2014, we have screened a selection of short films produced by participants in the Asian Counseling and Referral Service's (ACRS) Southeast Asian Young Men's group, which teaches documentary filmmaking as part of an outreach program for teens from refugee and immigrant families. We have made a point of not just highlighting our partnership with the program but also inviting the audiences to recognize the young filmmakers and ask them questions. ACRS does have a YouTube channel for sharing these films online in their entirety, but their channel is rarely cross-promoted in their social marketing efforts, so participating in the festival provides a productive way to grow our combined audiences. We have also found success in reaching younger audiences through social media channels including Facebook, Twitter, Instagram, and YouTube. We have at least two staff at any given time making sure to post content regularly, answer questions that we receive via private messages on these platforms, and respond to comments. In addition to film festival announcements, we use our social media platforms for sharing our thoughts on news and happenings that relate to Asian Americans, which helps in connecting our online spaces to the larger counterpublic sphere created by our film screenings and events. We select what we share on our channels with an eye toward piquing the interest of a wide range of people—from young K-pop fans to older followers who might be interested in a $250 per seat ticket to a community partner's gala. That way, we reach the younger audiences (18–34-year olds make up nearly half our Facebook fans) and social media-savvy older audiences as well.

We also try to establish relationships with people attending or teaching at all the neighboring colleges, particularly those located within just a few square miles—the University of Washington, Seattle University, and Seattle Central Community College. Members of the SAAFF staff take turns visiting Asian American Studies classes to promote the festival and encourage students to attend at our discounted student rate, or even volunteer and enjoy the opportunity to meet filmmakers and see films free. Alerting local faculty in Film and Ethnic Studies programs at neighboring colleges has also been a way for us to introduce students to film festivals. They generally attend to receive extra credit from these professors. As a result, we see many young faces in the audience. In addition, an unintended result of these efforts is that a number of high school and college students from these visits often apply to volunteer each year.

On the other hand, senior citizens do not make up the typical audience for online videos, but many are enthusiastic film festival goers. We have made it a priority to encourage our older audience members to come back year after year by moving to venues that are wheelchair accessible, offering a senior's discount on tickets, and programming films made by older filmmakers or about topics that might be of interest to them. Visual Communications in Los Angeles runs a Digital Histories program that teaches filmmaking to seniors from underserved Asian American communities. Every year, the manager of the Digital Histories program sends us a collection of documentaries to consider screening. We also specifically target older audiences who do not speak English at our free outdoor summer film screenings hosted in Seattle's CID in August. Oftentimes these residents of the neighborhood are walking by when they see us setting up the huge inflatable screen. They do not usually hesitate to ask one of us what is about to take place and what we are going to screen, and then take a seat for the evening. We sometimes program Chinese language films such as *Shaolin Soccer* (2000) as a direct effort to cater to these audiences. Elders in the CID also enjoy free performances by local Asian American groups, including kung fu and lion dance groups, hula dancers, tai chi practitioners, and musicians while we wait for the sun to set, which provides space and visibility to groups typically marginalized both in the mainstream public sphere and online. So, while the screening of an international film is not quite aligned with our mission to showcase "works by and about Asian Americans," it does help us reach a diverse audience and provide a space for the APA community to gather. Together, these strategies promote dialogue between filmmakers and audiences of all ages, backgrounds, and generations.

Programming

In the spirit of cultivating a counterpublic sphere, what we consider programming at SAAFF extends beyond just film. Having audiences gather in the same physical space means rich opportunities to include events of different kinds as part of our "film" festival. Starting in our second year, we have kicked off the annual festival with a big opening night party featuring spoken word poets, singers, dancers, hip-hop artists, and musicians. It is a big production held at a performance space separate from the theater. Local Asian American news anchors donate their time to emcee the event, which includes food, free whiskey tasting, a cash bar, and even a photo booth. At the 2015 festival, Geo (Prometheus Brown) of the hip-hop group Blue Scholars and Hollis Wong-Wear of the Flavor Blue delivered a riveting spoken word performance. Their piece about the connection between ethnic foods and history, family, music, and art was written especially for SAAFF's audience. This created an opportunity for the local festival goers to experience a truly unique performance in an intimate venue and spend time getting to know two artists from the community who made it big. This is one particularly memorable moment during our festival that could not have been replicated online.

Film festivals have traditionally hosted post-screening Q&A sessions for audiences. This format can be replicated by those who screen their work online by hosting live virtual Q&As that serve the same purpose. To enhance our own offerings, we decided to deepen the conversation and organize discussion panels at SAAFF that involve not just filmmakers, but also community organizers, activists, and scholars. Attendees have now come to expect the inclusion of in-depth discussions on such topics as immigration, reparations for past injustices, LGBTQ issues and identities, labor reform, and other topics concerning the APA counterpublic following films that feature those topics. On a few occasions, we also hosted some rather unexpected offline-only content. At our first event in 2013, held at the Wing Luke Museum, a well-known community leader named Bettie Luke was invited to serve on the discussion panel following the screening of Valerie Soe's documentary *The Chinese Gardens.* Luke, who is a chairperson for the Chinese Expulsion Remembrance Project, arrived for her discussion panel with a set of poster board displays that stood over six feet tall. The display was made up of historical photographs and detailed written descriptions mounted on cardboard that told the history of the anti-Chinese violence and government-sanctioned expulsions that took place in the Pacific Northwest in the late 1800s and led to the disappearance of the community discussed in Soe's film. Despite our reliance on sophisticated digital technologies to plan and promote the festival, we saw that some of the texts that drew the most audience attention were analogue.

SAAFF has also included content that blurs the line between text and audience, online and offline. In 2013, we opened with a documentary by local filmmaker Eliaichi Kimaro called *A Lot Like You* (ALLY). The film chronicled the filmmaker's trip to Africa to confront members of her extended family about issues of abuse. She wanted to capture the audience's thoughts on her film with a unique social photo project she called the ALLY Project. She had a small table at the festival's opening party where people could fill out a postcard with their responses to the question: "What did you leave our film thinking about?" The postcard instructed the audience members to take a photo of what they wrote and email it to them, tweet about it with a mention of their Twitter handle, or post it to Facebook and tag their Facebook page. We shared these posts with our audiences online as a way of inviting the audience to become co-producers in the extension of the film's meaning.

Operations

Beyond what is visible to attendees of the festival, there are also many ways in which the success of SAAFF is made possible through using new media technologies behind the scenes as well. Nearly every aspect of running this event has been made easier through the use of digital tools—including being able to network with other film festival organizers, work together virtually in the absence of an office space, sell tickets, dialogue with fans, study our audience, collaborate with our community partners, and, most importantly, publicize the festival. For instance, we have come to rely on the expertise shared within a private Facebook group called "Film Festival Organizers," which has nearly 1,200 members and is a treasure trove of information and best practices for running an independent film festival. Organizers ask and answer questions on the group about everything from how to convert digital film files, what to do with volunteers who harass other attendees, and how much to charge for a festival pass to finding the best online ticketing vendor and managing filmmakers' requests for fee waivers. Together we wrestled with a topic at the heart of this chapter—considering policies about not selecting films that are publicly available online. Competing with online film distribution is a challenge for most festivals, but the new digital landscape and social media have been a help as much as they can be considered a hindrance for traditional film festivals, because we can get on these networks to learn about and consult with our peers on the very issue of navigating the online–offline divide.

We also use an online platform for film submissions, which helps us attract submissions from across the country and lets the film community around the world know we exist. Launched in 2014, Film Freeway is a platform for filmmakers to submit their film in HD to multiple film festivals online. We also rely upon Gala Festival Engine, a platform for building our website and selling tickets online. Together, these software form the backbone of the operational pieces that our filmmakers and audiences interact with. Yet, we also use online tools among ourselves, which helps to overcome the difficulty of not having an office or dedicated meeting space. Online collaboration technologies help us to move tasks like brainstorming on a whiteboard, sketching out ideas on flip charts, or even keeping reminders on yellow sticky notes into the digital sphere. We use Google Drive to keep and access all our shared files, while our private Facebook group for festival staff serves as a hub for brainstorming, short conversations about logistics, reminders, and requests for help. We also use the Facebook Events function for planning staff meetings, and online scheduler Doodle for surveying staff on when they can staff shifts at an event or come together for a bigger meeting like a day-long planning retreat.

Our Facebook page provides a digital hub for a wide variety of engagements with our audience—including news about the festival, media articles about our filmmakers, reviews of the films we were screening, and promotional messages. During the event, Facebook and Twitter became our primary channels for communicating with festival attendees about sold-out shows, location changes, and other updates. Our community co-presenters' program had a social media component too. The community groups that we invited to speak to our audiences did so in exchange for tweets and Facebook posts about SAAFF to their followers. Based on the results of our audience surveys, most people heard about SAAFF through Facebook and continued to get updates about the festival from our newsfeed.

The 2,200 followers of our Facebook page also provided us with demographic data about who was interested in our event. We share this data in our sponsorship kit in order to attract companies to support us financially. Similarly, we gathered data from Twitter to see which of our messages and hashtags were getting retweeted the most in order to learn about the interests of our audience and to make better selections when curating stories to share on our social channels. Being able to conduct social media analysis and make sense of this data has given SAAFF the tools not only to publicize our festival and sell out our screenings, but also to study our audience, and use some of that information to program our festival and attract financial sponsors. Being competitive in the age of YouTube demands developing a social media strategy and using social media platforms and other online tools more effectively across all areas of the festival.

Strengthening Relationships and Building Community

Our strategy of combining online and offline models helps us to be more successful in refocusing on our goals of building relationships and communities. Rather than simply marveling at the number of views an online video can receive, we choose to focus on the multifaceted outcomes brought about by SAAFF. These values are epitomized by our opening event in 2016, which featured speeches by Mayor Ed Murray and Deputy Mayor Hyeoke Kim. Murray, who is married to Japanese American Michael Shiosaki, shared his husband's family's struggle to rebuild after Japanese internment during World War II, while Hyeoke discussed her own racial identity growing up as a second-generation Korean American. She relayed what it was like to watch mainstream movies and television and not find herself reflected in those productions. Both cited the lack of diverse portrayals of Asian Americans in mainstream media and the importance of SAAFF in providing that function. It was validating to hear their explicit support for SAAFF's mission, but their presence also meant that the filmmakers, community organizers, audiences, and activists could meet in person with these dignitaries and give their causes, needs, and concerns a face.

Having a physical space for people to gather and see films means we have been able to cultivate opportunities for serendipitous exchanges between all sorts of groups and individuals who might not otherwise run into one another. The theater vestibule concentrates most of our attendees in one place in between screenings, and when movies let out, it's bustling with attendees, press, filmmakers, staff, volunteers, sponsors, community partners, and discussion panelists. There was a particularly memorable moment that took place because of this funneling of most festival attendees into one space. Many friends of students from the ACRS Southeast Asian Young Men's Group arrived too late one afternoon to get a seat to see their friends' film. They decided to wait in the vestibule to rejoin them after the screening, but ended up running into filmmaker and YouTube celebrity Chris Dinh. The star-struck teenagers had no idea he would be there and ended up excitedly spending the duration of the screening chatting with Dinh and later attending the screening of his film *Crush the Skull*. It's in these chance encounters that the film festival comes to life—and such stories abound. One of the community co-presenters sparked a romance with a Bay Area-based filmmaker who came up to Seattle for the screening of one of his films in 2014, and the two were married in the summer of 2016. Several of our current staff members were either local filmmakers who screened a film at SAAFF in the past or volunteers whom we invited to join our staff. Artists who have performed at our opening night party have gotten gigs at other local area events after meeting leaders of other community organizations at SAAFF, and audience members who happen to work in government agencies that award grants to arts organizations have alerted us to grants that we qualify for. The value of these relationships is immeasurable.

Beyond the benefits for individuals, we have also endeavored to use the festival to strengthen the local APA community and the network of nonprofit organizations that support it. Because of the dispersed audience for films distributed online, media producers who operate popular YouTube channels or websites rarely engage in this kind of local work. One of the organizations that fall into this category is the *International Examiner* (IE), a nonprofit bi-weekly newspaper that serves the APA community. The editor in chief was eager to dedicate one issue of the IE to covering SAAFF, which meant they also published our printed program for us. We benefited in many ways from this relationship—free advertising for the festival to their 30,000 readers (as well as their 2,400 Facebook fans and 1,200 Twitter followers), our program being designed and published for us, and having a space to tell the stories behind the stories we were showing on the big screen. The *IE* publishes interviews with filmmakers and actors, reviews of our films, and stories about the subjects of the documentaries we screen. In return, we offer advertising discounts to our sponsors and encourage them to buy ads with the *IE*, we take out our own ads to promote the festival, we donate festival passes to auction off at their annual fundraiser, and we provide the editor with story ideas for the issue. There are many opportunities for partnerships with local APA nonprofits like this one, where there is mutual and long-term benefit.

The goals and missions of the groups we choose to partner with serve the community in a vast variety of ways, from organizing educational trips to sites of Japanese internment camps and operating summer programs for kids, to providing health, medical, and counseling services. The Asian Counseling and Referral Service (ACRS), the Japanese American Citizens League (JACL), the Organization of Chinese Americans (OCA), the Vietnamese Friendship Association, International Community Health Services (ICHS), Minidoka Pilgrimage, and the Japanese Cultural and Community Center are just a few of the organizations with which we have worked. The primary way we partner with them is through a community co-presenters program. We pair community groups with one to two film programs at SAAFF by topic, if possible. For example, Kollaboration, which operates an annual talent showcase for

Asian American entertainers, presented a 2016 feature documentary *Don't Think I've Forgotten: Cambodia's Last Rock and Roll* about the country's music movement of the 1960s before it was halted by the rise of the Khmer Rouge. Those groups promote the session to their membership lists and social media followers, who we hope will take an interest in the program we selected for them. In turn, we the list the organization on our online ticketing page, their representatives get a few minutes to speak to the audience at the start of the program, and we give them space at a community resource table to distribute flyers, meet other community leaders sharing the table, and talk to attendees. Often these groups run on a shoestring budget (if they have any marketing budget at all), struggle with making themselves known online, and rarely come across opportunities to speak to hundreds of people in their target audience. SAAFF affords them these important opportunities, and in return gets a chance to invite people from their membership lists to the festival.

When we are not gearing up for our annual festival in February, we look for ways to engage with the community year-round as well, which also serves the function of maintaining SAAFF's visibility during our "offseason." For example, in August each year, we work with Seattle Parks & Recreation to operate the free outdoor film series mentioned earlier. SAAFF is charged with programming and promoting the series, organizing live entertainment to play as we wait for the sun to set, and providing staff to help their employees set up and take down the inflatable screen and folding chairs. This is another partnership that we value, because it offers free film screenings to residents of the CID, many of whom are seniors on a limited income. As well, it drives people to the neighborhood for the event, which helps to bring business to the area's small shops and restaurants. When we are not focused on operating our annual festival in February, running the summer film series in August, or promoting our karaoke fundraiser in January, we also use our social media channels to publicize events promoted by groups we have worked with in the past. SAAFF shares the goings-on of other APA organizations so frequently, in fact, that we have effectively become a source of Seattle-area APA community and arts news and events, as well as a trusted advisor to many of these groups when they are looking to find a film to screen at one of their own events.

Concluding Thoughts

In this new media landscape, watching videos online has become ubiquitous. Popular videos are watched by hundreds of millions of people around the world. Traditional film festivals clearly need to learn how to navigate the changing social media terrain. But even more urgently, film festivals must figure out how to stay relevant when the primary functions they serve—connecting filmmakers and films to audiences—is done online at a larger scale and lower cost, with less labor and overhead. I have attempted to demonstrate that, while media circulating online can get a lot of views, there are limits to the kind of impact they can have. There is still a need for film festivals to showcase a wide range of films to a wide range of audiences, bringing independent film to the community. Because traditional film festivals actually do the work of bringing people together to the same space at the same time, they have the potential to facilitate a kind of engagement that can't be reproduced online.

SAAFF fosters unique opportunities for unlikely interactions among media producers, audiences, scholars, elected officials, artists, activists, and other community members, young and old. With our small festival, we have helped filmmakers to connect with audiences they do not typically encounter online and facilitate conversations that might otherwise not happen, between filmmakers, cast, crew, and audiences, between younger and elder members of the community, elected officials and their constituents, particularly of overlooked or marginalized communities, and even between YouTube and musical celebrities and their fans. SAAFF has gathered live audiences for up-and-coming musicians, older filmmakers, and teenage filmmakers from low-income, at-risk communities. Operating a traditional film festival has also created a space for tough conversations about historical and contemporary issues like immigration, mental health, sexual violence, finding bone marrow donors, and countless other concerns of the Seattle APA community. This happens through discussion panels, Q&As with filmmakers, and encounters with local nonprofits that aim to serve the community on those topics. While it might sometimes feel as if traditional film festivals are at odds with what is going on online in the digital world, it has become clear that there is still an important role that could be played by traditional "subaltern" film festivals: but only if they can traverse the new media landscape by effectively using digital tools to more effectively organize, collaborate, raise money, study their audience, partner with other organizations, publicize the festival, and overall strengthen their unique and vital form of advocacy and community support.

References

Anderson, Monica. 2015. "5 Facts about Online Video, for YouTube's 10th Birthday," Pew Internet Research, February 12. http://www.pewresearch.org/fact-tank/2015/02/12/5-facts-about-online-video-for-youtubes-10th-birthday/.

Fraser, Nancy. 1990. "Rethinking the Public Sphere: A Contribution to the Critique of Actually Existing Democracy." *Social Text* (25/26): 56–80.

Habermas, Jurgen. 1989. *The Structural Transformation of the Public Sphere: An Inquiry into a Category of Bourgeois Society*. Cambridge, MA: MIT Press.

Okada, Jun. 2005. "The PBS and NAATA Connection: Comparing the Public Spheres of Asian American Film and Video." *The Velvet Light Trap* 55: 39–51.

Pham, Vincent. 2011. Mobilizing "Asian American": Rhetoric and Ethnography of Asian American Media Organizations. Doctoral Dissertation, University of Illinois.

Wong, Cindy H.-Y. 2016. "Publics and Counterpublics: Rethinking Film Festivals as Public Spheres." In *Film Festivals: History, Theory, Method, Practice*, Marjike de Valck, Brendan Kredell, and Skadi Loist (eds), 83–99. New York: Routledge.

8

OVERCOMING BARRIERS TO REPRESENTATION

Lessons from Asian American Women Directors

Elaine H. Kim[1]

Launched in 2013, the television series *Orange Is the New Black* became the most-watched original series produced by Netflix that year (Gelt 2013). The show was heralded as feminist and progressive, particularly in its focus on women of color, trans women, and queer characters. In a *Salon.com* article, Wesley Yiin (2015) lauded *Orange Is the New Black* as "a huge step forward" for women and people of color in the television industry, pointing out how the show "[strips] away political correctness to more honestly depict complex social and power structures." However, Yiin observed that there were only two Asian women on the show, and only one who demonstrates any complexity. He concludes from this that "Asian-American stories either don't exist or don't matter." In an immediate backlash, irritated online commenters ignored the substance of Yiin's arguments and cited prison population statistics; almost without exception, they were unsympathetic, sarcastic, or hostile:

> Wow, do they work in the prison laundry by any chance?
> Is this a joke? Or more politely: an "us too-ism"?
> So-So [one of the two characters] is pretty hot.
> Wesley Yiin, you are an idiot and no one should be handing you an audience to listen to your drivel. Stop typing. Close the laptop. Never open it again.
> Why no white men? I'm insulted.

These comments demonstrate an indifference and, indeed, outright resistance to concerns about the invisibility of Asian American women in U.S. media, even at a time when imaginative representations of people of color and women have been appearing, and have been celebrated.

Asian American men have also often contributed to the silencing of Asian American women's efforts to address omissions and distortions by foregrounding Asian American masculinity. For instance, Jeff Adachi's documentary about Hollywood representations of Asian men, *The Slanted Screen* (2006), contains no footage of Asian women, whether as "experts" or as talent. Nor is there mention of Asian women in the narration or interviews. The implication that

Asian women don't matter is underscored by the fact that according to almost every Asian male actor interviewed in the documentary, an on-screen romantic pairing with a White woman would denote success and achievement for them more than anything else. More recently, while there has been much celebration of the accomplishments of Asian American male media pioneers such as director Justin Lin, YouTubers Kevin Wu and Ryan Higa, and blogger Angry Asian Man, there has been distinctly less focus on Asian American women and their successes in the realm of media.

These omissions and distortions regarding Asian women in U.S. society and culture are longstanding. In 1976, I co-founded, together with two Chinese and two Japanese American women, the now Oakland-based organization Asian Women United of California (AWU). The organization's credo is that if we want better representations, we should try to create them ourselves. For the past four decades, we have produced books and videos that provide self-determined representations of East, South, and Southeast Asian American women.[2] Yet, there is much more work to be done in this arena.

Asian American women documentary filmmakers—including, but not limited to, Christine Choy, Loni Ding, Felicia Lowe, Renee Tajima-Peña, Deann Borshay Liem, Debbie Lum, and Ramona Diaz—have used the genre of documentary film to share the stories of Asian American women, Asian American communities, or the community at large. But Asian American women's work in narrative features remains largely unrecognized. Rea Tajiri's avant-garde documentary, *History and Memory* (1991), is often screened and taught. But her narrative film, *Strawberry Fields* (1997), which portrays the lasting psychological effects of wartime internment on contemporary young Japanese American characters, is far less known, despite having been an Official Selection for the Venice Film Festival. Other important directors include Mira Nair, whose films include *Mississippi Masala* (1991) and *The Namesake* (2006), and Kayo Hatta, whose *Picture Bride* (1995) was a period drama about a Japanese woman who comes to live in Hawaii at the turn of the last century. *Picture Bride* won the Audience Award for best feature at the Sundance Film Festival and was an Official Selection for the Cannes Film Festival. Both Nair and Hatta utilized Asian actors and funding, and Hatta garnered support from Japanese American communities in Hawaii and California, as many viewers were eager to see their own stories on screen. Aside from Mira Nair, the only bankable Asian American woman filmmaker at present is Jennifer Yuh Nelson, who directed *Kung Fu Panda 2* (2011) and *Kung Fu Panda 3* (2016), while excellent films by new Asian American women filmmakers are booked in small art theaters for only a day or two.

Although Asian American documentary films are often recognized for their cultural and educational value, narrative feature films also need to be recognized for playing a key role in cultivating different ways of imagining the world. Moreover, feature filmmakers face a number of challenges and obstacles that stymie their success. To craft their stories—whether in a coming-of-age tale, a science fiction work, or a romantic comedy—Asian American women narrative filmmakers must negotiate the contextual minefield of misogyny and racial tensions. They must either adhere to or rebel against particular kinds of scripts, such as those having to do with sexuality, ethnic identities and communities, and interracial relationships. Since 2000, many Asian American women artists have made notable forays into independent feature-length narrative filmmaking that deserve attention due to both topic and formal strategy. This essay focuses on three women-centered feature films directed by Asian American women: Bertha Bay-sa Pan's *Face* (2002), Alice Wu's *Saving Face* (2004), and Jennifer Phang's *Advantageous* (2015). *Face* puts Asian American and global youth culture in conversation with each other while attempting to intervene in stereotyping of Asians and Blacks in the post-Los Angeles "riots" era. *Saving Face* focuses on the intersection of ethnicity and sexuality in a story about a Chinese American mother–daughter relationship. *Advantageous* places Asian American female characters at the center of a story that is not explicitly about race and culture.

Pan, Wu, and Phang present stories and characters that are rarely seen in mainstream American movies. Their films are about family and the complex relationships forged among mothers and daughters within the contexts of their larger communities. Although specificities of heritage, culture, and racial identity are important in *Face* and *Saving Face*, both Wu and Pan have emphasized in interviews that while these elements work to make the stories feel authentic and true, at a deeper level the stories are universal and can be fully appreciated and understood by a diversity of viewers. In the documentary video *Slaying the Dragon Reloaded* (2011), Wu states: "I don't think that the fact that I am an Asian American lesbian means that I can't relate to, you know, a 55-year-old European American middle class white male. I ultimately do think the human condition is fairly universal. Most people just really want a chance to love and a chance to belong to a community." To film critic David Edelstein's persistent questions about themes of "face" and cultural conflict in Chinese culture, Pan responds: "We've played in front of African-American audiences, Brazilian audiences, and in Italy for 1,200 teenagers. All these people would say, 'This is my story.' A Jewish gay man said, 'This is my story.' Whatever the clashes in this movie—between cultures, in families, in relationships—they are universal" (*New York Times*, March 20, 2005).

At the same time, in "authentic" and "true" stories about Asian American women, the part played by race, gender, and sexuality in personal struggles is difficult to ignore. The women in *Face* and *Saving Face* cannot fully distance themselves from their heritage, their culture, or their racial identities and the traumas they may impart, and although the characters in *Advantageous* inhabit some putatively postracial future, gender, class, and race are never far from relations of power. Each of the women characters in these three films addresses elements of race, gender, and sexuality or culture or class in her own distinctive way, reminding us of the unique and diverse ways in which Asian American women—both the characters and the filmmakers—insist that they can be simultaneously particular and universal.

Face: Chinese Traditions and American Youth Culture

Face (2002) features three generations of Chinese women who do whatever they can to control their own destinies, each from within the confines of her own cultural and generational context. While the film does not directly address cross-racial conflict, the immigrant generation is shown as narrow and unable to adapt to the contemporary American world in comparison to the younger generation—such as the Korean immigrant shopkeepers in the 1992 Los Angeles "riots," most of whom spoke limited English and were unaware of the historical and social contexts of their American lives. In this case, the missing context includes the history of anti-Black racism that is in the nation's bedrock, as is seen in institutions such as politics, health, labor, criminal justice, sports, education, and media.

In the late 1970s, young immigrant Kim (Bai Ling), who lives in a modest Flushing, New York apartment with her widowed mother (Kieu Chinh), has a Chinese American law school student fiancé (Ken Leung) and works as a student intern in an American bank. After Kim is raped and impregnated by a local Chinese American playboy (Will Yun Lee), her mother demands that the boy's wealthy family accept her in marriage. Eager for a grandchild, the boy's mother agrees despite her son's objections. Kim is mistreated by her husband and suffocated by her traditional mother-in-law, who plies her with Chinese foods for pregnant women and refuses to let her leave the house. When Kim surreptitiously flushes the Chinese food down the toilet and asks for ice cream, which to her represents the delicious treat that is American freedom, fun, and romance, the mother-in-law reminds her that cold foods are bad for the fetus and offers her Chinese herbal soup instead. Ultimately, Kim leaves the baby with her mother to raise and escapes to Hong Kong, where she becomes a glamorous international banker. Meanwhile, Kim's daughter Genie (Kristy Wu) grows up to be a lover of hip-hop culture in multiracial New York.

By the 1990s, Flushing is still peopled by Chinese immigrants, but it has blossomed into a bustling working-class community where immigrants from East and South Asia, Africa, and Latin America live and work side by side. Streetwise, comfortable in her social environment, and unselfconsciously feminist, Genie refuses to be sexually objectified. When a DJ named Michael shines a spotlight on her dancing in a club, Genie stops and moves out of the light, annoyed. Michael tries to apologize and she cuts him off; she will not be the passive recipient of his gaze. In a role reversal that challenges the stereotype that Asian women are sexually submissive and Black men are sexually dominant, it is she who sexualizes him, pushing into his apartment while pulling off his clothes. "Hey, whoa, can't we talk for a moment first?" he protests. Rejecting the Madame Butterfly role, Genie is the one who gets up to leave in the middle of the night while Michael wants her to stay. She is the one who casually promises to call sometime. Genie has no interest in marriage or even an exclusive relationship. Although she showers Michael with physical attention, she considers him "just a friend."

While *Face* challenges Chinese and American gender roles, it adheres to the familiar American narrative that to succeed as full social beings, the children of immigrants must leave behind the restrictive confines of the immigrant family and community that serve as a proxy for China. In this way, the film parallels the memoirs of women from all over Asia escaping from feudal patriarchal oppression into the heaven of American freedom, democracy, and equality for women.[3] To become a globetrotting independent woman, Kim has to leave behind the Chinese community—which includes her patriarchal boyfriend, her rapist and his ultra-Chinese family, her Chinatown uncle who won't employ her after she's married, and her mother, who considers her pregnancy a shame to the family even though it was the result of rape. To become an American, Genie must leave the "old world" of the immigrant generation behind. In one moment, she lurks behind a car to stare at and perhaps long for the very non-Chinese suburban home of her mother's rapist, her own father. Michael also represents her idealized version of America, with his music and clubs and pagers and mixtapes. When her grandmother refuses to accept her friendship with a Black man, Genie moves out. Though she loves her grandmother deeply, she knows she will never change her Chinese ways: "I don't eat American food," the grandmother repeats adamantly. To her, the only thing worse than Genie marrying a Black man would be for her not to marry at all.

For the viewer, Genie's world is infinitely more alluring and promising; the portrayal of American youth culture is stronger and more convincing than the representations of her mother's and grandmother's worlds. Even the soundtrack accentuates this binary: Chinese traditional music or Canto-pop songs accompany the "Chinese" scenes, while Genie's scenes feature a much more appealing soundtrack featuring music scored by Leonard Nelson Hubbard, known for his work with the Philadelphia hip-hop band The Roots. This perspective on American culture reflects Pan's own life experiences; although she was born in the United States, Pan attended Chinese schools in Taiwan from first to tenth grades. She heard of Malcolm X for the first time only when she went to see Spike Lee's film about him purely for entertainment. She was made aware of dehumanizing representations of Asian men in American popular culture when she received complaints, including hate mail, about the depiction of Asian men in *Face*. Indeed, the film's representation of Chinese American life in Flushing as something akin to entrapment in a claustrophobic time warp might reflect Pan's outsider view of Chinese Americans as trapped in what she calls "1960s and 1970s mindsets" brought with them when they immigrated to the United States, a view most certainly not shared by Chinese Americans themselves.[4]

Kim and Genie must traverse conventional cultural borders—single motherhood and interracial romance—to become the modern and independent women they wish to be. Although *Face* adheres to the familiar trope of East and West never meeting and of needing to leave the "old ways" behind to become American, becoming American does not mean striving for Whiteness in the film. Rather, the film's definition of becoming "American" means prioritizing individual identity and happiness over belonging in a community that only serves to limit and confine. In *Face,* the two kinds of Chinese masculinity that appear are the rapist and the domineering boyfriend, while the Chinese community means claustrophobic restriction, rigid prejudice, and closed-minded conservatism. And although a boundary between "China" and "America" has been traversed, it is the most permeable one, involving the Asian woman, the embodiment of desirable non-White femininity, with the Black man, the epitome of non-White masculinity.

In *Face*, mother–daughter relationships are more important than the romantic relationship between Genie and Michael. In a sense, the heterosexual relationship is mostly a vehicle for escape from family and community. Certain scenes, such as the scenes of, first, the mother as a young woman and then, later, the daughter standing by the subway track or going by or into the grandmother's room, convey a sense of both mother and daughter being stuck in unchanging time and in need of escape. But while we are encouraged to understand and identify with Genie's anger, we are not privy to the sources of Kim's discontent. She is effectively silenced throughout the film: her rape is brushed aside, and Genie never lets her speak, no matter how many times she earnestly tries. Although it's true that many Asian American mother–daughter narratives are crafted by and perhaps naturally tend to center on the daughters, the silencing of Kim is unsettling because we do not know whether it suggests the need for more plot and character development or derives from clichés about Chinese patriarchy and tradition. Also, the fact that Bai Ling, an experienced actor who has usually been confined to dragon lady roles in Hollywood films, depicts Kim as passionate and decisive to the point of being almost driven makes it harder for viewers to accept her silence.

Ultimately, *Face* is a story about youth, and the need to leave home behind—to strike out on one's own to become independent and autonomous, even if alone. Feeling rejected by both her daughter and her mother, Kim decides to relocate to Los Angeles. Genie moves out of the home she shared with her grandmother, leaving the old woman trapped, sweeping in her cramped apartment behind the door Genie constantly admonishes her to keep locked. In the end, all three women will go on alone.

Saving Face: A Chinese American Lesbian Romantic Comedy

Like *Face*, Alice Wu's *Saving Face* (2004) explores the relationship between Chinese immigrant family and community through exploring an individual Chinese American's happiness in America. Like *Face*, *Saving Face* decenters masculinity and Whiteness to feature strong and active Chinese American women as protagonists. It focuses on the mother–daughter pair of Ma and Wil as they both face difficult life situations—Ma is a widow who has accidentally gotten pregnant in her forties, and Wil is a lesbian who wants to be with her girlfriend Vivian. Both films tackle topics still deemed risky in risk-averse Hollywood: *Face* features an Asian–Black romance, while *Saving Face* centers on the deviant sexuality of its two Asian American leads. Both films foreground mother–daughter relationships[5] and are premised on the contrast between Chinese and American communities and identities. Yet, the focus in *Saving Face* is equally divided between mother and daughter. In doing so, the success and happiness of one is not predicated on the failure and unhappiness of the other. The goal is, then, for both women is to attain happiness for themselves and each other, all without giving up their Chinese family and community.

One of the film's important achievements is the degree to which young Asian American viewers are invited to feel intentionally included—something that may feel quite rare to many Asian Americans. The Chinese language and everyday practices in the Chinese American community are represented in affectionate detail, such as when Ma speaks in Mandarin and Wil immediately responds in English, and when Vivian tries to speak Mandarin using mostly long English phrases. References to Chinese food and herbal medicines, Chinese-language television, red and pink apartment décor, and some daily life accoutrements, such as tongue scrapers and facial masques, are likely to be highly recognizable to many Asian Americans. The film features an amusing role reversal as Wil tries to find a suitable husband for her pregnant mother, not only because of the common practice of parents trying to introduce potential spouses to their children but also because children of immigrants often find themselves acting as parents when they have to translate and interpret for immigrant parents and grandparents who do not speak English. Even more rare is that the story is not about Asians aspiring to Whiteness, unlike so many of the films directed by non-Asians that feature an Asian woman character. *Saving Face* refers directly to the hated "Asian fixation" of White men who fantasize about Asian women as exotic objects of desire when Wil tells her mother that Vivian is "a nice Chinese girl" and Ma hopes that Wil will not introduce her to "old ugly White men" as suitors.

Like *Face*, *Saving Face* invokes the familiar theme of "East–West" tensions between Asia and America and between the immigrant and "Americanized" generations. Wil's best friend, Jay (Ato Essandoh), has no backstory but, rather, exists so that Wil's character can express herself to the viewer. But Jay also represents the America to which she aspires. With him, she can smoke and speak English about whatever she is thinking. In contrast, the Chinese community in Flushing, though tightly-knit, can be suffocating and constricting. Wil keeps her sexuality a secret, Ma refuses to divulge the identity of her baby's father, and the starchy old grandfather ejects Ma from the home and tries to force her to marry—for the second time—a man of his choice whom she doesn't love, because he fears damage to his reputation in the Chinese community.

The incompatibility of old Chinese ways and contemporary American life is emblemized in the public park, where the grandfather practices his tai chi exercises, completely oblivious to the young Black men who want to play basketball in that space. Ma's very "Chinese" ignorance and mistrust of Black people cause her to cringe in horror when Jay doesn't remove his shoes at the door and seasons the food she serves with soy sauce. The clash between traditional "Chinese" closed-mindedness and "American" tolerance is epitomized when Ma, not knowing that Vivian is lesbian, assumes that Vivian does not want to date Jay because she is anti-Black.

But we can also see that America transforms Ma: after leaving her immigrant parents behind to move in with Wil, she discovers porn in the neighborhood video store. Eventually she is sitting on her sofa sharing fried chicken and Chinese takeout food while watching Chinese soap operas with Jay, who has become her friend. Seeing her "American" daughter recoil at the idea of permanently sharing the apartment with her after the baby is born, she decides to get a place of her own and try living as an independent woman. Ultimately, she accepts Wil's sexuality, encouraging her to be with Vivian. The familiar East–West tensions are displaced because of mother-and-daughter love and because the Chinese community in the film turns out to be more diverse and heterogeneous than anyone, including the audience, was led to assume. Wil's grandmother is more tolerant than her grandfather, and Vivian's mother and father readily accept their daughter's sexuality. The gossiping Chinese community, which provides cultural context by functioning something like a Greek chorus, is depicted with affection and humor. The film begins and ends at a community social gathering. Wil and Vivian can be lesbian and Chinese at the same time: they will not give up the Chinese community, but only certain patriarchal practices.

Saving Face has been castigated by some critics as "Disneyesque," complete with implausible happy endings for everyone (Holden 2005). The characters, they argue, are one-dimensional to the point of being types: a rigid Chinese patriarch, a fried chicken-loving Black friend without any backstory, a girlfriend, Vivian, who will drop everything if Wil will just say "yes." In real life, Ma would surely have married her father's choice of husband, or at least she would not have ended up a single mother enjoying an independent life in her own apartment. But the film is a perennial favorite with my young Asian American students, who point to the paucity of Asian woman-centered films.[6] They contend that *Saving Face*'s happy ending should be thought about in the context of most other films about LGBT experiences that end tragically and without hope, or that are made from a straight male perspective with two would-be lesbians struggling over a man or engaged in a love triangle that includes a man.

Some borders remain uncrossed in *Saving Face*: Wil and Vivian are "exceptional" upper-middle-class young women[7] who replicate a heterosexual couple, with Wil the busy surgeon in boyish clothing and Vivian the feminine ballet dancer. Clearly, only a certain degree of difference can be allowed in a film meant for a general audience, and gayness in mainstream media continues to be quite heteronormative. Facing the challenge of producing a film with universal appeal despite featuring many elements that would be novel to mainstream viewers, Wu seems to have made a bid for acceptance of Chinese American sexualities by representing Asian American lesbians as enormously appealing and relatable in the rather apolitical genre of romantic comedy entertainment, a choice that seems the most viable one in view of the almost insurmountable contextual barriers. But while the film might adhere to the formal constraints of the romantic comedy and conform to existing social structures, *Saving Face* succeeds in shifting expectations about female desire.

We must also recognize the struggles that Wu faced in creating this film at all. She first conceptualized the film in 2001 and wrote a prize-winning script, but industry executives only wanted to make the film if she would remove the Chinese language and make the gay Chinese American characters straight and White. Someone even suggested to her that Ellen Burstyn and Reese Witherspoon be cast as the mother and daughter (Leibowitz 2005). Wu ignored every single change that was suggested, and persevered in making the story as she originally intended. Yet, such choices are not without their own consequences; indeed, when I saw the film in a local movie theater just after its release, my companion and I were the only viewers except for a lone White man sitting a few seats from us. During a love scene between Wil and Vivien, we heard the man's chair squeaking loudly and realized that he was masturbating, which certainly speaks to the overrepresentation of Asian women in pornography. Despite this particular response to the film, we can nonetheless recognize that *Saving Face* makes a Herculean attempt to shift popular expectations of Asian American women's sexuality.

Advantageous: The Future of Gender and Class

While *Face* and *Saving Face* feature Asian women protagonists in humanizing social relationships, both films are premised on familiar assumptions about cultural difference. Like *Face* and *Saving Face*, *Advantageous* (2015) is a mother–daughter story. But *Advantageous*, an ultra-low-budget sci-fi film directed by Jennifer Phang and co-written by Phang and Jacqueline Kim, avoids the most obvious issues of cultural difference because it is set in the future, when a raceless society can be imagined. Asian American identity and race, though present and undeniable, can be read as contrapuntal undercurrent rather than as ethnic dressing. In the film's narrative, Gwen Koh (Jacqueline Kim) is the poised and elegant head of and spokesperson for the euphemistically named Center for Advanced Health and Living. The Center is developing a technology that will enable people to "become the *you* you were meant to be" by transferring the consciousness of an aging, disease-ridden person into the younger, better body of a cadaver. The procedure, Gwen chirps confidently, is "a pragmatic response to the impenetrable job market." According to her sales pitch, this technology makes it possible for a woman to be "defined by the totality of her choices," and not elements she does not choose, such as "race, height, and health." Gwen fully believes this credo, but she comes to see the irony that she actually has no choice when she is notified that due to "shifting desirability targets," she will be replaced in her job by a younger woman who is "a touch more universal looking." Like so many Asian American women, Gwen has striven for perfection and excellence, but once the moment of her surface appeal has passed, her competence is ultimately insufficient. "But I am capable," she protests, stunned that her only immediate option is what's left of her corporeal utility—to become a paid egg donor. Youth and beauty, which can be racially marked, are necessary for women unless they have wealth or social connections. In the future presented in the film, nothing has really changed in terms of class and gender inequality. In fact, stratification has intensified, and opportunities are scarcer than ever, especially for women.

In the late capitalist world of *Advantageous*, reality contradicts marketing. Continual newscasts in the background tout "bigger and better" skyscrapers and more and more "progress." These announcements are interspersed with stories about child prostitution and inexplicable explosions that undermine the narratives of technological advancement. There is no real escape from the surveillance of drones darting like mosquitoes through the dystopian cityscape, represented in the film by a drawing of angular structures in shades of gray or footage of the downtown Los Angeles Cal Trans building. On the street, people are shown in garish light, dwarfed by huge vertiginous buildings. Phang utilized computer-generated visual effects to create the huge headless woman-shaped Cryer Building with water flowing from the "neck" as if it were weeping as the torso turns sinuously from upside down to downside up. Steam spews from the nearby Orator Building and then dissipates, as if a crouching woman were trying to speak.

In *Advantageous*, society is in ruins. Even nature, under continuous siege, has been reduced to a palliative remnant that common people cling to for respite: in a graveyard scene near the beginning of the film, Jules, Gwen's 13-year-old daughter (Samantha Kim), finds a butterfly dead because of "pressure to be hyper-productive." "We have too many choices," the precocious girl observes, but "we are making the same ones over and over again, and they are the wrong choices, so it's like natural de-selection—our DNA is opting out." Because of environmental degradation (we assume), by the time she is 20, Jules will have no eggs left.

Gender, unlike race, is not just an undertow in this future world—as Jules states, "women are in trouble … going backwards going forward." Technology is stripping women of social opportunities, leaving them scrambling for the few spots in the shrinking job market. As company official Fisher (James Urbaniak) intimates to Gwen, the rulers of society fear a restive population. Putting women back into the home is "safer than putting millions of unemployed men in the street." Every night Gwen and Jules can hear women whimpering and crying, in either the apartment above or the apartment below. Outside, Gwen sees a homeless woman buried in the shrubbery, only her hand and part of her face visible under the leaves. "Take what you can get," she hisses when she hears that Gwen can sell her eggs. Another woman, bruised and bleeding, lies on a park bench as Gwen and Jules pass by. Public schools have closed, and billboards announce education lotteries. At 13, Jules' only chance for a secure future is to attend an expensive private school. She laments: "There is so much to do. I need to exercise more, study more, do more volunteer work … I need to be smarter, nicer, prettier, and classier—but what's the point?" Observing that everyone is either greedy or desperate, Jules wonders why she is alive and asks Gwen: "Why did you have me when you knew the world was so bad and you had to struggle so much?"

Yet, what we come to see is that Jules is Gwen's reason for living. She had been a self-assured and economically secure single mother, surfing along on her superficial excellence, unaware of the precariousness of her situation. She wants her daughter to have a secure and safe future instead of a life "without advantage," like so many women around them who are "so desperate that [they] would do anything." Having lost her job, she becomes desperate to pay Jules' tuition. Unable to get work or borrow money from estranged relatives, she finds that her only option is to become a guinea pig for the as yet unperfected brain cloning process. Her skills, tastes, personality, and memories will be transferred into the body of a racially ambiguous but certainly not Asian-looking young woman.[8] Ironically, Isa Cryer (Jennifer Ehle), the executive who decides to fire Gwen and maneuver her into undergoing the procedure for marketing effect, is not only a (White) woman but also an aging woman who seems completely unremorseful about how her executive decisions affect other women, despite the fact that her name is a pun. Social power and wealth, not technology, gender, or race, have created and sustain the trouble in *Advantageous.*

Unlike in *Face*, in *Advantageous*, comfort and solace are possible away from the menacing outside world of technology and putative progress, which is contrasted with intimate domestic scenes. Near the film's opening, we see a close-up of mother and daughter at a piano happily singing a duet in French. Instead of computers, there is singing and dancing and visits to the park. Scenes of Gwen serving Jules a homemade tart at the table or seated on the floor near a Christmas tree sharing a pecan pie right from the pie plate feature curves, color, and soft light. Inside the apartment, Gwen, who is fond of the past, listens to classical music, pores over old photographs, cooks homemade dishes, and decorates her home with Victorian objects. Her special gift to Jules is a fountain pen. When she is overwhelmed, she seeks refuge in a Quiet Room, where she can pay for some time away from sensory overload. In *Advantageous*, people's connection to the past, like their connection to nature and the earth, is becoming ever more tenuous and fragile. The contrast between the apartment and the cityscape parallels the contrast elsewhere in the film between surface appearance and inner qualities that have no value in the external world.

After Gwen's enormous sacrifice, not only of her appearance but also her "awareness" and thus her relationship with Jules, Jules cannot recognize her mother in the younger woman's body. Jules wonders twice, once with Gwen and again with her new mother, why she is alive. Gwen had exhorted her to know her own value: "Your ideas, wisdom, and kindness are the secret beauty everyone wants." When the new mother says: "Whatever you do will be worthwhile because you are kind. You are alive because of energy and empathy," Jules remarks: "You are beginning to sound like her." In the end, Jules will mother as Gwen mothered her. She decides to let "Gwen 2.0" live by bringing her medication, feeding her, and reviving her. That she can accept as her mother someone who looks nothing like Gwen underscores the contrast between surface appearances, which are valued above everything in the ruthless future world of increased social stratification and misogyny, and inner qualities, such as kindness, which have no value in that world. Ultimately, Jules chooses inner qualities over surface appearances. In *Advantageous*, then, race and ethnicity are superficial, while gender and class are not.

The film ends with the hope that "Gwen 2.0" will learn to love and protect Jules. She facilitates a bridge between Jules, who "always wanted a big family," and her birth father and her cousins' family, providing hope that unlike her mother, she will not be alone. Instead of this "happy ending," leaving Jules and her new mother unable to find connections with each other might have raised unsettling but challenging questions about maternal love and sacrifice, if not about the possible value of ideas, wisdom, and kindness—or anything else that is not merely superficial or directly marketable. Also, reading the film as being centered on the irrevocable connectedness of mind and body implies that erasing Gwen's race erases her "self," and shows race as irreducible despite technological innovation in the future world of *Advantageous*.[9]

Asian America has been abuzz for more than a decade now about the prevalence of cosmetic surgery for women in Asia. In an interview, Jennifer Phang commented that women are continually deemed not good enough, and are pressured to change themselves in order to survive. She states:

> It's funny though because, when you think about it, changing one's appearance seems like the lowest hanging fruit … obsession with surface appearance can take years, maybe decades, away from personal development, which could have greater importance in the long term.
>
> (Asch 2015)

Advantageous advances an important critique of neoliberal capitalism through a combination of its feminist proclivities, its ethical perspectives, and its formal strategies. In addition, the film is noteworthy for featuring Asian American characters in a story that is not about being Asian American, but about the human condition—demonstrating that it is possible for Asian American women to be the central characters in a universal story. This focus opens the door to explorations of themes such as Asian American maternal sacrifice, as Gwen's efforts to survive without a social support network recall how difficult it sometimes is for immigrants who are uprooted from their countries of origin to build social support networks in their adopted countries. Moreover, Gwen becomes susceptible to the pervasive notion of Asian Americans as a model minority, perhaps unaware of the limits of competence. The film also addresses the experience of Asian American girls, with its poignant questions about how daughters may be affected by their immigrant parents' values and attitudes, their mothers' sacrifices, and their treatment in the larger society, where they may strive to be perfect without ever really expressing their feelings or even knowing how to find and listen to their own voices.

Conclusion

Although Asian American women characters are at the center of *Face*, *Saving Face*, and *Advantageous*, all of these films sidestep a critique of racism. Perhaps Phang imagines a future in which race is merely incidental. In *Face*, Chinese and American "culture" stands in for race, with the grandmother serving as the racist because of her "racist" culture. In *Saving Face*, the Flushing Chinese American community is a world unto itself, replete with its own inner conflicts and untouched by issues like "American" racism. Yet, even if these directors want to emphasize the "universally human" over the cultural, common clichés and decontextualized stereotypes about Asian American model minority values demand attention, whether among producers or viewers, and generally have to be addressed by writers and directors. These include representations of the "tiger mother" and her ambitions for her children, a blind belief in school achievement as the only and guaranteed path to success, and the need to adjust to rather than challenge injustice.[10] Like *Face* and *Saving Face*, *Advantageous* refuses to engage in the kind of now tiresome identity politics felt necessary by many artists of earlier times, instead avoiding outright discussions of what it means to be Asian American or what kinds of racism Asian Americans have experienced.[11]

What these three films do is explore gender politics in the everyday lives of Asian American women. Despite the fact that they are charged with policing racial boundaries, enforcing heteronormativity, and reproducing the model minority, the older-generation women characters in the three films are quite similar. They are all single mothers who serve as role models for the younger women, and none of them seems destined for patriarchal, heteronormative, or any other kind of marriage. That they are differently gendered becomes clear when we consider their relationship to the general political context that equates feminism with choice and mobility.[12] The "right to choose" is apparently not the issue for any of the three films' single mothers. In *Face* and *Saving Face*, matters of choice have to do with race and sexuality: in *Face*, Kim and Genie choose between staying and leaving; in *Saving Face*, Hwei-Lan and Wil can choose everything, all without upsetting the social structure. But, as *Advantageous* makes clear, having choices may be really no choice at all, just as plastic surgery can erase idiosyncrasy in favor of conformity.[13] Moreover, in different ways, all three films lead us to think about reproductive labor in a political and structural sense[14] and raise questions about what roles Asian American women play in our national culture.

But overall, we must recognize that Asian American women feature filmmakers face difficult odds and enormous obstacles. According to Jacqueline Kim, independent filmmaking is about "investing in ourselves" and making what we want to see. Jennifer Phang adds:

> Success-driven filmmaking can actually lead to failure because you end up doing it for the wrong reasons … filmmaking isn't just about you and your success. It's about the story you're telling and what your viewers take from that story. It's very powerful to put fresh perspectives into the world, and I think that should be our focus.
>
> (Wall n.d.)

If becoming established in Hollywood is nearly impossible, competition among independent filmmakers is fierce: only a few hundred out of tens of thousands of applicants are chosen to screen their films at the Sundance Film Festival, and of those, only a dozen or so are picked up by studios. The rest, however, can be seen in the United States and other countries on Netflix and other video-on-demand platforms. The possibilities offered by Asian American studies classes should not be underestimated, as all three films will surely be screened and critically examined in Asian American Studies classes across the United States.

Asian Americans, like other immigrants and people of color in the United States, have the potential power to see the world from more than one perspective. Similarly to someone who is fluent in more than one language, this particular kind of "double consciousness" can expand our thinking to accommodate paradoxes because it can show us alternative ways of thinking. At the same time, as W. E. B. DuBois (1903) has suggested, "double consciousness" can require the disparaged to become familiar with dominant views of them, while the dominant do not generally have to be cognizant of perspectives other than their own. Armed with this "double consciousness" or "double vision" and their gendered perspectives, Asian American women directors have the potential of being able to address multiple publics, which might help explain the potential appeal of *Face*, *Saving Face*, and *Advantageous* to a wide array of viewers for sometimes quite different reasons.

While more Asian American women directors and actors would undoubtedly be a good thing, it is, of course, not simply a question of numbers. Rather, it is important to have stories that say something that other films do not, such as examining the "social and power structures" mentioned in Yiin's *Salon* essay. Bertha Bay-sa Pan's *Face*, Alice Wu's *Saving Face*, and Jennifer Phang's *Advantageous* negotiate the limits imposed by culture and gender or gender and class to interrupt the White male gaze that relegates to the sidelines Asian American women, who are otherwise viewed mostly as mere sex objects in pornography. They use filmmaking to articulate desires that have nothing to do with Whiteness or masculinity. While it is completely unreasonable to expect a film to be all things to everyone, these three films deploy different strategies to tell multiple stories about Asian American women to a diversity of viewers, and they have the potential to shift hegemonic expectations through insisting on a place for Asian American women in American media culture.

Notes

1 I am grateful to Peter Gwansic Kim, Lori Lopez, Vincent Pham, and especially Amy Kaihua Lee for reading this chapter and offering many insightful suggestions.

2 Among AWU's books are *With Silk Wings: Asian American Women at Work* (1983); *Making Waves: Writings by and About Asian American Women* (1989); *Maving More Waves: New Writing by Asian American Women* (1997); and *InvAsian: Asian Sisters Represent* (2003). Educational video documentaries include *Four Women* and *On New Ground* (1982), directed by Loni Ding; *Talking History* (1984), directed by Spencer Nakasako; *Slaying the Dragon: Asian Women in U.S. Television and Film* (1988), directed by Deborah Gee; *Art to Art: Expressions of Asian American Women* (1993), directed by Valerie Soe; *Labor Women* (2002), directed by Renee Tajima-Peña; and *Slaying the Dragon: Reloaded* (2011), directed by Elaine H. Kim.

3 See, for example, Ting-Xing Ye, *A Leaf in the Bitter Wind* (1998); Adeline Yen Mah, *Falling Leaves: The Memoir of an Unwanted Chinese Daughter* (1999); Elizabeth Kim, *Ten Thousand Sorrows* (2000); and Chanrithy Him, *When Broken Glass Floats* (2001). Many memoirs by Middle Eastern and North Korean young women about their suffering under native patriarchies and regimes have been received favorably by publishers.

4 Interview with author on July 21, 2016.

5 There are three love stories in *Saving Face*: the story of the two young lesbians; the story of the widow mother and her younger lover; and the mother–daughter story, which emerges as the most vivid and important, illuminated by the other love stories. Indeed, Alice Wu has said that the film is her "love letter" to her mother (Kim 2011).

6 Given that film criticism is mostly devoted to formal analyses that look at films as objects of study, very little attention has been paid to viewers, especially "minority" viewers like Asian American audiences.

7 In both *Face* and *Saving Face*, New York City is a lively character itself—gritty in *Face* and glittering in *Saving Face*, both largely ignoring working-class Chinese American life.

8 Phang made sure not to replace Gwen with a blonde but, rather, with a racially ambiguous woman. For her, race and ethnicity are superficialities. Being Asian (or Black or Latina), she points out, can be marketable; Gwen's Korean American looks might have been marketable in her moment, but when that moment passes, the market moves on to find something else, which, she adds, is not progress for diversity (Coffin 2015).

9 Thanks to Leilani Nishime for this insight at her presentation on *Advantageous* at the 2016 Association for Asian American Studies conference.

10 Phang has commented that simply accepting unfairness and helping one's own child or one's own social class is a problem because it's ultimately not good for the collectivity (Saito 2015).

11 Although *Face* might be read as responding to what Linda Williams has discussed as racial narratives of the 1980s and 1990s, such as the Los Angeles "riots" and the O. J. Simpson trial, that take the form of classic melodramas, Genie's interracial relationship only stirs up some trouble at home. She embraces hip-hop culture, but the film's racial tensions are elusive.

12 For many White Americans, trains moving west across the nation have served as a metaphor for mobility and modernity. For Chinese Americans, who completed the transcontinental railroad in the western states, they meant discrimination through lower wages and riskier work and lack of acknowledgment. Trains removed Japanese Americans eastward—or back—from the Pacific Coast to concentration camps during World War II. Nor was the paradigm of linear movement from east to west fitting for Filipinos and other Asian migrant farm

workers, who followed the crops and fishing seasons in circuits from Baja California to the Alaskan canneries. Trains did not denote progress for native Americans, as they cut through their lands, or for Mexican agricultural laborers. As seen in J. T. Takagi and Hye Jung Park's documentary film *#7 Train: An Immigrant Journey* (2009), the New York subway scenes in *Face* and *Saving Face* call to mind the train that links New York's Asian and other immigrant communities in circuits of encounter and connection between residential areas in Queens and worksites in Manhattan.

13 Like many other Asian Americans, I was accustomed to feeling superior to the Asian women who wish to change their faces and to the American view that they want the same features, making "all Asians look alike" seem truer than ever. Accustomed to the American—and Protestant—view of the individual as unique as opposed to the more common—and I suppose Confucian—Korean perspective that values the collectivity and fitting in with it, it never occurred to me, until a young Korean American AWU member suggested it, that perhaps I was thinking of looks as superficial compared with "what's inside," while maybe for the Korean women who elect to go under the knife, their looks, or at least their faces, are not equal to their identities, so that they view many plastic surgery procedures as being similar to clothing and hair styles, which can be changed without changing their identity. And I hear that Americans often prefer body surgery, such as breast augmentation, tummy tucks, and liposuction, to facial surgery. Does that mean that our faces are our individuality and our bodies are *not* ourselves? What, then, is inside and what is outside?

14 I am grateful to Amy Kaihua Lee for these observations about choice.

References

Asch, Mark. 2015. "The Woman in the Mirror: Talking to Advantageous Director Jennifer Phang." *The L Magazine*, June 17. http://www.thelmagazine.com/2015/06/woman-mirror-talking-advantageous-director-jennifer-phang/.

Coffin, Lesley. 2015. "The Mary Sue Interview: Advantageous' Jennifer Phang." *themarysue.com*, June 23. http://www.themarysue.com/the-mary-sue-interview-advantageous-jennifer-phang/.

DuBois, W. E. B. 1903. *The Souls of Black Folk*. Chicago: A.C. McClurg & Co.

Gelt, Jessica. 2013. "'Orange Is the New Black' is Netflix's Most Watched Original Series." *latimes.com*, October 21. http://articles.latimes.com/2013/oct/21/entertainment/la-et-st-netflix-orange-is-the-new-black-most-watched-series-20131021.

Holden, Stephen. 2005. "Juggling Her Chinese Clan, Gay Lover, Pregnant Mom," *New York Times*, May 27.

Kim, Elaine H. (director). 2011. *Slaying the Dragon: Reloaded*.

Leibowitz, Ed. 2005. "Kissing Vivian Shing," *New York Times*, May 29.

Saito, Stephen. 2015. "Interview: Jennifer Phang on Looking at the Past to see the Future in 'Advantageous'." *Moveable Feast*, June 26. http://moveablefest.com/moveable_fest/2015/06/jennifer-phang-advantageous.html.

Wall, Kylee. n.d. "Advantageous: Jennifer Phang on Making Way to Sundance." *creativecow.net*, https://library.creativecow.net/print.php?id=22525.

Yiin, Wesley. 2015. "Soso and Chang, Prison Bunkmates by Default: Why Won't 'Orange Is the New Black' Expand its Asian Cast?" *salon.com*, July 3. http://www.salon.com/2015/07/03/soso_and_chang_prison_bunkmates_by_default_why_wont_orange_is_the_new_black_expand_its_asian_cast/.

9

"PERPETUAL FOREIGNERS" IN AMERICA

Transnationalism and Transformations of Asian American Cultural Identities in Three Documentary Films

Valerie Soe

The history of Asian American media began with the creation of documentary films in the 1970s, when Asian American artists and activists used the filmic medium to tell true stories about their struggles, their triumphs, and their everyday lives. Yet, since the 1990s, as Brian Hu discusses in this collection, the documentary tradition has been somewhat eclipsed by the onslaught of feature-length Asian American fiction films. With the potential for bigger budgets and technical professionalization, these smaller, more personal pictures seemed to fade from the spotlight. Yet, the Asian American documentary tradition never truly disappeared—and as we can see from examining some of the more popular Asian American documentaries from the 2010s, such films are still being made in a way that calls attention to social issues facing Asian American communities. In this chapter, I give a brief history of Asian American filmmaking and the themes that characterized their storytelling. I then examine three Asian American documentaries—Ramona Diaz's *Don't Stop Believin': Everyman's Journey* (2012), Evan Jackson Leong's *Linsanity* (2013), and Tadashi Nakamura's *Jake Shimabukuro: Life on Four Strings* (2012)—in order to consider these shifting sensibilities and thematics.

In addition to expanding the definition of Asian American cultural identity to include more transnational perspectives, I argue that these films continue to examine and explicitly deal with countering the age-old stereotype that Asians in the United States are "perpetual foreigners," or outsiders who never truly belong in the United States or become part of American cultural identity. By diverging from discourses of assimilation, these films expand definitions of American identity to include those of Asian descent and demonstrate the internationalizing of Asian America via Asian American independent documentary film. Through this analysis, we can trace continuities across the long history of Asian American documentary film, while also considering some of the ways that contemporary transnationalism via nonfiction storytelling is transforming Asian American identities—in particular, with regard to the international salability of domestic celebrities. As we see in these three examinations of Asian American musicians, performers, and athletes, it is the harsh spotlight of international fame and the need to connect to mass audiences that allow these documentaries and their stars to truly push past the unwanted alienation and ostracization that have long marked Asian American experiences.

First-Stage Asian American Films and the Narrative Turn

Many Asian American media arts productions from the 1970s–1990s were social issue documentaries that looked at topics of concern from the Asian American community and reflected what Glenn Mimura calls a "community-based ethic, inspired and shaped by the decolonial struggles for self-determination that also profoundly influenced Third Cinema" (Mimura 2009: 40). The Third Cinema movement was distinctly international in its positioning, including the highly politicized films from Latin America, Africa, and Asia that focused on resistance and liberation. This ethos was taken up in the United States by minority groups whose oppression and subordination similarly demanded recognition, and film provided a platform for expressing these ideologies. Renee Tajima-Peña characterized the first historical stage of Asian American media arts production in the 1970s as "an urgent, idealistic brand of filmmaking that embodied the energy of the Asian American political movement and sought to be a voice for Asian American people" (Tajima-Peña 1992: 12).

Documentary filmmaking, in part because of its lower production costs in comparison with narrative filmmaking, dominated first-stage Asian American media arts production. In both aesthetics and content, these films reflected the political fervor and activism of the Asian American community at the time. As Tajima-Peña observes,

> The gritty Chinatown documentaries, fast and furious in style, captured San Francisco's burgeoning 'Chonk' Chinese American street culture in Curtis Choy's *Dupont Guy: The Schiz of Grant Avenue* (1975); in *Save Chinatown* (1973) Jon Wing Lum fuses provocateur filmmaking with the Philadelphia Chinatown community's fight again redevelopment; and Christine Choy's documentary about community struggles on New York's lower Eastside, *From Spikes to Spindles* (1976), expresses the confluence of Third World political culture.
>
> (Tajima-Pena 1992: 17)

This continued through the 1980s and 1990s, with films including Curtis Choy's *The Fall of the I-Hotel* (1984), which examined housing and displacement among first-generation Filipino Americans in raw portraits of the everyday lives of those who were most affected by the destruction of the landmark space. Christine Choy and Renee Tajima-Pena's *Who Killed Vincent Chin?* (1988) looked at anti-Asian violence in the United States, while Arthur Dong's *Forbidden City USA* (1989) explored culture and identity amidst the 1930s and 1940s San Francisco Chinese American nightclub scene. Spencer Nakasako and Sokly Ny's *AKA Don Bonus* (1995) used the format of the first-person video diary to reveal the challenges and concerns of a teenage Cambodian refugee in San Francisco.

Since the late 1990s, Asian American media production has expanded and diversified, moving away from documentary films and focusing instead on fiction films. This narrative turn was signaled by the arrival of "The Class of 1997," or the four Asian American feature filmmakers who were showcased that year at the San Francisco Asian American International Film Festival. A *New York Times* article with the headline "A Film Festival Focuses on Gener-Asian X" commented on how noteworthy it was for the 21-year-old festival to include more features made by Americans than by international filmmakers. The rarity of this selection pointed to how relevant the Asian American feature-length film had become. It seemed that the Asian American media arts community was joining the mainstream in privileging narrative fiction films over the documentaries that had previously been its strength. Yet, as Okada argues, many of these feature films "[de-emphasize] the social change ethos on which Asian American film and video was built," as she notes in reference to Justin Lin's 2003 film *Better Luck Tomorrow*. Okada calls this "the gerrymandering of Asian American film and video through the lens of marketability and mainstream success, which runs counter to the impulse of grassroots filmmaking of the past" (Okada 2015: 99).

The success of *Better Luck Tomorrow* and other feature-length narrative films such as *The Debut* (2000), *Colma: The Musical* (2006), and *The Motel* (2005), among many others, reflected a shift to narrative production on the part of many younger Asian American filmmakers. Along with the advent of digital media tools, which lower the financial burden of producing feature films, as well as the increase in Asian Americans completing professional film school training, narrative filmmaking has in some ways eclipsed the community-based, social issue documentaries that dominated the early years of Asian American media production.[1]

Yet, Asian American independent documentary film production continues to serve as an alternative to fiction films. Three documentaries from 2012–2013 seem particularly synchronous with the tradition of earlier nonfiction films in addressing relevant issues from the Asian American community: Ramona Diaz's *Don't Stop Believin': Everyman's Journey* (2012), Evan Jackson Leong's *Linsanity* (2013), and Tad Nakamura's *Jake Shimabukuro: Life on Four Strings* (2012). Each looks at the ways in which its respective subject rose to the top of his chosen field despite facing racism and racialized misperceptions of Asians in the United States. Philippines-born Arnel Pineda, as seen in Diaz's film; Taiwanese American Jeremy Lin, featured in Leong's film; and Japanese American Jake Shimabukuro, from Nakamura's film, all struggled for success in their respective fields of pop music and professional basketball. Both Pineda and Lin were perceived as foreign interlopers invading established U.S. institutions, while as a resident of the more multicultural Hawai'i, Shimabukuro was partially shielded from this type of discrimination. Through examining the lives of their high-profile celebrity subjects, these films expand perceptions of who and what counts as American, as well as Asian American.

The "Perpetual Foreigner"

The perpetual foreigner stereotype has been deployed countless times against Asians living in the United States as a way of denying civil rights. This often manifests in microaggressions similar to the one documented by Frank H. Wu, who states:

> "Where are you from?" is a question I like answering. "Where are you really from?" is a question I really hate answering. … Like many other people of color (or a few whites who have marked accents) who share memories of such encounters, I know what the question "Where are you really from?" means, even if the person asking is oblivious and regardless of whether the person is aggressive about it … I have been mistaken for a foreigner or told I cannot be a real American. … [These] comments and actions imply that I am not one of "us" but one of "them." I do not belong as an equal. My heart must be somewhere else rather than here. I am a visitor at best, an intruder at worst.
>
> (Wu 2003: 79–80)

Wu's experience reflects the belief that only "White" Americans are real Americans and that Asian Americans are "perpetual foreigners." They are not truly members of American society or culture, despite their long history within the United States. As Ron Takaki observes, "Asian Americans have been here for over 150 years, before many European immigrant groups. But as 'strangers' coming from a 'different shore,' they have been stereotyped as 'heathen,' exotic, and unassimilable" (Takaki 1993: 8). Takaki also states that although Asians have settled in the United States since the nineteenth century, Asian immigrants face more challenges than European immigrants to the United States when attempting to be recognized as Americans. Takaki notes:

> The Irish came about the same time as the Chinese, but they had a distinct advantage: the Naturalization Law of 1790 had reserved citizenship for "whites" only. Their compatible complexion allowed them to assimilate by blending into American society.
> (Takaki 1993: 10)

That is, while European immigrants to the United States look like native-born majority-culture White Americans, Asian immigrants do not and will never "look" European American, or White, and thus are more often seen as foreigners in their own country.

Various historical events in the United States emphasize the deleterious effect of the "perpetual foreigner" stereotype. In 1882, the United States enacted the Chinese Exclusion Act, which barred almost all immigration from China to the United States and described Chinese as "foreigners of a different race." It was the first U.S. federal law that barred a specific group from immigrating based on race. The act was not repealed until 1942 and led to widespread discrimination against the Chinese in the United States, as well as spawning several other similar laws limiting Asian immigration, including the 1924 National Origins Act, which specifically targeted immigration from Asian countries. In 1942, Executive Order 9066, decreed by U.S. President Franklin D. Roosevelt, resulted in the mass imprisonment in the United States of over 120,000 Japanese Americans during World War II on unfounded suspicions of disloyalty and treason based solely on their ethnic heritage. The order specifically played on fears of Japanese Americans as perpetual foreigners with loyalty to Japan instead of the United States.

Beyond federal legislation, the relationship between the United States and Asia has also contributed to acts of violence against Asian American individuals. In 1982, two unemployed White autoworkers murdered Vincent Chin, a Chinese American man from Detroit, in part because they associated him with the Japanese auto industry. According to testimony from the trial of the two men, one of them had stated just prior to the killing: "It's because of you motherfuckers that we're out of work," illustrating the conflation of Chinese and Japanese national identities as well as confusion between Japanese nationals and Asian Americans. In 2001, four days after the terrorist attacks on the World Trade Center, Sikh American Balbir Sodhi was shot and killed in Arizona by a man who thought Sodhi was Arab and who had earlier stated: "I'm going to go out and shoot some towel-heads" (Arora 2003). The perpetual foreigner stereotype thus has real and often dangerous consequences for Asian Americans.

Hollywood films also reinforce the perpetual foreigner stereotype, with Asian characters using heavy accents and remaining outside of dominant U.S. culture. Several films released in the 1980s and 1990s, including *Do The Right Thing* (1989), *Menace II Society* (1993), and *Falling Down* (1993), include depictions of Korean American shopkeepers as rude, unsociable, and bigoted in their behavior toward both White Americans and African Americans, and as defiantly unwilling to adapt U.S. cultural customs. More recently, in *The Hangover* (2009), the only Asian character, Leslie Chow, speaks in broken English, and his awkward and culturally inept behavior prevents him from joining the circle of friends featured in the movie.

In order to counter perceptions of their "otherness" or "foreignness," Asian Americans have historically been encouraged to deny their ethnic heritage and to assimilate. This manifests in immigrants and their descendants choosing to not speak their heritage languages and instead speaking only English, ceasing to observe Lunar New Year or other celebrations and rituals from their cultures, adopting English-friendly names, and otherwise molding themselves to fit into mainstream hegemonic U.S. culture, which leads to a loss of cultural identity and history. While the meaning and consequences of assimilation are complex and politically charged in ways that deserve much closer scrutiny, what I argue here is simply that these sentiments have clearly been represented and upheld through media representations. Yet, the three documentaries discussed here resist these ideologies of assimilation as a route toward success, and instead demonstrate the ways in which their subjects embrace transnationalism as a way of integrating their various cultural identities—a position that harkens back to the roots of Asian American activism, and the Asian American cinematic tradition itself.

Don't Stop Believin': Everyman's Journey

Ramona Diaz's 2012 documentary *Don't Stop Believin': Everyman's Journey* tells the story of singer Arnel Pineda's rise in U.S. pop music. Pineda was born and raised in the Philippines and began singing for the classic rock band Journey after guitarist Neal Schon found videos of Pineda covering Journey songs on YouTube. Diaz's documentary follows Pineda's first tour as Journey's lead singer as the band travels across the United States and around the world. His popularity began to rise in 2007 when he was picked to become the lead singer of Journey. Yet, he was continually pigeonholed by the perpetual foreigner stereotype and the perception that he was not "American" enough to be the lead singer for an iconic U.S. rock band. A comment on the YouTube clip of Pineda performing the Journey song *Don't Stop Believin'* demonstrates this point: "THIS SUCKS. TRYING TO REPLACE STEVE PERRY WITH A LITTLE ASIAN GUY JUST DOESN'T WORK, I FEEL LIKE I'M WATCHING A BAD EPISODE OF 'AMERICA'S GOT TALENT.' " A comment on another blog entry states: "pinoy mongoloid bad clone steve perry the new journey band is desperate." Pineda himself recalls: "One of the worst things I read on a fan messageboard said that Journey is an all-American band and it should stay like that" (Liberatore 2007).

The film documents Pineda's encounters with the perpetual foreigner stereotype even before he arrives in the United States. When Neal Schon first proposes the idea that Pineda audition for the band, other band members express some doubts about Pineda's ability to fit in with the band's culture—and, by extension, with U.S. culture. One band member wonders out loud: "Can he speak English?" and another refers to him as "someone from a third-world country." Pineda himself notes: "I'm so Asian! If you picture it, it was like I was just placed there using Adobe Photoshop—look, I'm in Journey!" Later in the film, Pineda reads from online criticisms that state: "Only filipinos [sic] will support this crappy singer!" which also suggests that some members of Journey's fan base regarded Pineda as an outsider. Together, these comments reinforce the perception that he was a "perpetual foreigner" and did not belong as the singer for the quintessential American rock band.

However, the film turns the perpetual foreigner stereotype around, showing that Pineda's Filipino heritage is a strength rather than a detriment. His participation comes to redefine Journey's culture and identity, and in turn affects American culture and identity. Throughout the film, Filipina director Ramona Diaz focuses on Pineda's Filipino roots, and in the film's interviews Pineda mostly speaks Tagalog. Diaz also emphasizes the transnationalism of Pineda's existence. In the film, Pineda makes no secret of where he considers home; for instance, we see a sequence shot in his brand new house in Manila, where he cooks dinner with his wife and sings to her. Pineda remains clearly rooted in the Philippines, which Diaz describes in an interview: "He refuses to live in the West" (Soe 2012). This acknowledgment of his choice to live in the Philippines can be seen as an act of resistance, as it comes well after his successful career and the mobility this would have brought him.

The film also underscores the Filipino and Filipino American reception of Pineda as reflecting a transnational connection. One sequence shows Pineda surrounded by adoring Filipino American fans requesting autographs, with one woman noting: "Arnel Pineda has made the world smaller. The impact on the Filipino community all over the world and in the Philippines! When Journey found him, they did not realize they inherited a nation." Here, the film reflects the way in which Pineda's presence makes the Filipino American community legible to the mainstream. As Journey guitarist Neil Schon notes later in the film, "I never noticed before there were so many Filipinos in the States." A group of White Journey fans also recognize a positive aspect of Pineda's Filipino heritage as they debate his qualifications to be the band's lead singer. One woman states: "I think he should be from here [the United States]." However, her opinion is quickly countered by another woman, who says: "I kinda like that he's not. Gives it more variety. Brings in more people." Or, as Journey bass player Ross Valory notes, "Having engaged someone from the other side of the world, it changed our reputation to be more international, beyond being an all-American rock band." The film emphasizes the ways in which Pineda's visibility as a Filipino singer in a U.S. band draws attention to the Filipino diaspora and its worldwide presence. It also recognizes the demographic impact of the Filipino American community, which is the second-largest Asian subgroup in the United States.

Notably, Diaz shot the scenes featuring Filipino fans at a Journey concert in Los Angeles. One fan also describes her affection for both Pineda and fellow Journey band member Jonathan Cain, who is European American. By locating Filipinos in Los Angeles and as followers of both Pineda and Cain, Diaz's film challenges the perpetual foreigner stereotype by presenting Filipino Americans as integrated into U.S. culture. As Celine Parreñas Shimizu observes in her examination of the film,

> The documentary form is used to cross distances of geography and structural location. It confronts new global realities and shows audiences the different and unequal ways in which we relate to each other. In other words, the documentary film by and about Filipina/os in the diaspora explores what bonds are possible in today's new social encounters as they are enabled by new media.
>
> (Parreñas Shimizu 2013: 55)

The film's ability to reveal transnational crossings via music, performance, and audience interactions is further demonstrated in its conclusion. Diaz ends the film with Pineda's climatic full-length rendition of the title song at a performance in Manila, with an audience full of adoring Filipino fans in Arnel Pineda t-shirts singing along and wiping away tears. By ending her film in Manila, Diaz emphasizes the way that Pineda's success with Journey counters the perpetual foreigner stereotype and redefines and expands definitions of American identity, as well as expanding the transnational scope of Filipino American and Asian American identity.

Linsanity

Evan Jackson Leong's 2013 film *Linsanity* looks at another celebrity who challenges common Asian American stereotypes and broadens depictions of Asian American identities. The film depicts National Basketball Association (NBA) basketball player Jeremy Lin's climb to stardom and the phenomenon known as "Linsanity," which occurred in a two-week period in February 2012 during which Lin shot to fame as the catalyst for the New York Knicks seven-game winning streak. Key elements of Leong's film depict Lin's struggles as he deals with racism and racialized expectations on and off the court, including the misperception that his Taiwanese background would prevent him from becoming a sports star in the United States.

At first glance, Jeremy Lin's background seems to contrast with Arnel Pineda's strong Filipino identity. Born and raised by immigrant Taiwanese parents in the San Francisco suburb of Palo Alto, California, Lin seems to be emphatically American—he has a blanket with pictures of the cartoon character Garfield on it, he shops at Target, and he plays songs from *The Lion King* at piano recitals. Yet, despite this, Lin is not exempt from perceptions that he is a "perpetual foreigner." The film notes that in high school Lin was Northern California Division II Player of the Year and led the Palo Alto High School team to the California state title, yet after graduation he was not recruited by any Division One college basketball teams. Commentators in the film's voiceover state: "He didn't fit the mold," and "He doesn't look the part." As one observer notes, "He's an Asian kid and he's not seven feet tall, and you don't see a lot of Asian point guards making it in Division One basketball." Was Lin perceived as being too foreign to be accepted in this all-American sport?

Later, the film documents his experiences on the Harvard basketball team as fans from other Ivy League teams harass him and shout racial epithets. Lin recounts some of the racial slurs from both high school and college, including "Take your ass back to China, you're a Chinese import" and "You chink, can you even open your eyes, can you even see the scoreboard?" Even after his success with the New York Knicks, Lin faced continued comments about his perceived unfitness to be in the NBA and his supposedly undeserved recognition. The film notes that boxer Floyd Mayweather, Jr wrote on his Twitter feed: "Jeremy Lin is a good player but all the hype is because he's Asian. Black players do what he does every night and don't get the same praise."

The film also includes a quick montage of various stereotypical Asian caricatures from U.S. media, including jokes on Conan O'Brien's show, where Lin's head is seen emerging from a fortune cookie. Another joke read: "He's only good at driving to the hoop"—as opposed to driving a car, referring to the stereotype that Asians are congenitally bad drivers. The sports entertainment network ESPN used the expression "Chink in the armor" in both broadcast and online news stories about Lin. Whether used intentionally or in ignorance, including the word "chink" in reference to Lin, whose grandparents are from China, demonstrates great insensitivity to the history of this racial slur. This overt and subtle racism illustrates the widespread perception that Lin is a "perpetual foreigner" and not qualified to play a quintessentially American sport like basketball. As one observer in the film notes, despite the success of Chinese star Yao Ming, "Basketball is not considered an Asian sport here in America."

However, rather than battling perceptions of his foreignness by attempting to assimilate and to erase his cultural heritage, the film shows that Lin is not afraid to embrace his Taiwanese American background. In one sequence, the film depicts Lin returning to Taiwan to visit his relatives there and to greet his burgeoning fan base in Asia. Lin expresses his pride in his Taiwanese background and discusses the importance of his ethnic heritage as he hangs out with his Taiwanese relatives and speaks rudimentary Mandarin to the Chinese and Taiwanese press. During this section of the film, Lin notes: "My roots are important to who I am and are a huge part of my identity. I'm very proud to be who I am." Leong's film denies the stereotype of the perpetual foreigner and shows that, rather than assimilating and renouncing his cultural heritage, Lin proudly embraces it. Lin expands definitions of American identity and culture to include Asian Americans—in particular, an Asian American who is comfortable with and in search of a transnational form of identity and community.

Jake Shimabukuro: Life on Four Strings

In *Jake Shimabukuro: Life on Four Strings*, a documentary profile of the ukelele virtuoso, director Tad Nakamura addresses the complex cultural identity of his main subject. Shimabukuro is of Japanese descent and was born and raised in Hawai'i. Although the perpetual foreigner stereotype would define Shimabukuro as Japanese and not American, in the film Nakamura clearly identifies Shimabukuro as Japanese American and a citizen of the United States or, more specifically, of Hawai'i. In the film, Shimabukuro's manager Kazusa Flanagan, who was born and raised in Japan, notes: "[Despite] coming from totally different backgrounds, different cultures, I guess Jake and I clicked." Although both share a common Japanese heritage, Flanagan's comment acknowledges the differences between Japanese and Japanese American identities. At the same time, later in the film, Shimabukuro acknowledges his connections to Japan and the cultural legacy of his Japanese heritage, stating: "Maybe it's the Japanese in me because culturally you don't know how to deal with praise or compliments—it makes you uncomfortable." The film also notes that Shimabukuro has toured extensively and enjoys great popularity in Japan, and includes a scene in which Shimabukuro leads a ukelele lesson in Japan, where he demonstrates his rudimentary Japanese language skills. Yet, the film continually emphasizes that Shimabukuro is not from Japan and isn't truly part of the culture there.

Instead, what we see is that Shimabukuro's identity is centered on his connection to Hawai'i. Shimabukuro notes his pleasure at "going home" to Hawai'i, observing that "Everything that's important to me is here." Following this statement, the film includes a sequence in which Shimabukuro's mother sings in the backyard of his family home in the Hawai'ian language. Here, Shimabukuro's mother becomes the embodiment to Shimabukuro of "home," which the film clearly delineates as Hawai'i, not Japan. In her interviews, his mother speaks in pidgin English, and Jake also briefly slips into the patois when talking with a group of small boys on a doorstep in his old neighborhood in Hawai'i. The film also associates Shimabukuro's mother with the ukelele, which she taught to Jake and which the film uses as a signifier for Hawai'ian culture. As Shimabukuro notes, "Playing the ukelele would remind me of her. Whenever I played the ukelele it—was like she was home with us." In this way his relationship with his mother, and by extension his relationship with the ukelele, becomes a metaphor for Shimabukuro's connections to his home in Hawai'i. As Tracy Terada, producer of Shimabukuro's first band, observes, "Outside of Hawai'i people didn't take the instrument seriously. In Hawaii we've always respected the instrument. It's a big part of our culture and it still is." Shimabukuro also notes: "Every time I played the ukelele or I heard it, I felt so at peace. It just brought me home."

The film concludes with Shimabukuro playing a concert in front of an ethnically mixed audience in New York City. Shimabukuro's voiceover notes: "You feel this tremendous responsibility to deliver," as the camera pans over faces of Asian American audience members. In this way, the film emphasizes Shimabukuro's broad appeal across cultures and ethnicities while at the same time focusing specifically on the great significance Shimabukuro's success holds for Asian Americans. He is an international star, but he is simultaneously firmly rooted in the Asian American community, where his work has a particular resonance. By delineating Shimabukuro's complex cultural identity and emphasizing his ties to Japan, the United States, and Hawai'i, the film illustrates the transnational connections of the Asian American community.

Conclusion

Don't Stop Believin', *Linsanity*, and *Life on Four Strings* emphasize the ongoing transformations of American identity and the ways in which immigrants and the children of immigrants from around the world in general, and Asia in particular, are redefining that identity. As the Asian American population continues to grow, these films aid in dispelling the damage of the perpetual foreigner stereotype as well as continuing to situate Asian Americans in a transnational context. They expand the definition of American culture, as shown in Pineda's gradual acceptance as Journey's lead singer, Shimabukoro's cross-cultural appeal, and Lin's success in the NBA. In addition, these films illustrate the increasingly transnational appeal of Asian American celebrities, who have embraced global perspectives and connections as a means of combating the perpetual foreigner stereotype.

The three films examined here continue in the tradition of earlier, first-stage Asian American media arts, advocating for and reflecting on pertinent issues in the Asian American community. At the same time, these films expand the parameters of Asian American media arts and internationalize the field by exploring the transnational identities of each of the film's subjects and their appeal beyond the boundaries of the United States. By focusing on individual Asian American celebrities, the films also reflect the ways in which Asian American identities have begun permeating the global pop culture consciousness. Rather than remaining locked into a U.S.-based identity, these individuals expand and increase the visibility of Asian Americans and situate them into a more transnational milieu. They reflect the ways in which the Asian American community continues to become more globally connected.

Note

1 For a broader reading of Asian American film history, see Okada's (2015) discussion of the more experimental and avant-garde programming by Daryl Chin and others in New York City's Asian Cinevision Asian American International Film Festival, as well as the schisms among film festivals in curating aesthetics-based or public television-oriented Asian American work.

References

Arora, Vasantha. 2003. "Trial opens in the Slaying of Sikh." *Tribune India*, September 4. http://www.tribuneindia.com/2003/20030905/world.htm#1.

Liberatore, Paul. 2007. "An Incredible Journey for Band's New Frontman." Marin Independent Journal, December 28. http://www.marinij.com/article/ZZ/20071228/NEWS/712289970.

Mimura, Glenn M. 2009. *Ghostlife of Third Cinema: Asian American Film and Video*, Minneapolis: University of Minnesota Press.

Okada, Jun. 2015. *Making Asian American Film and Video: History, Institutions, Movements*. New Brunswick: Rutgers University Press.

Parreñas Shimizu, Celine. 2013. "Can the Subaltern Sing, and in a Power Ballad? Arnel Pineda and Ramona Diaz's Don't Stop Believin': Everyman's Journey." *Concentric: Literary and Cultural Studies*, 39(1): 53–75.

Soe, Valerie. 2012. "Don't Stop Believin': An Interview with Filmmaker Ramona Diaz." *Beyond Asiaphilia*. http://beyondasiaphilia.com/2012/05/07/dont-stop-believin-an-interview-with-filmmaker-ramona-diaz/.

Tajima-Peña, Renee. 1992. "Moving the Image." In *Moving the Image, Independent Asian Pacific American Media Arts*, Russell C. Leong (ed). Los Angeles: UCLA Asian American Studies Center.

Takaki, Ron. 1993. *A Different Mirror: A History of Multicultural America*. Boston, MA: Little, Brown and Company.

Wu, Frank H. 2003. *Yellow: Race in America beyond Black and White*. New York: Basic Books.

Part III

HYBRID ASIAN AMERICANS

MEDIA AT THE MARGINS

10

QUEER EXPERIMENTAL ASIAN AMERICAN MEDIA

Eve Oishi

From one perspective, the category of "queer experimental Asian American media" can be understood to inscribe a self-evident and self-defining category: a body of work by media artists who identify as both queer and Asian American and who work within an experimental aesthetic or form. This perspective takes "queer" and "Asian American" as categories of identity, while "experimental" and "media" are understood to be terms of aesthetics and technology. Bringing these terms together in this way is linked to a project of visibility, as it is understood that the art and the artists included in this category occupy a marginalized position within art scholarship and criticism and are worthy of attention as a distinct body of work. This essay is not an argument against such a perspective; I have published several articles and curated numerous film and video programs that were motivated by this premise (Oishi 2000, 2003). However, the development of the field of Asian American studies over the last 20 years, particularly the influence of poststructuralist theories of language and identity, has put these terms under increasing pressure, requiring alternative methodological approaches.

While the modifiers "queer" and "Asian American" seem to refer primarily to the physiology of a particular text's producer, they also represent historically specific developments that have provided new lenses through which work can be read and classified. "Asian American" is a term coined in the late 1960s as a way of joining cultural history, experience and political affiliation into one integrated category of identity. "Queer" came into common use as a marker of personal and political identity in the 1990s as a more inclusive umbrella term that could encompass the growing diversity of the LGBT community. It is also an anti-essentialist term, shaped by poststructuralist theory, which understood sexuality as a fluid and contextual category formed out of and in response to social, cultural, and political conditions. The same political and theoretical factors that produced the rise of queer theory also significantly reshaped the field of Asian American studies, challenging not only its tendency to focus on the United States but also any uncritical acceptance of the idea of Asian American subjectivity as ahistorical or existing outside of cultural and political structures, both global and domestic.

Kandice Chuh has suggested doing away with the reliance on a central "subject" of Asian American studies, as it becomes a means of obscuring the larger processes through which the category of Asian American has been produced and through which it functions. She writes:

> If we accept a priori that Asian American studies is subjectless, then rather than looking to complete the category "Asian American," to actualize it by such methods as enumerating various components of differences (gender, class, sexuality, religion, and so on), we are positioned to critique the effects of the various configurations of power and knowledge through which the term comes to have meaning.
>
> (Chuh 2003: 10–11)

As Jun Okada argues, Asian American media, like Asian American studies, must be understood through the institutions and structures that have supported its development. Defining Asian American film and video as "that which is interwoven with the rise of public broadcasting and thereby identified intimately and inextricably with questions about institutional parameters, funding, programming, and artistic freedom," Okada argues that the history, form, and content of Asian American media must be understood as overlapping and mutually constitutive elements (Okada 2015: 3).

If the category of Asian American media emerges from and is made legible through its institutional history, it is also necessary to understand how this history has drawn boundaries of inclusion and exclusion. Daryl Chin has documented the ways in which the establishment of a critical canon within experimental cinema led to expanding opportunities in exhibition, distribution, and funding for certain (mostly White, male) filmmakers and the increasing marginalization of others, in particular women and people of color. He notes that during the 1970s and 1980s, in response to this marginalization, "feminist artists and artists of color developed alternative media collectives and festivals, but those spaces did not develop with room for experimental cinema" (Chin 1991: 222). Thus, Asian American artists working within experimental modes have often been overlooked within scholarly considerations or institutional support of Asian American film and video.

My previous explorations of queer experimental Asian American media have taken "Asian American" or "queer Asian American" as the starting point for an analysis of media production that then looks for the unifying themes or aesthetic strategies that its constituents employ. This approach makes strategic use of categories such as Asian American art or Asian American media as classifications that emerge out of and depend upon a logical alignment between artist, medium, and content. This chapter, however, begins with the recognition of the impossibility of envisioning "Queer Experimental Asian American Media" as a coherent category of media production, and instead takes the incoherence of the category as a productive lens through which to understand the function and status of certain visual and formal signifiers within Asian American media art practice.

This chapter examines the terms of the larger title ("queer," "experimental," "Asian American") through specific texts in order to understand some of the ways that each component modifies and illuminates the others. Such an approach focuses on the ideological and critical work that each of these terms performs, both in collaboration with and in opposition to the other terms and to the construction of the field as a whole. Seen this way, the terms function as "collaborative antagonisms," to borrow Kandice Chuh's description of Asian American studies, "collaborative in the doubled sense of working together and working subversively against, and antagonistic in the ways in which diverse approaches to knowledge critique and identify each other's limits" (Chuh 2003: 28). I have deliberately chosen works that stand in oblique relationship to the term "queer Asian American experimental media" as a way of avoiding any attempt to perform a stabilizing taxonomy and instead exploring the critical usefulness of the term(s) in question. The texts I consider are *Chinese Series* (2003), the last film made by Stan Brakhage, and *Doom Generation* (1995) and *Splendor* (1999), two "heterosexual" films by queer Japanese American director Gregg Araki. Taking a closer look at the ways in which these films seem to embody or disembody the accepted definitions of "queer," "experimental," or "Asian American" media allows us to understand the ways in which these categories are produced in tandem with and in opposition to one another, depending on the historical and institutional context. Whereas the canonization of U.S. experimental cinema involved the exclusion of Asian American and, to a certain extent, queer artists, Asian American media developed as a visible and viable category in part through institutions that funded more traditional (non-experimental) narrative films, a trend that accompanied the rise of an increasingly mainstream queer cinema.

Stan Brakhage: Disembodied Form

Stan Brakhage would seem an obvious choice to illustrate the keyword "experimental," as he is widely considered to be the father of American experimental cinema. His connection to queer Asian American cinema is less apparent, since his own identities are neither Asian American nor queer. From the 1950s until his death in 2003, he revolutionized non-narrative filmmaking, experimenting with multiple exposures, collage, and hand-processing the film itself, in particular hand-painting and scratching the celluloid to produce forms and colors that translated abstract expressionism into a cinematic idiom that introduced rhythm, movement, and time to the medium of painting. As the editors of Critical Visions in Film Theory write,

> Brakhage forces viewers to move away from the habitual way of processing movie images that focus on content and narrative and instead refocus their attention toward less obvious pictorial and sensory qualities, such as light, movement, and texture.
>
> (Corrigan et al. 2011: 667–668)

Brakhage's last film *Chinese Series* (2003) was made in the months before his death and was made by wetting a filmstrip with his saliva and making scratches with his fingernails. The finished film, just over two minutes long, consists of a black background across which the scratch marks appear as white linear shapes, rimmed faintly with lines of green, yellow, and blue. As one film blogger writes,

> The images resulting from this literally hands-on process are as minimal and stark as one would expect: abstract hieroglyphics stuttering across the frame, seeming to spell out words in some indecipherable language. It's calligraphic and graceful. This not-quite-language is a poignant metaphor for Brakhage in the last days of his life, painstakingly (and maybe painfully) scratching out his last communication to the world, the very last images he'd create.
>
> (*Only the Cinema* 2012)

The filmmaker's wife Marilyn Brakhage writes that the film "flickers across the screen as suggestions of Chinese ideograms" (M. Brakhage 2010). She quotes Courtney Hoskins, who printed the film, as writing that the film evokes a sense of "running through a humid bamboo forest … [in which] green and yellow stalks create these glowing shadows as they cut across the sunlight" (cited in M. Brakhage 2010).

In his essay "In Consideration of Aesthetics," Brakhage writes: "I am primarily interested in the aesthetic possibilities of the medium, and these are those which promote mental reflection (rather than reflective recollection)" (S. Brakhage 1996: 60). In the context of a career eschewing representation in favor of form, color, and pattern, Brakhage's *Chinese Series* references the Chinese ideograph not for its linguistic or calligraphic meaning, but *as* pure form. Framed within the viscerality of the dying filmmaker's physical manipulation, "Chinese" thus becomes an aesthetic category, a medium, a scooping out of light through a mark on the film, a vital illumination against the obliteration of death. At the same time, there is a seemingly paradoxical figurativeness referenced by the descriptions of the film that identify in the abstract shapes, ideographs, and the shadows of bamboo stalks, both staples in classical Chinese figurative painting. Without the signifying status of language, however, the ideograph is presented, like bamboo, as a metaphoric signifier of China. Like the kanji tattoo whose literal translation is subordinated to the function of the ideograph as decorative object, the ghosts of Chinese characters function as anti-representation, the signs that, through their unreadability, affirm the alterities of black vs. white, life vs. death, Chinese vs. Western. In "In Consideration of Aesthetics," Brakhage extends this binary, suggesting that Chinese culture contains the ability to produce the abstract notion of Film but not the object itself: "The Chinese have a beautiful glyph for their movie-designation: 'Electric Shadows.' But it hasn't seemed to help them make anything of lasting visual value in their whole known filmic history" (S. Brakhage 1996: 60).

Brakhage has relied on a similar aestheticization of the writings of non-Western cultures in other series, such as what P. Adam Sitney calls the "cinematic mediations on hieroglyphics and calligraphy in his *The Egyptian Series, Babylon Series,* [and] *The Persian Series*" (Sitney 2015: 171). In the titling of these series, which are marked by aesthetic richness, saturated colors, and swirling forms, cultural and geopolitical markers similarly function as aesthetic ones.

While it would be a stretch to cite a film by Stan Brakhage as an example of Asian American experimental media, his *Chinese Series* helps to illuminate the ways in which the category of Asia remains if not a ghostly, then at least a formally structuring, presence within American experimental cinema. Conversely, in the essay cited earlier, Daryl Chin has pointed out the ways in which Brakhage, as the preeminent example of experimental cinema in the United States, represents an institutionally structuring presence in the formation and direction of Asian American experimental media, as his position of dominance created a narrative about experimental film that narrowed the funding, exhibition, and distribution opportunities for Asian American artists. Chin writes:

> Thus, once it was established that Stan Brakhage was central to one definition of "the avant garde" (which is not homogeneous, by the way), Stan Brakhage's work became dominant within the network of nonprofit media centers. I am not arguing that there is no reason for this ascendancy during that time; certainly, given the alternative nature of experimental cinema, Stan Brakhage has defined one of the most impressive non-narrative aesthetics in the cinema. However, that dominance meant the de-emphasis of further alternatives.
>
> (Chin 1991: 222)[1]

Trying to find the place of Stan Brakhage within a genealogy of "queer experimental Asian American media" allows us to understand the multiple aesthetic and institutional contexts in which such a category comes into coherence.

Gregg Araki: Formally Disavowing Embodiment as Identity

Gregg Araki's work evades placement within several of the categories considered here. In fact, much critical discussion of Araki's work concerns the difficulty of placing him within established categories of cinema, leading Jun Okada to describe him as a "meaningfully ambivalent figure standing both inside and outside of the institution, challenging its entire existence" (Okada 2015: 9). Since his first feature film *three bewildered people in the night* (1987), Araki has been known for work that conforms to the general definition of narrative feature film yet employs aesthetic and narrative strategies borrowed from a long tradition of avant-garde cinema. In a 1989 letter of introduction to Jim Hubbard, co-director of the New York Experimental Gay and Lesbian Film Festival, Araki, who at that point had completed two feature films, acknowledges the generic indeterminacy of his work, while stating a clear commitment to remaining outside of the (independent) mainstream. He writes:

> I frequently find myself falling into a sort of limbo: my films are really not what you could classify as avant-garde or experimental—they are fictional, (meandering) narrative, and I guess some people find them dramatic. But at the same time, they are definitely not the commercialized, AMERICAN PLAYHOUSE-reject flotsam being passed-off as "New Independent Cinema" these days either.
>
> (Araki 1996 [1989]: 123)

However, despite Araki's focus on formal and aesthetic categories in his descriptions of his own work, it is the content of his films, and its relationship to his personal identity, that have been given the most critical attention. Daryl Chin sums up the problem this way: "Gregg Araki is an Asian American filmmaker who does not make Asian-American films. He is a gay filmmaker whose films do not configure solely gay concerns" (Chin 1993: 103). In this sense, he has come to stand in for an academic and political "problem," which Peter X Feng had dubbed "The Gregg Araki question": namely, "If an Asian American filmmaker makes a movie which doesn't engage with Asian American issues, would you include it in your definition of Asian American cinema?" ("In Search of Asian American Cinema," cited in Okada 2015: 79).

While Araki's racial representation is seen as a problematic within Asian American film criticism, his position within queer cinema, while much considered, is less vexed. Araki identifies as queer even while publicly distancing himself from the dominant institutions of queer culture, saying: "my outlook is not exactly embraced by the gay community. I am in no way a spokesman for gay people in the 1990s" (quoted in Levy 1999: 469).[2] Despite this disavowal, and despite the fact that the "Gregg Araki question" is understood to refer only to his treatment of Asian American themes and not his treatment of sexuality, most academic scholarship on Araki accepts him as a queer filmmaker and a member of the New Queer Cinema or Queer New Wave that was first identified as a movement by B. Ruby Rich in 1992. If his position within that movement is, as Rich has dubbed him, the "bad boy of the New Queer Cinema" (Rich 2013: 92), it has generally been due to his failure to cast actors of color or directly address issues of racism and racial identity. In the words of critic and festival programmer Kimberly Yutani, "his 'lacking of color' in his films is a point that deems him controversial, particularly in the Asian American community" (Yutani 1996: 178).[3]

Some scholars and reviewers have been critical of his work for featuring predominantly or fully White casts or of his decision to move queer sexuality back into the subtext in later films.[4] A different approach has been to read for the queer or the Asian American sensibility or voice hidden within his films. For example, Glyn Davis reads Araki as working within an aesthetic of "queer camp," a postmodern mode he identifies as a strategy of the New Queer Cinema of the 1990s, developed partly in response to the cooptation of older "gay camp" by Hollywood cinema.[5] Jun Okada reads the biraciality of Araki's favorite actor, James Duval, as a "covert signifier of problematic Asian American masculinity" (Okada 2015: 96). I consider the overlap and divergence of both critical lenses—those that are critical of his failure to address issues of race or sexuality and those that find that absence or ambivalence productive—as obverse sides of the same analytical model that presumes or seeks out a connection between a filmmaker's formal strategies and biography, between author and auteur.[6] This chapter is not intended as a critique of this approach, which comes out of and engages with longer and more complex considerations of the politics of field formation, theories of spectatorship (within both psychoanalytic and audience studies), and film history. Rather, I am suggesting that this critical framework, itself a product of histories of ethnic and queer visibility, political organizing, institutionalization, artistic production, and advocacy, provides a significant context within and against which Araki develops his distinctive style.

I am interested in what can be revealed if, instead of thinking about what is queer or Asian American about his films, we consider his oeuvre in terms of irresponsibility: a deliberate identification with avant-garde practices and sensibilities, which are understood as and through a frustration of mainstream aesthetic and generic conventions as well as a frustration of ideological readings that assume a link between artistic expression and personal identity or politics. The ambivalent representations of queer and Asian American subjectivity in his films (exemplified by sexual frustration, ambiguity, or excessively offensive stereotype) are figured as formal tropes and intertextual references to avant-garde cinema, and those cinematic strategies become, in turn, a way of disavowing categorization within identity- or genre-based categories and declaring a polymorphously perverse attachment to the history of cinema writ large.

Doom Generation and *Splendor*: Axis of Irresponsibility

For this analysis I examine two of Araki's films, *Doom Generation* (1995) and *Splendor (1999)*, which emphatically evade categorization as Asian American, queer, or even experimental, and which can be seen to mark a turn in his filmography away from queer-centered content and, in the case of *Splendor*, toward a more conventional Hollywood style. Araki's first four films deal explicitly with queer themes and characters: *three bewildered people in the night* (1987) follows a love triangle between a heterosexual couple and their gay male friend; *the long weekend (o' despair)* (1989) tells the story of two female friends, one lesbian and one straight, who, along with their partners, visit their gay male friend in Los Angeles over a long weekend; *The Living End* (1992) is a road movie about two HIV-positive men on a crime spree; and *Totally F***ed Up* (1993) centers on six gay teenagers in LA. The opening credits for *The Living End* introduce it as "An Irresponsible Film by Gregg Araki," signaling the director's deliberate disavowal of the positive gay and AIDS imagery that was an ascendant characteristic of queer cinema in the early 1990s.[7]

Unlike his previous films, neither *Doom Generation*, a dark comedy about three disaffected drifters and the second of Araki's "teen apocalypse trilogy,"[8] nor *Splendor*, a breezy comedy about a love triangle between two men and a woman, features explicitly gay characters. In fact, the opening credits for *Doom Generation* introduce it as "A Heterosexual Movie by Gregg Araki," an ironic reference to the title sequence from the earlier *Totally F***ed Up*, which reads: "Another Homo Movie by Gregg Araki." From one perspective, the move from an all- or largely queer cast in his first four films to ostensibly heterosexual plotlines in these two films signifies a progression in which queer sexuality is evacuated or converted from surface to subtext. Similarly, in contrast to *Nowhere*, which is situated chronologically between *Doom Generation* and *Splendor*, and which features a multicultural cast almost parodically tailored for a mid-nineties multiculturalist agenda, these two films can be read as capitulating to mainstream treatments of racial difference (elision or offensive stereotype). However, reading these films within the larger context of Araki's "Godard-damaged" oeuvre (Chua 1992), in particular its formal referentiality and its recurring visual and narrative motifs, such as his focus on the erotic triad, suggest an alternate reading of these two films as representing antipodal yet complementary strategies. Whereas one depends upon exploitation tropes of shock, excess, and offensiveness, the other is extreme in its appropriation of mainstream romantic comedy conventions, hewing to them in excess. Both can be seen as "irresponsible" strategies, part of Araki's larger practice of enacting and connoting resistance to identity-based readings through form.

Doom Generation features a teenage couple, Jordan White (James Duval) and Amy Blue (Rose McGowan), in Los Angeles, who pick up an alluring drifter named Xavier Red (Johnathon Schaech) on their way home from a club. Stopping at a Quickie Mart, Amy and Jordan are threatened at gunpoint by the hostile and suspicious store proprietor. X grabs the store owner from behind in an attempt to save his friends and is attacked by the store owner's wife. In the confusion, and under the impassive gaze of the owner's three children, the store owner's head is shot off. Fleeing the scene, the three characters eventually begin a *ménage a trois*, but their sex is interrupted when Amy has to go outside to urinate. At that point they are set upon by neo-Nazis, who rape Amy on an American flag and castrate Jordan with garden shears before Amy is able to grab the shears and kill them. Amy escapes with X, leaving Jordan, presumably, to die.

With the exception of James Duval's racially ambiguous character (more on him later), *Doom Generation* is Araki's only film to feature Asian American characters. Given the repeated attention given to "the Gregg Araki question" by critics, Araki's refusal to cast Asian Americans, as well as his choice of exception to this rule, is striking: the Asian Quickie Mart husband and wife embody the most reviled stereotypes of Asian immigrants in urban American spaces—namely, the surly, suspicious, and often violent liquor or convenience store owners featured in Spike Lee's *Do The Right Thing* (1989) and news coverage of the 1992 urban uprising in Los Angeles. Even after the exploitative gore of the husband's beheading in the Quickie Mart, the characters learn that the owner's wife has disemboweled her children before committing suicide with a machete. The fact that these characters are played by Dustin Nguyen and Margaret Cho, two pioneers in Asian American popular culture who starred in primetime network television shows (*21 Jump Street* and *All American Girl*), performs yet another wink (or slur) at the idea of positive images and mainstream racial representation.

In examining this scene, whose over-the-top violence and gore feature a disembodied head spewing what looks like split pea soup and a cash register ringing up the numbers 666, one must first note its overt references to cinematic history. The film itself cites Jean-Luc Godard's 1964 *Bande à Part*, which also features two young men and a woman and a robbery shootout. The Quickie Mart scene contains allusions to the famous Odessa Steps sequence in Sergei Eisenstein's 1925 silent film *Battleship Potemkin*, in which a young boy is splattered in blood and a woman is shot in the face, as well as the 1973 horror classic *The Exorcist*. However, the blatant play on the stereotype of the Asian convenience store owner, brought to a head within public discussion after the shooting of 15-year-old Latasha Harlins by liquor store owner Soon Ja Du in 1991 weeks after the beating of Rodney King, signals that Araki's reticence about dealing with race in his earlier films does not stem from an investment in model minority images. In fact, this scene can be read as the filmmaker's answer to "the Araki question," in which representations of Asian Americans are subject to the same deliberately tasteless satire as the narrative expectations of love and a happy ending, as conventions to be skewered in the most extreme fashion.

Araki has expressed his disappointment at the poor reception his films have gotten from queer and Asian American audiences, saying:

> As a gay Asian American, I consider myself a card-carrying (albeit controversial) member of two, count 'em two, "oppressed" subcultural groups, and I've been screened on the circuit under both "umbrellas." While, like any struggling independent, I'm always grateful to have my work shown/seen/discussed, I've found that the response to my films within those contingents is often, surprisingly, more hostile and xenophobic than even that of the Mainstream.
>
> (Araki 1991: 69)

Reading the Quickie Mart scene as a response to this marginalization involves an analytical framework that considers Araki's biography as a salient element in the analysis of his films but reads it through his awareness of and resistance to the channels into which queer and Asian American filmmakers were being funneled through institutional and critical pressures in the 1990s.

The only other Asian American to appear in Araki's films is also his most frequently cast actor: James Duvall, a mixed-race actor of Vietnamese, French, Native American, and Irish descent. Duval stars in all three of the "teen apocalypse" films as well as *Kaboom* (2010) and is something of a muse for Araki, or, as he puts it, "my Joe Dallesandro" (Yutani 1996: 180). The characters that Duval plays in the trilogy are notable for their innocence and idealism—in contrast to the more jaded or nihilistic characters surrounding him—and, ultimately, for his failure to achieve the love that he is searching for. In all three films, Duval's character arc provides the resolution of the film, in each case the antithesis of a happy ending. In *Totally F***ed Up* (1993) the film ends with his character, depressed over the failure of a gay romance, drinking Drano and drowning himself in a swimming pool; *Doom Generation* ends with his murder via castration; and in *Nowhere* he seems to finally find the monogamous relationship he had been searching for, only to have his lover explode and be replaced by a giant alien cockroach.

Jun Okada argues that "the films' frequent focus on the biracial actor Duval's sexual ambivalence also shows a racial ambivalence" (Okada 2015: 96). I agree with this analysis insofar as Duval's racial indeterminacy functions as an analogue of the larger strategies of indeterminacy and disavowal within the film. But I also follow Daryl Chin's assessment that Araki's ambivalence is, above all, in relation to narrative convention. The characters that Duval plays are not, in fact, ambivalent. They wholeheartedly and naively yearn for a sexual and romantic resolution, and in this they are repeatedly denied and frustrated, as is the viewer. Chin writes that "Araki remains ambivalent about his negations of and resistances to narrative convention. This ambivalence then finds a correlative in his depiction of frustrated desire" (Chin 1993: 107).

Central to Araki's trope of frustrated desire is the love triangle, a narrative device that makes its appearance in his first film *three bewildered people in the night* and recurs in both *Doom Generation* and *Splendor*. Beyond the narrative trope of the romantic triangle, the threesome is a recurring visual motif throughout Araki's early films, whether including a grouping of friends or lovers, and occurring even in the Quickie Mart scene with a repeated medium shot of the three small sons of the store owners shown watching television and watching their father's murder with the same blank expressions, suggesting that these are both scenes of meaningless spectacle.

Araki's erotic triads always consist of two men and a woman; sex between the men is never explicitly shown, remaining either unconsummated or merely suggested. While Robin

Wood reads the *ménage a trois* in *Doom Generation* as "passionate and positive, deeply romantic" (Wood 1998: 338) and at the heart of why he considers this film to be "one of the most radical political statements in American cinema" (Wood 1998: 339), I argue that it is its status as unconsummated and unsolvable dilemma that makes it the signature trope for Araki's oeuvre.

The love triangle receives a slightly different treatment in *Splendor*, in which the three-way dynamic occurs between Kathleen Robertson, Matt Keeslar, and Johnathon Schaech (X from *Doom Generation* in another intra-oeuvre echo.) As in *three bewildered people in the night*, it remains ambiguous whether the homoerotic attraction between the two men is acted on. The three characters are often shown in frame together, but the female character, Veronica, is always positioned visually and alphabetically between Abel and Zed, preventing them from actually touching. Veronica is torn between two lovers and resolves the situation by living with both of them. As they become increasingly comfortable in their domesticity, Veronica discovers that she is pregnant and cannot know who the baby's father is (in an echo of the scene from *Totally F***ed Up* in which the gay boys collectively donate sperm to inseminate their lesbian friends, ensuring that the actual donor will remain unknown). She meets a third man and becomes engaged to him, leaving Abel and Zed to live together in a farcical parody of heterosexual domesticity. The climax comes when the two men interrupt her wedding *The Graduate*-style, and convince her that they are responsible enough to care for her baby. The film ends with Abel, Zed, Veronica, and their twin babies living happily ever after.

Because of the queer content in Araki's early films, the lack of explicit sexual contact between the two men in *Splendor* reverberates as a voluble silence, with the image of the bisexual love triangle in *Doom Generation*, and its subsequent rape and castration scene, never far away. With much of the film taking place in bed, the repeated visual and narrative focus on who is having sex serves as a constant reminder of who is *not* having sex. While the film most obviously references the 1933 screwball comedy *Design for Living* directed by Ernst Lubitsch and based on the 1932 play by Noel Coward and Godard's 1961 love triangle film *A Woman Is a Woman*, the tongue-in-cheek repression of queer sexuality in turn inflects Araki's reference to Elia Kazan's 1961 film *Splendor in the Grass*, in which repressed teen sexuality literally drives Natalie Wood's character insane.

Araki's films are, above all, referential, to the history of cinema and to his own larger body of work. In a series of visually and narratively vectored references to both Hollywood films and his own, *Splendor* links both Whiteness and heterosexuality to the death drive, casting a queer light over a tradition of classic Hollywood heterosexuality but refusing to offer homosexuality as an antidote. Drawing on his own oeuvre as visual archive, he is able to inflect a fluffy Hollywood rom-com with darker edges, linking it to a tradition of avant-garde experimentation in which the cinematic form itself serves as pressure or threat to the borders of any particular film. What emerges is a critical engagement with cinematic genres, including the presumed connection of identity to aesthetics that resulted from the institutional and critical sorting of film and video work into identity-based categories for the purposes of funding, distribution, and exhibition.

Another key difference between the two films is their setting. Although both are set in Los Angeles, *Doom Generation*'s version is Araki's usual dystopic and "alienating city filled with 7-Elevens, minimalls, and parking lots" (Levy 1999: 466–467), while the mise-en-scène of *Splendor* is, like the story, glossy and brightly lit. Despite their many differences, *Doom Generation* and *Splendor* can both be read as responses to the ways in which the renegade aspects of New Queer Cinema were beginning to be eclipsed by more mainstream fare. Both end excessively: one in an overload of violence and iconoclastic desecration, and the other in a surfeit of heterosexuality and narrative closure (two husbands and two babies).

This brings us back to the reading of Stan Brakhage and the keyword "experimental." Where Stan Brakhage's film shows how the Asianist presence (to borrow and adapt Toni Morrison's term from *Playing in the Dark*) haunts and shapes the form of U.S. experimental cinema, Araki deliberately erases (or explodes into farce and exploitation) the traces of his ethnic autobiography, making a formal argument for the ways in which biographical readings constrain the possibilities for aesthetic expression. This resistance to ideological treatment is linked to experimentation in form; it is transmuted into form itself. Inherent in this paradigm lies the critique that identity-based criticism holds at its heart a binary logic, a notion of identity that is both sought and confirmed in the reading of an "Asian American" or "queer" film, identity as a construct that is necessarily binary in designating what is and what is not a part of the category. Araki's framework replaces the binary with the threesome, a looped configuration, endlessly mirrored and never resolved.

Comparing these vastly diverse films offers some partial insights into how aesthetic categorization is the product of both material and ideological histories. The fact that there is a body of artistic production that can be labeled "queer experimental Asian American media" itself depends upon the collaborative and antagonistic histories that inscribe queer media, experimental media, and Asian American media. In one version of this story told here, the history of classical experimental media in the United States has involved the simultaneous marginalization of Asian American artists and reification of Asia as empty form, while Asian American and queer media have emerged in the margins, wherein identity is produced as form and vice versa. While not disavowing the importance of canons, this chapter makes an argument for the value of reading texts against the grain of their most obvious or common groupings as a way of remaining conscious of the utility and limits of these categories. Why are certain artists allowed the privilege of transforming geopolitical markers into a formal experimentation evacuated of bodies, while for others politicized bodies are the most potent signifiers linking together an aesthetic language? Fixing our gaze on the myriad institutional and political contexts within which our objects of study gain coherence and legibility allows us to see some of these questions more clearly.

Notes

1 A similar argument could be made for the erasure of queer artists in the establishment of an experimental cinema canon with Brakhage as its figurehead. Similarly, B. Ruby Rich pointed out that the critical work establishing this canon failed to note the queer subcultural influences or sensibilities of much postwar avant-garde cinema, including Kenneth Anger, "Jack Smith, Gregory Markopoulos, Taylor Mead, George Kuchar, Nathaniel Dorsky, José Rodriguez-Soltero, and the most famous and successful of them all, Andy Warhol … The American avant-garde was a very queer place indeed, hiding in plain sight for years until it was safe to come out" (Rich 2013: 4).

2 "'Being gay in the 1990s is not just a matter of what you do when you have sex,' Araki said. 'It has to do with your outlook, your place in society; homophobia is so prevalent, it becomes ingrained in your personality on all levels. It really informs my films'" (quoted in Levy 1999: 469).

3 Jun Xing writes: "As an Asian American, Araki's queer sensibilities are informed by a gay agenda rather than one of ethnic activism" (Xing 1998: 202).

4 Lawrence Chua takes him to task for the all-White casting of his first three films (Chua 1992). Kylo-Patrick Hart critiques *Splendor* for hewing too closely to the taboos of the Production Code-era screwball comedies that it references, saying that his failure to include transgressive sexual representations in this film, "especially given the sorts of daring, unapologetic representations of sexual couplings and forms of sexual expression featured in his preceding films which his fans had come to expect, is one of *Splendor's* most substantial shortcomings" (Hart 2010: 63).

5 Davis defines queer camp as "(1) [a self-consciously "bad"] performance style; (2) the role of trashy ephemera; (3) the use of parody; (4) political aims; and (5) the references to earlier (queer) camp filmmakers" (Davis 2004: 59).

6 Another iteration of this can be found in Todd McCarthy's review of *Totally F***ed Up* for *Variety*, in which he writes: "there is a dichotomy between Araki's radical, activist attitude and the passive, victimized mind-set of his characters" (McCarthy 1993).

7 Araki has stated that the "Irresponsible" tagline was a reference to Robin Wood's analysis of irresponsibility in the comedies of Howard Hawks, particularly *Bringing up Baby*, one of his numerous citations and homages to earlier cinema and to film theory. Wood wrote that Hawks' "comedies derive much of their tension and intensity from the fascination exerted by irresponsibility" (Wood 2006: 62).

8 The other films in this trilogy are *Totally F***ed Up* (1993) and *Nowhere* (1997). In making an argument that *Doom Generation* and *Splendor* represent a move away from queer-centered content, I realize that I am conveniently skipping over *Nowhere*, which was produced between *Doom Generation* and *Splendor* and which features several gay and bisexual characters and relationships. While I have chosen to focus on these other two films for the sake of space, *Nowhere* fits squarely within Araki's larger auteurist oeuvre, particularly, as I mention later in this chapter, in the anti-resolution it shares with the other three films in the trilogy figured through the death or frustration of the idealistic character played by James Duvall.

References

Araki, Gregg (director). 1987. *Three Bewildered People in the Night.*

Araki, Gregg (director). 1989. *The Long Weekend (O'Despair).*

Araki, Gregg (director). 1991. "The (Sorry) State of (Independent) Things." In *Moving the Image: Independent Asian Pacific American Media Arts*, Russell Leong (ed.). Los Angeles: UCLA Asian American Studies Center, Visual Communications, Southern California Asian American Studies Central.

Araki, Gregg (director). 1992. *The Living End.*

Araki, Gregg (director). 1993. *Totally F***ed Up.*

Araki, Gregg (director). 1995. *Doom Generation.*

Araki, Gregg. 1996 [1989]. Letter to Jim Hubbard, reprinted in *MIXZINE 96.* New York.

Araki, Gregg (director). 1997. *Nowhere.*

Araki, Gregg (director). 1999. *Splendor.*

Brakhage, Marilyn. 2010. "Some Notes on the Selection of Titles for *By Brakhage: An Anthology, Volume Two*," May 25. https://www.criterion.com/current/posts/1471-some-notes-on-the-selection-of-titles-for-by-brakhage-an-anthology-volume-two.

Brakhage. Stan. 1996. "In Consideration of Aesthetics." *Chicago Review* (47–48): 56–61.

Brakhage, Stan. 2003. *Chinese Series.*

Chin, Daryl. 1991. "Moving the Image, Removing the Artist, Killing the Messenger." In *Moving the Image: Independent Asian Pacific American Media Arts*, Russell Leong (ed), 219–226. Los Angeles: UCLA Asian American Studies Center, Visual Communications, Southern California Asian American Studies Central.

Chin, Daryl. 1993. "Girlfriend in a Coma: Notes on the Films of Gregg Araki." In *Queer Looks Perspectives on Lesbian and Gay Film and Video*, M. Gever, J. Greyson, and P. Parmar (eds), 103–107. New York: Routledge.

Chua, Lawrence. 1992. "Gregg Araki by Lawrence Chua," http://bombmagazine.org/article/1581/gregg-araki.

Chuh, Kandice. 2003. *Imagine Otherwise: On Asian Americanist Critique.* Durham, NC: Duke University Press.

Corrigan, Timothy, Patricia White, and Meta Mazaj (eds). 2011. *Critical Visions in Film Theory.* Boston, MA: Bedford/St. Martin's.

Davis, Glyn. 2004. "Camp and Queer and the New Queer Director: Case Study—Gregg Araki." In *New Queer Cinema: A Critical Reader*, Michele Aaron (ed), 53–67. Brunswick, NJ: Rutgers University Press.

Feng, Peter X. 1995. "In Search of Asian American Cinema" *Cineaste* 21(1–2) (Winter–Spring): 32–35. Cited in Okada 2015.

Hart, Kylo-Patrick R. 2010. *Images for a Generation Doomed.* Lanham, MD: Lexington Books.

Levy, Emanuel. 1999. *Cinema of Outsiders: The Rise of American Independent Film,* New York: New York University Press.

McCarthy, Todd. 1993. "Review: *Totally F***ed Up*," *Variety*, http://variety.com/1993/film/reviews/totally-f-ed-up-1200433814/.

Morrison, Toni. 1993. *Playing in the Dark: Whiteness and the Literary Imagination.* New York: Vintage.

Oishi, Eve. 2000. "Bad Asians: New Film and Video by Queer Asian American Artists." In *Countervisions: Asian American Film Criticism*, D. Hamamoto (ed.), Philadelphia: Temple University Press.

Oishi, Eve. 2003. "Bad Asians, the Sequel: Continuing Trends in Queer API Film and Video." *Millennium Film Journal* 39: 221–243.

Okada, Jun. 2015. *Making Asian American Film and Video: History, Institutions, Movements*. New Brunswick: Rutgers University Press.
Only the Cinema. 2012. http://seul-le-cinema.blogspot.com/2012/04/persian-series-1-3chinese-series.html.
Rich, B. Ruby. 2013. *New Queer Cinema: The Director's Cut*. Durham, NC and London: Duke University Press.
Sitney, P. Adams. 2015. *The Cinema of Poetry*. Oxford: Oxford University Press.
Wood, Robin. 1998. *Sexual Politics and Narrative Film: Hollywood and Beyond*. New York: Columbia University Press.
Wood, Robin. 2006. *Howard Hawks*. Detroit: Wayne State University Press. Originally published 1968 by Martin Secker and Warburg in association with the British Film Institute.
Xing, Jun. 1998. *Asian American through the Lens: History, Representations, and Identity*. Lanham, MD: Alta Mira Press.
Yutani, Kimberly. 1996. "Gregg Araki and the Queer New Wave." In R. Leong (ed), *Asian American Sexualities: Dimensions of the Gay and Lesbian Experience*, 175–180, New York: Routledge.

11

REWRITING HISTORY

Adoptee Documentaries as a Site of Truth-Telling

Kimberly D. McKee

Transnational adoption of Asian children profoundly impacted the American landscape. The face of Asian America radically changed as the majority of adoptees entered White families. From the earliest adoptions of children from Hong Kong and Japan in the 1940s and 1950s to the adoption boom sparked by the Korean War, Americans embraced Asian children with open arms. South Korea maintains the longest-running adoption relationship with the United States from the post-Korean War period to the present day, and with an estimated 130,000 Korean adoptees in the United States, they are the largest population of adoptees from Asia. No longer can we assume Asian Americans are raised in households by biological/social parents of Asian descent. As these adoptees enter adulthood, their cultural productions (documentaries, literature, theater, art) provide a new avenue to understand the Asian American experience. They redefine what it means to be Asian American (McKee 2016a).

The narrative that has dominated adoption discourse for the last half of the twentieth century supported a narrow mythology: if it were not for adoption, adoptees would face lives of poverty and degradation. Ideologies of rescue, democracy, and Christian Americanism intertwined themselves with international adoption rhetoric (Oh 2005). This chapter elucidates how adoptee-authored cinematic productions intervene and recast a 50-year history of adoption that had relied on reductive narratives concerning the Western humanitarian rescue of orphans. In doing so, adoptees are now claiming their space in Asian American history. Viewers must grapple with the complexities of adoption and consider it as a method of family making, unmaking, and remaking. Catherine Ceniza Choy (2013) notes that adoptee-authored films reflect both the personal losses of individual adoptees and the collective losses of the broader adoption community, including adoptees, birth families, and adoptive families. Yet, their messages concerning adoption-related losses are not limited to members of the adoption community, as seen in the PBS series P.O.V's screening of domestic and international adoption-related films (e.g. *Off and Running*, Opper 2010; *Wo Ai Ni Mommy*, Wang-Bical 2010). Moreover, adoptee-authored films are finding wider viewership. Netflix recently released the documentary *Twinsters* (Futerman and Miyamoto, 2015), which follows the reunion of two Korean adoptee twins, Samantha Futerman and Anaïs Bordier, who were separated at birth and raised in the United States and France. Adoptee-authored cinematic productions are also gaining traction on non-traditional media platforms to share their work with the broader community, such as John Sanvidge's *Adoptees in the Wild* series (2013–2015) for the now defunct web-based magazine *Gazillion Voices* and Dan Matthews' YouTube docu-series—*aka Dan* (Maxwell 2014).

In this chapter, I examine two Korean adoptee-authored documentaries: *In the Matter of Cha Jung Hee* (2010) and *Resilience* (2009), directed by Deann Borshay Liem and Tammy Chu, respectively. These films illustrate the complexities of what it means to be adopted transracially and internationally, as well as how an adoptee's reunion with their biological parents does not end neatly upon the initial meeting. *In the Matter of Cha Jung Hee* (2010) reveals the complicity of orphanages in rendering children adoptable for transnational and transracial parents. *Resilience* foregrounds the perspective of birth mothers, which is commonly elided from discussions of reunion, as the focus most often is on the adoptee and their adopted parents. These documentaries expose the messiness inherent in adoption, elucidating how adoptees are forever linked to mainstream perceptions of adoption as they contend with conflicting emotions and discourses throughout their search and reunion experience.

Cultural Productions about Adoption Experiences

Documentaries provide a pseudo-realistic view of people's lived lives that viewers usually treat as if they were impartial arbiters of truth rather than a narrative framework.[1] Mike Ball and Greg Smith (2001) note: "Documentary is about reporting, not inventing, whatever is in the world … The realist impulse is paramount: documentary photographs and film aim to exhibit the facts of a situation" (304). They discuss these characteristics as being similar to ethnographic texts in their ability to shape conclusions about the world. Ball and Smith also advance the arguments of Michael Renov (1993) concerning the fictional aspects of nonfictional film. Renov contends that in the construction of a documentary's narrative, regardless of how intimate it may feel, the film relies on "fictive" elements (e.g. poetic language, voiceover, or musical accompaniment) and provides a particular lens for viewers to explore a community or issue. Documentaries mediate viewers' experience with the subject. In the case of the adoption community, Korean adoptee-authored productions have the power to influence perceptions of transracial, international adoptees' identity negotiations, experiences with birth search and reunion, and the growing adult adoptee community. These documentaries offer pieces of truth into the adoption experience and often serve as an entry point for individuals' engagement with broader communities such as adoptive parents and other adoptees.

The clearest example of documentaries' impact on public perceptions of Korean adoption is Borshay Liem's first film *First Person Plural* (2000), which chronicles her personal experiences as a transracial, international adoptee growing up in California. *First Person Plural* (2000) was groundbreaking for its inclusion of Borshay Liem's birth search and reunion, as it was one of the earliest cinematic productions to do so. The characterization of the text as "autoethnographic" and "documentary film memoir" by Barbara Yngvesson (2010) and Kim Park Nelson (2007), respectively, underscores how documentaries are read as forms of historical truth. Park Nelson (2007) notes that adoptive parents, adoption agencies, and adoptees often recommend *First Person Plural* (Liem 2000) to current and prospective adoptive parents, adoptees, and those interested in adoption because of its candid examination of the effects of assimilation on adoptee development of positive racial and ethnic identities during childhood and adolescence. The documentary's reach was aided by its screening on PBS as part of their P.O.V. series. Additionally, the film's distribution through the Center for Asian American Media located her work not only as part of Adoption Studies scholarship, but also within the field of Asian American Studies.

This chapter joins Korean Adoption Studies research that locates adult adoptees as experts on the adopted person's experience and critiques practices of international adoption (E. Kim 2010; Park Nelson 2016; Pate 2014). Such scholarship is invested in understanding the role of cultural artifacts in shaping and reshaping public perceptions of transnational adoption. In her examination of Korean adoptee performances and artwork in South Korea, Eleana J. Kim (2010) finds that these productions contest narratives of adoption that routinely elide the contradictions between South Korea's sustained participation in international adoption and its growing economic power. These projects also expose the emotional consequences of adoption in the lives of adult adoptees, including the disclosure of suicide rates among adoptees and the language and cultural inadequacies adoptees experience when they return to South Korea. Kim Park Nelson (2009) notes: "[Korean adoptee artists] have been among the first to challenge dominant White narratives of transnational adoption as an emotionally seamless act of child salvation; instead, these artists wrestle with the grittier reality of identity crisis, displacement, birth family loss, and American racism" (262). Building upon this work concerning cultural productions as a mode of contestation, I use documentaries as a tool to better understand the ways in which adoptees situate themselves within broader histories of adoption and simultaneously claim their expertise concerning the adoption experience.

Talking Back: Adoptees Construct Counterstories

Borshay Liem's second adoption film, *In the Matter of Cha Jung Hee* (2010), dismantles assumptions that adoptable orphans are parentless children in its examination of how fabricated orphanage documents facilitated her entry into the United States Borshay Liem's adoptive parents applied to adopt a child named Cha Jung Hee after sponsoring her through the Foster Parents Plan. However, Borshay Liem was sent in place of the original child. She was told by orphanage workers not to reveal that she was not in fact Cha Jung Hee prior to her airplane journey to the United States. She lived her life with Cha Jung Hee's birth date and adoption case history as her own. David Smolin (2006) calls this practice "child laundering," noting that "the current intercountry adoption system frequently takes children illegally from birth parents, and then uses the official processes of the adoption and legal systems to 'launder' them as 'legally' adopted children" (115). Borshay Liem's journey to uncover the truth about her Korean identity stemmed from discovering a photo of another girl in adoption documents at her parents' house. Written on the back of this photo was a single name, Cha Jung Hee. The same name was also written on the back of a different photo, one of Borshay Liem.

This line of inquiry builds on the work of Catherine Ceniza Choy (2010) and Jodi Kim (2015) that locates *In the Matter of Cha Jung Hee* (2010) as part of Cold War, militarized, and gendered logics framing kinship and diaspora. Yet, I depart from Choy and Kim's examination of the film as a site of Cold War politics and an exploration of family dynamics between Borshay Liem and her adoptive and biological families. Instead, I examine the film's illumination of the commodification of children within adoption and the impact of learning that children are seen as interchangeable objects in the lives of adoptees.

These disruptions to mainstream adoption narratives can also be seen in *Resilience* (2009), a film that remains understudied as an adoption text. *Resilience* (2009) offers a searing depiction of the experiences of birth mothers as it follows the reunion between Myung-ja and her son, Brent Beesley, who was adopted as an infant by a couple living in South Dakota. Birth mothers (and birth parents more generally) are routinely overlooked and elided in discussion of Korean adoption. Prior to the release of *Resilience* (2009), U.S. audiences only had access to the voices of Korean birth mothers who resided at the Ae Ran Won unwed mothers' home featured in *I Wish You a Beautiful Life* (1999), which was released by a small publisher in St Paul, MN. A companion volume (*Dreaming a World: Korean Birth Mothers Tell Their Stories*, 2010) was released a decade later. Together, *In the Matter of Cha Jung Hee* and *Resilience* provide a counter-discourse in their opposition to what Catherine Ceniza Choy (2010) calls "received venues of knowledge—archival records, case files, ethnographic spectacle, government-sponsored reportage, authoritative talking heads, and history textbooks—that gird national memory" (159–160). Adoptees produce counterstories, redefining a past that incorrectly characterized their experience (Lindemann Nelson 2001, 18).

These films also deploy what bell hooks (1989) terms "talking back," where adoptees locate themselves as experts of their experiences and reframe what it means to be a knowledge producer. Talking back is a form of resistance, shifting an understanding of adoptees in the eyes of the public imaginary. *In the Matter of Cha Jung Hee* (2010) and *Resilience* (2009) reject dominant discourse's construction of adoption as a method of rescue. Their presence as both actors in the documentary and filmmakers provides a counterpoint to Western, White depictions of adoption. Adoptee-authored documentaries rely upon a critical lens in examining adoption from multiple perspectives and locations.[2] These Korean adoptee-authored documentaries are similar to the films produced by Asian American/Canadian women, such as *Slaying the Dragon* (1988), *Yellow Tail Blues: Two Asian American Families* (1991), and *Sally's Beauty Spot* (1990), that, according to Marina Heung (1995), "seize on an alternative way to appropriate, revise, and re-envision the possibilities of representing herself" (84–85). This analysis furthers Heung's contention that "identities are constructed and communicated always within the historical nexus of competing and contingent representations, and that once we acknowledge this, we will understand the ways in which stories and texts speak to each other—and indeed, the reason why they speak to us" (85). Through this mode of knowing, *In the Matter of Cha Jung Hee* (2010) and *Resilience* (2009) unearth previously silenced perspectives on adoption.

One Adoptee, Multiple Orphans

These documentaries shine light upon the mechanized pipeline created by the adoption marketplace, whereby there is a deeper emphasis on financial profit and satiating (prospective) adoptive parents' needs than on the rights of biological parents and adoptees (McKee 2016b). Many adoptive parents and allies of adoptees do not consider the real and imagined consequences of adoption and its deep impact on biological families. Yet, what we see in *In the Matter of Cha Jung Hee* (2010) is that Deann Borshay Liem's arrival to the United States in March 1966 dramatically altered the course of two families. She, like other adoptees, represented family and the future to her waiting adoptive parents. At the same time, for her biological family, the child once known as Kang Ok Jin was forever lost at the exact moment it was determined that she would replace Cha Jung Hee. This was due to the fact that adoptees are seen as interchangeable—a perspective wherein their status as objects available for consumption erases their personal agency and personhood. In this film, adoption can no longer be seen as simply about rescuing children and placing them in "good" homes.

To understand why the orphanage sent her in place of Cha Jung Hee, Borshay Liem sought answers from Sun Duck Orphanage and Social Welfare Society. The workers at Sun Duck Orphanage were unable to clarify the discrepancies that occurred with her adoption. In fact, when viewing the orphanage intake photo of Cha Jung Hee, Borshay Liem discovers a third girl named Cha Jung Hee. This girl is the original Cha Jung Hee, which means the girl in the photo that Borshay Liem found at her parents' house was a second girl, who was also given the name Cha Jung Hee. Upon this revelation, Borshay Liem compares the photos of the three girls named Cha Jung Hee. The three photographs expose the ways in which adoptees become interchangeable objects for the consumption of adoptive parents. The orphanage renamed two other young girls as Cha Jung Hee to fulfill the fantasy of the original Cha Jung Hee as a young orphan in need of Western humanitarian aid.

The discovery of this act of duplicity exposes how the orphanages firmly believed that adoption was the only option for these children, even though many of the children placed for adoption were never legal orphans, as they had at least one living parent. Orphanages officials believed that if adoption could no longer save the original Cha Jung Hee, another child should not miss out on the opportunity. The forged documents cemented Borshay Liem's social death—the dissolving of biological/familial ties to Korea. Social death facilitates the creation of orphans in name only, as many adoptees, like Borshay Liem, have living biological parents. However, disruption in name is enough, as this social death simultaneously disrupts adoptees' ability to maintain ties to their birth culture (McKee 2015; Pate 2014). Jodi Kim (2015) writes: "Stripped bare, the orphan could then presumably establish family connections and sociality as if they had not existed before" (811). Operating in conjunction with this social death is adoptees' social and cultural isolation due to the inability to integrate ancestral lived experiences to inform present-day social reality.

Yet, what is most salient at the end of *In the Matter of Cha Jung Hee* (2010) is the fact that Cha Jung Hee is no longer a specific child, but the model adoptable orphan. Cha Jung Hee's function as an orphan archetype is echoed in the common practices of many orphanages' deployment of a manufactured template to describe a child's origins. This particular narrative features a story of a vulnerable child found abandoned by local police and placed into an orphanage, where orphanage officials provided a date of birth and name (McKee 2016b). Variations of this account may note the child's date of birth as written on a slip of paper with the child's belongings. This contrived narrative highlights how abandonment facilitates the adoption industry's continuance.

Cha Jung Hee becomes a template of an adoptable child through a seemingly unique narrative that is instead a recycled and repurposed fiction describing more than one child's biological origins. Tales of vulnerability allow orphanages to market children to prospective adoptive parents as helpful waifs and orphans. A mother dying during childbirth and a father killed during the Korean War seems plausible. Throughout her childhood and young adulthood, this account seemed feasible. After all, when placed into a wider historical context, many of the earliest adoptees were orphaned during the Korean War. Yet, when Borshay Liem realizes that Korean War fighting ceased in 1953, she realizes that it is impossible for this narrative to be hers, given her birth occurred a few years later. This fictional story went unchallenged because it fit within a particular narrative celebrating child rescue. A war orphan is much more appealing than a child placed in an orphanage by loving biological parents because they lacked the economic means to effectively feed, clothe, and educate the child. The trope of the war orphan was so engrained in society that it was accepted even though it defied historical and biological reality.

In the Matter of Cha Jung Hee (2010) provides a clear critique of the manufactured nature of adoptee identities. The documentary demonstrates how adoption is a process of commodification based on the selling of fetishized objects—children. This departure from narratives of rescue requires orphanages, adoption agencies, adoptive parents, and pro-adoption supporters to grapple with the social, economic, and political reasons fueling adoption. Borshay Liem exposes not only the racial trauma of anti-Asian racism on the adoptee, but also the mechanized and fraudulent nature of the international adoption process. Catherine Ceniza Choy (2013) notes: "Viewers also see images of love *and* of commodification of Korean children—images that are often discussed separately—placed alongside one another" (138). Challenging the widely held norms concerning adoption as a touted form of child-saving and rescue, whereby previously abandoned children find happiness in Western families, Borshay Liem exposes the fallacy of such humanitarian logic. She, like thousands of other adoptees, was never in fact a *true* orphan. Rather, Borshay Liem was a social orphan produced to fulfill a Western desire for the perfect child readily available for consumption.

When children become identical objects instructed not to speak of their actual names and birthdays, they are told that their original identities are irrelevant and unimportant. More importantly, the disappearance of one child to replace another may have a profound impact on the adoptee. Identity is no longer limited to an individual's intersectional identity (e.g. race, class, gender). Rather, identity becomes mired in questions of living someone else's life. Borshay Liem reflects: "I arrived in America walking in Cha Jung Hee's shoes." She experiences dissonance while grappling with what it means to literally become someone else. Borshay Liem's intrinsic understanding of self "has been held captive to [the original Cha Jung Hee's] name and her identity" (In the Matter of Cha Jung Hee 2010). She comments: "Even today, her birth date is the one that appears on my driver's license and legal documents. She's a stranger who continues to be my legal identity" (Ibid.). Learning of 101 individuals named Cha Jung Hee provides Borshay Liem with the groundwork to imagine herself as someone else: the life of not only the original Cha Jung Hee placed at the Sun Duck Orphanage, but all those named Cha Jung Hee. At the same time, recognizing the what-ifs of being Cha Jung Hee creates an opportunity for Borshay Liem to further consider what might have been if she had remained Kang Ok Jin and not been sent in the place of another child. Here, we see that an adoptee's identity cannot be viewed in a singular lens. Rather, as Jodi Kim notes, Borshay Liem maintains a "complex subjectivity vis-à-vis multiple filiations and affiliations, whether familial, cultural, racial, or national" (J. Kim 2010, 172). To overlook the contradictions produced by the interchangeability of adopted children's bodies elides the histories of deceit that generated Borshay Liem's adoption. After all, it was only due to duplicitous actions by the orphanage that she gained entry to the West. Meeting several of the women named Cha Jung Hee in South Korea offers Borshay Liem a new understanding of what life could have been like if it had not been for adoption. She is connected to a generation of Korean women whose lives were profoundly impacted by the legacy of war, poverty, and slow economic recovery.

Borshay Liem's desire to learn more about the circumstances that led to her shedding her identity as Kang Ok Jin to become Cha Jung Hee and then Deann Borshay is further complicated when considering the random nature of adoption. Adoption is arbitrary, which means that the family and even the country one is sent to are not predetermined. Given slightly different circumstances, she could have been raised in Sweden, Denmark, France, or countless other receiving countries of Korean children. While *In the Matter of Cha Jung Hee* (2010) constructs a story of the many lives and possibilities of Borshay Liem, it also offers adoptees, more broadly, an opportunity to consider the discrepancies and irregularities of their own adoptions. Borshay Liem's experience cannot be seen as an anomaly. This cathartic production provides her with the opportunity to attempt to "string [the lost moments of the past] together into one unbroken history" (*In the Matter of Cha Jung Hee* 2010).

Not the Only Birth Mother

Another aspect revealed by these documentaries is the experiences of Korean birth mothers and birth families, whose voices are routinely elided or maligned in South Korean adoption lore. When birth mothers have entered the conversation, adoptive parents routinely invoke the mythic prostitute birth mother as a method to affirm the fact that had it not been for adoption, the adoptee would most likely have lived a licentious life in squalor. The mythic prostitute birth mother is rooted in Orientalist stereotypes of Asian women's hypersexuality and the fact that many of the initial Korean adoptees were products of mixed-race liaisons between Korean women and American or United Nations soldiers during the post-Korean War era. These women were assumed to be prostitutes, suffered condemnation, and were labeled "U.N. madams," "comforters," or "Western queens" (D. S. Kim 2007: 10).

Yet, mediated conversations around birth families are already beginning to shift these discourses. The activism of adoptees in South Korea, including Jane Jeong Trenka, Shannon Heit, and Tammy Chu, as well as organizations including TRACK (Truth and Reconciliation for the Adoption Community of Korea), Adoptee Solidarity Korea, and the Korean Unwed Mothers' Families Association, helped to bring birth families into the media spotlight. The rise of social media (e.g. Facebook, Twitter) and video sharing sites (e.g. YouTube) also allows adoptees and unwed mothers in South Korea to connect with other adoptees and their allies across the globe. These conversations continue in the documentaries made by Korean adoptee filmmakers, including the way that Tammy Chu constructs a new narrative for birth mothers and their experiences with relinquishment in *Resilience* (2009).

Through humanizing a single birth mother, *Resilience* (2009) propels viewers into examining adoption reunion from two perspectives—those of birth mother Myung-ja and adoptee son Beesley —as Chu follows the family after 30 years of separation. In contrast to the growing number of female adoptee-authored cultural productions that were produced in the same time frame as *Resilience* (2009), Beesley's reunion narrative is one of the few centering on a man's perspective on Korean adoption.[3] An accomplished filmmaker, Chu first entered adoption media with her award-winning documentary *Searching for Go-Hyang* (1998), which was broadcast in the United States on PBS and on the Korean television station EBS, and screened at film festivals across the world. *Searching for Go-Hyang* (1998) chronicles Chu's adoption experience from South Korea to the United States with her twin sister and their reunion with biological family after a 14-year absence. Her personal experiences allow her subjects to project and engage in raw honesty that a non-adoptee filmmaker would most likely not be privy to because of her status as an insider informant.[4] Chu serves as a bridge between Beesley, an adoptee lacking cultural knowledge of South Korea, and Myung-ja because Chu maintains contact with her biological family and stays engaged with the adoptee activist community in South Korea, where she currently resides.

Tracing the nuances of the reunion, Chu's narrative exposes the sadness of moments that are literarily lost in translation between mother and son. Their reunion demonstrates the unspoken costs endured by both biological families and adoptees through the film's focus on a single relationship. All adoptions involve a rupture of bonds between child and biological parents, but in the case of international and transracial adoption, adoptees enter a new culture and grow up with parents of a different racial/ethnic background. Racial dissonance and racial melancholia magnify adoption's cultural losses, as White parents of Korean children were routinely told to "raise them as your very own" and deploy colorblind parenting (Eng 2010; Park Nelson 2006; Song and Lee 2009). At the same time, within the traditional adoption narrative, there is a pervasive assumption that birth parents are like ghosts, or absent figures from the adoption triad. In reality, these are individuals who desire the right to parent and who often desire to parent. Birth parents grapple with the anguish of parent–child separation as adoptees encounter loss and sadness as a result of their adoptions.

Chu's film exposes these realities, as well as more generally reinserting the birth parent as someone possessing a valid voice in the adoption narrative. By merely including Myung-ja and interviewing her more than once for the documentary, Chu incorporates birth mothers beyond tokenized figures. Their voices are seen as equal to the voices of adoptees. Yet, Chu goes even further, featuring footage of Myung-ja speaking candidly to the camera during her reunion with her son, from his earliest visit to South Korea to meet with her to when he lived for a short time in South Korea. Viewers hear her honest fears and desires after her son's adoption. Myung-ja discusses Beesley, noting: "I needed to see him before I died. I wanted to tell him how I lived, that I didn't send him away, but tell him what really happened. He needs to know his roots. But how was I supposed to find him? I thought he was with a rich family in Korea who didn't have a child of their own." In these interviews, we are privy to an array of new and complicating details. For instance, she never consented to the adoption of the son she knew as Sungwook, as other family members placed him in an orphanage. Relinquishment was not an altruistic decision.

Revelations about the experiences of the birth mother are not without their cost, as we see when Beesley ends up on the South Korean television series *Beautiful Forgiveness*, which helps with reunions, as a source to fund his reunion visit. His episode of the show contains a voyeuristic, dramatized re-enactment of the hardships Myung-ja endured as a low-income parent. While we are again given a chance to consider the perspective of the birth mother, Hosu Kim (2007) argues that it is through the witnessing of birth mothers' shame that these women may reclaim their status as mothers. She notes: "[T]hrough her very shame, she once again is recognized as a mother who *aspires* to live up to that ideal. She is now acknowledged as a birthmother" (135; emphasis original). Asked by the *Beautiful Forgiveness* hosts whether she looked for Sungwook (Beesley), Myung-ja notes: "Of course I did. But I couldn't find him. Everyone just said that he had been sent away. We were so poor so I just assumed that he was living with a wealthy family. It was only recently that I found out he was adopted overseas." This re-enactment may seem sensationalizing, but it does get to the heart of what fuels many international adoptions—the absence of opportunities, both in terms of income and social support, for low-income families.

The lack of support for low-income families reflects South Korea's troubled history with social services. In 1993, at the end of Korea's peak engagement with adoption, social security expenditures only accounted for 2.3% of the gross domestic product (GDP), and central government spending on social welfare amounted to 10.2% in 1995 (Woo 2004). Social welfare expenditures remain low. In 2008, only 10.9% of the country's GDP was spent on social welfare (Jung 2010). Unfortunately, the fact that South Korea historically and presently lacks meaningful support for unwed mothers and low-income families is overlooked in conversations regarding South Korea's continued participation in international adoption. Dominant narratives of adoption overemphasize the need to rescue children from poverty without examining the systemic factors that may result in a preponderance of adoptees originating from low-income households. This, coupled with a rhetoric of saving female adoptees from "a more putatively pernicious Asian patriarchy," fueled Orientalist beliefs about adopting children from the backward East for lives in the privileged West (J. Kim 2010: 169).

Viewers witness how financial disparities affect Myung-ja's interactions with her son following their reunion. Beesley experiences a dissonance between Myung-ja as a biological tie and Myung-ja as a mother because a metaphorical distance exists between the two of them. To bridge this chasm, Myung-ja, like other birth parents, employ gifts as a method to connect herself with her son. Yet, these gifts come at a price (Prébin 2013). She cannot afford the gifts for Beesley and his family without supplementing her existing income with work as a maid and borrowing $1,000 from her father. Addressing the fact that she paid for nearly everything, Beesley said: "I understand why she's doing it. She can't replace time. You can't go backwards and make up. So all you can do is work on the present and the future. So if that's her way." This does not mean he is comfortable with the gesture. Instead, he is invested in getting to know her, as their reunion was never about gifts. The exchange of material goods exposes how adoption, even in reunion, becomes commodified. Capitalism persists as a method of family making. No longer are adoptees the commodities; rather, it's the love that the gifts signify that becomes available for consumption. This is not to minimize the love offered by Myung-ja, but to call attention to the fact that objects cannot replace the time and intimacy taken away from mother and child. Myung-ja ruminates that she does not know her son's likes and dislikes. Typically, this information is basic knowledge between parent and child, but biological parents only gain access to their child's unique personalities upon reunion. There is no guarantee that these gaps in familiarity will be bridged between biological parent and child.

On the adoptee's side, we also hear about the lack of diversity Beesley experienced due to his upbringing in the United States Rarely exposed to other Asian Americans or to Korean culture during his formative years in South Dakota, he invokes nostalgia for White America when describing his childhood. Despite his all-American, idyllic childhood experience, Beesley still had unanswered questions concerning why he was adopted and what it would have been like if he had been raised by his birth parents in South Korea. He reveals: "In the back of my mind I thought it would be cool if I could find my mother or my father or someone from my biological family." Beesley has low expectations about what he will learn, because, like many adoptees, he believed the adoption story provided in the paperwork received by his adoptive parents was true. There was never a reason to question the circumstances presented by his adoption agency. Viewers of *Resilience* (2009) and those watching Beesley's episode of *Beautiful Forgiveness* witness the multiple deceptions that took place to facilitate his adoption. Birth search also demands grappling with the messiness of South Korea's economic rise, as it was built on the legacy of the Korean War and the devastation it wreaked on families for generations. The story of Myung-ja and Beesley's reunion explores the lasting impact of separation upon communication. Myung-ja wants to talk openly with her son, but she admits in defeat and resignation: "It's too difficult for me to learn English at my age. So if Sungwook [Beesley] could learn Korean ... Talking through a translator is not the same as talking just the two of us" (*Resilience* 2009). Her comments poignantly illustrate what has been literally lost in translation. Even if their nonverbal communication demonstrates their love and longing for one another, mother and son are forever powerless in the face of verbal language deficiencies. A gulf of questions separates the two of them as the disembodied nature of translation fails to capture the truths one learns when speaking the same mother tongue. Addressing the limitations of their communication, Beesley notes: "Once we're able to have a direct conversation. I think that will heal some of the wounds that my mother has that she can explain her past directly to me to make her feel a little more at ease with it." These moments of frustration, loss, and words left unspoken reveal to viewers the costs of adoption in the lives of birth mothers and their adult adopted children.

Conclusion

The Korean adoptee community has witnessed a growing trend of adoptee birth searches in the last 20 years, and documentaries such as these possess many important lessons about reunion. These films complicate the notion that adoptees' searches for biological family end neatly with reunion. Reunion is just one starting point in a lifelong process: the beginning of a new era for both the adoptees and their families. *Resilience* (Chu 2009) foregrounds the effects of reunion on birth mothers and their families, while *In the Matter of Cha Jung Hee* (Liem 2010) elucidates the consequences of reunion on one's identity. Together, these adoptee-authored documentaries offer nuanced portrayals of relinquishment and reunion that illuminate the complexities of reunion as more than just meeting one's biological relatives. Moreover, adoptees reassert their authority within the adoption experience by locating their voices in these narratives.

This rewriting starts with the relationship that adoptees have to Korea, as adoption disrupts their identities as Korean nationals. These stories about reunion and return to South Korea, more broadly, shift how Korean identity is understood. The metaphorical motherland is not what it seems for adoptees, as the concept of "home" is complicated by language and cultural competency deficiencies. As overseas Koreans, adoptees represent a new articulation of Korean identity—a neoliberal, cosmopolitan ideal with Western privilege due to their English-language proficiency and/or knowledge of a European language. Borshay Liem is encouraged to look to the future, not to the past, as the orphanage workers she meets believe adoption provided opportunities that would not have been available if she had remained in South Korea. This positioning as a Western subject indicates that adoptees' homes are the nations of their adoptive parents. Raised in primarily White families, adoptees are cultural Whites, fluent in English, and benefit from privileges associated with their Western upbringing.[5] Yet, the searches themselves and the pain that inspires them remind us otherwise.

Through these cultural productions, adoptees craft new histories of Asian American immigration to the United States. These texts provide grounds for marginalized populations to claim and shift narratives to reflect their own interests. Together, Borshay Liem and Chu ask viewers to see what it means to be an adopted person through adoptees' eyes. However, this does not mean erasing the past or denying the humanity of those who parted with their children, as we see in Chu's recentering of biological parent experiences from ghostly figures to actual people. Documentary thus allows adoptees to fully participate and engage in a form of knowledge production that validates and honors the various truths and realities of their community.

Notes

1 For an examination of South Korean cinema that explores adoption themes, please see Ji Young Yoo and Keith Wagner's (2013) work on films that incorporate adoption and adoptee characters into their storylines.

2 Similarly, Shakuntala Banaji (2010) deploys bell hooks' oppositional gaze in his examination of viewers' outsider and insider status concerning their reception of *Slumdog Millionaire.*

3 Female Korean adoptee writers, performers, and artists including Kate Hers, Sun Mee Chomet, Nathalie Mihee Lemoine, Marissa Lichwick, Jennifer Kwon Dobbs, Katy Robinson, Jane Jeong Trenka, Sun Yung Shin, and Jeannine Joy Vance also contribute to the rise of female adoptee-authored cultural productions.

4 In a rare instance, adoptee insider status was bestowed on Eleana J. Kim (2010). Consequently, it remains a deep privilege to gain entry to these spaces, as other scholars studying Korean adoptees have yet to make these inroads. Nandini Sikand (2015) discusses the complexities of one's position as an ethnographic documentary filmmaker. This reflection is useful when considering one's insider status in the community.

5 For a discussion of cultural Whiteness, see France Winddance Twine's (1996) article "Brown Skinned White Girls: Class, Culture and the Construction of White Identity in Suburban Communities."

References

Ball, Mike and Greg Smith. 2001. "Technologies of Realism? Ethnographic Uses of Photography and Film." In *Handbook of Ethnography*, Paul Atkinson, Amanda Coffey, Sara Delamont, John Lofland, and Lynn Lofland (eds), 302–320. London: Sage Publications.

Banaji, Shakuntala. 2010. "Seduced 'Outsiders' versus Sceptical 'Insiders'?: Slumdog Millionaire through Its Re/Viewers." *Participations: Journal of Audience and Reception Studies* 7(1): 1–24.

Choy, Catherine Ceniza. 2013. *Global Families: A History of Asian International Adoption in America*. New York: New York University Press.

Chu, Tammy (director). 2009. *Resilience*.

Eng, David L. 2010. *The Feeling of Kinship: Queer Liberalism and the Racialization of Intimacy*. Durham, NC: Duke University Press.

Futerman, Samantha, and Ryan Miyamoto (directors). 2015. *Twinsters*.

Heung, Marina. 1995. "Representing Ourselves: Films and Videos by Asian American/Canadian Women." In *Feminism, Multiculturalism, and the Media: Global Diversities*, Angharad N. Valdivia (ed), 82–104. Thousand Oaks, CA: Sage Publications.

hooks, bell. 1989. *Talking Back: Thinking Feminist, Thinking Black*. Boston: South End Press.

Jung, Ha-won. 2010. "Korea's Welfare Expenditures Lag at 1/10 of GDP." *Korea JoongAng Daily*. http://koreajoongangdaily.joins.com/news/article/article.aspx?aid=2916606.

Kim, Dong Soo. 2007. "Contextualizing Adoption from a Korean Perspective." In *International Korean Adoption: A Fifty-Year History of Policy and Practice*. M. Elizabeth Vonk, Dong Soo Kim, and Marvin D. Feit (eds), 3–24. New York: Haworth Press.

Kim, Eleana J. 2010. *Adopted Territory: Transnational Korean Adoptees and the Politics of Belonging*. Durham, NC: Duke University Press.

Kim, Hosu. 2007. "Television Mothers: Lost & Found in Search and Reunion Narratives." In *Proceedings of the First International Korean Adoption Studies Research Symposium*, 125–145. Seoul: Dongguk University.

Kim, Jodi. 2010. *Ends of Empire: Asian American Critiques and the Cold War*. Minneapolis: University of Minnesota Press.

Kim, Jodi. 2015. "'The Ending Is Not an Ending at All': On the Militarized and Gendered Diasporas of Korean Transnational Adoption and the Korean War." *Positions* 23(4): 807–835. doi:10.1215/10679847-3148418.

Liem, Deann Borshay (director). 2000. *First Person Plural*.

Liem, Deann Borshay (director). 2010. *In the Matter of Cha Jung Hee*.

Lindemann Nelson, Hilde. 2001. *Damaged Identities, Narrative Repair*. Ithaca: Cornell University Press.

Maxwell, Jon (director). 2014. *Korean Adoptee Story—"aka DAN" KOREAN ADOPTEE DOC Pt. 1*. Produced by Mayrok Media, Arirang TV, and ISAtv. Performed by Dan Matthews. YouTube. March 6. https://youtu.be/OzGHY6enzDs?list=PL2T8s_i7PmAEYOiss64MnSQwsv6EwlymD.

McKee, Kimberly. 2015. "Real versus Fictive Kinship: Legitimating the Adoptive Family." Essay. In *Critical Kinship Studies*, Charlotte Kroløkke, Lene Myong, Stine Wilum Adrian, and Tine Tjørnhøj-Thomse (eds), 221–236. London: Rowman & Littlefield International.

McKee, Kimberly. 2016a. "Claiming Ourselves as 'Korean': Accounting for Adoptees within the Korean Diaspora in the United States." Essay. In *Click and Kin: Transnational Identity and Quick Media*, May Friedman and Silvia Schultermandl (eds), 159–179. Toronto: University of Toronto Press.

McKee, Kimberly. 2016b. "Monetary Flows and the Movements of Children: The Transnational Adoption Industrial Complex." *Journal of Korean Studies* 21(1): 137–178.

Oh, Arissa. 2005. "A New Kind of Missionary Work: Christians, Christian Americanists, and the Adoption of Korean GI Babies, 1955–1961." *Women's Studies Quarterly* 33(3/4): 161–188. http://www.jstor.org/stable/10.2307/40004423?ref=search-gateway:3df1d86b17b216330b413fc1562a45ba.

Opper, Nicole (director). 2010. *Off and Running*.

Park Nelson, Kim. 2006. "Shopping For Children." In *Outsiders within: Writing on Transracial Adoption*, Jane Jeong Trenka, Julia Chinyere Oparah, and Sun Yung Shin (eds), 89–104. Cambridge: South End Press.

Park Nelson, Kim. 2007. "'Loss Is More than Sadness': Reading Dissent in Transracial Adoption Melodrama in The Language of Blood and First Person Plural." *Adoption and Culture* 1(1): 101–128.

Park Nelson, Kim. 2009. *Korean Looks, American Eyes: Korean American Adoptees, Race, Culture and Nation*. Dissertation, University of Minnesota.

Park Nelson, Kim. 2016. *Invisible Asians: Korean American Adoptees, Asian American Experiences, and Racial Exceptionalism*. New Brunswick: Rutgers University Press.

Pate, SooJin. 2014. *From Orphan to Adoptee: U.S. Empire and Genealogies of Korean Adoption*. Minneapolis: University of Minnesota Press.

Prébin, Elise. 2013. *Meeting Once More: The Korean Side of Transnational Adoption*. New York: New York University Press.

Renov, Michael. 1993. *Theorizing Documentary*. New York: Routledge.

Sanvidge, John. 2015. "Adoptees in the Wild." *Gazillion Voices Magazine*. http://gazillionvoices.com/category/film-essays/#.vphuspmrkrs.

Sikand, Nandini. 2015. "Filmed Ethnography or Ethnographic Film? Voice and Positionality in Ethnographic, Documentary, and Feminist Film." *Journal of Film and Video* 67(3–4): 42–56. doi:10.5406/jfilmvideo.67.3-4.0042.

Smolin, David. 2006. "Child Laundering: How the Intercountry Adoption System Legitimizes and Incentivizes the Practices of Buying, Trafficking, Kidnapping, and Stealing Children." *Wayne Law Review* 52(1): 113–200.

Song, Sueyoung L. and Richard M. Lee. 2009. "The Past and Present Cultural Experiences of Adopted Korean American Adults." *Adoption Quarterly* 12(1): 19–36. doi:10.1080/10926750902791946.

Twine, France Winddance. 1996. "Brown Skinned White Girls: Class, Culture and the Construction of White Identity in Suburban Communities." *Gender, Place and Culture: A Journal of Feminist Geography* 3(2): 205–224. doi:10.1080/09663699650021891.

Wang-Breal, Stephanie (director). 2010. *Wo Ai Ni Mommy.*

Woo, Myungsook. 2004. *The Politics of Social Welfare Policy in South Korea: Growth and Citizenship*. Lanham: University Press of America.

Yngvesson, Barbara. 2010. *Belonging in an Adopted World: Race, Identity, and Transnational Adoption*. Chicago: The University of Chicago Press.

Yoo, Ji Young and Keith Wagner. 2013. "Transnational Adoption in Korean Cinema: Partial Citizens and Nationalism on Screen." *Third Text* 27(5): 659–673.

12

STUNNING

Digital Portraits of Mixed Race Families from *Slate* to Tumblr

Leilani Nishime

As the *New York Times* declared over ten years ago, we have entered the age of the Ethnically Ambiguous,[1] an era that seems to be primarily characterized by the currency and marketability of mixed race beauty. In this context, the celebration and promotion of artist CYJO's series of photographs of mixed race families in the *Slate* article "Stunning Portraits of Mixed Race Families"[2] and in the *Huffington Post*[3] was not entirely surprising. The slide show on *Slate* featured brightly lit, posed photographs of attractive adults and children in their homes. The photographs identify the people in the pictures by their family name, followed by a list of citizenships, ancestries, languages, and geographic locations. The accompanying articles repeated the usual clichés about the browning of America and changes to the 2000 Census that allowed individuals to check off multiple races. These familiar refrains are paired with the increasingly popular positioning of mixed race individuals as people who are beyond national boundaries and symbolic of a globalized future.

The reaction among race scholars was a great deal more ambivalent. Of particular note is the post by the academic blogger Chauncey DeVega, who argues that the entire project harkens back to "race science and eugenics" and "images of the human zoo at the Great World's Fair."[4] As a longtime reader of DeVega and as a critic who has also written about the legacies of eugenic visual culture for mixed race people,[5] I was glad to see that I was not the only person made uncomfortable by the praise heaped on the photo series. Indeed, like other photo-based art depicting mixed race people, CYJO's images seem to reference the eugenicist practice of photographing mixed race people in order to catalog and categorize their hereditary deviance. Early scientific photography, however, is not the only generic antecedent to the photo series. The pictures simultaneously invoke racist scientific photography *and* what would seem to be an entirely different photographic genre, the family portrait.

Drawing from the images edited and showcased by *Slate* and from *Mixed Blood*, the larger project from which these pictures were chosen, I set both collections in conversation with another visual culture project, the crowdsourced Tumblr blog *We Are the 15%*.[6] The blog's title references the purported 15% of families who are mixed race in the United States. It regularly publishes images sent to the owners of the site by families to show, in the words of the blog, "portraits of American interracial families and marriages." These projects may be working within the idiom of one of the most banal photographic genres, but they enter into the conversation at a moment of fundamental change in the nature and use of the genre of family photographs.

Just as the conventions of the family photo were transformed through the dissemination of snapshot technologies throughout the twentieth century (Chalfen 1987: 15; Sarvas and Frohlich 2011: 59; West 2000: 167), the swift adoption of phone cameras and the ease of image uploads have again destabilized the meaning and circulation of the family photo, allowing us a temporary space to question its social function.

Through this assemblage of texts—including popular press articles, the art project *Mixed Blood*, and the *We Are the 15%* Tumblr—we can trace the transformation of the family photo through the imbrication of racialized narratives of hierarchical difference with the aesthetics of the family portrait. The photographs can also help us to understand how the image and imaginary of the mixed race family visually depict ideologically invested and rapidly shifting social attitudes toward mixed race families within the context of globalization. These images evidence changes to the fluid, if longstanding, conjoining of family and nation. A detailed examination of these pictures as part of the visual culture of family photographs forces us to reconsider the easy collapse of globalization with an imagined transcendence of both national and social boundaries and the concurrent equation of the nation with a singular and repressive familial ideal.

The Mixed Race Family and the Nation

The family has long stood in metonymic relation to the nation. While DeVega argues that structures of looking dictated by the pairing of photography and eugenic "science" in the fin de siècle continue as part of our collective visual memory, the *Mixed Blood* series more directly references the family album—a distinct but contemporary project located at the nexus of eugenics and nation. Shawn Michelle Smith (1999) argues that family pictures, especially those depicting children and "Republican Motherhood," worked to secure the place of White middle-class women as both the symbol and the source of national identity (113–132). These idealized images enshrined patriarchal, heteronormative, reproductive, White families as a national—and naturalized—ideal.

In contrast, "deviant" family formations worked to justify inequitable citizenship policies. This was certainly the case for Asian Americans, as we can see in early photographs of Chinese American and Filipino American men pictured as asexual or sexually perverse. The staging of Chinatown as exotic bachelor communities visually confirmed popular narratives that placed Asian males outside of the nuclear family as temporary sojourners. The broad dissemination of popular images of Chinatown rendered invisible the state policy barring Asian female immigration and laws against miscegenation and racial intermarriage, both of which legislated against Asian male family formation (Lee 2001: 141). Instead, viewers of mainstream American media would see "bachelor" communities and alternative socialities as the natural or cultural inclination of Asian men (Eng 2001: 14; Hamamoto 1994: 6–10). The stereotype of Asian men as romantic failures barred them from the U.S. ideal of the reproductive family then and in the foreseeable future. The image of the Chinese as a "race so different from our own that we do not permit those belonging to it to become citizens of the United States"[7] was made manifest in Chinatown images and served to justify racially specific citizenship laws that excluded the Chinese and, later, all Asians from the national body.

The mixed race family, and more specifically the mixed Asian family, has had a similarly troubled relationship to the visual representation of U.S. citizenship. Although there is a dearth of images of Asian mixed race children, there is an abundance of images of Asian female/White male couples. In her comprehensive study of cinematic representations of these couples, Marchetti (1994) argues that throughout the twentieth century, films allegorized the relationship of the United States to Asia. The mythology of the "white knight" who rescues the downtrodden Asian woman fit well with U.S. colonial aspirations. The persistent popularity of Hollywood films such as *The World of Suzie Wong* (1960), *Rambo: First Blood, Part 2* (1982), and *Pacific Rim* (2013) encouraged viewers to emotionally invest in an interracial and transnational romance. Those relationships take place in exotic lands and the films end before the couples travel to the United States, emphasizing their distance from the familial and domestic realm. The most famous of all narratives of interracial Asian relationships, the opera *Madame Butterfly*, ends with the Asian heroine's suicide—a plot twist that allows her child to move to the United States with two White parents.

The rare images we have of mixed race Asian American families have been dominated by the stories of White adoptive families, and have similarly tended to affirm notions of the superiority and expansiveness of a U.S. familial ideal. Scholars of transnational adoption argue that popular representations of transnational adoption replicate the salvation narratives that characterized earlier images of White men and Asian women (Anagnost 2000: 399; Dorow 2006: 176–178). The roots of transnational and transracial adoption in U.S. wars in Asia are evident in persistent images of children rescued from Asian poverty and misogyny set in contrast to the benevolence and assimilative power of the White U.S. family (Klein 2003: 146; Shome 2011: 338). In his examination of media displays of transracial families, Guterl describes the press coverage of the Angelina Jolie/Brad Pitt mega-celebrity family and argues that they "offer instead a new ethics for the twenty-first century. Their rainbow tribe is not an American product but a global one" (Guterl 2013: 102). He concludes, however, by saying: "It is, though, nothing but an old masterpiece traced onto new paper. The basic premise is unchanged from 1951 … the deeply symbolic establishment and orchestration of racial difference within the family, all of it premised on the stark juxtaposition of supposedly divergent types" (103). While it is true that visual racial difference remains central to the depiction of the "colorblind" mixed race family, we still need to tease out the significance of this shift from a U.S.-centric to a global ideal—an ideal posed as the liberatory opposite of the limits of nation.

The worldwide fascination with the glamorous and cosmopolitan Jolie-Pitt family is part of a larger convergence between the symbolic meaning of images of mixed race couples and their biological children and transracially adopted children. Envisioning mixed race families as harbingers of the supposed utopia of a post-race future has become the dominant mode for imagining mixed race. Like the mixed race adoptive families in the mid-twentieth century, contemporary mixed race families have come to symbolize American racial exceptionalism. What does it mean to visualize mixed race families as a global rather than American ideal in the case of the "Stunning" article and the "Mixed Race" exhibit? And what does it mean to adhere to a nationalist framework while offering up a visual message that undermines a unified familial ideal in the case of the *We Are the 15%* Tumblr? In both cases, their images must engage with the legacy of the family photo both as an aesthetic practice and as an archival project, and it is within that tradition that mixed race family photographs can challenge the notion of globalization as the solution to the boundaries of nation, while also proposing an intervention into and revision of the family as nation.

"Stunning," *Mixed Blood*, and the Global Family Portrait

Even as it quotes from the visual language of the family, *Mixed Blood* asserts a more polemical challenge to earlier formal family portraiture conventions. The *Mixed Blood* series sidesteps the middlebrow embrace of snapshot photography that dominates the twentieth century to employ the technologies and visual vernaculars of an earlier period. The return to this earlier photographic language lends legitimacy to an idealized image of the racially mixed family with many of the attendant constraints of the form. In the mid-1800s, when family photographs first became popular, cameras were still an expensive piece of equipment requiring special skills to operate. Owning a family photograph depended upon professional photographers well versed in the visual cues that would differentiate these images from the other widespread use of photographic images—police and medical photography. Tagg argues that during this period, images split into two categories: scientific photographs, which sought to remove the photographer to assert the objectivity and truth of the image, and, in contrast, artistic photographs, which showed the skills of the photographer to cultivate greater cultural capital (Tagg 1988: 63–64).

Mixed Blood similarly depends upon its status as art to gain legitimacy for its images. The photographer as artist is evident in both the content and the aesthetics of the images. The pictures are carefully composed, with the artist organizing the space so that each family member stands square to the camera and, with the notable exception of mothers who carry their babies, the subjects do not touch each other. Their expressions are similarly standard, without the strange contortions or blinking that characterize so many personal family photographs. The bright, even lighting across disparate settings lends a sense of perfection to the images that underlines the professional status of the photographer.

Like early portraits, these images do more than preserve a family memory. They also confer a social relation between the artist, the photographic subject, and the viewer. According to Smith (1999), the popularity of family photographs in the latter half of the nineteenth century was fueled by the upper-class aspirations of the bourgeoisie (93–94). Although the families may not have been able to afford the traditional oil paintings of the most elite class, these photographs did serve as markers of rising social class, since they required disposable income on the part of the subject. The poses were highly codified, and since the images were primarily taken at the artist's studio, there were only a limited number of available backdrops. The homogeneity of those early family photographs, like the repetitions we see in *Mixed Race*, wordlessly argue for the subjects' place in a newly emergent economic and social class.

In the case of *Mixed Race*, the images work to rewrite the narrative of the mixed race family from deviant or socially abject to fully fledged members of a cosmopolitan elite. While the families are photographed in both Beijing and New York City, the U.S.-based photos are notable for their glossy commercial surface, with the subjects in fashionable hipster-chic clothing and airy industrial or minimalist décor. In recuperating the history of visual representations of mixed race families, CYJO offers up an alternative to demeaning images or the erasure of mixed families from our shared visual culture. Instead, CYJO's pictures seem to consolidate a new vision of mixed race relations. This is especially true for images of mixed race Asian families, which are almost entirely absent from U.S. collective memory. The pictures' deep depth of focus and fine details index the care taken to create the image, emphasizing both their descriptive power and their permanence. These, like the family portraits placed in albums or framed for the mantelpiece, are to be saved and revisited. We are meant to examine each carefully as elements of a permanent archive.

Even as the pictures revise traditional images of the idealized White family, they still return to the visual rhetoric of a singular family norm. Beyond the narrowness of their class identifications, the images also adhere to a highly gendered, heteronormative ideal. In her study of the scientific discourses of race and sexuality in the late nineteenth century, Somerville (2000) argues that the "pervasive climate of eugenicist and anti-miscegenation sentiment and legislation" worked in conjunction with the developing science of sexology to define both interracial and non-heteronormative relationships as deviant (31). The White heterosexual familial ideal, then, served as an antidote to these twinned threats to racial and sexual boundaries.

Images from *Mixed Race* decouple those narratives to promote an iconic vision of the mixed race family in contradistinction to queer or gender non-normative family formation. Of the 18 pictures in the series, only two stray from familiar depictions of the heterosexual nuclear family. Of the six images in which members of the family are touching, all of them are mothers and their children. These traditional gender roles are also reinforced by the ordering of the family lineup. As the viewer faces the pictures, the parents are on the left side of the image and the children stand to the right, so that we can clearly identify the role of each member of the nuclear family. The men are farthest to the left with the youngest child farthest to the right, imbuing the father with the highest ranking in the household.

The gendered and classed nature of these images of the mixed race family is further exacerbated by the incomplete set of pictures reproduced for the *Slate* "Stunning" slide show and for a similar article in the *Huffington Post*. Both articles chose only a few of the pictures from the series to showcase, and their representative choices are telling. Among those images, none are of men of color paired with White women, although half of the women of color are paired with White men. Nor do the articles include a single image depicting African American men as the head of a mixed race family, despite the fact that such images do appear in the original *Mixed Blood* series. Fewer of the decidedly less fashionable images of the Beijing families are showcased, which ultimately promotes a more upscale and sophisticated image.

In the interview that accompanies the article, CYJO says that the project was inspired by an interest in "the idea of a global identity." *Slate* author David Rosenberg's accompanying description notes the setting of each of the images in the family's home. He writes: "It is also possible to get a glimpse into the family's living environment, another example of how cultures are shared." The *Huffington Post* article quotes CYJO, as saying that "these portraits and narratives illustrate how their love naturally crosses boundaries." It then concludes with: "We couldn't have said it better ourselves. Check out some of the stunning photographs below." The emphasis on the distinctions between the individuals within each photograph may reinforce racial differences, but the comparative work of the series overall leads to a flattening of differences in these articles. Instead, we are presented with a "global identity" premised on an essential similarity between families. The families shown in the articles are surprisingly homogeneous: adhering to norms of gender and racial hierarchies, drawn from a limited economic class, and omitting any alternatives to the heterosexual reproductive family formation, with the exception of one image of a single-parent household. The articles' emphasis on similarities despite racial and geographical differences also keeps the families in a perpetual present. In this case, global identity appears to mean an identity free of history or any social force beyond a love that transcends national boundaries.

The abstraction of the images from their original context for the online slide show shuts down the possibility for more subversive interpretations of the project. The singular, successive images with the ethnicities and nationalities listed below the families' photos in the "Stunning" article differ from the presentation of the images on CYJO's own webpage.[8] There, the pictures are set in two groups, one from New York and the other from Beijing, with each group arranged in a three by three grid of nine families. The organization of the images on the website encourages the reader to see each group collectively and to contrast the families along geographical lines. While one or two images in each group might fit seamlessly in the other, the majority of the images signal distinct differences between mixed families in the United States and China. While still very similar in terms of gender hierarchies and heteronormative family formations, differences in both race and class begin to emerge.

The houses in Beijing, for example, appear to be smaller and less artistically curated. While only one of the rooms in the New York images is small enough to view three walls in a single picture, six of the nine images in Beijing are. The New York homes have little to no furniture, and many are dominated by large-scale pieces of art. The rooms in the Beijing homes are crowded with chairs and desks, some with toys and household goods covering most of the surfaces, indicating less room to spread out and store objects as well as the need for each space to accommodate multiple uses. The ethnic makeup of the Beijing families is also distinct from the New York pictures. For instance, the Beijing families do not appear to include any people of African descent, reminding us that social and historical circumstances facilitate or prohibit romantic ties across racial lines—as Myra Washington reminds us in her chapter on Blasians in this collection. Further, some of the families included in the Beijing photos, such as the Chinese and Japanese family, would simply be considered "Asian" in the United States and not mixed race at all. The cultural underpinning of the meaning of racial difference itself is evidenced by these images, where what counts as mixed race shifts from one national context to the next. By reading these images collectively and against each other, we can find an alternative narrative to *Slate* and *HuffPost*'s naturalization of racial difference and the simultaneous dismissal of those same differences in the name of transcendent love. Reading these images together might prompt us not to see these families as a series of individuals or even a collection of a new kind of family formation, but instead see the powerful influence of context, history, economics, and national politics in shaping the domestic space of the family and the definition of racial difference. These readings are far less possible in the context of the *Slate* slideshow.

Tumblr and the Transformation of the Mixed Race Family Portrait

In order to make the ideological limits of the *Slate* and *HuffPost* articles more visible, I turn to a contrasting visual representation of the mixed race family. The Tumblr blog *We Are the 15%*, like the "Stunning" article, provides a public forum for the visual display of mixed race families. It too draws from the familiar genre of family pictures, but it differs significantly in its production, distribution, and aesthetics—differences that create an alternative visual language of mixed race families. *We Are the 15%* revises the genre of the family portrait, this time not through the elevation of the image to the status of art, as in *Mixed Blood*, but by inhabiting Tumblr's liminal spaces between the public and the private, the permanent and the disposable.

We Are the 15% is a visual blog where married couple Alyson West and Michael David Murphy post crowdsourced images of multiracial families. Started in June 2013, the site posts a new picture several times a week and now has hundreds of images. While clearly a curated collection—West and Murphy often arrange images thematically, such as the series on families with pets or families hiking—taken together, the pictures are a heteroglossia of visual languages. The site includes images ranging from glossily artistic professional photographs to the rigidly normative family portraits one might find at a storefront studio, but the feed is dominated by amateur snapshot-style photographs and the occasional selfie. It is these photos, with their codes of authenticity and ephemerality, that are the most promising in their challenge to a White, upper-middle-class, heteronormative family ideal.

Unlike the *Mixed Blood* photos, which draw from the visual language of formal family portraits and fine art, many of the images from *We Are the 15%* follow what Sarvas and Frohlich (2011) describe as the Kodak Path. Due to changes in both the technology and the social meaning of photographs after Kodak expanded its marketing to a broad swath of American consumers, snapshot photography codified the family photo to "properly" commemorate specified events and similarly dictated appropriate body and facial gestures. Though frequently dismissed as cliché and repetitive, these photographs work to suture the photographer and the subject being photographed into a larger social context. Bourdieu (1996) writes that the family photograph "is always aimed at the fulfilment of social and socially defined functions, ordinary practice is necessarily ritualistic and ceremonial, and therefore stereotyped as much in its choice of objects as in its expressive techniques …" (39). Unlike art photography, which "is defined by the definition of its objects" (39), Bourdieu views family photographs as an act of submission to the social imperative of what one *must* photograph. Pictures of vacations and weddings, for example, are not understood to be aesthetic objects but documentation and evidence of social belonging.

The pictures in *We Are the 15%* signal the participation of the mixed race family in a national body through this visual quotation of other family photos. The photographs are often grouped together by themes such as Halloween or Fourth of July, or social rituals such as graduation. The images share in familiar national sartorial traditions and symbols like wearing red, white, and blue, posing by pumpkins, or waving flags. The site also brings its audience and the families shown on the site into the national fold through its timeliness. Like the newspapers which Benedict Anderson (2006) saw as central to imagining the nation (34–35), the Tumblr site participates in national calendrical time. Halloween pictures begin appearing in October, for example, and the site ran a series of pictures of same-gender couples following the Supreme Court decision legalizing same-sex marriage. Significantly, it is these ritual and shared chronologies that indicate each family's national belonging rather than the racial or gender, or even the generational, makeup of the family. The binding of the images to a U.S. context, however, is troublingly ideological. It risks reinforcing an American exceptionalism that characterizes so much of the rhetoric around mixed race families as an emergent form. The "only in America" sentiment that attaches to mixed race public figures like President Obama and pre-scandal Tiger Woods positions the United States as a postracial space. Asian bodies are particularly vulnerable, given their historical use in promoting what Robert Lee (1999) calls "cold war liberalism" (145–149). As many Asian American scholars have argued, in post-World War II U.S. politics, Asian Americans were transformed from enemy alien to model minority and used as evidence of racial progress in the U.S. (Klein 2003: 5; Marchetti 1994: 114–115; Simpson 2001: 11). Claiming this moral high ground was crucial to U.S. claims to global leadership. We can see similar arguments today, justifying our current imperial project by contrasting U.S. society with the racism, sexism, or homophobia of the enemy Other (Puar 2007). While the dangers of rampant nationalism remain relevant, they do not foreclose on the possibility of generating alternatives to a repressive family ideal. That ideal, after all, is equally at home in images promoting an extra-national or global ideology. Even as *We Are the 15%* uncritically reproduces the visual grammar of the proper place and context of normative family photos and the boundaries of national identity, it presents a far more indeterminate and heterogeneous vision of mixed race families than *Mixed Blood*.

The site not only includes a range of familial configurations; it also highlights the incompleteness of its image archive even as it builds that archive. As Barthes (1981) has argued, photographs are intimately tied to death, memory, and history (31–32). Family snapshots were meant to be saved, entombed in photo albums (although this often failed to happen), and made part of a family narrative—eulogizing and memorializing the moment that was materially captured even as it disappeared. While the photographs in *We Are the 15%* fit within the generic conventions of images meant for the family photo album, they are recontextualized and revalued when they join the Tumblr site. In her article on everyday aesthetics in photo sharing sites, Murray (2008) argues that we are seeing a shift in our affective relationship to photographs. Instead of the mourning that accompanied earlier imperatives to keep and catalog our private images, she asserts that the constantly refreshing feed on sites like Flickr embrace the images as "fleeting, malleable, and immediate." Further, she argues, "There is less narrative coherence in the practice of 'strict groups' and much more of a fascination with the process of compilation and comparison" (155). Her discussion of photo sharing sites dovetails neatly with Rettberg's (2014) study of serial selfie streams. Rettberg argues that they require a different understanding of narrative, one that emphasizes its incompleteness and contingency (36). The blog always implies the possibility of another entry and resists narrative closure.

The element of time, then, comes to play an important role in how audiences view and consume the images in both "Stunning" and *We Are the 15%*. The articles in *Slate* and *Huffpost*, while perpetually available online, follow the tradition of a magazine feature, as they are meant to be read from beginning to end at a single point in time. In contrast, the Tumblr site is meant to be experienced over time, with snapshots capturing an ephemeral moment. They participate in an aesthetics of momentary pleasure, asking us to enjoy the images of families that slip by in a continual stream. These are not to be viewed as a definitive archive, but, rather, immediately experienced as part of our everyday visual culture. Instead of a corpus of images of a singular timeless ideal family, we have a temporally contingent, continually growing catalog of images. What the Tumblr site loses, then, is the aura that accrues around the "Stunning" images. The "Stunning" article presents CYJO's photographs as unique and precious. The *Mixed Blood* project can claim belonging and even beauty in spaces usually closed to non-White bodies. This legitimizing force is abandoned in *We Are the 15%* by the collection of images that make no claim to the traditional histories of works of art. Although Benjamin (1968) would have categorized both photography collections as mechanically reproduced art or art without aura, the sheer ease of presentation and access to the Tumblr site emphasizes its impermanence and reproducibility. The Tumblr images risk devaluation by losing their ritual function. Tumblr replaces the compulsion to slow down to contemplate art and experience the sublime with the rapid consumption and equally rapid dismissal of images as they flow across our screens.

The loss of cultural capital, however, also opens up a space for an alternative vision of family made manifest in image aesthetics, as well as the framing of the content. The heterogeneous aesthetics of the site, like the logic of the blog feed, resist closure. Unlike the carefully lit and composed pictures we find in *Mixed Blood*, the Tumblr images are frequently imperfect, poorly focused, unconventionally cropped, too bright or too dark, or tilted. The individuals in the picture might be grimacing or, in the case of the selfies, have eyes focused on the camera image rather than the lens. There are the professionally and artistically photographed wedding images, but we also find wedding pictures where the bride is turning away from the camera, the flowers are out of focus, and guests seem oblivious to the camera and stand in disorderly clumps in the background. Bourdieu (1996) argues that snapshots are often ideographic, harnessing shared symbols like the Eiffel Tower and cropping out "circumstantial and temporal aspects, such as people moving, in short, everything that constitutes life" (37) to portray a Paris outside of time and without a history. Many of the images from *We Are the 15%* fail to adhere to snapshot conventions and instead highlight the everyday and the mundane. In their very ordinariness, these images push for a broader definition of family. Rather than cropping out contextual clues, the images are insistently located in a specific place and era, unable or unwilling to transcend larger historical or social forces. For instance, the site will occasionally run a series of images of interracial families from earlier eras, upsetting narratives that continually locate mixed race people in a utopic future.

Further, the subjects being photographed often disrupt the assumption of the heteronormative nuclear family or leave familial relationships ambiguous. The images are labeled with a single last name (e.g. The Smiths) or with a list of first names, further obscuring the relationships between people in the photograph. The feed is weighted toward images of heterosexual couples and nuclear families, but also includes what seem to be families blended through marriage, single-parent families, and large groups that include multiple generations. One of the images shows three people who appear to be in the same generation with only their first names as identifiers. Are they siblings? Cousins? A couple and a friend? A plural relationship? Whether or not these family formations exceed the boundaries of the heteronormative nuclear family, the site allows for the ambiguities of the image. The disorder of the photographs impedes the audience's ability to categorize and reify a singular family structure. Certainly, the framing of this diversity of family formations within a nationalist rhetoric might promote the kind of American exceptionalism that justifies U.S. colonialism, yet the aesthetics of the images themselves, their mode of delivery, and the subject of the photographs also work to broaden our concept of family beyond the narrow heterosexual, normatively gendered, White, middle-class ideal that has so often come to represent *the* American family.

Conclusion

Mixed race families occupy a fraught space in visual culture. The historical roots of photographic images of mixed race people in eugenicist projects, which incited a will to know and fix race through visual scrutiny, taints the project of visualizing mixed race. While never completely leaving this legacy behind, scholars can enrich our understanding and analysis of the implications of visual images of mixed race families by looking outside of this specific aesthetic and historical trajectory. Contextualizing *Mixed Blood* and *We Are the 15%* within the evolving genre of family photographs—from early family portraiture of the late 1800s through the mid-twentieth-century Kodak path to our current moment when the family photos are once again being transformed, this time through the advent of digital photography and photo sharing sites—makes clear the crucial role mixed race families play in shared narratives of both family and, by extension, nation. The insertion of mixed race families into the codified visual language of the family photo, then, invites a questioning of globalization, nation, and the gendered, racialized, and classed ideals that characterize the national family.

The enduring forever-foreigner stereotype of Asian Americans, in conjunction with legal and institutional histories that tacitly encouraged interracial relationships, places mixed race Asian families at a crucial pivot point in the discourse of both family and nation. The inclusion of Asian mixed race families in both of these photography series—one depicting a globalized future and the other documenting the diversity of contemporary U.S. families—offers a rare opportunity to track and compare the representational flexibility as well as the limits of these images. While some have argued that the emphasis by media activists on promoting the visual representation of mixed race families is misplaced because it leads to the exoticization or objectification of mixed race people, these examples show us that the meanings of visual representation are contingent and contextual. Assumptions about the liberatory or reactionary significance of the display of images of mixed race families, especially as they intervene in discussion of nation and globalization, must be revised as they encounter the specific genres, histories, and dissemination of these images. Rather than cede the space of visual representation, we would do better to look to the shifting norms of photo production and sharing online and ask how we might use those changes to revise and expand our vision of both mixed race families and broader familial and national norms.[9]

Notes

1 La Ferla, Ruth. "Generation E.A.: Ethnically Ambiguous," *New York Times*, December 28, 2003, www.nytimes.com/2003/12/28/style/generation-ea-ethnically-ambiguous.html.

2 Rosenberg, David. "Stunning Portraits of Mixed-Race Families," *Slate.com*, June 24, 2014, www.slate.com/blogs/behold/2014/06/24/cyjo_mixed_blood_is_a_series_of_portraits_of_individuals_and_families_of.html.

3 Bologna, Carolyn. "Photographer Captures the Future with Mixed Race Family Portraits Series," *The Huffington Post*, July 15, 2014, www.huffingtonpost.com/2014/07/15/mixed-race-families-photo-series_n_5564714.html.

4 DeVega, Chauncey. "Stunning Portraits of Mixed Race Families," *Indomitable: The Online Home of Essayist and Cultural Critic Chauncey DeVega*, June 25, 2014, www.chaunceydevega.com/2014/06/stunning-portraits-of-mixed-race.html.

5 The last chapter of *Undercover Asian: Multiracial Asian Americans in Visual Culture* is an extensive analysis of Kip Fulbeck's art photographic piece *The Hapa Project*. The chapter argues that Fulbeck's work intervenes in the visual language of eugenicist photography to reimagine the multiplicity of ways we attempt to categorize and reify race as a biological truth rather than a cultural fiction (Nishime 2014).

6 Tumblr. "We Are the 15%," http://wearethe15percent.com/.

7 This quote echoed a widely held belief about the inherent alien-ness of the Chinese people that was used in support of the Chinese Exclusion Act. It appeared in the dissenting opinion of Supreme Court Justice Harlan in the case of *Plessy v. Ferguson* (1896).

8 CYJO, "Mixed Blood," www.cyjo.net/index.php?/work/mixed-blood/.

9 I would like to thank the editors, Lori Lopez and Vincent Pham, and my colleagues at the University of Washington Habiba Ibrahim, Ralina Joseph, and Sonnet Retman, for reading and commenting on earlier versions of this chapter.

References

Anagnost, Ann. 2000. "Scenes of Misrecognition: Maternal Citizenship in the Age of Transnational Adoption." *positions: east asia cultures critique* 8(2): 389–421.

Anderson, Benedict. 2006. *Imagined Communities: Reflections on the Origin and Spread of Nationalism*. New York: Verso Books.

Barthes, Roland. 1981. *Camera Lucida*. New York: Hill and Wang.

Benjamin, Walter. 1968. *Illuminations*. New York: Schocken Books Incorporated.

Bologna, Carolyn. 2014. "Photographer Captures the Future With Mixed Race Family Portraits Series," *The Huffington Post*, July 15. http://www.huffingtonpost.com/2014/07/15/mixed-race-families-photo-series_n_5564714.html.

Bourdieu, Pierre. 1996. *Photography: A Middle-brow Art*. Translated by Shaun Whiteside. Stanford. CA: Stanford University Press.

Chalfen, Richard. 1987. *Snapshot Versions of Life*. Bowling Green: Bowling Green State University Popular Press.

CYJO. n.d. "Mixed Blood." http://www.cyjo.net/index.php?/work/mixed-blood/.

DeVega, Chauncey. 2014. "'Stunning Portraits of Mixed Race Families," *Indomitable: The Online Home of Essayist and Cultural Critic Chauncey DeVega*, June 25. http://www.chaunceydevega.com/2014/06/stunning-portraits-of-mixed-race.html.

Dorow, Sara K. 2006. *Transnational Adoption: A Cultural Economy of Race, Gender, and Kinship*. New York: New York University Press.

Eng, David L. 2001. *Racial Castration: Managing Masculinity in Asian America*. Durham: Duke University Press.

Guterl, Matthew Pratt. 2013. *Seeing Race in Modern America*. Chapel Hill: UNC Press Books.

Hamamoto, Darrell Y. 1994. *Monitored Peril: Asian Americans and the Politics of TV Representation*. Minneapolis: University of Minnesota Press.

Klein, Christina. 2003. *Cold War Orientalism: Asia in the Middlebrow Imagination, 1945–1961*. Berkeley: University of California Press.

La Ferla, Ruth. 2003. "Generation E.A.: Ethnically Ambiguous," *New York Times*, December 28. http://www.nytimes.com/2003/12/28/style/generation-ea-ethnically-ambiguous.html.

Lee, Anthony W. 2001. *Picturing Chinatown Art and Orientalism in San Francisco*. Berkeley: University of California Press.

Lee, Robert G. 1999. *Orientals: Asian Americans in Popular Culture*. Philadelphia: Temple University Press.

Marchetti, Gina. 1994. *Romance and the "Yellow Peril": Race, Sex, and Discursive Strategies in Hollywood Fiction*. Berkeley: University of California Press.

Murray, Susan. 2008. "Digital Images, Photo-sharing, and Our Shifting Notions of Everyday Aesthetics." *Journal of Visual Culture* 7(2): 147–163.

Nishime, Leilani. 2014. *Undercover Asian: Multiracial Asian Americans in Visual Culture*. Urbana-Champaign, IL: University of Illinois Press.

Plessy v. Ferguson. 1896. 163 U.S. 537 (Harlan, J., dissenting).

Puar, Jasbir. 2007. *Terrorist Assemblages: Homonationalism in Queer Times*. Durham: Duke University Press.

Rettberg, Jill Walker. 2014. *Seeing Ourselves through Technology: How We Use Selfies, Blogs and Wearable Devices to See and Shape Ourselves*. London: Palgrave Macmillan, 2014.

Rosenberg, David. 2014. "Stunning Portraits of Mixed-Race Families," *Slate.com*, June 24. http://www.slate.com/blogs/behold/2014/06/24/cyjo_mixed_blood_is_a_series_of_portraits_of_individuals_and_families_of.html.

Sarvas, Risto and David M. Frohlich. 2011. *From Snapshots to Social Media: The Changing Picture of Domestic Photography*. New York: Springer Science & Business Media.

Shome, Raka. 2011. " 'Global Motherhood': The Transnational Intimacies of White Femininity." *Critical Studies in Media Communication* 28(5): 388–406.

Simpson, Caroline Chung. 2001. *An Absent Presence: Japanese Americans in Postwar American Culture, 1945–1960*. Durham: Duke University Press.

Smith, Shawn Michelle. 1999. *American Archives: Gender, Race, and Class in Visual Culture*. Princeton, NJ: Princeton University Press.

Somerville, Siobhan B. 2000. *Queering the Color Line: Race and the Invention of Homosexuality in American Culture*. Durham: Duke University Press.

Tagg, John. 1988. *The Burden of Representation: Essays on Photographies and Histories*. Minneapolis: University of Minnesota Press.

Tumblr. n.d. "We are the 15%." http://wearethe15percent.com/.

West, Nancy Martha. 2000. *Kodak and the Lens of Nostalgia*. Charlottesville: University Press of Virginia.

13

BLACK/ASIAN HYBRIDITIES

Multiracial Asian/Americans on *The Voice*

Myra Washington

Verse: Introduction

In 2013–2014, mixed race Asian/American[1] and Black (Blasian) contestants were prominently featured on the popular singing competition show *The Voice*. Judith Hill, who until the show had been known mainly as a back-up singer for Michael Jackson, made it to the top eight on Season 4. Tessanne Chin, already popular in her home country of Jamaica, went on to win Season 5. Rarely have two Blasian women occupied the eyes and ears of a television audience on a weekly basis. On the contrary, Blasians have often suffered from exclusion and disavowal, particularly at the hands of other Asian/Americans. But we are now beginning to see a shift toward recognition and a sense of belonging. This visibility has been helped by the popularity of the term "Blasian," as well as the rise of Blasian celebrities in popular culture. Yet, the experiences of celebrities like Hill and Chin are also rife with contradiction; they are often faced with criticisms and questions about their claims to racial authenticity, even as their abilities to negotiate multiple spaces and productively leverage their mixed race identities are simultaneously construed as a benefit (Dagbovie 2007).

The multiple histories and experiences of Blasians have long gone unacknowledged, as they have predominantly been understood through overly simplistic discourses of pathology, celebration, binaries, and essentialisms (Washington forthcoming). Contemporary shifts in narratives about Blasian identities give us the opportunity to challenge and shift these rhetorics, particularly with regard to recognizing the multiplicities of Asian/American representations and subjectivities. Blasians are challenging the hegemony of race that is constructed around the lives of not just Blacks and Asian/Americans, but all members of U.S. society, as we are all embroiled in the nonsensical discourses of race framing our identities. If, as Stuart Hall (2007) notes, "the future belongs to the impure," then Blasians offer us a glimpse into what a potentially different racial terrain might look like by challenging hegemonic constructions of race.

In this chapter I examine how discourses of Black and Asian connections, racial mixing, and global racial politics come to be inscribed on the bodies of singers Tessanne Chin and Judith Hill. By examining how narratives frame these Blasian contestants on *The Voice*, I reveal the need for spaces in which mixed race Asian/American identities can be articulated. I start the chapter with a review of Asian/American performances on reality shows in light of the common ways that they have been articulated with racial tropes. I then focus on Afro-Asian connections in an examination of mixed race Asian/Americans who are also Black, complicating the idea that racial mixing in the Asian/American community occurs only around Whiteness. I conclude with an analysis of Hill and Chin's presence on *The Voice*, analyzing audience tweets that discussed their racial identities as they performed on the show. Ultimately, the recognition and popularity of these Blasian performers troubles the idea that Asian/Americans are merely wedges used to further the divide between Whiteness and Blackness, and provides a welcome indication that U.S. racial logics have begun to shift in ways that challenge existing racialized hierarchies.

Accompaniment: Asian/Americans and Singing Competition Shows

Asian/Americans are largely underrepresented on ensemble reality television shows, but have become somewhat visible on competition reality shows like *Survivor*, *Top Chef*, *Project Runway*, and other talent shows. Grace Wang (2010) attributes this to the fact that reality television competition shows that reward "supposedly neutral concepts such as talent and skill are racialized" (406). That is, competition shows rely on racialized (and gendered) tropes to render the contestants familiar to viewers: technically skilled/robotic Asian/Americans, angry Blacks, emotional women, fiery Latinxs, etc. Asian/Americans, like other marginalized groups of color, are relegated to token status, meaning there is never an overrepresentation of people of color on these shows. Despite the celebratory rhetoric from media watchers about the visibility of Asian/Americans on reality television (Lam 2014), the presence of more than one Asian/American in the same season of a competitive reality show has warranted either narrative arcs that provide explanation (e.g. exes Jun Song and Jee Choe on *Big Brother*) or solidarity (e.g. Mei Lin and Melissa King on *Top Chef*).

We have seen some Asian/Americans participating in singing competition shows, such as William Hung, who auditioned for *American Idol* in 2004. Hung became an internet meme and a media punchline (Meizel 2009) after his heavily accented and out-of-tune version of Ricky Martin's "She Bangs" went viral. Since then, only a handful of other Asian/Americans have become popular on these talent shows as contestants (rather than audition jokes). Out of the 15 seasons of *American Idol*, approximately seven Asian/Americans have made it to the top ten,[2] and there have been no Asian/American champions. East Asian/American singers Paul Kim, John Park, and Elijah Liu all made it to the semi-finals (top 14), while Korean singer Heejun Han cracked the top ten in Season 11. South Asian singers Sanjaya Malakar (Season 6) and Anoop Desai (Season 8) both placed seventh in their respective seasons. Sonika Vaid is the first South Asian/American to make it to the top five. There have been a number of Filipinas or mixed race Filipinas within the top ranks of *American Idol*, including Thia Megia, Melinda Lira, Jasmine Trias, Ramiele Malubay, and Jessica Sanchez. Jasmine Trias (Season 3) placed third, and Jessica Sanchez was the runner-up for Season 11. How audiences and judges reacted to both the presence and the performances of these Asian/American singers provides a framework for understanding the reception that would greet Chin and Hill during their turn on reality television.

Both Anoop Desai and Heejun Han provide perhaps the best illustration of how these shows and their audiences have received Asian/American contestants. During Desai's audition, judge Simon Cowell greets Desai by mispronouncing his name, and Desai corrects him by using rapper Snoop Dogg's name as a pronunciation key. When Desai sings an R&B song from Boyz II Men, all of the judges express their surprise at how "soulful" his singing was, how "unexpected" it was to hear that "come out of him." As the judges compliment his singing, Cowell chimes in to declare: "It's all a bit geeky at the moment though, the look. He looks like he just came out of a meeting with Bill Gates or something. You know what I mean, it's all a bit Silicon [Valley], high tech." Desai's outfit during his audition is a button-down shirt and khaki shorts, which another judge more correctly refers to as "preppy." Cowell relies on narratives of what I have called *yellow peril 2.0* (Washington 2016), or the need to connect Asian/American men to the tech sector as an explanation for their dominance.

Heejun Han similarly exposes the judges for their continued reliance on clichéd tropes of Asian/Americans. Han, wearing glasses and fidgeting, is shown in the package leading up to his audition as awkward, geeky, and nervously truthful. While the show does not explicitly link him to William Hung, the comical treatment of both singers offers a clear comparison. In his slightly accented English, Han compliments the judges while he shakes out his nerves through his arms. The judges mimic his arm shaking during his audition. When Han tells them that he sings soul music and launches into Michael Bolton's "How Am I Supposed to Live without You," judge Jennifer Lopez exclaims with surprise: "He sings really nice! … I'm surprised he can really sing, no?" When he is finished singing, the judges do the shaky hands again and cheer. Judge Steven Tyler remarks: "That was great, man you sing great!" Lopez says: "You have a beautiful voice!" To which Randy Jackson adds: "Surprisingly!" He goes on to say: "I am really impressed and shocked! You have a really, really good voice, I am impressed." The judges' surprise highlights how primed they are for poor or comedic auditions from Asian/Americans; they were obviously expecting Silicon Valley rather than Motown.

Desai and Han's reliance on R&B/soul songs for their auditions serves to signal that they are "American enough," despite the expectations of the judges. The understanding that R&B/soul music is rooted in the experience of Black people in the United States confers on them the Americanness they need—regardless of whether or not they are already American, as was the case for Desai. Drawing on symbolic Blackness also confers on them a modicum of "cool" to counter the robotic, nerdy, uncreative, and unemotional stereotypes of Asian/Americans (Chun 2013). Their own Asian/American masculinity is burnished through its relationship to the Blackness that roots R&B/soul. Additionally, because this is a competition show and not an ensemble reality show, the need to perform race in order to build a narrative frame is mostly abrogated. Yet, through their song choices, these singers demonstrate the vital importance of racialized performances viewers will find recognizable, or at least familiar.

Interlude: Afro-Asian Connections

This brief comparative racialization on *American Idol* sets the stage for moving past using Asian/Americans as merely a third term for disrupting the Black/White binary, and toward thinking of Blasians as an example of how to more fully account for the "multiplicity of racial logics and racism" (Lye 2008). Hill, Chin, and other mixed race Blasians trouble the idea of what authenticity means for both Asian/Americans and Blacks by embodying hybridity's "both/and" function. Furthermore, their representations open up the possibility of a "neither" option, reminding us how powerful both cultural and biological definitions of race continue to be. Audiences must work to render their identities familiar within current racial logics, despite the fact that they do not quite fit within them. *The Voice* is a U.S.-centered show, and I analyze Chin and Hill within this specific racial paradigm that supports the Black/White binary, but we must also recognize that these singers emerge from Afro-Asian contexts.

Like the term "Asian/American," which conflates a hugely diverse geographic region of the world under the umbrella "Asian," "Blasian"[3] also lumps together disparate groups of people. While Tessanne Chin and Judith Hill have different histories and experiences and are more dissimilar than they are similar, within our current racial paradigm they both are generally considered, not incorrectly, mixed race Black and Asian. As such, these contestants from *The Voice* epitomize the transnational nature of Black and Asian connections. Scholars like Vijay Prashad (2000, 2001, 2008) have traced the ways African and Asian countries have interacted, and continue to interact, with each other. From early trade routes connecting East African countries to East Asian ones (Sheriff 1987), to the Indian Ocean slave trade[4] (Harris 1972), to Afro-Asian solidarity from the late nineteenth century into the twentieth century, there exists an extensive history of Black and Asian occupations, conquests, intermingling, networking, and community-building.

To understand the emergence of Blasians like Tessanne Chin from Jamaica, we must acknowledge the many Afro-Asian connections that occur in the Caribbean. Jung (2006) notes that coolies, or unskilled/indentured laborers from mainly China and the Indian sub-continent working in the Caribbean, exceeded the numbers of free Chinese laborers who traveled to the United States. In addition to recognition of their presence as analogous to that of slaves in the U.S., the presence of coolies in the Caribbean became a precursor to current discourses about race (Kim 2000; Washington 2012). These coolies in the Caribbean were held up as an exemplar of what a non-slave-dependent industrious labor force would look like. Alternately, abolitionists also used coolies as examples of an exploited labor force comparable to slaves in the United States. The Chinese laborers, both in the United States and in the Caribbean, were socially organized into bachelor communities. Since they were prohibited by law from mixing with White women, the laborers married into the neighboring Black and indigenous communities. The presence of Asians in the Caribbean as parallel to the presence of Blacks in the United States lays the foundation for Black/Asian racial mixing and offers a means of contextualizing these interracial relationships on the islands.

Jamaica's official motto, "Out of many, one people," reflects this racial mélange. The 1955 Miss Jamaica pageant, reconfigured after calls for a more racially egalitarian contest to reflect the population, highlights how the island has structured itself racially. The organizers announced that the pageant would separate and crown the women according to "ten types":

> Miss Ebony for black-complected women, Miss Mahogany for women of "cocoa-brown complexion," Miss Satinwood for "girls of coffee and milk complexion," Miss Golden Apple for "peaches and cream" Jamaican women, Miss Apple Blossom for "a Jamaican girl of white European parentage," Miss Pomegranate for "white Mediterranean girls," Miss Sandalwood for women of "pure Indian parentage," Miss Lotus who was to be "pure Chinese," Miss Jasmine for a Jamaican of "part-Chinese parentage," Miss Allspice for "part-Indian" women.
>
> (Barnes 1994)

The separation of women by ethnicity, color, and parentage and its subsequent embrace (Cooper 2012) has resulted in the preference for *brownings*. Brownings are the "just-right mix" found in light-skinned Jamaicans thought to reflect "all the elements and sources that produced such diversity" (Moss 2012). Chin and her musician parents—both of whom themselves are racially mixed (Chinese/Indigenous father and Black Jamaican/English mother)—are part of the idealized version of Jamaica that proclaims itself a multiracial nation.

Although Judith Hill's Black father and Japanese mother met as members of the same funk band in the United States (Kreps 2009) and not via U.S. military occupation in Asia, her particular Blasian mixture is oftentimes a reflection of the militarized American presence in Asia. A very brief history of Black U.S. soldiers in Asian countries includes fighting in the Philippine–American War in 1898, the Korean War, the Viet Nam war, and continued military presence in various Asian countries. Additionally, the anti-miscegenation laws in the United States resulted in the War Brides Act, which allowed soldiers to bring back their foreign-born (mostly Asian) wives and children. However, U.S. soldiers have been so omnipresent in Asian countries that this has produced its own trope of the absentee/abandonment-prone American father leaving behind the Asian mother and mixed race child(ren). Adding Blackness to that trope lays bare the anxieties over the sexualities and sexual practices of Black men and Asian women. The relationship between these Black soldiers and the Asian women in these countries has been responsible for the large jump in the Blasian population in the last few decades. With projections estimating that one out of five Asian/Americans will be multiracial by 2020 (Le 2016), the politics that undergird this particular Black and Asian mixture are necessary in making sense of contemporary Blasian experiences.

Fugue: Finding Their *Voices*

The premise of NBC's popular singing competition show, *The Voice*, is fairly simple: there are four judges/coaches who sit with their backs to the contestants for a "blind" audition. If a coach likes a contestant's voice, they will turn their chair around to claim the singer for their team. By the end of the auditions, there are four teams belonging to each of the coaches, and each team is whittled down week by week until there is one final singer left.[5] The judges for Season 4 were Adam Levine of Maroon 5, country singer Blake Shelton, R&B singer Usher, and Colombian pop star Shakira. In Season 5, all of the original judges returned, with Cee-lo Green and Christina Aguilera replacing Usher and Shakira.

Both Judith Hill and Tessanne Chin entered their respective seasons as recognizable performers with careers pre-dating the show. As a back-up singer for Michael Jackson, Hill was featured singing a duet with him in his concert documentary *This Is It*. After Jackson's death, Hill went from being a relative unknown to the subject of countless queries after singing "Heal the World" at his funeral. During her audition for *The Voice*, she impressed all four judges when she sang a stripped-down version of former judge Christina Aguilera's "What a Girl Wants." During her audition, we see her family and friends waiting backstage for her—including her Black father, Japanese mother, and Blasian brother, who of whom offers clues about her racial background.

Tessanne Chin came onto the show as a recording artist with a few hits in her native Jamaica, where she and her sister Tami were pop and rock/reggae stars. During her audition, she sang Pink's "Try" and impressed all four judges. As she sang, the camera cut from her performance to her Chinese Jamaican father, her Black Jamaican husband, and her Black best friend. Without the visual cue of her mother's body, Chin's actual racial mixture remains ambiguous. This ambiguity then becomes apparent in comments from the judges—rather than effusively praising her universally attractive talent or voice, they can't help but comment on her background. Country singer Blake Shelton tries to place this visibly Asian woman in Jamaica, awkwardly commenting: "I'm so fascinated by you … because you've been to Jamaica." Shelton's confusion is palpable as he tries to resolve the dissonance between the Asian Jamaican woman in front of him and his own assumptions about what Jamaicans look like.

While the responses from the judges are examples of how these two Blasians were racialized on *The Voice*, the real-time Twitter feed during the airing of their respective seasons provided a glimpse into how audiences racially read Hill and Chin. Tweets containing #thevoice and the singers' names (#JudithHill and #TessanneChin) during their respective seasons reveal the way that the audiences frame and contextualize these Blasian singers, largely in terms of race. For example, there was a flurry of tweets about Hill that addressed her mixed race identity during her audition:

@g_taylor41: "Asian and black might be the best combo ever!!!!!!! #JudithHill"
@Kae_Kashelle: "Oooooooh. She's beautiful :) #blasian #black #asian #judithhill"
@Super_Negra: "@Judith_Hill is a gorgeous mix of Japanese/Black. #thevoice #teamJudith"

Since viewers saw Hill's parents prominently featured during her audition, they were able to categorize her as both Black and Asian, and in *@Kae_Kashelle's* case, as Blasian. These tweets are part of the discursive framing around racial mixing that imagines mixed race people as exceptionally good looking because of their racial mixture. Hill's racial identity, specifically her Asian/American identity, was also praised by many viewers. Up until her elimination, mentions of her Japanese and/or Asian identity were almost universally brought up as a form of praise, pride, and inclusion:

@Im_Van_T: "Judith Hill on #TheVoice. Winner. That's right. Blasian the path with #TeamAdam! There's good, then there's #Asian.")
@NeetaManishaa: "Judith Hill #asian #awesome #TeamAdam"
@guafahnako: "Im rooting for @Judith_Hill. I only go for the Best, Goodluck Asian Barbie Doll!"
@audreymagazine: "Two Asian women on The voice tonight – including one of our faves @judith_hill: wp.me/p15az9-b8l #VoicePremier".

These tweets foreground Hill's inclusion within the pan-ethnic Asian/American umbrella, reifying Blasians' place within Asian America. The now defunct *Audrey* magazine, which promoted itself as the "nation's premier Asian American women's lifestyle magazine," claimed Hill as Asian/American from the beginning of the show. *Audrey*'s embrace of Hill meant that Blackness did not negate her claim to an Asian/American identity, and it gave Blasians entrée into the symbolic Asian/American community.

These comments contrast with the treatment of Chin in the following season, when the tweets following her performances hardly ever mentioned any Blasian or Black identity and focused almost exclusively on her Asianness:

@ccstewy: "Ha ha #TheVoiceIsBack @TerriKarelle: @nbcthevoice is gna b like wtf? An Asian who has a Jamaican accent & sings Rock! @Tessanne #teamjamaica"
@AlexMarieSen: "yes finally showing an Asian Jamaican on mainstream American television #TheVoice @Tessanne #meltingpot"
@StephanHomer: "Jamaican born, Caribbean grown, Asian powered. Well done @ Tessanne"
@asianinny: "We love @Tessanne of the @The_VoiceUSA… you make us #Asian proud!"

Unlike Hill, whose parents were both visible during her audition, Chin's Black Jamaican/English mother was not present. Her Asian last name and the presence of her mixed race Asian/American father resulted in a nearly singular focus on her Asian/American identity. While the Twitter feed for Hill featured dozens of tweets referring to her as Blasian or Black and Asian, there were very few Blasian, Black, or Black and Asian references to Chin through her entire run on *The Voice*. Moreover, the few attempts to racialize her as Black focused on the aesthetic extraordinariness of racial mixing, or used Blackness to talk about her body:

@Sparkiebaby: "@tessanne THIS #Win RT @DamYouSiico: Tessane wid the chiney face and black gyal body and adele voice at Dem to bloodclaah #TeamTessane"
@Xo_AsianBaby: "@Tessanne is soooo pretty to me she's Asian & black <ok and heart emojis>"
@theonly_Doasay: "This is what [black x Asian] looks like guyssss! @Tessanne <heart eyes emoji x 4>"
@GrindAffiliate1: "#Tessanne Chin on #theVoice…tho..u go gal! She Jamaican and Asian, got the body of a African queen and Asian in eye…#watchout now"
@kamdeeders: "If Tessanne Chin is what all black and Asian people look like they should all have babies together"
@Gem_Belle "Most women of the Asian persuasion are genetically thin. Not this broad. She got Jamaican! #yeamon! #thevoice #tessannechin"

Since the bodies of Asian/American women are represented (or disciplined, as Margaret Cho has reminded us) as thin, Chin was a conundrum. To explain why this phenotypically Asian/American woman was presumably not thin enough, audiences turned to her Blackness. These tweets reinforced familiar narratives of bodies, particularly Black bodies, in visual culture, as excessive and spectacular. Instead of considering the fact that Chin's body served to expand the ways racialized bodies are represented, we instead see a preponderance of exoticization and admiration that deems her body non-normative for an Asian/American woman.

While these responses to Hill and Chin's auditions reveal some of the ways that Blasian identities are differently celebrated, responses to their eliminations may reveal their potential for shifting racial paradigms. Hill was projected to win her season, so her surprising elimination became an "upset" that inspired emotional outpouring and cries of racism against her. While the tweets discussing the unfairness of her elimination could not agree on whether Hill did not garner enough votes because she was Black or because she was Asian/American, they were unified in their critique of White supremacy and the racist system that allows it to flourish. There were some who felt she was eliminated because she was Black *or* Asian/American and the show is rigged in favor of White contestants:

@francis_cola: "I don't watch the show, but I can bet u its because she is black. Blond country will win. That's USA"
@softkittenhes: "WTF JUDITH HILL WASN'T SAVED.. COS SHE'S ASIAN ISNT SHE.. I SMELL RACISM"
@blujayrain: "How many times are we going to see this? They will vote for a black or white person with less talent"
@RivkaSimons: "She's off cuz white people (n jews) r scared to death of black women in Mohawk hairdoos"
@bryanlimwc: "Kris Thomas and Judith Hill are such good vocalists. They're amazing singers. But they're black… #StopRacism"

These tweets all raise the issue of racism, but are split between blaming it on anti-Blackness and anti-Asian sentiment. The lack of consensus from fans about which racial identity was responsible for her elimination offers a clear example of how Blasians mount a challenge to the current racial and racist paradigm. Importantly, these Blasians also do not create their own rung in the racial hierarchy of the United States, but their presence contests its existence. The tension between whether to recognize Blasians as either Black or Asian/American opens up a space to critique the racial order for its inability to account for multiracial subjectivities such as theirs. For her fans, Hill's Blackness does not take away from her Asian/American identity—in fact, some use it in order to position her as a wedge between Black and White people. Some tweets specifically talked about her elimination in terms of being Blasian:

> *@TygaPostss*: "Judith hill didn't go through cause the voice is racist they didn't want another black person to win. And she's Asian. <angry face emoji> #thevoice"
> *@Randyisthinking*: "The Country folks didn't know what to do with Judith Hill Black AND Asian?! Minds blown. #TheVoice"

Understanding "country folks" as a stand-in for Whiteness, we can see through these tweets how difficult it is to make sense of Hill and Chin because of their mixed race identities. Other than the audition packages that aired in the premier episode of their respective seasons, *The Voice* itself did not otherwise explain their racial identities. In a post-elimination interview, Hill authenticates the confusion audiences felt upon seeing her on screen: "It's difficult, I think that in Hollywood it's hard being a woman of color, and especially mixed when people aren't really familiar with your face or what you represent" (Williams 2013). That these singers are both Black and Asian/American results in audiences trying to figure out how and where to fit them racially in familiar categories.

Harmony: Blasians as the Third Space

Beyond examining the reactions from viewers to the presence of Chin and Hill on *The Voice*, it is also important to consider how these two women understand and represent their own racial identities. In interviews given after their appearances on the show, both women spoke about their racial mixture in global terms, gesturing to the expansiveness of their reach. But they differed on how to situate their particular mixtures—Chin claimed her mixture as old and familiar, while Hill rooted hers in the future because of its unfamiliarity. Both declarations are true, and that Blasians are both familiar and not. Obviously, the history of Afro-Asian connections has shown Blasians to be a mixture that is old and familiar to some, while the reception these singers received on *The Voice* proved Blasians to be largely unfamiliar to U.S. communities. Yet, this incommensurability points to the way that Hill and Chin subvert dominant discourses of race—specifically, by escaping what Bhabha (1991) called the "politics of polarity," and creating what we might see as a third space where they can transgress rigid racial categories.

The connection between being multiracial and drawing on global influences has long been part of the narrative for how mixed race people are positioned as bridges to connect disparate groups. Hill alludes to this in her own words, particularly during an interview for the *Huffington Post* after she was eliminated. One caller asked Hill how her biracial identity has influenced her music and her career, and she replied:

> being half black and half Japanese it's always been about celebrating world music and cultures … Also growing up in a biracial home my parents were very open-minded and the house was full of musicians from all over the world.
>
> (Williams 2013)

Hill's connection of the global feeling in her music to growing up Blasian in an interracial household works to situate Blasians as translators who help render the unfamiliar and foreign into something familiar. Chin makes a similar move in her radio interview with former MTV VJ Sway. Sway enters the conversation by declaring: "The world hadn't seen anything like you. They don't understand in Jamaica, with your last name being Chin, of Asian descent as well, how that came to be. Can you explain that history how that came to be?" Chin replies:

> Well I am fourth generation Jamaican, so that means my grandmother's parents were the ones that came to Jamaica, from China, directly from China … In our little country we are a huge melting pot, I think suits our motto very well "out of many, one people." I'm a mixed up girl, I have a little bit of everything in my culture, my heritage, my race, I'm very proud of it.
>
> (Zobe 2014)

Chin's reply shows how Jamaica's racial pastiche transformed what it meant to be Jamaican. She later talks about how Jamaica as a country bought the rights to broadcast *The Voice* in order to support her run on the show, which it only does on a national scale for things like the Olympics. Bhabha makes clear that the third space is about how disparate elements are transformed once they encounter each other. In Chin's comments, we can see Jamaica's embrace of the third space created by racial mixing, as this Blasian singer has allowed it to progress past the segregated beauty pageants of its past to truly embracing the "melting pot" analogy and national motto.

This hybrid space enables challenging essentialist notions of identity, particularly of Black or Asian/American hypersexuality and body politics, through the refusal of these Blasian singers to singularly embody either Asian/Americanness or Blackness. Sakamoto (1996) notes that "giving up the desire for a pure origin, hybridity retains a sense of difference and tension between two cultures, but without assuming hierarchy. It is not just new identity but a new form of identity" (115–166). When asked how her multiracial identity has either helped or hindered her career, Hill observes:

> It takes a little bit of them getting used to it, you have to spoon-feed it to them or gradually introduce it to them. I think that *The Voice*, that was something I felt … I did feel my ethnicity, it was very clear that this is not straight down the middle, my path has always been I've sort of been in my own lane … I've always had that struggle where I've got one foot here and one foot there, and always representing, and being on *The Voice* I felt that, I'm not really in a lane that they can identify and be like "ok we know exactly what you are and we going to put you in this box" so I was constantly breaking the box …
>
> (Williams 2013)

She helps visualize this third space as she talks about being in her "own lane." Her explanation that she has never been "entirely" Black or Asian/American forces questions about how we think about race: such as whether race is mainly a visual marker, and if so, how do we determine the best and true markers of race? Or is there a cultural component of race that is predicated on performances of authenticity, and how then will we determine authentic performances? As such, the inclusion of Blasians expanded the visual and performative possibilities for Asian/Americans, which did in fact "break the box" for how Asian/Americans were represented on the show.

Hill continues on to further explicate what it means to be "betwixt and between" (Turner 1969) racial identities as a Blasian when she recalls how "Even growing up I'd be accepted in the Black community or the Asian community but not entirely, sort of like in the cracks." Being in the cracks allows these Blasian singers to subvert and resist racial boundaries through their inability to be categorized. The cracks also represent how Blasians sit outside essentialist ideas of both Black and Asian/Americans. Hill ends the interview by reasserting that the visibility and increased popularity of Blasians is the future. She states about her presence and reception on *The Voice*: "It's just a celebration of our new culture, and I love that, and I want to continue in that and I'm not ashamed of it. I know it's going to be hard to break new ground, but I want to do that and do it slowly and gradually so people can get used to it."

Coda: Conclusion

The utility and benefit of acknowledging Blasians within discussions of Asian/American media centers on hybridity and the possibilities it engenders for rethinking representation. In these conversations about Chin and Hill, we can see the challenge Blasians mount against the U.S. racial paradigm and the racial order of things, as the inability to categorize Blasians as either Asian/American or Black upends the racial hierarchy. Furthermore, that inability becomes a counter-narrative helmed by Blasians to force an expansion of how Asian/Americans are represented. The visibility of these Blasian singers on *The Voice* challenges the essentialist notions that rigidly racialize both Asian/Americans and Blacks by forcing viewers to imagine Asian/Americans and Blacks beyond these notions connected to the past. The show offers a different and new representation of the Asian/American experience that does not fit within cultural familiar narratives.

These differences are visible within even the most basic framing of cultural mixing by these two women—while Chin points out that the racial mixing between Blacks and Asians has been happening for generations, Hill refers to her exposure (and the subsequent exposure of other Blasians) as a "celebration of our new culture." Both statements can be seen as true. As Hill claims, these representations reveal a new culture that eschews both grand narratives and recognizable categories for audiences who are not familiar with seeing Blasians in media. Yet, Chin provides a necessary and important reminder that the diasporic movements of both Blacks and Asian/Americans mean that Blasians themselves are not new. Rather, they play a potentially new role in allowing us to move past current notions of race and into creating new ones.

Notes

1 I use "Asian/American" to highlight the conflating of Asian American with Asian despite their status in the United States and the refusal to acknowledge the citizenship and/or immigrant status of the group writ large. I opt to use the slash instead of writing "Asian" and "Asian Americans" because, as Palumbo-Liu (1999) notes, the slash represents "a choice between two terms, their simultaneous and equal status, and an element of indecidability, that is, as it at once implies both exclusion and inclusion" (1).

2 This number is approximate because it is based on their self-disclosed racial identities, but it is quite possible there have been other Asian/American *Idol* singers in the top ten who have not identified themselves as such.

3 The term itself is a replacement for the outdated "Afro-Asian" label and the clunky "Cablinasian" label popularized by Tiger Woods, and is frequently used culturally by people to define themselves as well as by academics whose research focuses on mixed race Black and Asian people.

4 While not as massive as the Atlantic slave trade, the Indian Ocean slave trade still moved large numbers of bodies.

5 The whittling is done through a combination of votes via telephone, text message, *The Voice* application, the NBC website, and/or Facebook, along with iTunes purchases of the songs sung during each episode.

Further Reading

Bow, Leslie. 2010. *Partly Colored: Asian Americans and Racial Anomaly in the Segregated South*. New York: New York University Press. (Historicization of Asian/Americans within the U.S. racial hierarchy.)

Ho, Jennifer A. 2015. *Racial Ambiguity in Asian American Culture*. New Brunswick: Rutgers University Press. (An extended treatment of mixed-race Asian/Americans.)

King-O'Riain, Rebecca C., Stephen Small, Minelle Mahtani, Miri Song, and Paul Spickard (eds). 2014. *Global Mixed Race*. New York: New York University Press. (A contextualization of the movements and lives of mixed race people.)

Nishime, LeiLani. 2014. *Undercover Asian: Multiracial Asian Americans in Visual Culture*. Urbana: University of Illinois Press. (An extended treatment of mixed race Asian/Americans.)

Williams-León, Teresa and Cynthia L. Nakashima. 2001. *The Sum of Our Parts: Mixed-Heritage Asian Americans*. Philadelphia: Temple University Press. (Canonical anthology of key research on mixed race Asian/Americans.)

References

Barnes, Natasha B. 1994. "Face of the Nation: Race, Nationalisms and Identities in Jamaican Beauty Pageants." *Massachusetts Review*, 35(3/4): 484.

Bhabha, Homi K. 1991. *The Location of Culture*. London: Routledge.

Chun, Elaine W. 2013. "Ironic Blackness as Masculine Cool: Asian American Language and Authenticity on YouTube." *Applied Linguistics*, 35(5): 592–612.

Cooper, Carolyn. 2012. "Who is Jamaica?" *New York Times*, August 5. www.nytimes.com/2012/08/06/opinion/who-is-jamaica.html.

Dagbovie, Sika Alaine. 2007. "Star-Light, Star-Bright, Star Damn Near White: Mixed-Race Superstars." *The Journal of Popular Culture* 40(2): 217–237.

Hall, Stuart. 2007. "Subjects in History: Making Diasporic Identities." In *The House That Race Built*, Wahneema Lubiano (ed.), 299. New York: Vantage Books.

Harris, Joseph P. 1972. *Africans and Their History*. New York: New American Library.

Ho, Fred and Bill V. Mullen (eds). 2008. *Afro Asian: Revolutionary Political & Cultural Connections between African Americans and Asian Americans*. Durham: Duke University Press.

Jung, Moon-Ho. 2006. *Coolies and Cane: Race, Labor, and Sugar in the Age of Emancipation*. Baltimore: Johns Hopkins University Press.

Kim, Claire Jean. 2000. *Bitter Fruit: The Politics of Black–Korean Conflict in New York City*. New Haven: Yale University Press.

Kreps, Daniel. 2009. "Judith Hill: 'Heal the World' Singer from Jackson Memorial Revealed." *Rolling Stone*, last modified July 7. http://www.rollingstone.com/music/news/judith-hill-heal-the-world-singer-from-jackson-memorial-revealed-20090707.

Lam, Andrew. 2014. "The 'Bamboo Ceiling': Hollywood Shuns Asians while New Media Embraces Them." *New America Media*, last modified January 26, 2014. http://newamericamedia.org/2014/01/the-bamboo-ceiling-hollywood-shuns-asians-while-new-media-embraces-them.php.

Le, C. N. 2016. "Multiracial/Hapa Asian Americans." *Asian-Nation: The Landscape of Asian America*, last updated March 1, 2016. http://www.asian-nation.org/multiracial.shtml.

Lye, Colleen. 2008. "The Afro-Asian Analogy." *PMLA* 123(5): 1732–1736.

Meizel, Katherine. 2009. "Making the Dream a Reality (Show): The Celebration of Failure in *American Idol*." *Popular Music and Society* 32(4): 475–488.

Moss, Adam. 2012. "It's Not Black and White – Race Relations a Grey Matter." *The Jamaica-Gleaner*, January 22. http://jamaica-gleaner.com/gleaner/20120122/focus/focus5.html.

Palumbo-Liu, David. 1999. *Asian/American: Historical Crossings of a Racial Frontier*. Stanford: Stanford University Press.

Prashad, Vijay. 2000. *The Karma of Brown Folk*. Minneapolis: University of Minnesota Press.

Prashad, Vijay. 2001. *Everybody Was Kung Fu Fighting: Afro-Asian Connections and the Myth of Cultural Purity*. Boston, MA: Beacon Press.

Prashad, Vijay. 2008. *The Darker Nations: A People's History of the Third World*. New York: The New Press.

Sakamoto, Rumi. 1996. "Japan, Hybridity and the Creation of Colonialist Discourse." *Theory, Culture & Society* 13(3): 113–128.

Sheriff, Abdul. 1987. *Slaves, Spices and Ivory in Zanzibar*. Dar es Salaam: Tanzania Publishing House.

Turner, Victor. 1969. *The Ritual Process: Structure and Anti-Structure*. London: Transaction Publishers.

Wang, Grace. 2010. "A Shot at Half-Exposure: Asian Americans in Reality TV Shows." *Television & New Media* 11(5): 404–427.

Washington, Myra. 2012. "Interracial Intimacies: Hegemonic Construction of Asian American and Black Relationships on TV Medical Dramas." *Howard Journal of Communication* 23(2): 253–271.

Washington, Myra. 2015. "Because I'm Blasian: Tiger Woods, Scandal and Protecting the Blasian Brand." *Communication, Culture & Critique* 8(4): 522–539.

Washington, Myra. 2016. "Asian American Masculinity: The Politics of Virility, Virality, and Visibility." In *The Intersectional Internet: Race, Sex, Class and Culture Online*, Safiya Noble and Brendesha Tynes (eds). New York: Peter Lang.

Washington, Myra. Forthcoming. *Blasian Invasion: Mixed-Race Blacks and Asians in the Celebrity Industrial Complex*. Jackson: University Press of Mississippi.

Williams, Tiffany. 2013. "Judith Hill Talks *20 Feet from Stardom.*" *Huffpost Live*, last updated June 21, 2013. http://live.huffingtonpost.com/r/highlight/51c50761fe34444dba00054f.

Zobe, D. J. 2014. "2013 Winner of *The Voice* Tessanne Chin's Chinese Jamaican Mixed Background and the Forgotten Story of the Coolie Trade." *The Microscopic Giant*, last modified January 7, 2014. http://themicrogiant.com/2013-voice-winner-tessanne-chin-mixed-chinese-jamaican-coolie-trade/.

Part IV

ASIAN AMERICAN NEW MEDIA

DIGITAL ARTIFACTS, NETWORKS, AND LIVES

14

ASIAN AMERICA GONE VIRAL

A Genealogy of Asian American YouTubers and Memes

Lori Kido Lopez

Throughout YouTube's first decade, Asian Americans were clearly recognized as some of the platform's most notable breakout stars. Since 2007, enterprising youth such as KevJumba, Michelle Phan, and Nigahiga have used their self-produced videos to woo fans by the thousands, and to launch their careers. Asian American YouTubers have been able to parlay their popularity into a wide variety of outcomes, including feature film productions, corporate sponsorships, record deals, television roles, concert series, makeup lines, and more. Academic scholarship and mainstream media reports abound on the Asian American YouTube phenomenon, with countless writers and theorists celebrating how Asian Americans are evading the systemic racism of media institutions through digital outlets and their unique affordances. Their success stories particularly stand out in comparison with the struggles historically faced by Asian Americans in more traditional media industries. As is discussed elsewhere in this collection, Asian American professionals have always been rare within the world of film and television, where a "bamboo ceiling" still limits possibilities. While it may be questionable how much any one of these Asian American YouTube superstars has actually crossed the threshold into mainstream visibility and recognition, their stories remain legend within Asian American communities.

Yet, what comes next? In an era when Asian American YouTubers are already well established and have been widely recognized for their successes, it is time to look beyond this "first generation" and explore what Asian American online engagement means in a post-KevJumba era. Asian American youth may no longer need to ask whether or not someone like them can participate in online media production and distribution, as they have long had access to Asian American images with a click of the mouse. In productively building upon the successes of those who came before them, they can instead focus their energies on producing their own "viral" hits. In this chapter, I investigate up-and-coming Asian American YouTubers as a way of expanding our understanding of how digital Asian America is progressing, particularly focusing on the shape of dialogues that are being fostered as a result of the increased potential for new voices to participate. The concept of dialogue takes on a particular meaning within the digital sphere, as participants create a traceable thread that serves to document its own history. But if we can now identify a progression from YouTube's early days until today, it is important to then ask how Asian American digital histories have been documented, referenced, and given meaning through these digital forms of dialogue. While the histories of minorities and people of color are always in danger of being coopted or lost, the digital context must be assessed for the way its affordances can serve to either record or negate its own historical traces.

I specifically investigate a YouTube channel called SuperBadFilm, which was created by a collective of second-generation and 1.5-generation (those who came to the United States as children) Hmong American youth from central California. Between 2011 and 2014, they posted 34 videos in an array of genres, including dramatic narratives and love stories, documentation of community activities, group vlogs, and humorous sketches. By 2016, they had acquired over 15,000 subscribers, and the hundreds of "likes" and comments on their videos indicate that they have a relatively small but dedicated fan base. Assessments of SuperBadFilm are particularly useful in terms of these questions about the way that today's Asian American YouTubers build upon and are in conversation with other widely visible online participants, because their videos are rich in intertextual references. In fact, all of their most popular videos can most accurately be categorized as memetic, or based on memes that deliberately participate in a digital dialogue that extends far beyond their own creations. Moreover, their identification as Hmong Americans, who are already marginalized within Asian America, and in particular with little visibility in U.S. media (Schein and Thoj 2009; Wilcox 2012), provides a unique perspective on Asian American media. But this investigation moves beyond asking how Asian Americans are representing themselves online; instead, I put forth new lines of inquiry—asking about the political function of online memes as a way of encouraging participation, tracing the production of digital citational practices as a way of shaping and documenting lineages, and uncovering a genealogy of the "next-generation" Asian American YouTube community and their videos. In doing so, this chapter illuminates the complexities of the digital arena as a space for recording and transforming Asian American histories.

YouTube's Asian American Celebrities

The success of Asian Americans on YouTube has followed a notably different trajectory from the careers of more traditional Asian American media professionals. Throughout the history of Asian American cinema (and other independent film genres), it has always been the case that filmmakers of color who focus on stories about their own specific communities face an uphill battle for recognition and professional success (Okada 2015). Yet, the advent of digital media production has already begun to open new possibilities for challenging the industrial status quo, and Asian Americans provide a clear example of the way that these opportunities can dramatically shift the possibilities for media production and distribution. This is partly related to the fact that many Asian Americans have eagerly adopted digital technologies, with their collective rates of internet usage and mobile phone adoption eclipsing those of all other racial groups (Pew Research Center 2011). A report by the Nielsen Company describes Asian Americans as "digital pioneers, adopting technology faster than any other segment. With higher rates of smartphone usage, online video consumption, and internet connectivity, they are redefining the way they watch, listen, and interact" (Nielsen Company 2013). It is also now commonplace for amateur media consumers to have access to high-quality cameras and editing software on their laptops and mobile devices. Together, the hunger for representations (Balance 2012) and the capacity for easily creating content to engage with these newly accessible audiences opened the door for artists such as two of YouTube's earliest stars, Kevin Wu "KevJumba" and Ryan Higa "Nigahiga." Their comic shorts—both scripted gags and more confessional-style vlogs—rocketed their fledgling channels to internet stardom, particularly within the metric of most-subscribed YouTube channels. Makeup guru Michelle Phan was another early stand-out, helping to pioneer the genre of the makeup/beauty vlogger and eventually becoming the first woman to reach one billion views on YouTube (Sawyer and Jarvis 2015). Other early stars included comedian Christine Gambino "HappySlip," rapper/comedian Timothy Delaghetto, filmmakers Freddie Wong and the trio comprising Wong Fu Productions, musicians David So and Kina Grannis, and many others who have together provided a wealth of Asian American artists and channels for audiences to follow.

Scholarly investigations of Asian American YouTubers have largely sought to address the question of how this new digital venue serves to alleviate the political shortcomings of mainstream media industries. For instance, we might hope that these self-representations would counter the preponderance of troublesome racial stereotypes that have long saturated film and television. Textual analyses of KevJumba's and Nigahiga's videos have shown that they do challenge some stereotypes, but have come to rely upon others (Chun 2013; Guo and Lee 2013). There is more optimism around the impact that YouTube videos have had on the careers of Asian American artists, who have long struggled to cross over into professional positions. In my own work I have argued that the successes of Asian American YouTubers has often been located at the level of the talented few, but that these highly visible celebrities are using their digital networks to call attention to Asian Americans working in both mainstream and independent media (Lopez 2016). The creation of partnerships between artists, videographers, musicians, dancers, and actors from the digital and traditional media realms interpellates an Asian American audience who will support and sustain the production of creative works. YouTube has also provided a powerful tool for Asian American musicians to use in circumventing institutional racism and taking advantage of transnational audiences in the development of their careers (Jung 2014). Yet, digital media can also serve as a counterpart to or criticism of mainstream media, as Pham and Ono find in their investigation of KevJumba's network television debut—they praise the agency he shows in using his YouTube videos to provide ancillary commentary that reframes his television performance (Pham and Ono 2016).

While these individual investigations have set out to understand the political consequences of these digital performances, together this literature more broadly affirms the brief—but meaningful—history of the rise of Asian American YouTube and acknowledges its social significance. As with so many forms of anti-racist cultural labor, participating in media production of such a personal nature can take its toll on the individuals at the helm (Lopez 2014), and we have already seen some of the most popular Asian American YouTubers take a break or step away from their YouTube channels to focus on other projects. To name just a few, the celebrated channels of KevJumba, HappySlip, and YOMYOMF are no longer regularly updated. Yet the success of these early participants has inspired many others, and a cadre of Asian American YouTubers has risen to take their place. Together, the works of both longstanding and more recent participants compose a deep and growing repository of Asian American digital narratives. The existence of so many hypervisible Asian Americans online must be acknowledged as a profound change within the mediated landscape, particularly for youth audiences who primarily rely upon YouTube, Facebook, Snapchat, and other streaming platforms for entertainment content. A decade after the rise of the Asian American YouTuber, we can now begin to look beyond these early success stories to ask how later generations of YouTubers continue making use of digital affordances to participate and shape the platform in new ways—and how these new interlocutors are rewriting the way that we understand Asian American digital histories on their own terms.

The Memetic Videos of SuperBadFilm

While perusing YouTube videos about Hmong Americans, I came across the channel "SuperBadFilm" and was instantly charmed. The videos produced by this collective of Hmong American college students and young adults are recognizable as being inspired by and in conversation with the cohort of Asian American YouTubers described above. Yet, they clearly speak from a perspective that is rarely seen within mainstream Asian American media—an enthusiastic emphasis is placed on their Hmong identities and cultures. Their videos include romantic shorts ("Give Me More Time" and "Silent Love"), humorous compilation videos ("You Know You're Hmong If" and "Fantasy vs. Reality"), and vlogs ("YouTube Q & A" and "Chubby Bunny Challenge"). In 2015, I contacted SuperBadFilm and was able to meet up with six members for a group interview in Fresno. We discussed the origins of their channel, the goals that motivated their participation on YouTube, and the connections they saw between themselves and other YouTubers. In the analysis that follows, I examine the content of their videos and statements from their interviews in order to connect their work to the contemporary Asian American digital landscape.

While there are a variety of genres represented in the videos posted to SuperBadFilm's YouTube channel, their most popular videos can largely be categorized as memetic—that is, the style and content of their videos are derived from and based upon other popular internet memes. The idea of a "meme" comes from Richard Dawkins (1976), who took a biological approach to theorizing how small units of culture adapt, survive, and are replicated. Although originally used to describe analogue memes such as songs or images, the idea has been taken up in the digital realm to refer to the way that phrases, images, and videos invite copying and imitation in order to rapidly spread from user to user (Shifman 2013). While many common internet memes like "lolcats" or "philosoraptor" consist solely of photos with user-generated captions, the practice of slightly modifying a very popular framework can also be applied to the creation of videos, as we can see with SuperBadFilm's YouTube channel. For example, the second video posted by SuperBadFilm is called "Shit Hmong Dads Say," and features quick cuts between a long list of brief quips, advice, admonishments, and funny fatherly statements edited together into a three-minute sequence. This is based on the memes "Shit My Dad Says" and "Shit Girls Say," which are broader in scope but use the same tone and style of editing for comedic effect. Both of these memes circulated widely; in fact, the Twitter account for "Shit My Dad Says" became so popular that it inspired a sitcom called *$#*! My Dad Says* starring William Shatner. Posted in early 2011, the SuperBadFilm video "Shit Hmong Dads Say" was one of hundreds of memetic videos that followed up on this particular meme, including a host of YouTube videos such as "Shit Asian Girls Say," "Shit Drunk Guys Say," or the more politically themed "Shit White Girls Say To Black Girls."

We can also see this reliance on internet memes in their video titled "Hmong Songs in Real Life." It is based on popular YouTube user SteveKardynal's comic video series "Songs in Real Life," which inserts lyrics from popular songs as dialogue in real-life situations. Riffing on this formula, SuperBadFilm's videos use a blend of popular and traditional Hmong songs to similarly create comedy through juxtaposing melodramatic or humorous lyrics into banal everyday situations. They created three versions of "Hmong Songs in Real Life" with different songs, but also moved beyond music to include videos such as "Hmong Movies vs In Real Life," "Hmong Girls in Real Life," "Hmong Parents in Real Life," and "Hmong Guys in Real Life." In each, the videos take up the task of explaining stereotypical or generalized attributes of Hmong gender roles or familial roles through humorous depictions of everyday life. Some of their other memetic videos include "Hmong Be Like," "Harlem Shake [Hmong Store Edition]," and "You Know You're Hmong If." While many studies of memes examine a collective body of memes as a way of understanding the work that a single meme can perform (Gal et al. 2016; Soha and McDowell 2016), here we can ask why a single video source would focus on memetic videos, and in particular, why this next generation of Asian American YouTubers chooses to focus so heavily on memes.

One way of understanding the significance of formal and aesthetic mimicry to minority media producers is revealed in the case of *Better Luck Tomorrow* (2002). The Asian American independent film became a breakout hit for first-time director Justin Lin in large part due to its confident, proficient take on the genre of the mainstream teen comedy. Despite its shoestring budget, it was easily recognizable as fitting within a constellation of familiar tropes, aesthetic conventions, and plotlines—the nerdy and unnoticed teenager lusting after a romance with the cheerleader and social acceptance from the popular crowd, the thrill of developing and undertaking a complicated heist, and the dramatic downward spiral following the allure of drugs, money, and violence. In her analysis of *Better Luck Tomorrow*, Margaret Hillenbrand (2008) argues that Lin deploys enthusiastic mimicry as a way of moving Asian American cinema from the arthouse into the mainstream. She does not see this as demonstrating a wholehearted capitulation to mainstream or hegemonic norms and values, as she is able to read certain moments from the film as counter-hegemonic and subversive. Yet, her argument helps to reveal the political value of aesthetic and stylistic imitation in an uneven mediated landscape where Asian Americans are often disregarded.

If we apply Hillenbrand's analysis of mimicry to SuperBadFilm's video oeuvre, we can similarly see the use of memetic videos as a way of attracting audiences, because their videos are, as with *Better Luck Tomorrow*, "fluent in the lexicon of popular film, [they display their] proficiency, like an apt pupil, through enthusiastic mimicry—of genre, stock character, and dramatic structure" (Hillenbrand 2008: 51). Both Lin and SuperBadFilm ostensibly deploy mimicry as a way of gaining access and increasing popularity, given that potential alternatives (such as avant-garde experimentation, or the expository mode of documentaries) are assumed not to be crowd-pleasers. Internet memes and memetic videos, in contrast, are designed for wide propagation and longevity because they are so easily understood and appreciated, which prompts circulation. Individual entries can then more easily become swept up in the larger momentum of sharing and spreading that propels meme cultures. While this phenomenon is popularly described as "going viral," Jenkins et al. (2013) remind us that this epidemiological term can serve to deny the agency of human actors in making decisions about what content to share. There is nothing "natural" about the circulation of ideas; audiences decide to engage with texts that mean something to them, and they share those texts when something is gained in doing so. In asking what SuperBadFilm's memetic videos mean, we must, then, ask how they resonate with actual audiences.

Inserting Hmong Americans into Digital Asian America

Beyond their reliance on memes, another remarkable characteristic of SuperBadFilm's videos is a strong voicing of their Hmong identity. Their videos are filled with explicit references to their ethnic identity, with over half of their films specifically mentioning the word "Hmong" in their title and one completely in Hmong ("Ua Siab Ntev Tos Kuv"). This explicit identification is unusual among the early Asian American YouTubers, who rarely created works with the word "Asian American" in their title and often seemed to shy away from making any claims to Asian American identification. In contrast, the videos of SuperBadFilm stand apart in their desire to build pride for identifying as Hmong. Nearly all of the comical videos are scripted in Hmong, but in addition, the jokes from videos such as "Hmong Songs in Real Life," "Hmong Love Movie Stereotypes," and "Hmong Medicine from China" depend upon a familiarity with Hmong music, Hmong movies, and Hmong commercials. SuperBadFilm also create documentary-style videos about their participation in cultural activities such as Hmong New Year. We can see from these videos an earnest affection for many aspects of Hmong culture, including Hmong language, cultural traditions, and a variety of media objects. These choices reveal the target audience for their videos, as well as some of their broader goals in what they hope to communicate to them—they seem to be speaking primarily to those who speak Hmong and are familiar with cultural norms, and they encourage the maintenance of an affective, potentially nostalgic connection to Hmong cultural texts.

Shifman (2013) distinguishes memes from virality because they are characterized by modification and reinterpretation, rather than simply their ability to spread rapidly. Yet, the two concepts are connected in the sense that slight modification to an easily understood, recognized, and appreciated meme is what might encourage its popularity in a competitive environment. If transformation is a key component of the resilience and power of memes, we can then better understand the power of SuperBadFilm's memetic videos—they are meaningfully transforming the original content in a way that is specific to a new audience. In this case, it seems clear that the unique signature of their videos is simply applying the memetic content to their own Hmong identities. While the decision to often speak only in Hmong serves to limit their audience to only Hmong (or Hmong-speaking) viewers, it also constitutes the meaningful and attractive "transformation" that is integral to the appeal of memetic content. Yet, Shifman's work on memes also reminds us that the creators of memetic videos can also shift the meaning of the video. Since digital memes often focus on the "performative self" by including the uploader's face and body as part of the message (Shifman 2013: 30), they can represent a body or perspective that shifts our understanding of the digital landscape. For instance, in Shifman's (2011) examination of the "Leave Britney Alone" meme, she argues that the video itself "[conveys] the message that being gay and effeminate is a legitimate practice" (14). This is clearly the case for racialized memes—that is, both those who use the visibility of a racialized body to disrupt the normatively White media landscape, and those whose message is outwardly focused on anti-racism or racial specificity, are working to legitimize their mediated existence and participation. Indeed, Shifman defines a meme as being "incorporated in the body and mind of its hosts" (Shifman 2013: 56), rather than simply spreading in an unchanged way from user to user.

This insertion of Hmong American bodies, languages, cultures, and perspectives into the digital landscape is particularly meaningful for a community that is largely absent from the digital networks of millennial Asian America. As mentioned earlier, Asian Americans are often recognized as early adopters of digital technologies and are celebrated as full participants within the online realm. Yet, Hmong communities are among those falling under the heterogeneous umbrella of Asian America who are conspicuously missing from this data. Pew Internet Research and other mainstream research bodies routinely use studies on only the largest six ethnic populations of Asian Americans to stand in for the entire group (Pew Research Center 2012), and Hmong are the ninth largest ethnic group of Asians in the United States. With a population of only 260,000 as of 2013 (Pfeifer and Yang 2013), Hmong communities and their media practices are rarely discussed in academic scholarship, mainstream media discourses, or online venues. The digital participation of Chinese Americans, Japanese Americans, Filipino Americans,

Vietnamese Americans, Indian Americans, and mixed race Asian Americans has been fairly common within YouTube's popular channels. In comparison, there are currently no Hmong YouTubers cracking the ranks of top performers, among other markers of digital power, which mirrors the lack of Hmong artistic performers in general who are available within the entertainment media realm.

Taken together with the attributes of aesthetic mimicry and digital fluency, we can see that SuperBadFilm are able to use their production of memetic videos as a tool for challenging the boundaries of digital Asian America. This relationship between SuperBadFilm and other Asian American YouTubers is important in making sense of the intertextuality of SuperBadFilm's work. Hillenbrand sees Justin Lin's mimicry as reflective of tensions between Asian American cinema—a latent cinema that had largely failed to break into the mainstream until *Better Luck Tomorrow*—and the mainstream, with depictions of "violent heteromasculinity and bourgeois materialism" (65) serving as intertextual referents to similar themes that are omnipresent in such genres as teen flicks and gangster movies. Hillenbrand calls Lin's implicit critique of such generic norms "parodic," as they can serve to remind viewers that Asian American bodies are so often denied access to these kinds of roles. In replicating the style and voice of popular Asian American YouTubers, the work of these Hmong American artists reflects a similar tension in asserting their own distinctive voice as an ethnic group that has long been marginalized and left out of dominant characterizations of Asian America.

In interviews with members of SuperBadFilm, they explicitly discuss the fact that they have seen no Hmong predecessors leading the way in creating YouTube videos for or about Hmong Americans. When talking about the absence of Hmong Americans within the online media world, one member stated: "Our generation is still trying to catch up to society. We have to promote ourselves." Just as *Better Luck Tomorrow* uses the style of mainstream cinema to rectify the absence of Asian Americans in that space, so SuperBadFilm use the style of Asian American YouTube videos to create an online space for Hmong Americans. They render visible a Hmong presence within digital realms wherein their technological and artistic proficiency serve to legitimate their membership and affirm a sense of belonging. This desire and struggle for digital recognition reminds us that participatory cultures online are not equally open and available to everyone; digital spaces and cultures reflect many of the exclusions and social stratifications of the offline world (Nakamura 2008). For Hmong Americans, as with many diasporic communities, digital spaces have opened up a wealth of opportunities for connecting to other Hmong Americans and affirming their own identities within a larger Asian American collective that often does not recognize their cultural specificities.

Participating in Memetic Citational Practices

We have seen the way that SuperBadFilm's memetic videos serve to expand the boundaries of digital Asian America to underrepresented communities, but the question remains as to how later generations of YouTubers such as these participate in the creation of an Asian American digital history. This line of inquiry is important for a number of reasons. First, we must acknowledge the political significance of citational practices in general, due to a recognition of the fact that minority labor has systematically been obscured and erased throughout history—an injustice that Asian Americans have long worked to rectify (Okihiro 2014). The very origins of Asian American Studies as a field of research and teaching stem from the political necessity of documenting widely overlooked Asian American histories and contributions to American society and culture (Chan 2005). Given that Asian Americans played a pioneering role in the early days of YouTube and are a vital part of the platform's history, we can, then, ask how their influence has left a trace and what it means in the context of what came afterward.

Digital media provides its own challenges and opportunities for conducting historical analyses. Digital data can easily be deleted or moved, rendering links inactive or broken, replaced by dummy pages created by cybersquatters or 404 error pages (Gitelman 2006). Yet, digital data is also prone to leaving a trace, both through being archived by the crawlers of the Wayback Machine and through the complex network of links that create paths from one site to another. All forms of media are figuratively connected through intertextuality, homage, and other artistic devices, but online forms of media use hypertext and other forms of digital linking to create literal pathways from one site to another. Many of the most common social media platforms build opportunities for direct links into their algorithm—for instance, when Facebook messages are shared, a tweet is retweeted, or a Tumblr post is reblogged, an automatic link is created to the original content. Yet, we still see many instances of digital theft, failure to correctly give attribution or credit, and other forms of exploitation, particularly surrounding the labor of those who are disenfranchised in the offline world as well (Felix 2015). For instance, the three Black women who created #BlackLivesMatter in the wake of Trayvon Martin's murder have discussed their frustrations with those who have failed to correctly acknowledge their contributions to the project. In an online article discussing the origins of the movement and the "Theft of Black Queer Women's Work," Alicia Garza states: "When you adopt Black Lives Matter and transform it into something else … it's appropriate politically to credit the lineage from which your adapted work derived" (Garza 2014). This call for proper citation is particularly significant when the failure to do so risks shifting the political goals and outcomes of a project.

These questions about how to properly give credit for the contributions of minority workers and cultures have arisen around memetic videos in particular. The example of the "Harlem Shake" meme is helpful because it has been widely discussed in terms of both cultural theft/appropriation and digital citation practices. Originating in 2012, this meme is based on a version of a song called "Harlem Shake" that was produced by Harry Rodrigues. A comedian named Filthy Frank posted a video of a wild dance party breaking out at the moment the beat drops, and within days, over 12,000 variations of dance parties set to the song had been posted to YouTube (Allocca 2013). Yet, a slew of criticism quickly followed, denouncing the viral trend for appropriating the Black cultural roots of the dance form sharing its name (Palmer 2013). With each new iteration of the meme, knowledge of the dance form that originated in the 1980s seemed to recede and become obscured from the conversation.

These two cases remind us that digital content is both resilient and tenuous. It is resilient in the sense that digital copies are easy for any user to create and repost, making it difficult to scrub the internet of any particular content. Online searches can be used to unearth even the smallest, most limited references, and the long tails of internet databases rely upon digital storage space to preserve content. In this sense, Garza's story about the origins of #BlackLivesMatter and videos of Harlem Shakers from the 1980s can persist alongside the later iterations and transformations of their work that necessitate these arguments. Yet, their complaints about the ways in which origin stories and histories can be rewritten or obscured remind us that not all internet content is equal. Due to vast disparities in the popularity of certain sites and the role that search engine algorithms play in ranking and highlighting content, users are likely to encounter certain content more commonly than others (Halavais 2009). Highly ranked YouTube videos are those that are popular in terms of views, comments, and ratings, that are widely linked to by external sites, and that deploy relevant keywords and descriptions. Moreover, YouTube's platform—unlike Facebook, Twitter, and Tumblr—does not provide a space for content creators to automatically link content or videos, leaving it up to the discretion of individuals to perform this citational act.

Within this context, it becomes clear that memes and memetic videos themselves can constitute weak vehicles for citational practices. As discussed earlier, memes flourish when they are instantly recognizable, and then spread through the modifications and interventions made by individual users in a way that extends or reinterprets the original message. These two practices do not require any knowledge of the meme's originator or the original context for the meme itself, and practices of citation have not become commonplace. In their simplicity, memetic videos rarely offer opportunities to even link to similar content. Yet, as with all practices of appropriation, there are clear political consequences for the disenfranchised communities whose sense of ownership and history is obscured in the digital arena, buried beneath thousands of videos, channels, and pages that search algorithms rank above theirs. We can see here that there are both technological and cultural barriers in place that make memetic videos poor tools for looking backward and creating traceable histories.

Digital Genealogies of Asian America

If this linear form of tracing history is fraught, it may be more productive to consider a genealogy of the memetic videos by SuperBadFilm—asking how their own histories are either made visible or obscured, and how this connects to their own goals and stated interventions. I use the Foucauldian idea of "genealogy" here to highlight the way that the histories are deeply ideological and cannot be extricated from the power dynamics that shape their development. The use of this term in the context of Dawkins' metaphor of the meme is particularly ironic, as the genealogical method eschews the linear evolutionary path of biological genes. Rather than searching for an unbroken narrative of evolution, Foucault sees the search for history as one in which we must "identify the accidents, the minute deviations—or conversely, the complete reversals—the errors, the false appraisals, and the faulty calculations that gave birth to those things that continue to exist and have value for us" (Foucault 1977: 146). The genealogical method is particularly appropriate for seeking histories in the digital realm, where "what has value" is often impossible to trace directly to its source, given the ephemerality of so much internet storage. Wendy Chun reminds us of this in her examination of the future of digital media:

> Memory, with its constant degeneration, does not equal storage; although artificial memory has historically combined the transitory with the permanent, the passing with the stable, digital media complicates this relationship by making the permanent into an enduring ephemeral, creating unforeseen degenerative links between humans and machines.
>
> (Chun 2008: 148)

This framework offers a powerful means for excavating the enduring legacy of the Asian American digital pioneers who shaped YouTube in its earliest days, yet who are often completely neglected in mainstream accounts of the platform's rise and development.

There are a number of ways that we can uncover the history of SuperBadFilm, their channel, and their memetic films. First, we can consider the memes that they are referencing and trace their specific origins. As is common with most memes, there is not much direct citation to the meme conversations in which they are participating. The only example of direct citation is a line in the description of their "Hmong Songs in Real Life" video, which reads: "THIS VIDEO WAS INSPIRED BY Steve Kardynal, THE FIRST GUY WHO MADE "SONG'S

IN REAL LIFE" :)"Yet, there is no link to Kardynal's videos, and this line is directly beneath a description of their own sequel video, "Hmong Songs in Real Life 2," which does contain an active link—directing traffic back to their own channel, rather than to their actual predecessor. In all of their other mimetic videos ("Shit Hmong Dads Say," "Hmong Be Like," "Harlem Shake [Hmong Store Edition]," and "You Know You're Hmong If"), there is no discussion of a connection to other memetic videos at all. As mentioned earlier, memes are often able to spread because they are part of an interconnected digital conversation that links from one version of a meme to another. In this case, SuperBadFilm do nothing to indicate knowledge of these memes or a desire to participate in any ongoing conversation—they are simply using the meme as inspiration for their own Hmong-centric videography.

This lack of interest in participating in a memetic conversation was also made clear in my conversations with the members of SuperBadFilm. When asked about who inspired their work, they do not mention any of the names of the White YouTubers such as Steve Kardynal, Kyle Humphrey and Graydon Sheppard, or Justin Halpern, who originally created the memes that they are explicitly referencing in their videos. Moreover, they do not mention the works of Black videographers on YouTube or the video sharing app Vine, whose works provided the source material for their videos "Harlem Shake (Hmong Store Edition)" or "Hmong Be Like." In some sense, the absence of these referents can be seen as an instance of misattribution or a failed citational practice, as there does not seem to be any recognition of the broader conversation in which these videos are playing a role.

Yet, it is also interesting to note who they do discuss as the inspiration for their videos—they were eager to point to their fandom and affection for Asian American YouTubers including Wong Fu Productions, Nigahiga, and Just Kidding Films. These are the YouTubers whom they claim to emulate, and whose works inspire their own participation as videographers and YouTubers. We can see from these comments that their involvement is not premised on the content of their videos or the love of memes and memetic videos, but, rather, on the act of participating in YouTube itself. In the wake of the first generation of Asian American YouTubers pioneering a mode of online storytelling that opened doors and transformed possibilities, the next generation of participants affirm and acknowledge these accomplishments. One of the ways that they do so is by playing an active role in establishing their own histories. In the case of SuperBadFilm, they eschew the literal connections between their work and non-Asian YouTubers—instead, they affirm the ideological consequences that Asian American YouTubers have had in reframing the identities of those who belong within digitally mediated spaces. They hope to join in with and continue the conversation started among those media producers, even if their actual videos evolved from and reference a different body of work.

YouTube 2.0 and our Digital Futures

Another potential site for mapping digital citational practices is in the direct links provided within the different subpages of SuperBadFilm's channel, as all YouTube pages contain spaces for promoting other channels. While it is possible for the owners of YouTube channels to designate their own related channels on the tab called "Channels," SuperBadFilm do not enter any information into this area. The only links to other channels are those listed under the heading "Related channels"—a short list of other channels that is created automatically by YouTube's algorithms based on what is believed to be similar content (Figure 14.1).

In this case, we might guess that related content would include channels hosting similarly memetic videos, or the Asian American YouTubers whom they describe as their inspira-

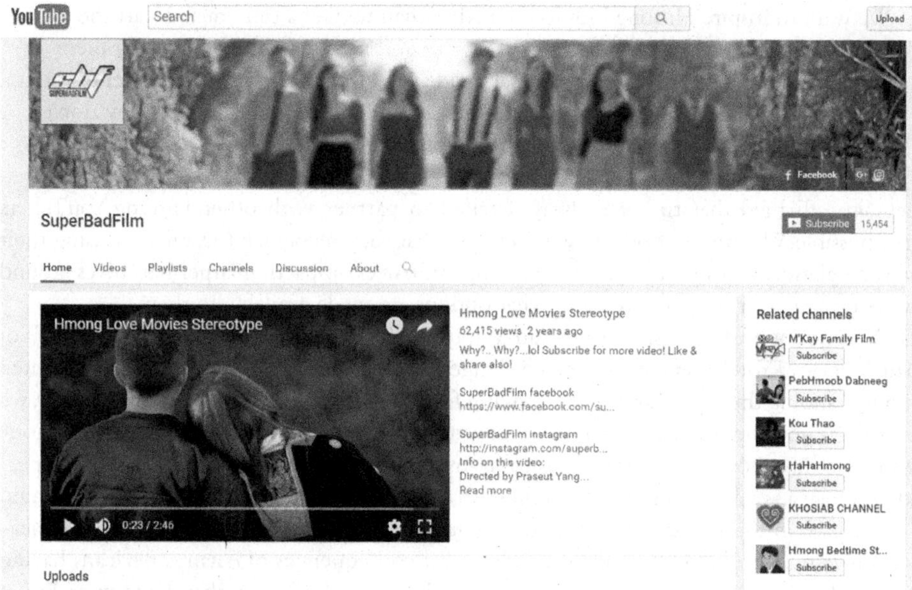

Figure 14.1 The YouTube channel for SuperBadFilm automatically links to similar channels under the heading "Related channels."

tion. Instead, the six videos selected by YouTube's algorithms consist of six Hmong-themed channels: PebHmoob Dabneeg, Kou Thao, M'Kay Family Film, HaHaHmong, Khosiab Channel, and Hmong Bedtime Stories. The same is true for the videos that pop up as "Up Next" on the right-hand side of the video player page—rather than linking to other "Songs in Real Life" videos, nearly all of the links are to Hmong-themed videos. The centrality of Hmong identifications in the names and content of these related channels and videos again reminds us that the act of inserting Hmong language, narratives, and bodies into the online realm is noteworthy—such that YouTube categorizes their videos as primarily Hmong, rather than primarily Asian American, as they would characterize their own oeuvre. YouTube's algorithms serve to delimit their own genre as "Hmong," prioritizing their ethnic/cultural markers as somehow more significant than these other possibilities.

If SuperBadFilm's memetic videos allow limited paths for tracing their own digital histories and predecessors, they nevertheless open new possibilities with regard to the opposite side of the temporal equation—looking forward, and inviting future participation. Indeed, the channels of these "competitors" or other Hmong videos evidence this particular phenomenon, as the allure of SuperBadFilm's "Hmong Songs in Real Life" video inspired other Hmong YouTubers to also participate in the meme. The channel HahaHmong produced its own "Hmong Songs in Real Life" video, M'Kay Family Film produced a "Hmong New Year Songs in Real Life" video, and If you are… produced a parody video called "Hmong Songs in Real Life, MASK HMONG PARODY." Together, these videos serve to promote the visibility of many different Hmong cultural producers, including the videographers themselves, but also the artists whose song clips are featured and listed in this meme. While the members of SuperBadFilm position their works as being inspired by the first generation of Asian American YouTubers, they are also attentive to the role that they play in inspiring other young Hmong artists. One member stated:

> We want to inspire Hmong kids to go further than us. Get a camera and start shooting, step out of the box. Instead of getting out and racing cars or being gang members or getting in trouble, they can make videos and have fun with their friends. In the Hmong community the actors support the people in Thailand, but they don't support the actors over here in the U.S. I think that would be cool.

They also affirmed that they are always excited to partner with other Hmong YouTubers when possible. We can see from these statements that they recognize the value of using their YouTube platform to speak to and for Hmong audiences, impacting larger narratives around how Hmong youth are perceived and what options are made available to them.

This genealogy of an Asian American YouTube channel from "the next generation" of Asian American YouTubers reveals the challenges and discontinuities that must be negotiated in understanding the digital archive. In looking for traces of SuperBadFilm's digital history, we see that it is not important to accurately reconstruct the particular branches of the evolutionary process that provided the inspiration for any one meme. The memetic videos of SuperBadFilm play a weak role in linking to those that came before them, and can scarcely be said to participate in the broader conversations engendered by any one meme. Rather, a genealogical investigation helps to reveal the ideological consequences of Asian Americans having established a digital presence. Moreover, this genealogy reveals the way that the temporality of this history can be reversed—memes and memetic videos can be seen to more productively issue a call to the future for future participation, and for unique voices to continue to challenge the ideologies that had previously rendered their identities invisible. In this sense, the lack of direct citation by memes is not necessarily a negative attribute. Rather, the memetic videos of SuperBadFilm are but one node in a constellation of digital participants who are together impacting our understanding of both the past and the future.

References

Allocca, Kevin. 2013. "The Harlem Shake Has Exploded." *YouTube Trends*, February 15. http://youtube-trends.blogspot.com/2013/02/the-harlem-shake-has-exploded.html.

Balance, Christine Bacareza. 2012. "How It Feels to Be Viral Me: Affective Labor and Asian American YouTube." *Women's Studies Quarterly* 40(1/2): 138–152.

Chan, Sucheng. 2005. *In Defense of Asian American Studies: The Politics of Teaching and Program Building.* Urbana: University of Illinois Press.

Chun, Elaine. 2013. "Ironic Blackness as Masculine Cool: Asian American Language and Authenticity on YouTube." *Applied Linguistics* 34(5): 592–612.

Chun, Wendy Hui Kyong. 2008. "The Enduring Ephemeral, or the Future is a Memory." *Critical Inquiry* (35): 148–171.

Dawkins, Richard. 1976. *The Selfish Gene.* Oxford: Oxford University Press.

Felix, Doreen St. 2015. "Black Teens Are Breaking the Internet and Seeing None of the Profits," *Fader*, December 3. http://www.thefader.com/2015/12/03/on-fleek-peaches-monroee-meechie-viral-vines.

Foucault, Michel. 1977. "Nietzsche, Genealogy, History." In *Language, Counter-Memory, Practice: Selected Essays and Interviews*, Michel Foucault, 139–164. New York: Cornell University Press.

Gal, Noam, Limor Shifman, and Zohar Kampf. 2016. " 'It Gets Better': Internet Memes and the Construction of Collective Identity." *New Media & Society* 18(8): 1698–1714.

Garza, Alicia. 2014. "A Herstory of the #BlackLivesMatter Movement by Alicia Garza." *The Feminist Wire*, October 7. http://www.thefeministwire.com/2014/10/blacklivesmatter-2.

Gitelman, Lisa. 2006. *Always Already New: Media, History, and the Data of Culture.* Cambridge: MIT Press.

Guo, Lei and Lorin Lee. 2013. "The Critique of YouTube-Based Vernacular Discourse: A Case Study of YouTube's Asian Community." *Critical Studies in Mass Communication* 30(5): 391–406.

Halavais, Alexander. 2009. *Search Engine Society.* Cambridge: Polity Press.

Hillenbrand, Margaret. 2008. "Of Myths and Men: Better Luck Tomorrow and the Mainstreaming of Asian American Cinema." *Cinema Journal* 47(4): 50–75.

Jenkins, Henry, Sam Ford, and Joshua Green. 2013. *Spreadable Media: Creating Value and Meaning in a Networked Culture.* New York: New York University Press.

Jung, Eun-Young. 2014. "Transnational Migrations and YouTube Sensations: Korean Americans, Popular Music, and Social Media." *Ethnomusicology* 58(1): 55–82.

Lopez, Lori Kido. 2014. "Blogging while Angry: The Sustainability of Emotional Labor in the Asian American Blogosphere." *Media, Culture and Society* 36(4): 421–436.

Lopez, Lori Kido. 2016. *Asian American Media Activism: Fighting for Cultural Citizenship.* New York: New York University Press.

Nakamura, Lisa. 2008. *Digitizing Race: Visual Cultures of the Internet.* Minneapolis: University of Minnesota Press.

Nielsen Company. 2013. *Significant, Sophisticated, and Savvy: The Asian American Consumer.* New York: The Nielsen Company.

Okada, Jun. 2015. *Making Asian American Film and Video: History, Institutions, Movements.* New Brunswick, NJ: Rutgers University Press.

Okihiro, Gary. 2014. *Margins and Mainstreams: Asians in American History and Culture.* Seattle: University of Washington Press.

Palmer, Tamara. 2013. "The Harlem Shakedown," *The Root*, February 15. http://www.theroot.com/articles/culture/2013/02/the_harlem_shake_viral_video_craze_what_about_the_original/.

Pew Research Center. 2011. *Asian-Americans and Technology.* January 6. http://www.pewinternet.org/Presentations/2011/Jan/Organization-for-Chinese-Americans.aspx.

Pew Research Center. 2012. *The Rise of Asian Americans.* Washington, DC: Pew Social & Demographic Trends.

Pfeifer, Mark, and Kou Yang. 2013. "Hmong Population and Demographic Trends in the 2010 Census and 2010 American Community Survey." *State of the Hmong Community.* Washington, DC: Hmong National Development.

Pham, Vincent and Kent Ono. 2016. "YouTube Made the TV Star: KevJumba's Star Appearance on The Amazing Race 17." In *Global Asian American Popular Cultures*, Shilpa Davé, Leilani Nishime, and Tasha Oren (eds), 74–88. New York: New York University Press.

Sawyer, Nicole, and Rebecca Jarvis. 2015. "YouTube Star Michelle Phan: 7 Things You Didn't Know About Her." *ABC News*, March 19. http://abcnews.go.com/Business/youtube-star-michelle-phan-things/story?id=29753510.

Schein, Louisa, and Va-Megn Thoj. 2009. "Gran Torino's Boys and Men with Guns: Hmong Perspectives." *Hmong Studies Journal* 10: 1–52.

Shifman, Limor. 2011. "An Anatomy of a YouTube Meme." *New Media and Society* 14(2): 187–203.

Shifman, Limor. 2013. *Memes in Digital Culture.* Cambridge: MIT Press.

Soha, Michael and Zachary J. McDowell. 2016. "Monetizing a Meme: YouTube, Content ID, and the Harlem Shake." *Social Media + Society* 2(1): 1–12.

Wilcox, Hui Nui. 2012. "The Mediated Figure of Hmong Farmer, Hmong Studies, and Asian American Critique." *Hmong Studies Journal* 13(1): 1–27.

15

ASIAN AMERICA ON DEMAND

Asian Americans, Media Networks, and a Matrix Stage

L. S. Kim

Introduction

The racial politics of the fall television season in the United States are pondered each year: Which programs include characters of color? Are there people of color hired as producers, writers, or directors? How does the new lineup look overall, in terms of diversity? There's a rhythm to the revisiting of these questions, a ritual that holds both drama and a quiet ending: the improvements are not enough, but it's a little better than last year. The demand for expanding what racial representation looks like is often misunderstood as complaining. As a result, small gestures of (public relations) placation are made, despite the fact that what is needed is a deeper historical and conceptual consideration. Yet, change is not inherently a goal for a mainstream media industry that functions on derivative content; creating what they already know has met certain (financial) criteria for success becomes a tautological justification for a conservative approach to making "new" films or television programs. There are three false premises on which Hollywood operates, and that viewers tend to believe:

1. Talking about race and the media is interpreted as "complaints" about racism, and diversity is about political correctness (rather than creativity). The conversation is already cast as negative.
2. Change automatically comes with time, and progress in racial representation is teleological. Being progressive, then, is displaced by passivity, with the belief/excuse that "things will get better in the future."
3. Viewers identify with characters who are "like" them,[1] so only Asian Americans can identify with Asian American lead characters on screen. This defies the reality of innumerable non-White people who have identified with main (that is, White) characters since the birth of cinema, as well as wholly underestimating the ability of White people to identify with characters of color and to have compassion for their stories or experiences.

Asian American representation is both a practice and a subject of inquiry that can stand to be better understood by Asian Americans, by broader audience members, by media producers, and by financial decision-makers.[2] For those who think that images are ideological and operate within a semiotic system, or at least who can accept that images signify and are not blithely neutral, the realm of film, television, and media is key to delivering (or correcting) information, fostering equality, and in some cases, inspiring justice. What is exciting about Asian Americans working in the media—as artists, producers, critics, consumers—is that doing so also contributes to making social change possible. What is problematic about Asian American representation is that through 100 years of American image culture, there remain relatively few and unvaried images of and imaginings about who and how Asian Americans can be in society.

In this chapter I address these concerns about Asian Americans and the media, asking: How can we remember a history of exclusion, both lived and cinematic, and yet also understand and assimilate popular cultural forms that are not directly politicized as part of what could be conceived of as the Asian American media movement? How can we expand the vocabulary related to Asian Americans and the media, and extend racial discourse to those not intuitively concerned about racial representation? I define representation as linked to what is at stake in Asian American cultural production and cultural citizenship: Representation is about the power to self-express, the power to belong, the power to command respect, and the power to demand equality within difference. I argue that Asian American representation and an engagement with popular media (both broadcast television and online) can be advanced through a collaborative (though not necessary a coordinated) effort among artists, producers, critics, and consumers. This is now taking place within what I call a *matrix stage*, a space where different forms of producing and consuming media overlap and blend, opening up new possibilities for collaboration and meaning making. It is this practice of participating in a matrix stage that can lead to cultural change through Asian American media.

After offering a historical background of Asian Americans and television that highlights the rise and fall of Asian American cable channels as failed forms of Asian American networks, I analyze a comparative case study that exemplifies the potential for the matrix stage: ABC's Asian American-centered sitcom *Fresh Off the Boat,* and an online counterpart, *Fresh Off the Show*, hosted by Phil Yu and Jenny Yang on Yu's YouTube channel. Blogger Yu (Angry Asian Man) and comedian Yang also have their own online show, *Angry Asian America*, on ISAtv. These examples of Asian American cultural production can be seen to shift the media landscape—or at least the place of Asian Americans within it—through a deep and necessary connection with fans and viewers, demonstrating a double meaning for "Asian American network." A growing awareness of the critical mass constituted by both makers and consumers will be essential in creating, challenging, enriching, playing with, and moving Asian American representation into different spaces and new directions.

Historical Background: Struggles with and against Representation

In thinking about Asian Americans and their relationship to media and visual culture, we can identify two primary struggles: with being represented at all, and with combating images that disempower, disparage, or dismiss the humanity of individuals of Asian descent. There is a desire for representations, but there is also a pre-conditioned fear that they will be damaging or humiliating. Expressing characters with complexity within standard genres is not easy, but generic limitations have not been a barrier for White characters and actors. In contrast, creating characters of color and acknowledging one's engagement in representing race produces angst for image producers, and is often avoided.

When the concept of diversity entered mainstream public discourse coupled with the (pejorative) term "politically correct" in the 1990s, the representation of race was taken more as a burden than as an opportunity. It didn't come "naturally" to an industry or culture accustomed to a representational system based on social hierarchy,[3] and there were few, if any, models of success. Rather, racial representation relied on the use of easy or racist tropes, the absence of portrayals in the first place, and the seeming refusal to allow for range in personalities, in genres, and in the kinds of relationships characters of color could have with White characters or with one another. Roadblocks include the areas of both writing and casting, as well as the fact that industry professionals and viewing audiences may have heard calls for diversity without understanding their meaning or value. By the 1990s, increasing attention was drawn to reports and protests by media organizations with regard to the lack of diversity on American screens (Lopez 2016). Studios and networks did respond—programs "colored up" by adding (supporting) characters, and several major television studios established writing programs to provide training and mentoring for screenwriters of color. Both of these, even if seemingly forced, were significant—especially given that the late 1980s and early 1990s marked the start of anti-affirmative-action legislation and sentiment.

The motivation for improvement generally comes from outside the industry, rather than from within. Media organizations and "watchdog groups" such as the Media Action Network for Asian Americans (MANAA) and the civil rights legal organization the Asian Pacific American Media Coalition (APAMC) push and protest for change. This includes staying vigilant in looking for specific films and television programs that practice racism, as well as weighing in before the fall television season begins. More recently, deliberate media activism has been joined by less formal social media activity constituted by a more ephemeral viewer-consumer. Opinions on social media range from superficial love-it-or-hate-it statements, to comments that serve as feedback to media makers, to political critiques that spark debate and generate news buzz. In the past, networks and their advertisers made decisions based on research on viewing habits and ratings; however, in an expanded social media world, their decisions are now taking into consideration online and digital media culture. As a result, fan-driven campaigns or dissatisfaction can be mobilized much more swiftly.

Within this context, we can then ask how a television program like *Fresh Off the Boat* emerged, and how it maintained a place on the broadcast schedule. Television has always been a more immediate "everyday" medium than film, due to film's long pre-production and production processes. Social and national events are quickly adapted and assimilated into television storylines, which makes programs intimate, familiar, and a closer part of our lives. There isn't the same kind of cinematic, voyeuristic distance as there is in the film experience. Viewers have become more discernibly participatory, putting into practice my earlier assertion that "Asian Americans need to communicate to networks the specific kinds of representations they desire" (Kim 2004). *Fresh Off the Boat* and its ancillary texts, such as *Fresh Off the Show*, demonstrate this form of communication. The fact that producers, agents, and others look to the internet to see how a television episode or performance/performer is doing, and that Asian Americans are forging a presence in those spaces, marks new possibilities for racial representation. Yet, we cannot understand these newer texts without first considering the history of Asian American television and the problems that have made these forms of representation difficult.

Asian American Cable Television Channels: Alternative Programming—the Problems of Categorization

Near the beginning of the 2000s, a new space emerged for Asian American representation through a handful of cable channels founded to provide content for an Asian American and Asian immigrant viewership. In March 2005, Comcast rebranded its International Channel to

AZN Television. The channel targeted fast-growing, young, affluent, English-speaking Asian American communities. Its programming included popular imported Asian films, dramatic series, documentaries, music, and anime, as well as a slate of original programming. AZN promoted itself as "the network for Asian America" and declared that "it speaks your language." In doing so, it began to stake out a space of belonging for Asian America, while its direct address served to acknowledge and value Asian Americans as viewers.

ImaginAsian Entertainment premiered in 2004 and focused on entertainment featuring Asian performers. The channel competed with AZN in some markets, such as New York, Los Angeles, and the San Francisco Bay Area. The company also operated The ImaginAsian, a renovated movie theatre in Midtown Manhattan. First-run and classic East Asian films were shown there, and it also hosted film festivals that allowed independent filmmakers to exhibit their films on a limited basis. Other ventures included an online magazine, iaRadio, and a film/DVD distribution division that released iaTV original programs and one of the more famous Asian American feature films, *Journey from the Fall* (2006), by Vietnamese American director Ham Tran.

During this era, MTV Networks launched several channels targeting specific national audiences: MTV-Desi, MTV-K, and MTV-Chi. Within two years, these three channels were cancelled for not attracting audiences or advertising revenue. Despite the decision also being shaped by corporate restructuring, Aswin Punathambekar concluded: "Given the fact that all other attempts to carve out a space for Asian American programming on television—AZN, American Desi, South Asia World, and ImaginAsian—had failed or struggled to remain viable, the dismay among Asian American groups was understandable" (Punathambekar 2009). AZN was shut down in January 2008, and ImaginAsian's offices were closed in late 2009. In 2011, ImaginAsian became the MNet television network, focusing on K-pop music and culture, which is not quite akin to Asian American programming or representation.

Myx TV is an Asian American cable television network based in Los Angeles and launched in 2007. It is available in cities including New York City, Los Angeles, and Honolulu on Time Warner Cable, and in Chicago and Seattle on Comcast. In May 2013, Myx TV launched an on-demand app on Roku. It has a website, Facebook page, and YouTube channel.[4] MyxTV's broadcast programming includes acquired material such as a Japanese sports game show, a K-pop variety show, and an original reality series called *I'm Asian American and …* that aired in 2014. The ten-episode docu-series focuses on "the Asian American diaspora, promising to show the 'lives of very different, very real people.' Each episode will follow a different person, including a lawyer who fights human trafficking, someone who does not identify as male or female, and a triplet whose siblings are autistic." Myx TV also produces events such as Myx Mash, a concert performance held in San Francisco in May 2010. Myx TV's *K-pop Takeover* was the first K-pop dance convention in the United States featuring K-pop choreographers and *America's Best Dance Crew* winners, Poreotics. The network does not have wide distribution and the fare is not highbrow, but Myx TV has its hands in several areas of pop culture; it is currently the only Asian American cable television channel.

Comcast/Xfinity has dedicated broadcast space and time to Asian American programming in the form of an on-demand movie service launched in 2010, "Cinema Asian America." Curator Chi-hui Yang had previously been the director and programmer of one of the largest Asian American film festivals in existence, the San Francisco International Asian American Film Festival, now known as CAAMFest (Center for Asian American Media Fest). Cinema Asian America is the only series or collection of its kind, and focuses on independent films.

These have all been important efforts. The fact that independent cable channels for Asian American audiences and programming did not take off tells us that it does not work to follow a traditional model of being one-sided and ratings-dependent. Moreover, I would argue that the channels were not successful or sustained because "Asian American" is not a genre. Yet, what these traditional broadcast channels have revealed is that there is an audience of culturally aware Asian Americans who are gaining a sense of cultural pride and status, and wanting to help define "Asian American" beyond what a limited set of well-intentioned and corporate-sanctioned producers were able to showcase. Perhaps the lesson is that the notion of niche is not fitting when it comes to the production and consumption of Asian American representation. Asian American content and audiences are not neatly categorized or strictly located as one small market segment. Rather, the consumption and enjoyment of media material by Asian Americans are polymorphous; Asian American cultural production and consumption are transmediated and historically informed—not simply part of a technological trend.

Asian Americans Taking the Stage: "A Matrix Stage"

Asian Americans have long demonstrated facility with media production, as other authors from this collection have shown. As a result, there is often a contradictory dynamic between an understated ("quiet") usage of media by Asian Americans as political/representational minorities and as adventurers experimenting and playing with, even intervening in, media culture. Asian Americans are playing with the simultaneity of margin and center. The dichotomy between margin and center is both mythic and real. On the one hand, because of social and political exclusion, historical erasure, and ignorant dismissal of the contributions Asian Americans do and can make to U.S. society and culture, Asian Americans are disallowed high status in U.S. society. On the other hand, Asian American performers and artists are proving that operating on the margins—often by choice and by design—can be a strategy for entry, though "going mainstream" is not necessarily the goal. Furthermore, as bell hooks (1990) reminds us, being on the margin, or being a minority, is not necessarily a position of powerlessness.

Artists who distribute work via the internet acknowledge (usually obliquely, or by virtue of their chosen alternative platform) that there are institutional barriers, but they show both a desire for wider recognition and a satisfaction and gratitude for the subcultural support generated. For example, a number of YouTube musicians have income-generating careers apart from the dominant music industry, including Clara C., Kina Grannis, David Choi, and Jane Lui. There are top YouTube channels with figures such as comedians Ryan Higa/Nigahiga and Kevin Wu/KevJumba, Christine Gambino/Happy Slip, the producers of Wong Fu Productions, filmmaker Freddie Wong, director Jon Chu, and makeup artist and entrepreneur Michelle Phan, for whom the internet has been a forum to forge successful careers both on- and offline. YOMYOMF, both a blog and a group YouTube channel, is another example of a platform(s) through which Asian American artists have demonstrated defiance, confidence, craft, and community. Inspired and supported by director Justin Lin, one of their projects was a short film competition designed to offer access to professional filmmaking industries. The competition, called "Interpretations," was announced at the Asian American film festival in San Francisco, CAAMfest, and was officially presented by YOMYOMF and sponsored by Comcast, NBC/Universal. Justin Lin described the impetus behind the competition:

> There might be a talented filmmaker living out someplace like the Midwest and they just don't have any industry contacts or know how to get started but they love to make films and videos … This is a way to find those filmmakers who we may

> otherwise never stumble upon and who may not know how to take their career to the next level. We believe the talent is out there and we want to provide them with access.
>
> (Bai 2016)

These different media figures do not follow the presumed uni-directional margin-to-center trajectory. Rather, Asian American artists are creating alternative models of stardom, fandom, and the marketplace. In turn, there is movement, back and forth, between the margins and the so-called center.

I call this space where margin and mainstream intermingle a *matrix stage*: where work can be consumed, grown, scouted, funded, added to, reiterated, and transferred to different physical and virtual platforms. While not completely tactical or directly political, I define Asian American media practices both in terms of consumers and as products consumed, and with the relationship between margin and mainstream forming a matrix rather than a linear spectrum. Within the matrix stage, the perceptual environments of Asian Americans shift—for example, from film to television to online, from the direct performative texts to the criticism of/critical response to these texts, and from mainstream to what is generally understood as ethnic programming. At the same time, we can also note that there has been a propensity for race-neutrality within Asian Americans, whereby race consciousness slips in and out of Asian American artistic and aesthetic discourses. The matrix stage is a practice and a method whereby Asian Americans can collaborate and maneuver, as minorities and as non-essentialized, across spaces and venues, to represent Asian American perspectives and themselves—often deliberately, but not always so. There is overlap and simultaneity of racial identification, cultural awareness, ethnic specificity, and also "just wanting to be."

The matrix stage is comprised of venues such as broadcast television, cable television, online series, internet channels, and live performances. It includes stars, artists, directors, producers, writers, and bloggers, as well as informal participants such as commentators, audiences, and fans. Asian American television culture in the age of new media is marked by an intermingling of all of these, facilitated by the still relatively small number of Asian American media artists who are able to be or become acquainted with one another. Asian American viewers-producers who watch a program or follow a favorite star are able to access a surprisingly close network of other Asian American productions, performers, and fellow fans. In entering "the matrix," one is joining a community. This experience is often a welcome invitation to see and celebrate "people like me" taking up the screen. Furthermore, it is a form of affirmation, a statement of optimism about Asian American social presence, and a call to power.

This strategy of uniting multi-platform performers and calling upon viewer participation through various forms of fandom can be seen as part of a larger movement to develop, grow, and make known Asian American audiences. In order to increase Asian American visibility, the visibility of Asian American viewers-consumers must also be raised. Asian American audiences must become involved, because this user-savvy minority group is starting to catch the eye of executives and decision-makers, and because dependence on mainstream/White audiences is not going to bring about change. The growing percentage of Asian Americans within the United States population is not quite relevant, as the calculus regarding media consumption has changed and become more complex. Strict Nielsen ratings and other measurement data are being augmented by viewing practices that include engagements with new media, social media, and alternative media. These activities, when framed within a matrix stage, demonstrate a cultural practice in which Asian American artists and fans are engaging that can potentially provoke changes in the larger media culture.

Fresh Off the Boat and *Fresh Off the Show*: A Contingent Practice

We can now examine a multifaceted case that reveals the potential for such a matrix stage, particularly as it has become dependent on digital media cultures. The International Secret Agents (ISA) are the members of the band Far East Movement and the members of Wong Fu Productions, who together co-founded a concert series in 2008. In 2013, they came together again to produce a YouTube channel called ISAtv, which they describe on their website as a "premiere platform for celebrating Asian Youth Culture and its global influence." ISAtv has garnered millions of online views and fans from around the world, who tune in for interviews, music videos, premieres, short films, and game shows. As television scholars are beginning to recognize, the question of where TV resides and what it can achieve has expanded beyond what the industry has traditionally understood (Lotz 2014). Yet, the philosophy of ISAtv returns to a kind of democratic idealism in believing that television can help facilitate community, identity, and coalition, though on a minor/ity scale rather than a sweeping national or "mass" scale. It is and it isn't "television." The engagements through ISAtv are both popular and culturally specific, with mainstream musical art forms or genres, for example, and also "marginal" senses of style, humor, and aesthetics.

ISAtv producers approached Phil Yu, who had developed credibility through his popular and longstanding news blog angryasianman.com, to create a new show for their channel in 2014. Along with his co-host comedian Jenny Yang, they created *Angry Asian America*. The 12 episodes of its first season cover informal conversations about topics such as bullying, racist rants against Asians, what the events in Ferguson, MO and #BlackLivesMatter mean for Asian Americans, and questions such as "Is the golden age for Asian Americans on YouTube over?" and "Do your tweets create social change?" Yu and Yang invite and interview guests, together discussing acting and casting vis-à-vis Asian Americans, critiquing media, film, and television, MTV, and Disney. ISAtv renewed *Angry Asian America* for a second season (though Yu and Yang do not receive payment, as this is a different model of production). *Angry Asian America*'s first episode of the second season is titled "More Asian Americans on TV!?" ISAtv and *Angry Asian America* were thus in full swing in the fall of 2015, when ABC became the first network in history to have three series featuring first-billed Asian American leads on air at the same time (as well as 18 recurring roles played by Asian American actors). In addition to *Fresh Off the Boat*, the network debuted *Dr. Ken*, a sitcom featuring Ken Jeong, and an FBI thriller called *Quantico*, headlined by Bollywood star Priyanka Chopra. (Although Priyanka Chopra is an Indian actress, rather than Asian American, she is noted here because her character in *Quantico*, Alex Parrish, is Asian American.) According to the advocacy organization APAMC, *FOB*'s success depended on the fact that 60 percent of its audience is White, and that it is the No. 1 television program among Asian Americans. APAMC co-chair Daniel Mayeda stated: "It's a culmination of years of advocacy … Finally people figured out diversity is not just something you do to get community groups off your back, this is a way to make money. This is something we've been telling them for over a decade. The data is now bearing that out" (Ge 2015).

Although these explanations center advocacy and profitability, the show's success also reveals a new structure that is now in place and practiced—that is, a matrix stage, on and through which Asian Americans are engaging in self-representation. A thriving social media culture enhances this possibility for self-representation and for a kind of feedback: specifically, for Asian Americans to "talk back" to industry professionals. For example, through campaigns started by organizations such as @18millionrising, or through the outcry surrounding #CancelColbert,[5] we can see that Asian Americans are reacting in a context where numerous or anonymous voices previously were not recognized.

The power of this form of participation has been openly recognized by the television networks, as became apparent at a special advanced screening event of the pilot at Visual Communications, an Asian American media organization in Los Angeles. During the Q & A panel after the screening with network executives, I raised my hand and asked: "Considering all the excitement already generated for *FOB*, in particular by Asian Americans, what will be the measure of success for the show from the network's perspective?" Samie Kim Falvey, executive vice president of Comedy Development at ABC, answered that ratings would not be the only measure. She said that "ABC is looking to see what buzz" the show generates. She also implied that there was an expectation that the "buzz" would be informal and grown from Asian Americans. In other words, informal community response mattered, and would impact formal decision-making about the future of the primetime enterprise. A community screening such as this one in Little Tokyo was not merely a fringe event; rather, the Asian American gathering was also part of a mainstream marketing plan. It was both self-celebratory and a kind of focus group intended to help create excitement about the new series. Asian American subcultural and social media networks were specifically understood as a potential mechanism for helping this program take off. Likewise, a number of people (bloggers, writers, online artists) understood tacitly what was being asked of them.

On February 10, 2015, a week after *FOB* premiered, Phil Yu and Jenny Yang started hosting *Fresh Off the Show*. This unofficial *Fresh Off the Boat* aftershow streamed live after every episode. It was created by hosting a Google Hangout during which viewers/participants could send in or live-tweet questions and comments, and these fresh-off-the-air videos would be preserved on YouTube. In the first episode, Yu and Yang state that "there's a conversation to be had" around what *FOB* was conjuring up: for example, questions about representation, production, Eddie Huang,[6] and claims/criticisms about what is authentic, as well as themes or experiences brought up in the episodes. More importantly, they emphasized that "we're going to keep the conversation going."

The aftershow provides a forum for viewers to react and share; for its two smart, informed, and funny hosts to comment, contextualize, praise, and ask guiding questions; and to feature guests including the cast and writers of *FOB* along with additional special guests, such as Asian American actors. The tone is generally upbeat, informal, and humorous, providing the opportunity for questions to be raised regarding the production but also keeping things positive and fairly light. A range of emotions are shared—including amazement, elation, and appreciation of the fact that representations are deeply affirming. Nostalgia and cultural pride also are part of the feel of the aftershow, which is a little like an afterparty with Asian snacks. I see it as a concerted effort to extend the life of the broadcast television program, and to demonstrate to network executives the kind of buzz it was looking for. It is not necessarily the case that *FOS* reaches mass audiences, but, rather, that it invites and inspires generative engagements with *FOB* through viewers who are tweeting and retweeting, liking various Facebook pages, Googling subjects related to and including the show, posting comments online, talking with friends about the show, and watching episodes on demand. Yu's Angry Asian Man blog receives nearly half a million hits each month, and so his posts about the show and its content are potent. Additionally, I think I am not the only professor who has created assignments connected to *Fresh Off the Boat* for students to watch the program, log in to the aftershow, and study the *FOB* Facebook page. I even had a student who live-tweeted throughout various broadcasts. Although there is a sense of immediacy and liveness to *FOS*, Yang jokes that they count "Live +3"—meaning that viewership is gauged three days after the initial air/post date. Similarly to ABC, Yu and Yang are not so much concerned with the initial number as with keeping *FOB* circulating in popular culture.

FOB is groundbreaking in a number of ways. It is culturally and ethnically specific, showcasing Chinese and Taiwanese American culture while also not arguing that all Taiwanese immigrants are like the Huangs; the three children are different from each other; an intergenerational household is shown without the assumption that assimilation is eventual and inevitable; Randall Park's accent faded away by the end of the first season, while Constance Wu's stayed; the costuming and periodization in the 1990s reinforce their Americanness; the Huangs are a loving couple and a caring family; the members of the Huang family live and work and go to school in an integrated context, portraying Chineseness or Asian Americanness as a negotiated part of an American experience; Asian is not Other, and Whiteness is not necessarily the ideal.[7] Finally (or first), the producing and creative teams include Asian Americans, some of whom have actively tapped into the networks of Asian American independent or informal cultural producers.

Network decision-makers can see that audiences are engaged with the series in ways that expand beyond the broadcast. *FOB* performed well in its first season, although weekly ratings and viewership decreased slightly. Nevertheless, the series was renewed for a second season. *FOB* had its second season premiere on September 22, 2015, and *FOS* followed with the Huang brothers (the three actors who play Eddie, Emery, and Evan) hanging out with Yu and Yang, catching up like old friends after summer and talking about the episode. Yu also admitted that he was offering "free plugs" for ABC by telling viewers that the *FOB* DVD would soon be available.

This is how Asian Americans are engaging in Asian American representation—and in doing so, helping to forge a matrix stage in which Asian Americans as consumers-producers matter. The "Asian America" that AZN and ImaginAsian struggled to aim for has not crystallized through the passage of time or the development of new digital and affordable/accessible technologies, and "Asian American identity" has not necessarily stabilized or unified politically. Rather, a more confident self-claiming of Asian America comes through a shared experience of producing-and-consuming among people who have a sense of familiarity and equality, and who feel in relationship with one another. Asian Americans as audiences finally feel needed, because this is the case. Their role in increasing and improving the representation of Asian Americans has finally been recognized as significant and potent.

Conclusion: Redefining the Limits of Television and Producing the Self

Why are we seeking Asian American representation? The root answer from the time when Hollywood cinema was born remains: that invisibility and misrepresentation are disempowering and dangerous. But in a new digital viewing/consuming universe in which Asian Americans have demonstrated incredible facility (as well as pleasure) with new media cultures, we can re-ask and re-answer the question of what is at stake in seeing Asian Americans on screen. I caution those wanting to believe in a teleology of progress when it comes to racial representation—that things get better over time—as this idea is false and passive. At the same time, the increase in Asian American cultural production and the multi-fold ways that it is happening demand recognition.

The kind of "direct address" contact with viewers that the cable channels previously attempted now happens with ease via the internet. Familiar, friendly, DIY, humble, with an articulated sense of "community," and with great display of appreciation for online supporters, Asian American content is provided in relation to what viewers seem to like and enjoy—what they "demand." Asian Americans are seeking alternative spaces for visibility, as viewers and as makers. In terms of media culture, Asian Americans are solidifying and amplifying their networks, and in doing so, they are asserting what Lori Kido Lopez (2016) has theorized as different forms of cultural citizenship. Asian American artists and viewers-producers are taking up transmedia mechanisms to establish themselves as performers, fans, critics, and above all, as citizens. They are interacting in a matrix where race is made and unmade, credited and dismissed, discussed and negotiated. Comment threads can be (and often are) vitriolic, unabashed, raw "conversations" about the significance of race and the very merits of how race matters.

In order for there to be more Asian American representations, Asian Americans must participate in generating visibility on screen(s), and as media viewer-producers. We see this taking place in the fact that while Asian Americans have access to an infinite number of viewers, they work to create a more defined sense of community. This includes fans, but Asian American viewers also feel they are a part of an inspired group who know that their support (their views, their "likes," their retweets) is helping to build Asian American representation. It is a collaboration. The trajectory of Asian Americans in television culture, and for Asian American Studies more broadly, involves a number of figures: artists, performers, producers, critics, curators, and consumers who also produce culture. What has helped to bring about more, and more varied, Asian American representation is the creative control, the impulse to collaborate, and the ability to participate among all of the above-named positions.

We must recognize the emergence of a new mode of production—a matrix stage, whereby Asian American viewers are active and participatory in generating a legible response to mainstream texts. They are creating content primarily for Asian Americans via alternative platforms, which possess complicated relationships to mainstream media. The dialectic between margin and mainstream is being addressed in a matrix space where Asian Americans are representing, creating, consuming, and even enjoying themselves. What "television" beyond TV encourages is a mode that is not aspirational but relational. With a sense of intimacy and possibility that Asian American media creators share in such forums as *Fresh Off the Show*, *Angry Asian America*, and ISAtv, as well as through instructional or competitive opportunities to literally enter media production, Asian American cultural production is invitational. It is an invitation that we must heartily accept.

Notes

1 Or disidentify in attempt to reject racialization, or in an act of self-loathing.

2 Scholars, such as Kent Ono, Vincent Pham, Lori Kido Lopez, Leilani Nishime, Tasha Oren, Shilpa Davé, Lisa Nakamura, Peter Feng, Darrell Hamamoto, Renee Tajima-Peña, Sylvia Chong, Jane Park, Gina Marchetti, and Jun Okada, who continue to theorize and write about it provide one kind of advocacy.

3 By hierarchy, I mean patriarchy and White supremacy/White privilege, the notion of a meritocratic middle class, and Western religion and heterosexuality as the desired norm.

4 AZN and ImaginAsian had websites, both of which are no longer running; ImaginAsian's Facebook page is still up, with accessible videos posted in 2007 and 2008.

5 #CancelColbert was a hashtag that responded to the use of a fake Asian accent and (intentionally) "bad Asian joke" on *The Colbert Report* in May 2015.

6 Celebrity chef Eddie Huang, on whose memoir the television series is based, has engaged in his own buzz/static, ultimately seeming to disown the show. He has made statements (earlier on) in support of the effort for there to be an Asian American program, as well as making scathing comments about how far the program has strayed and sold out; Huang no longer provides the voice-over narration.

7 These are almost point-by-point differences from *All American Girl* (1994–1995), which was made, and canceled, 20 years before *Fresh Off the Boat* on the same network. See Margaret Cho's show *I'm the One That I Want* to learn about the demoralizing, health-threatening experience and how she "failed" at performing herself.

References

Bai, Stephany. 2016. "Justin Lin Revives 'Interpretations' Asian-American Short Film Initiative," *NBC News*, March 11. http://www.nbcnews.com/news/asian-america/justin-lin-revives-interpretations-asian-american-short-film-initiative-n536941.

Cho, Margaret. *Margaret Cho: I'm the One That I Want*. Cho Taussig Productions, 2000.

Ge, Linda. 2015. "How ABC Is Trailblazing Path for Asians on TV with 'Fresh Off the Boat,' 'Dr. Ken,' 'Quantico'," *TheWrap.com*, 29 September. http://www.thewrap.com/how-abc-is-trailblazing-path-for-asians-on-tv-with-fresh-off-the-boat-dr-ken-quantico/.

Hamamoto, Darrell and Sandra Liu. 2000. *Countervisions: Asian American Film Criticism*. Philadelphia: Temple University Press.

hooks, bell. 1990. "Choosing the Margin as a Space of Radical Openness." In *Yearning: Race, Gender, and Cultural Politics*. Boston, MA: South End Press.

Jacobs, Gary. *All American Girl*. Sandollar Television, 1994–1995.

Khan, Nahnatchka. 2015. *Fresh Off the Boat*. Fierce Baby Productions.

Kim, L. S. 2004. "Be the One That You Want: Asian Americans in Television Culture, Onscreen and Beyond." *Amerasia Journal* 30(1): 125–146.

Lopez, Lori Kido. 2016. *Asian American Media Activism: Fighting for Cultural Citizenship*. New York: New York University Press.

Lotz, Amanda. 2014. *The Television Will Be Revolutionized*. New York: New York University Press.

Okada, Jun. 2015. *Making Asian American Film and Video: History, Institutions, Movements*. New Brunswick, New Jersey: Rutgers University Press.

Ono, Kent and Vincent Pham. 2009. *Asian Americans and the Media*. Cambridge; Malden, MA: Polity.

Punathambekar, Aswin. 2009. "What Brown Cannot Do for You: MTV-Desi, Diasporic Youth Culture, and the Limits of Television," *FlowTV* 10 (2), http://www.flowjournal.org/2009/06/what-brown-cannot-do-for-you-mtv-desi-diasporic-youth-culture-and-the-limits-of-televisionaswin-punathambekarthe-university-of-michigan/.

16

REFLECTIONS ON #SOLIDARITY

Intersectional Movements in AAPI Communities

Rachel Kuo

On December 15, 2013, Suey Park started a conversation about Asian American feminism on Twitter under the hashtag #NotYourAsianSidekick. The hashtag pushed conversations around Asian American feminism to the forefront of both Asian American and feminist online communities, and demanded a space where the two digital publics could converge. #NotYourAsianSidekick produced many conversations in mainstream media, popular media, and academic outlets about the efficacy of hashtags in activism and the many ways that Twitter has been used by racial justice activists. Since its origins in 2006, the platform has provided opportunity for discourse, education, demonstration, organization, and community-building. It is positioned within the larger realm of social media such as Facebook posts, Tumblr blogs, and Instagram images, which re-mediate print media materials like flyers, newsletters, and posters. As part of a strategic and intentional process, the use of hashtags on Twitter can drive discourse about race and racism to generate more visibility for racial justice movements. The hashtag's power lies in the massive number of contributors, as more tweets enhance a message's complexity and elevate its reach. While hashtag activism is relatively new to social movement practice, the messages of #NotYourAsianSidekick are not new (Fang 2013; Ma 2013). Hashtags extend and expand ongoing struggles to shift cultural politics around racial discourse, and in this particular case, help us to better understand the intersection between anti-racism and feminism.

In this chapter, I compare samples of print and digital media materials that articulate discourses of solidarity from the lens of Asian American and Pacific Islander (AAPI)[1] women who are working to build a more intersectional feminist, anti-racist movement. These discourses can be seen as examples of intersectionality and solidarity in practice, and reveal the ways that hashtags on Twitter function as a tool for unity and specificity. The print materials come from Asian Women United (AWU)'s archives (1976–1989) and the archives of the Asian American Legal Defense Fund (1973–1993) and Asian Cinevision (1978–1990). They include letters, newsletters, pamphlets, article clippings, and brochures that reflect attempts on the part of these organizations to form women's coalitions and participate in broader movements. These archival materials help provide the background for this specific historical moment in intersectional identity-making and community-building within the Asian American feminist movement. I then compare these findings with contemporary hashtags on Twitter that represent gestures of solidarity either within the AAPI community or as extensions beyond. These include #NotYourAsianSidekick, #ModelMinorityMutiny, and #APIs4BlackLives/#Asians4BlackLives. These hashtags follow a narrative arc from December 2013 to December 2014 and can be seen as contributing to the formation of an AAPI feminist counterpublic that can "engage in debate with wider publics to test ideas and perhaps utilize traditional social movement tactics" (Squires 2002: 448).

Hashtags operate as social movement tools for AAPI feminist communities to collectively disseminate information, discuss their needs, and make demands. Making subversive use of both visibility and invisibility, AAPI feminists who have been perceived as "invisible" can use hashtags to make their presence and message more visible to mainstream publics dominated by whiteness. Hashtags also generate counter-discourse around racial hierarchies and demonstrate effective ways of building solidarity. They are a specific tool whose use at specific moments can extend and expand existing movements and discourse, particularly when focusing on forging bonds of solidarity and addressing intersectionality. In considering linkages between AAPI feminists and other activist collectives, I am interested in moving away from isolating the hashtag as a "singular confrontation racialized/gendered users are having with white audiences within a white space" (Kim 2015). In reading these tweets alongside archival print materials, I argue that hashtags can be seen to represent relationships—between the AAPI feminist counterpublic disseminating the message, other AAPI and feminist counterpublics, and also activist counterpublics, including Black Lives Matter activists. When working toward forming solidarity with other racial communities, AAPIs must examine the intersectionality of their own identities and communities and consider who is currently excluded or silenced among themselves. Through this investigation, we can see how hashtags draw attention to intersectionality and function as material forms of solidarity during a particular historical moment, as well as how hashtags function as limited tools in a long, ongoing movement.

Generating Feminist Consciousness among Asian American and Pacific Islander Women

The AAPI community is made up of many communities that are vastly diverse, which also means that the ways these different communities experience oppression can be very different from one another. Their divergent histories of oppression due to U.S. imperialism and xenophobic racism have created barriers to collective identification and organization (Chow 1982). As a result, AAPI social justice organizers have often sought to create unity in their work, including promoting solidarity among themselves and with other communities of color. Yet, one of the difficulties of creating solidarity is that identities such as race and gender can seem to be at odds with one another. For instance, AAPI women have needed to address sexism and heterosexism from within the larger AAPI movement, as well as racism from within the larger feminist movement (Chow 1982).

The mainstream feminist movement has long been criticized for being driven by the needs and desires of middle-class White women. This focus on addressing sexism from a White middle-class cultural context excludes women of color because White feminism operates from an assumption that all women share similar experiences—ignoring oppressions due to race, socioeconomic status, nationality, religion, and history (Chai 1985). Gender becomes constructed around White gender norms, which creates racialized gender constructions for women of color. Yet, the issues AAPI women face are distinctly racialized—they are perceived as hyperfeminine, passive, weak, submissive, and exotic objects. This portrayal of femininity and sexuality for consumption by men narrowly restricts AAPI women's expressions of gender and sexuality (Pyke and Johnson 2003). Alice Yun Chai (1985) further notes that AAPI women have not been given the time and space to reflect on experiences and evolve consciousness around oppression as Asians and as women, and that they have been socialized "to believe they did little worth writing about" (62). As a result, AAPI women began developing a feminist consciousness outside of the experiences of the mainstream feminist movement (Chow 1982), organizing informally to develop racial and gender consciousness and increase visibility. They also began to participate and align with women of color organizations in creating counterpublics.

Catherine Squires' model of the Black public sphere (2002) accounts for the many different ways a marginalized group can respond to the mainstream—recognizing that marginalized groups are not homogeneous, and in fact create multiple spaces for communicating among themselves and with others. Her models draw on Nancy Fraser's idea of "subaltern counterpublics" (1992), where members of marginalized groups circulate "counter discourses" that create different interpretations and representations of identities and interests. Both Fraser and Squires indicate ways that public spheres can be fragmented and intersectional, but Squires' model is particularly useful in the way it acknowledges the political intersections of identity. Theories of intersectionality are premised on the multiple axes of situated knowledge, evidence, and experiences at the intersection of sexism, racism, classism, nativism, and language discrimination (Chun et al. 2013; Crenshaw 1989). A framework of intersectionality offers a "both/and" approach to identity-making and supports the creation of a strategic, collective, and political struggle that allows AAPI women to start forging coalitions within their identity group and also extend outward toward coalitions across other identity groups to align strategically with other women of color.

Beyond coalitions, or strategic organizational partnerships around a singular issue, solidarity, then, depends upon the practice of intersectionality. Atshan and Moore (2014) state that "solidarities are formed through multidirectional relationships—connections that require a type of self-reflexive work on both the person who is directly impacted ... and the ally" (680). Solidarity statements are material forms of these reciprocities. We can define a solidarity statement as one that follows a simple formula: defining the communities involved, defining the relationship, and articulating the existing system of oppression. Often, motives of solidarity are depicted as the offering of specific experiences of struggle faced by one community and sharing how this connects with the specific experiences faced by the other community—the solidarity statement is, then, a recognition of mutual interlocking oppression. Below, we will see ways that AAPI women have negotiated solidarity with each other as well as with other women of color communities. In order to better understand the formation of AAPI feminist counterpublics and the meaning of solidarity within them, we can look at documents from the AWU during the 1980s.

AWU and the Claiming of Intersectional Solidarity

The Coalition of Asian Women's Groups' statement of purpose opens with a nod to the multiple identities possessed by Asian women. It describes diversity across ethnicity, national origin, age, sexuality, class, citizenship status, politics, and more:

> We are women of Chinese, Japanese, Korean, Filipino, Indian, and other Asian ancestry—young women and older women ... workers and professionals; heterosexual

> women and lesbians; American-born and Asian born; women who hold diverse political beliefs. We are Asian women who have similar histories and share similar experiences. Identifying with one another, we have come together to explore and attempt to resolve issues that affect all of us as Asian women in America.
>
> (Coalition of Asian Women's Groups 1980)

Despite all the different representative identities, the coalition purports to foster solidarity through finding commonality in experience and history. In establishing a community of "Asian women in America," this statement of purpose expresses both unity as well as specificity. It further states:

> Our voices have all too often been turned into whispers, and our faces into invisible masks. Through simplistic caricatures, racism denies us the right to be who we are. We Asian women will fight for self-determination, for the right to define our own situations and to act accordingly. Sexism is like racism in that it exploits our images and transfixes us in stereotypes. However, as Asian women we are marred doubly by xenophobia and misogyny.
>
> (Coalition of Asian Women's Groups 1980)

Here, the coalition discusses the invisibility of Asian women from both the Asian American and the feminist movement, as well as the way invisibility has led to the false construction of Asian American femininity into stereotypes. Racial stereotyping denies recognition and representation of both identity and experience. The coalition's statement continues to unify the struggle of Asian American women through calling attention to the dual oppression of racism and sexism:

> We have benefitted from the struggles of the predominantly White feminist movement. However, we must necessarily expand our vision to integrate and develop our Asian and female identities.
>
> (Coalition of Asian Women's Groups 1980)

While feminists and Asian American activists have supported Asian American women in a general way, the coalition asks for their own space for identity formation and community-building, and then a way for those identities and communities to be recognized and represented—made visible—to existing movements.

We can see this desire reiterated in a *New York Times* article in 1980, whose headline reads "Asian-American Women: A Bid for Visibility" (Special to *The New York Times* 1980). The article discusses the first National Asian/Pacific American Women's Conference, where 400 women of Japanese, Chinese, Korean, Filipino, Burmese, Vietnamese, Samoan, Tongan, Hawaiian, and Guamanian descent came together to create a politicized national network focused on addressing inequities in employment and education. The network sought to make Asian Pacific American women more visible in the political sphere. Although the group were predominantly middle class, they were concerned with addressing the "model minority myth." An article published in *Ms. Gazette* quoted Tin Myaing Thein in discussing how the myth created tensions between "Asians" and "Pacific Islanders": "Asians are thought of as the goody-good, exotic, sexy, real smart, never rock-the-boat types, while textbooks portray Pacific Islanders as the good-natured but not very smart people" (Thein quoted in Look 1980). Thein captures the different ways that Asians and indigenous Pacific Islanders have been stereotypically racialized, which created intra-community fractures. Much of the work of the inaugural National Asian/Pacific American Women's Conference and formation of the Coalition of Asian Women's Groups was to create a space for AAPI women to unite as one community, while simultaneously specifying the many identities and experiences represented within this community.

Beyond deconstructing the myth of the model minority, we can also see the way that these organizations worked toward building solidarity with other women of color organizations. For instance, AWU worked with WREE (Women for Racial and Economic Equality) in proposing a women's bill of rights. Like other solidarity statements, the bill opens by defining the community:

> We are Black, white, Chicano, Puerto Rican, Asian and Native American women. We are workers, trade unionists, unemployed, housewives, welfare recipients, professionals, students and senior citizens.
>
> (Women for Racial and Economic Equality 1980)

The bill then defines the oppression experienced by the community and their demands. In this statement, we can see the way that political intersectionality addresses oppression across multiple systems:

> We are women witnessing a daily deterioration of our living standards as the economic crisis in our country grows deeper.... We are women demanding a say in the future of our country and an end to all forms of male supremacy. We are women whose experiences have shown that racism is the major obstacle to bettering our living conditions in any real or meaningful way. Our organization strives for unity of all women based on a principled program of struggle to end racism in all its forms. We are women who are united with our sisters throughout the world under the banner of world peace and equality for women.
>
> (Women for Racial and Economic Equality 1980)

Later, in 1978, AWU drafted a statement in support of affirmative action movements, which read:

> Whereas as Asian American woman we feel a double prejudice, as women and as minorities; whereas poverty exists in a society controlled by the wealthy; whereas political and economic racism and sexism exist to limit the opportunities and the equal status of minority and poor men and women in a predominantly white and male oriented society.
>
> (Asian Women United 1978)

This statement expresses solidarity across race and gender, addresses intersections of racism, sexism, and classism faced by AAPI women, and demonstrates consciousness around power dynamics controlled by White masculinity.

Decades later, these power dynamics remain. Despite post-Civil Rights discourses about the United States as a "postracial" multicultural society, racism, sexism, and other forms of systemic oppression continue to disenfranchise women of color. Digital discourses must be recognized as a continuation of this work in fostering the visibility of AAPI feminism. Yet, these relationships also operate differently in digital spaces, as intersectional formations of solidarity across multiple identities manifest in networked relationships. On Twitter, hashtags can reflect specific racial and cultural codes, mediating individual participation in a larger community and collective discourse in real time (Brock 2009). Hashtags provide the opportunity for participants in a community to be visible to one another and occasionally for the interests to be visible to the dominant public, whether intentionally or unintentionally. But let us consider in particular the way that hashtags can be used to develop solidarity.

Hashtags as Articulations of Solidarity and Disruptions

Solidarity is built upon an ongoing and consistent commitment. According to hooks, "Solidarity is not the same as support. To experience solidarity, we must have a community of interests, shared beliefs and goals around which to unite" (hooks 2012). Sustained support cannot be based on self-interest, such as guilt or merely wanting to feel good about helping. From this understanding of solidarity, we can see that Twitter hashtags alone do not form solidarity and cannot be the only expression of solidarity. However, hashtags can nevertheless be interpreted as signifiers of solidarity, as their collective digital presence becomes a material record of reciprocal commitments. Quick, one-button acts of retweeting and liking demonstrate that a user is in agreement, and also further circulate a message to different networks. Other types of responses, such as writing a new tweet or replying to a tweet, demonstrate this as well, and also additionally provide material labor by producing discourse. These forms of participation offer an "experience of 'real time' engagement [and] community" (Bonilla and Rosa 2015: 7).

Hashtags can also serve to disrupt dominant ideologies. Mainstream media cultures have repetitively constructed people of color into racial stereotypes. Hashtags can be used by racial justice movements as media counterpoints, offering different representations and perspectives that disrupt harmful racial logics. Because ideologies work most effectively when they are unconscious practice (Hall 1981), strategically constructed hashtags are well positioned to intervene and disrupt the dominant public's complacency around certain ideologies. As participants connect their own experiences, identities, and perspectives to the hashtag, the hashtag also archives and links together discourse as part of an "intertextual chain" that represents a heterogeneous community of many voices (Bonilla and Rosa 2015). The articulated discourse under the activist hashtag begins to connect with the many complicated social conditions of racial injustice (Hall 1981). To give a few examples: #BlackLivesMatter first launched to disrupt the normalization of police targeting and brutality against Black bodies; #SayHerName disrupts the accepted erasure of Black women in media narratives about police violence; #Solidarityisforwhitewomen disrupts embedded White feminist logics that excluded women of color; #IAmNotYourWedge disrupts the ways Asian Americans are used as a tool for oppression by the White dominant public to deny justice for others. When these racial justice activist hashtags are used over and over again, they become part of a counter-ideological discourse about whose bodies and rights are valued.

The particular hashtags I investigate with regard to AAPI activism function as articulations of solidarity and disruptions of hegemonic ideologies. Moreover, they offer AAPIs a way to unite while also expressing specificity. The unity and specificity combined give hashtags the potential of bringing intersectionality into movements and practicing cross-community solidarity. #NotYourAsianSidekick aims to both unite Asian and Pacific Islander American women together as well as to designate space for expressions of various intersecting identities. Later, #ModelMinorityMutiny and #Asians4BlackLives aim to unite AAPIs through reciprocal solidarity practices with the Black counterpublic. As Lisa Lowe (1991) states, the "articulation of an 'Asian American identity' as an organizing tool has provided a concept of political unity [but] essentializing Asian American identity and suppressing our differences … inadvertently supports the racist discourse that constructs Asians as a homogeneous group" (30). Tweets using hashtags allow participants to express their many identities, histories, and experiences to the digital public while also expressing unity with one another.

AAPI Hashtag Activism

We can now examine some of the specific conversations that took place using hashtags that centered on Asian American feminism and activism. First, #NotYourAsianSidekick focused on intersectional feminism in the AAPI community. This hashtag followed closely after #Solidarityisforwhitewomen, which was a wider counterpublic critique of White feminism by feminists of color. Suey Park, who originated the #NotYourAsianSidekick hashtag, began the conversation by creating and claiming space and visibility for AAPI women:

> #NotYourAsianSidekick: This is beginning because for too long I've complained about not having an AAPI space that represents me.
> Suey Park (@sueypark), December 15, 2013, 10:42 am
> Nobody will GIVE us a space. We need to MAKE a space, to use our voices, build community, and be heard. #NotYourAsianSidekick.
> Suey Park (@sueypark), December 15, 2013, 10:43 am

Park then moves to acknowledge the need for intersectionality in the feminist movement and in the AAPI community:

> #NotYourAsianSidekick is a convo to discuss the problems within the AAPI community and issues with white feminism.
> Suey Park (@sueypark), December 15, 2013, 10:45 am
> #NotYourAsianSidekick is MAKING room for those of us silenced by the AAPI mainstream. Queer/disabled/mixed/South Asian/sex-positive. All.
> Suey Park (@sueypark), December 15, 2013, 10:45 am

The discussion expanded in many directions across different issues including mental health, violence, body image, family, immigration, and more. These tweets represent the broad range of interests for AAPI feminists, and also serve as points of unity and reciprocal solidarity-making. As the conversation continued, different participants maintained the claimed space as one for AAPI feminism:

> Friendly reminder that while the popularity of #NotYourAsianSidekick is great, it originated as talk on Asian American FEMINISM. #dontderail
> Juliet Shen (@juliet_shen), December 15, 2013, 11:10 pm

Here, Shen claims the digital space as one for AAPI feminism. Her reminder specifies the parameters of discourse while unifying the conversation under the AAPI feminist counterpublic. Under #NotYourAsianSidekick, participants highlighted the diversity among AAPI women to confront how AAPI women have typically been represented only as East Asian:

> When East Asian becomes the default for Asian identity, we neglect other subgroups (Nepali, Afghani, Uzbek) in convos

Maureen Ahmed, (@maureenjahmed), December 15, 2013, 11:39 am

Myth: we're all Mandarin-speaking Chinese. Pro tip: it's never OK to go up to a random Asian stranger & say "ni hao."

Tracie (@txc84), December 15, 2013, 10:17 am

Participants also moved to provide a historical context for this discourse, which then allowed entry into the larger, ongoing movement of AAPI feminism. Many circulated an image of a group of young Asian American women holding a sign that reads: "We need feminism because we're not your mail order brides, the cure to your yellow fever, your fantasy sex toys, or your subservient housewives. We are strong, independent, and capable Asian American women." The sign clearly alludes to stereotypes rooted in histories of fetishization and objectification.

Lawyer, scholar, and activist Mari Matsuda posted an image of a 2008 poster that featured a historic image from 1969, in front of Oakland's Alameda County Courthouse in Oakland on the opening day of the Huey P. Newton trial. The protest sign reads "Power to the People. Black Power to Black people. Yellow Power to Yellow People," and the rest of the poster text reads: "Your Asian Wasn't Quiet. She wasn't Nahnatchka a model minority. Wasn't your Asian fantasy. Maybe chose a path other than motherhood. She speaks truth to power. This is what Asian America looks like. Get used to it. Not created in your image. And she thinks critically about media propaganda." (See Figure 16.1.) Other tweets using the hashtag #NotYourA-

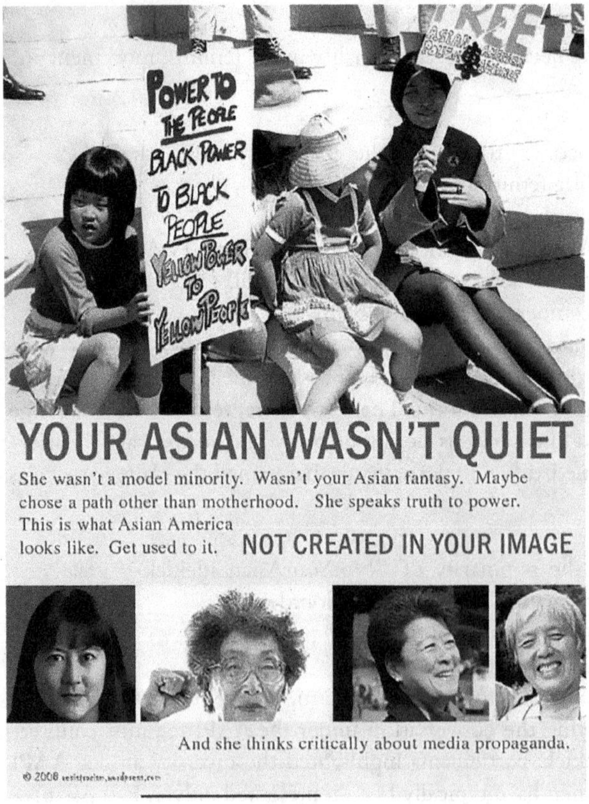

Figure 16.1 A 2008 poster from Resist Racism (resistracism.wordpress.com) reposted by Mari Matsuda during #NotYourAsianSidekick that depicts herself and other AAPI activists Yuri Kochiyama, Helen Zia, and Grace Lee Boggs.

sianSidekick began to discuss the specific racialization of Asian Americans under the White supremacist racial hierarchy.

> I need Asian feminism that confronts, rejects, and dismantles the Model Minority Myth as a tool of anti-black racism #NotYourAsianSidekick
>
> Julia Carrie Wong (@juliacarriew), December 15, 2013, 12:09 pm
>
> Being "honorary whites" ≠ a compliment or a good thing. Also not something to aspire to #NotYourAsianSidekick #racialjustice #realsolidarity
>
> Christine M. Samala (@samala), December 15, 2013, 2:28 pm
>
> #NotYourAsianSidekick don't make me ur "model" minority cuz ur tryna say OTHER ppl of color r BAD. IM NOT UR DIVIDE & CONQUER.
>
> Jenny Yang (@jennyyangtv), December 15, 2013, 2:29 pm
>
> #NotYourAsianSidekick there IS internalized anti-black/ness racism within my communities. makes some of us LIKE being the "model minority."
>
> Jenny Yang (@jennyyangtv), December 15, 2013, 3:40 pm

#NotYourAsianSidekick became a tool for protesting oppressive ideologies as well as a way to begin marking the AAPI feminist counterpublic. While the myth of the model minority has been damaging to Asian Americans by falsely assuming uniform success and accomplishment, here we can additionally see the emphasis on how it upholds anti-Blackness. By creating a narrative that hard work equates success, the model minority myth negates past and present structural barriers that interrupt success for different marginalized groups. Racial myths and stereotypes are often used as a "wedge" to divide groups, whether it's creating unfair racial hierarchies or emphasizing elements of cultural and racial superiority and/or inferiority. In this case, the model minority myth is successful because it constructs Black people as a "problem" minority. It creates juxtapositions and racial binaries; as Stacey Lee (2005) states, "the achievements of Asian Americans are used to discipline African Americans … the success of Asian Americans proves that the United States is free of racial bias and inequality" (5). Additionally, the model minority myth also allows non-Black East Asians and other Asian peoples to escape the social and structural White supremacy enacted against Black people and gain "proximity to and power from whiteness and settler colonialism through our conscious and unconscious participation in anti-Black racism and ongoing occupation" (Yang-Stevens and Quan-Pham 2016).

Continuing the #ModelMinorityMutiny

Since the murder of Trayvon Martin in 2012, the use of the hashtag #BlackLivesMatter has been reflective of a widespread critique of police brutality against Black bodies and systemic anti-Black racism. The hashtag #BlackLivesMatter was started by three queer Black women—Alicia Garza, Opal Tometi, and Patrisse Cullors—and has become a critical framing tool that centered Blackness when discussing racial injustice. Garza states:

> Black Lives Matter affirms the lives of Black queer and trans folks, disabled folks, Black-undocumented folks, folks with records, women and all Black lives along the gender spectrum. It centers those that have been marginalized within Black liberation movements.
>
> (Garza 2014)

She reminds participants of the intersectionality within movements even as they work to center the Black experience. Garza also writes about how other communities of color must position themselves if they are operating in solidarity with the Black community:

> When Black people get free, everybody gets free … #BlackLivesMatter doesn't mean your life isn't important—it means that Black lives, which are seen as without value within White supremacy, are important to your liberation … to keep it real—it is appropriate and necessary to have strategy and action centered around Blackness without other non-Black communities of color, or White folks for that matter, needing to find a place and a way to center themselves within it.
>
> (Garza 2014)

Here, Garza criticizes the appropriation of the #BlackLivesMovement project into #AllLivesMatter, which distracts from the cultural and political project of making Black lives matter in the United States. She also provides a specific entry point for other communities of color to engage with this particular racial justice movement: that to fight for racial justice is to fight against anti-Black racism.

After the non-indictment verdicts of the police officers who murdered Michael Brown and Eric Garner in late 2014, the AAPI community started widely using #ModelMinorityMutiny. This hashtag was a way to reject the racial hierarchies that have created community complicity in anti-Black racism, and express solidarity with the #BlackLivesMatter movement. The phrase "model minority mutiny" was first used by Soya Jung in an online article, "The Racial Justice Movement Needs a Model Minority Mutiny." She recaps the creation of the model minority myth as a "racial invitation" that White supremacy offered Asian Americans: "If you come here and assimilate into this anti-black settler state, if you behave properly, we will let you hustle for your prosperity. You won't be white, but you might get close, and at least you won't be black" (Jung 2014a). Jung calls for AAPIs to "kill the programming" of the myth. What Jung suggests is neither new nor radical, but it is a reminder of the role AAPIs can play in racism and racial justice. #ModelMinorityMutiny extends the argument against the model minority myth and becomes an example of Asian and Black solidarity that demands AAPI communities address their own complicity in reinforcing both white supremacy and anti-Black racism. #ModelMinorityMutiny extends out of #BlackLivesMatter and aims to transform the cultural politics around racism both within the Asian American community and with the White American public.

Grassroots organizing from Asian American groups across the country, including Seeding Change, Southeast Freedom Network, CAAAV Organizing Asian Communities,[2] DRUM, SAALT, NAPWAF, 18 Million Rising,[3] and many more moved online calls for solidarity to offline, on-the-ground actions that demonstrated solidarity. As Asian Americans joined #BlackLivesMatter protests and direct actions, #ModelMinorityMutiny made its way from the digital realm into the streets, as participants started writing it on protest signs. When Asian Americans participated in these actions, these signs expressed their specific relationship to the movement. Jung writes:

> Model Minority Mutiny is a call not only to those of us with class, skin-color, or gender privilege to examine our complicity in the system. It is an opening to acknowledge the marginalization of those Asian Americans who are most vulnerable to state violence—refugees of war; those targeted by state surveillance and profiling; those trapped in low-wage jobs and the informal economy; those who are incarcerated and formerly incarcerated; those who are undocumented; those who are trans,

> disabled, queer, cis-women, dark-skinned, Sikh, or Muslim. It is an invitation for Asian Americans to unite across difference for the long-term work to dismantle the apparatuses of state violence.
>
> (Jung 2014b)

Here, Jung is uniting Asian Americans by specifically acknowledging the different marginalizations faced by the community due to systemic oppression across gender, race, disability status, class, and more identities.

Explicitly Expressing Solidarity through #Asians4BlackLives

The limits of organizing solely around one's own specific racial identity were revealed in November 2014, when Akai Gurley, a 28-year-old Black man, was shot and killed by Chinese American NYPD officer, Peter Liang.[4] While some members of the Chinese American community rallied for the officer in their own community, others moved to recenter Black lives. As a response to the hashtag #JusticeforAkaiGurley, the hashtags #APIs4BlackLives and #Asians4BlackLives were deployed. They called for solidarity from the AAPI community in the larger struggle toward racial justice and an end to police violence. A letter from CAAAV Organizing Asian Communities clearly explicates the need for cross-racial solidarity:

> We stand with Akai Gurley's family and all those who have lost loved ones to police violence. We firmly believe that Peter Liang must be held accountable for his actions … Police violence against Black communities is a systemic problem … This should be unacceptable to all of us, especially as many of our own community members, from South Asians post-9/11 to Southeast Asian communities, are also targeted by police departments across the country. Our history shows us that when Asian communities work together in solidarity with Black communities, we all benefit. We also recognize that the Asian community in the US has historically benefited from Black-led movements for racial and economic justice.
>
> (CAAAV Organizing Asian Communities 2014)

In the statement, the authors make a direct connection between violence against Black bodies and violence against members of the Asian American community, as well as reminding the community that liberation for Black lives means liberation for Asian Americans. These and other statements using the hashtag #Asians4BlackLives echoed discourse from AWU's archives of how the model minority myth has created a divide between Asian communities and Black communities, homogenized the AAPI community and erased specific experiences and histories of oppression at the hands of the U.S. government, and acknowledged the specific racial hierarchy created by White supremacy that gives Asians "relative privilege" within this hierarchy.

On September 11, 2015, a collective of South Asian organizations, including the National Queer Asian Pacific Islander Alliance, Muslim American Women's Policy Forum, and Bay Area Solidarity Summer, created a similar solidarity statement using the hashtags #SouthAsiansforBlackPower, #JusticeforMuslims, and #ModelMinorityMutiny. They posted a statement addressing the consequences of conflating racial and religious identities in ways that criminally racialized "Muslim" and highlighted the intersections of Islamophobia, caste-based oppression, xenophobia, racial profiling, and anti-Blackness in the United States. They wrote:

> We understand that police terror, colonialism, and imperialism are all intricately connected to anti-Blackness. The U.S. was built on the ideology that Black bodies were less than human, disposable, and deserving of violence ... We must struggle with the fact that we have benefited off of and been complicit in this stolen labor and harm, not just in the past but also presently, within and outside of our own diaspora. We stand with the Black Lives Matter movement, knowing that Black power is inextricably tied to our own liberation as well.
>
> (Queer South Asian National Network 2015)

The use of these hashtags in the solidarity statement accomplishes three things. First, they unite the liberation of South Asian and Black communities as a mutually interdependent struggle. Second, they specify the oppressive conditions of Islamophobia targeted toward South Asians, and even more specifically, the Muslim community. Finally, they challenge the ideology of the model minority myth and acknowledge community complicity in settler colonialism and anti-Black racism.

Conclusion

This investigation of solidarity statements in both print and digital materials across historical moments from AAPI feminist racial justice organizing shows the complexity of solidarity work. By looking at the development of intersectional feminist consciousness in Asian American women's groups and through #NotYourAsianSidekick, this chapter revealed the formation and emergence of specific AAPI counterpublics at different moments in history. While seemingly recent, hashtags like #NotYourAsianSidekick, #ModelMinorityMutiny, and #Asians4BlackLives are continued messages from an ongoing struggle for justice—reminding us that this work is part of a larger process. Contemporary messages are simply being distributed and circulated via digital technologies. In recognizing this overlap, we can see that different technologies offer continued opportunities for transforming cultural hegemony within and across different networks and publics. Rather than looking at hashtags and digital media activism as a brand new moment, I situate this work within a historical and ongoing narrative arc, wherein the politics of solidarity, community, and identity are constantly being navigated and negotiated. This analysis has also revealed the ways that communities operationalize intersectionality through articulating and developing solidarity across identity categories, and specifically the way that hashtags can represent bonds of solidarity. Assessing the broader racial context of digital activism reveals the way that AAPI communities can effectively create solidarity with other communities of color in working toward justice. AAPI solidarity statements are reminders that working toward liberation for Black lives means working toward liberation for AAPIs as well—their liberation is inextricably bound together. As solidarity statements also reflect the diversity within a community, they are constant reminders that communities must commit to being accountable to all their members in order to foster a more inclusive movement and strive for liberation in a way that doesn't oppress others. Solidarity statements often call attention to members of communities that are most excluded and least visible. For example, in the Asian American community, these include Indigenous Pacific Islander communities, South Asian communities, refugee communities, Sikh communities, Muslim communities, queer and trans communities, and more.

While hashtags function as gestures of solidarity between both individuals and communities, they are also just a small piece of a movement. As such, they must be used alongside a variety of tools as well as on-the-ground action. If #Asians4BlackLives only existed on Twitter, solidarity would only be performative discourse. Although hashtags can demonstrate intentions for solidarity and political intersectionality, future scholarship could examine ways that solidarity statements are put into practice versus just examining expression and articulation. Uniting under the term "people of color" allows building solidarity between movements that also allows for different racial histories (Balasubramanian, 2013); challenging colonialist and racist systems of oppression to disrupt anti-Black racism and settler colonialism must also be practiced in everyday life, beyond the hashtag, and beyond "activist moments."

While solidarity and commitment to fighting oppression between and across communities of color become crucial for decolonization processes, social movement-building and inter-community solidarity from an intersectional and reciprocal perspective are often easier said than done. There is a lot of work to be done that considers the ways racial justice movements in AAPI communities can prioritize dismantling anti-Black racism and settler colonialism, as complicity in a racist system would continue to cost Asian Americans real solidarity and justice. We need to think about how to create and maintain partnerships that are truly fluid, reciprocal, critical, and intersectional—partnerships that include and address multiple perspectives and issues.

Notes

1 I use "Asian American and Pacific Islander" (AAPI) to unify the communities, while attempting to avoid combining the two groups together. This is to recognize Pacific Islanders as a distinct pan-ethnic group, and specifically that Indigenous Pacific Islanders have sovereignty and land claims beyond civil rights and have experienced specific oppression under U.S. colonialism (Kehaulani Kauanui 2008).

2 CAAAV (Committee Against Anti-Asian Violence) was originally founded in 1986 by working-class AAPI women as a response to hate crimes against Asian Americans throughout the United States. Their work has focused on addressing institutional racism, rather than specific individual cases, and has centered the needs of women and those who identify as queer, trans, and poor.

3 18MillionRising.org (18MR) was launched in September 2012, addressing how the 18 million plus Asians and Pacific Islanders in the United States were also the most politically under-organized and under-represented. Led by founding director Christine M. Samala, 18MR.org promotes AAPI civic engagement through technology and social media.

4 In February 2016, Liang was convicted of manslaughter. In Brooklyn, New York, nearly 15,000 people protested Liang's conviction—there were more than 40 protests throughout the nation, with most of the protestors being Chinese American. Liang was sentenced to 800 hours of community service in April 2016.

References

Atshan, Sa'ed Adel and Moore, Darnell L. 2014. "Reciprocal Solidarity: Where the Black and Palestinian Queer Struggles Meet." *Biography: An Interdisciplinary Quarterly* 37(2): 680–705.

Balasubramanian, Janani. 2013. "What Do We Mean When We Say Colonized?" *Black Girl Dangerous*, December 2. http://www.blackgirldangerous.org/2013/12/mean-say-colonized/.

Bonilla, Yarimar and Jonathan Rosa. 2015. "#Ferguson: Digital protest, hashtag ethnography, and the racial politics of social media in the United States." *American Ethnologist* 42(1): 4–17.

Brock, Andre. 2009. "Life on the Wire: Deconstructing Race on the Internet." *Information, Communication, and Society* 12(3): 344–363.

CAAAV Organizing Asian Communities. 2014. "#JusticeforAkaiGurley National Sign on Letter." CAAAV, April, http://caaav.org/justiceforakaigurley-national-sign-on-letter.

Chai, Alice Yun. 1985. "Toward a Holistic Paradigm for Asian American Women's Studies: A Synthesis of Feminist Scholarship and Women of Color's Feminist Politics." *Women's Studies International Forum* 8(1): 59–66.

Chow, Esther Ngan-Ling. 1982. "The Development of Feminist Consciousness among Asian American Women." *Gender and Society* 1(3): 284–299.

Chun, Jennifer Jihye, George Lipsitz, and Young Shi. 2013. "Intersectionality as a Social Movement Strategy: Asian Immigrant Women Advocates." *Signs - Intersectionality: Theorizing Power, Empowering Theory* 38(4): 917–940.

Coalition of Asian Women's Groups. 1980. Statement of purpose for Coalition of Asian Women's Groups, 1980s, Box 1, Folder 12, Asian Women United Records and Photographs, Tamiment Library and Robert F. Wagner Labor Archives, New York University.

Crenshaw, Kimberle. 1989. "Demarginalizing the Intersection of Race and Sex: A Black Feminist Critique of Antidiscrimination Doctrine, Feminist Theory and Antiracist Politics." *University of Chicago Legal Forum* 140: 139–167.

Fang, Jenn. 2013. "#NotYourAsianSidekick: Can a Social Movement Start on Twitter?" *Reappropriate.co*, December 20. http://reappropriate.co/2013/12/notyourasiansidekick-can-a-social-movement-start-on-twitter/.

Fraser, Nancy. 1992. "Rethinking the Public Sphere: A Contribution to the Critique of Actually Existing Democracy." In *Habermas and the Public Sphere*, Craig Calhoun (ed.), 109–142. Cambridge, MA: MIT Press.

Garza, Alicia. 2014. "A Herstory of the #BlackLivesMatter Movement." *The Feminist Wire*, October 7. http://www.thefeministwire.com/2014/10/blacklivesmatter-2/.

Hall, Stuart. 1981. "The Whites of Their Eyes: Racist Ideologies and the Media." In *Media Studies: A Reader*, Paul Marris and Sue Thornham (eds), 271–283. New York, NY: New York University Press.

hooks, bell. 2012. "Sisterhood." In *Feminist Theory: From Margin to Center*. New York, New York: Routledge, 43–68.

Jung, Soya. 2014a. "The Racial Justice Movement Needs a Model Minority Mutiny." *Race Files*, October 13. http://www.racefiles.com/2014/10/13/model-minority-mutiny/.

Jung, Soya. 2014b. "What does a Model Minority Mutiny Demand?" *Race Files*, December 12. http://www.racefiles.com/2014/12/13/what-does-model-minority-mutiny-demand/.

Kehaulani Kauanui, J. 2008. "Where Are Native Hawaiians and Other Pacific Islanders in Higher Education?" *Diverse Education*, September 8. https://diverseeducation.wordpress.com/2008/09/08/where-are-native-hawaiians-and-other-pacific-islanders-in-higher-education/.

Kim, Eunsong. 2015. "The Politics of Trending." *Model View Culture*, March 19. https://modelviewculture.com/pieces/the-politics-of-trending.

Lee, Stacey. 2005. *Up against Whiteness: Race, School, and Immigrant Youth*. New York, NY: Teachers College Press.

Look, Alice. 1980. "Model Minority Makes Waves: Asian/Pacific American Women on the Move." *Ms. Gazette*, November, Box 1, Folder 11, Asian Women United Records and Photographs, Tamiment Library and Robert F. Wagner Labor Archives, New York University.

Lowe, Lisa. 1991. "Heterogeneity, Hybridity, Multiplicity: Marking Asian American Differences." *Diaspora: A Journal of Transnational Studies* 1(1): 24–44.

Ma, Kai. 2013. "#NotYourAsianSidekick Is Great. Now Can We Get Some Real Social Change?" *Time*, December 18. http://ideas.time.com/2013/12/18/notyourasiansidekick-is-great-now-can-we-get-some-real-social-change/.

Pamphlet for Women for Racial and Economic Equality (WREE) and Women's Bill of Rights, 1980s, Box 2, Folder 18, Asian Women United Records and Photographs, Tamiment Library and Robert F. Wagner Labor Archives, New York University.

Pyke, Karen D., and Denise L. Johnson. 2003. "Asian American Women and Racialized Femininities: Doing Gender across Cultural Worlds." *Gender and Society* 17(1): 33–53.

Queer South Asian National Network. 2015. "South Asians for Black Power: On Anti-Blackness, Islamophobia, and Complicity." September 11. https://queersouthasian.wordpress.com/2015/09/11/south-asians-for-black-power-on-anti-blackness-islamophobia-and-complicity/.

Special to the New York Times. 1980. "Asian-American Women: A Bid for Visibility." *New York Times*, August 18.

Squires, Catherine. 2002. "Rethinking the Black Public Sphere: An Alternative Vocabulary for Multiple Public Spheres." *Communication Theory* 12(4): 446–468.

Wong, Julia Carrie. 2015. "Which Side Are You On?": #Asians4BlackLives Confronts Anti-Black Prejudice in Asian Communities." *Salon*, March 8. http://www.salon.com/2015/03/08/which_side_are_you_on_asians4blacklives_confronts_anti_black_prejudice_in_asian_communities/.

Yang-Stevens, Kat, and Alex Quan-Pham. 2016. "Akai Gurley the 'Thug,' Peter Liang the 'Rookie Cop' and the Model Minority Myth." *Truthout*, February 26. http://www.truth-out.org/opinion/item/34988-akai-gurley-the-thug-peter-liang-the-rookie-cop-and-the-model-minority-myth.

17

ORDERING A NEW WORLD ORIENTALIST BIOPOWER IN *WORLD OF WARCRAFT: MISTS OF PANDARIA*

Takeo Rivera

Of what relevance are video games to Asian American Studies? Besides the fact that a significant portion of the video game-playing community is Asian American,[1] and that some Asian American literary forms have recently been characterized as gameic or ludic (Fickle 2014), North American video games have had a long, contentious history with regard to Asian racialization. With varying degrees of epistemic violence, Asian racialization is present in the grotesquely racist *Shadow Warrior*, the techno-orientalist cyberpunk *Deus Ex* series, the essentialist and stereotypical portrayals in Sid Meier's *Civilization* series and *Alpha Centauri*, the comparatively benevolent but romanticizing *Jade Empire*, and the redemptive but masculinist *Sleeping Dogs* (to name but a handful of easy examples). Because of this, an Asian American Studies lens is imperative for critically scrutinizing video games.

This chapter specifically examines Blizzard Entertainment's 2012 *Mists of Pandaria*, an expansion set to the company's famous massively multiplayer online role-playing game (MMORPG) *World of Warcraft* (*WoW*). It takes place in a virtual racial fantasyscape inhabited by a form of panda-people called "Pandaren," who are arguably racialized as Asian. Although *Mists of Pandaria* is not overtly anti-Asian, it nevertheless extends *WoW*'s preexisting tendency toward non-White dehumanization into the realm of the Asiatic, producing essentialist cybertypes that are at once legible, inhabitable, and targetable. It was met with a collective response from active players who desired fidelity toward an essentialist Orientalism. Consequently, the event of *Mists of Pandaria*'s introduction to the preexisting gamescape of *WoW* illustrates a peculiar pleasure of Orientalist mastery that emerges from the game structure, the fan culture, and Columbian fantasies of discovery.

This chapter critically examines the implications of deriving ludic pleasure from essentialism and the broader biopolitical regime to which it belongs. Rather than being an incipient moment of racial play, *Mists of Pandaria* represents an expansion of an established fantasy racial order that reflects a biopolitical tendency toward the cultural incorporation and marketization of otherness. *Pandaria* does so through building upon a preexisting fantasy racial logic that imbues racialization itself with agentic pleasure, and, through the Orientalized cartography of the land of Pandaria itself, subjects a virtual Orient to a regime of essentialized knowledge and targetability. I first provide an overview of video game theory in relationship to biopower. Next, I situate *WoW* and its *Mists of Pandaria* expansion within both a system of racial legibility and a Euro-American colonial fantasy of Columbian discovery. In drawing attention to the specific Asian racialization within the *WoW* paradigm, I explore how *Mists of Pandaria* produces a peculiar epistemic violence even through its apparently benevolent mode of representation. Finally, I close with a brief examination of *WoW* fan culture and how *WoW*'s very participants all work to perpetuate the pleasures of racial fantasy.

Biopower as Immersion in the Age of the World Target

Before delving into an analysis of *WoW* itself, I must situate this discussion within a broader theoretical context regarding games and biopolitical theory. After all, any discussion of *WoW* cannot be fully appreciated without attention to its medium-specific dimensions. First and foremost, *WoW*, as a game, must be understood as defined fundamentally by action; as Alexander Galloway has concisely declared, "If photographs are images, and films are moving images, then *video games are actions*" (Galloway 2006: 2). Video gaming depends fundamentally on player participation, and the mode of direct interactivity of the player is the central basis of video game analysis. Beyond what a player does in a game, video games can be analyzed in terms of the range of actional possibilities the game provides to the player, as well as its more traditionally literary narrativistic dimensions. Compared with literature, video games provide interactivity that is simultaneously more direct and tangible (the player can concretely see her direct impact on the game and directly affect the course of its progression) and more limited in possibility (whereas the reader is free to imagine, disidentify, and reinterpret with relative ease without any boundaries, the gamer is limited to specific outcomes dictated by the programmatic constraints of the game). Consequently, an analysis of video games must incorporate what Ian Bogost (2007) has termed "procedural rhetorics"—what the game "says" or "does" through multiple freedoms and constraints that enable or prevent particular actions by the player.

Furthermore, *WoW* derives much of its pleasurable power from what Janet Murray describes as *immersion*:

> The experience of being transported to an elaborately simulated place is pleasurable in itself, regardless of the fantasy content … Immersion is a metaphorical term derived from the physical experience of being submerged in water … The sensation of being surrounded by a completely other reality, as different as water is from air, that takes over all our attention, our whole perceptual apparatus.
>
> (Murray 1997: 98)

Within the actional paradigm of the video game, the sense of being fully transported within the logic of the gameworld is a tremendous anchor for gamers. Many factors can contribute to this sense of immersion. One aspect, for example, is the fugue of the challenge within particularly fast-paced video games that require concentration not unlike that of a competitive athlete. However, I focus on another dimension that produces immersion: the production of in-game lore and the procedural rhetorics of the gameworld itself. This is particularly salient within the role-playing game category of video games, or narrative-driven types of games in which the player assumes the role of a character and develops and strengthens that character throughout the game's narrative arc, as well as making decisions and dialogue choices while exploring the gameworld. Specifically, I propose that *WoW* unsettlingly succeeds at producing a procedural logic of biopower that is both immersive and pleasurable.

I refer primarily to the original formulation of biopower articulated by Michel Foucault (1978, 2003), who defines biopower as power over life through a combination of individuating anatomo-politics and biopolitical analysis of the species body. As Foucault notes, biopower is related to "state racism" in enabling the logical paradigm of racial war. State racism derives from war, since "modern" war is understood as a war between races, though Foucault's notion of "race" is quite expansive, including what appears to be the formulation of class by what Marx would call class consciousness. However, the rise of modernity and the decline of sovereign power brought the notion of life itself under state control in the nineteenth century in the form of biopower: "One of the basic phenomena of the 19th century was what might be called power's hold over life. What I mean is the acquisition of power over man insofar as man is a living being, that the biological came under State control" (Foucault 2003: 239–240). This contrasts with the sovereign power prior to the nineteenth century, exemplified by the sovereign's right to "take life or let live" (241). Biopower, in contrast, represents "the power to 'make' live and 'let die'" (241), ultimately justified by seeing humankind not just in terms of bodies, but as a *species* whose attributes of life and well-being had to be regulated and maintained.

In the context of Foucault's (1972) larger theorizations about power and knowledge, it is also important to understand biopower as not simply a top-down manifestation of systemic regulation; rather, it produces its own epistemic grid of intelligibility. Specifically, biopower, when understood as an *optic*, produces what Rey Chow (2006) has deemed "targetability." Chow argues that postwar knowledge production occurs in the "Age of the World Target," and that area studies "capitalize on the intertwined logics of the world-as-picture and the world-as-target, always returning the results of knowing other cultures to the point of origin, the 'eye'/'I' that is the American state and society" (Chow 2006: 14–15). Such a view assumes that otherness is viewed and evaluated as a potential target, in military as well as epistemic terms. Indeed, continues Chow, the world-as-target, the world as targetable and thus "bombable," paired with the rise of high-speed communication, "*virtualizes* the world. As a condition that is no longer separable from civilian life, war is thoroughly absorbed into the fabric of our daily communications—our information channels, our entertainment media, our machinery for speech and expression" (34). With the dawn of the information age, visuality also becomes destructibility; to render visible is to render susceptible to annihilation.

As I discuss here, *WoW* produces its immersive pleasure largely through its own codified episteme of biopower, in which racialization itself becomes procedural rhetoric. Utilizing fantasy races as an analogy, *WoW* presents a system of racial attributes that renders race as both targetable and legible, and thus subject to the regulatory schema of gameplay. Consequently, this discussion interrogates the relationship between gameic fantasy and biopower more generally, addressing the possibility that the pleasure of fantasy racialization is, in fact, intrinsic to the genre.

World of Warcraft as Racial System

When Blizzard Entertainment released the *Mists of Pandaria* expansion in 2012, it was adding to a game and an online community of players that had been in operation since 2004. *WoW*, with between six and ten million monthly paying subscribers since 2006,[2] currently holds the Guinness Book of World Records title for Most Popular MMORPG in history. As an MMORPG, *WoW* enables millions of players to interact in a virtual fantasy world by assuming various avatars and taking up quests and objectives. Players begin by creating avatars with specific attributes and visual characteristics (which I will describe in further detail later). This helps *WoW* players become more deeply immersed in the open-world setting of *WoW*, where they have the agency to conduct an entire repertoire of actions at will, at their own pace. Although there is a central storyline in *WoW*, consisting of a series of interlocking quests, players are free to perform activities within the constraints of its digital world, such as challenging other opponents, managing their inventories, or raising pets or crops, among other activities. *WoW* constitutes a virtual world in which its players reside for hours, days, or weeks on end, participating in a setting in which players can spend time battling extraordinary villains together, socializing, or selling goods to acquire more in-game currency, in whatever combination or order each player desires.

Since *WoW* is massively multiplayer and has microphone headset capabilities, players commonly form "guilds" who play together at regularly scheduled times of the day. Consequently, in the fullest sense of the phrase, *WoW* is an online community complete with its own rules, social norms, fanfictions, and even pornography. *WoW* demonstrates that unlike other forms of media—including other types of video games—the MMORPG has a unique capacity to build a virtual world that is mediated not only by the programming structure of its gameworld and its procedural rhetorics, but by a social community within the world itself, effectively combining the immersive imaginative quality of the role-playing game with the electronic sociality of the chatroom.

A broad contingent of this community is not just invested in the gameplay of *WoW*, but in its "lore," or its internal mythologies and history: that is to say, its narrative (as opposed to ludic) dimensions. As Tanya Krzywinska (2006) writes, "any fantasy-based game draws on a range of preexisting sources relevant to the invocation of the fantastic to lend breadth and depth to a game world and make use of players' knowledge" (383). *WoW* is technically the fourth game release in the *Warcraft* franchise developed by Blizzard, beginning with the 1994 release of the first title, *Warcraft: Orcs and Humans.* The lore developed by Blizzard is extensive and transmediated; its primary "canon" emerges from its PC video games, but has been extended into a series of licensed novels, a card game, and a tabletop role-playing game. The premise of the *Warcraft* universe is familiarly Tolkienesque, revolving primarily around a racial war between humans and their allies (the "Alliance") and orcs and their allies (the "Horde") transpiring on a mythical world called Azeroth. Players choose to play as a character of a particular race within the Alliance or the Horde, and then customize the character appropriately, including phenotypic features, attributes like physical strength, intelligence, and dexterity, and their class—"class" understood here as referring to the gameplay type of combatant, such as "Mage" or "Warrior." Each race and class in *WoW* possesses specialized advantages and disadvantages; for example, not all classes are open to all races, and some races possess higher "intelligence" or "strength" than others.

Crucially, as is common within the Western fantasy genre, "humans" are coded as White (Corneliussen and Rettbergh 2008; Langer 2008; Monson 2012; Packer 2014). Although players can choose from a range of phenotypic options, humans project primarily Western European aesthetics, as reflected in their plate mail armor and stone castles, and are described as possessing hegemonically White-liberal ideals such as "honor and justice."[3] Furthermore, humans generally speak with British accents. Human characters can also activate a "racial power" called "Every Man for Himself," which "removes all movement impairing effects and all effects which cause loss of control of your character."[4] This mode metaphorically naturalizes and biologizes an individualist "bootstraps" capacity to free the character from external constraints.

White humanity, or human Whiteness, is co-constituted by the other races present in the game, which are analogous with a U.S. racial logic, though all races have particular attributes, both culturally and statistically. Notably, Horde races such as orcs, trolls, and tauren are the furthest from White normativity, while non-human Alliance races such as elves and dwarves tend to reflect ethnicized White groups. Jessica Langer (2008) writes:

> Trolls correspond directly with black Caribbean folk, particularly but not exclusively Jamaican; tauren represent native North American people (specifically Native American and Canadian First Nations tribes); humans correspond with white British and white American people; and dwarves correlate to the Scottish.
>
> (Langer 2008: 89)

Dwarves speak with Scottish accents, and are shorter and stouter than the tall, slim humans, though they also possess pale skin and straight hair. Meanwhile, racial otherness and abjection is assigned primarily to races of the orc-led Horde, culturally marked by overt shamanism and barbarism. The Horde's trolls speak with Jamaican accents (ending their sentences with "mon") and utilize various forms of black magic. Orcs, in line with representations in fantasy literature since Tolkien, represent a culmination of masculine chaos and barbarity, coded variously as Hun, Mongol, Islamic, and Black; they are characterized by their massive muscles, warrior culture, protruding canine teeth, green skin, tribal political organization, and, of course, bloodlust. Orcs, who in the lore were once led by a chieftain named Ogrim Doomhammer, are capable of dancing a "racial dance" that directly references the choreography of 1990s pop rapper MC Hammer, solidifying orc coding as "Black." Thus, in total, the longstanding lore of *WoW* constructs a conflict between White human civilization and non-White orc barbarism.

Importantly, this racialization is not lost on its players. Scholars have demonstrated a wide range of examples of players' active participation in racial discourse (Higgin 2009; Monson 2012; Packer 2014). To add to this heap of examples, I add this comment from *WoW* player "Djsne" on the official *WoW* website, informally describing the game's racial typology:

> Here's how each race is influenced by
>
> 1 Humans-medieval Europe
> 2 Night-elves-mostly Celtic with some Gree, amazon and to a lesser extent some Chinese and Japanese culture
> 3 Gnomes -?
> 4 Dwarves-scottish [sic]
> 5 Draenel-Turkish despite everyone saying they're Russian (only thing Russian is their accents)
> 6 Worgen-English
>   1 Orc-Mongols
>   2 Trolls-Jamacian [sic]
>   3 Undead-?
>   4 Tauren-native American [sic]
>   5 Blood elves-?
>   6 Goblin-jews [sic]
>
> Pandas chinese obviously [sic]

As this comment indicates, some racial analogies are more obvious than others—tellingly, Djsne writes "Pandas chinese [sic] obviously," referring to the Pandaren race featured in *Mists of Pandaria*. Yet, other racial analogies are contentious, as evidenced by Djsne's characterization of Draenei as "Turkish despite everyone saying they're Russian." Others, such as gnomes and undead, may not have obvious analogues in the hegemonic U.S. racial system. Nevertheless, the freedom of players to assume a role on either side of this conflict represents what Lisa Nakamura (2002) has termed "identity tourism," which describes the pleasurable capacity to assume a different (usually racialized and gendered, and often eroticized and essentialized) role online without having to experience the oppressions of that group in the material world. However, with the articulation of fantasy fictional races as proxies for race, players can obscure their identity tourism not just beneath the perceived anonymity of the internet, but beneath a fantasy fiction of "unreal" races. The pleasure implicit in choosing and developing such characters implies that the *act* of racial essentialization is pleasurable itself, even when the analogy to "real-world" races is ambiguous. Choosing to be undead may not index specific racial attributes that have material-world analogs, but the undead are still racialized and given particular attributes. This establishes capabilities and limitations on the player's character that give the player an agentic pleasure of ownership and identity tourism. Yet, even when alterity does not have a clear non-White analog, it is still constituted against Whiteness, given the presence of humans who are only White, squarely centering Whiteness in the digital racial system. All humanity is White; all non-Whites are non-human.[5] As has been a norm across gameified role-playing contexts since the analog tabletop RPG era of *Dungeons and Dragons*, *WoW* assigns each race a set of innate strengths and weaknesses across attributes and skills during the player's avatar character creation, positioning racial essentialism as an axis of strategic, ludic pleasure.

Beyond the troubling proposition that racial essentialism provides a source of pleasure within the game, we can also see racial hierarchization at work. Out of all of the races, the (White-reading) humans are the most "balanced," with every starting base attribute (including Intellect) at 20. In contrast, Black-reading orcs begin with an Intellect of 19, indigenous-reading tauren begin with an Intellect of 15, and Caribbean-reading trolls begin with an Intellect of 16, although, of course, they all compensate with higher statistics than humans in more physical attributes like Strength, Stamina, or Agility. Humans thus occupy the space of normative Whiteness against which all difference is premised, while other non-White races are relegated to the all-too-familiar stereotype of the subaltern, bestial savage, or, to gesture to Fanon (2008), the Black man who is nothing but the biological. All the while, *WoW* quantifies its normativity, numerically representing humans as the unmarked White.

The construction of fantasy races within *WoW* and the larger genre can be conceptualized via biopower. The replacement of "actual" human racial categories with biologically distinct races—possessing quantifiable differences in attributes between them—reflects a desire for species mastery and management, from both the game developer who establishes the parameters of such difference and the players who don the avatars as identity tourists. Nick Dyer-Witheford and Greig de Peuter (2009) argue that the *WoW* virtual world exercises a regulatory power over the anatomo-politics of individual player avatars as well as the species body of its entire community. Further, the circuits of power circulate upward, with players exercising " 'biopolitical production' from below" (127). Following in the long tradition of Orientalist depictions of the Other, *WoW* thus offers not only fantasy as genre, but *the* fantasy of biopower itself, presenting other-races-as-other-species that are inhabitable, controllable, and (in relation to players of the opposing faction) targetable. In *WoW's* context of existential war between Alliance and Horde, the essentialist, racially marked Others can be players' friends or enemies based on race alone, but are already in effect knowable through the same character creation system that each player has gone through.

Pandaria: Expanding Biopower into the Virtual Orient

It was to this nearly decade-old digital racial system that *Mists of Pandaria* was added in 2012. The expansion was introduced during a panel at BlizzCon 2011, the annual public convention for Blizzard Entertainment's developers and fans. Blizzard developers explained that the expansion pack would add Pandaria as an entirely new continent to the world of Azeroth, populated by the anthropomorphized (and Orientalized) panda bear Pandaren. Situating Pandaria in relation to *WoW* lore, the developers describe how Pandaria has been "shrouded in mist" until the apocalyptic "Cataclysm" unveils the continent; both the Alliance and the Horde accidentally "discover" the continent after mutually shipwrecking each other through a massive naval battle. As lead content designer Cory Stockton stated in his *Mists of Pandaria* presentation, "Pandaria's been around for a long time. The thing is, it's been shrouded by mist since the Sundering, so no one's had access to it. The Pandaren had been alone there for all this time. They've been undiscovered."[6]

The Pandaria narrative is not simply yet another Western redeployment of *Robinson Crusoe*, or a mere representation of discovery and survival. The stakes are indeed higher: *Mists of Pandaria* literally adds a new continent to a world where people "actually live." As Deleuze and Parnet (2007) have powerfully argued, the distinctions between the "virtual" and the "actual" blur constantly:

> the mirror takes control of a character, engulfs him and leaves him as just a virtuality; hence, there is coalescence and division, or rather oscillation, a perpetual exchange between the actual object and its virtual image: the virtual image never stops becoming actual. The virtual image absorbs all of a character's actuality, at the same time as the actual character is no more than a virtuality.
>
> (Deleuze and Parnet 2007: 150)

The ten million-strong gaming community of *WoW* had developed a virtual racial system and cultural logics and mapped out the original Europeanized territory to a fault, pushing the limits of the European-fantasy imaginary as far as Blizzard's gameworld designers had programmed them. Yet, if the virtual is constantly becoming the actual (and conversely, as Deleuze argues, the completely actual never exists), the virtuality or immateriality of the *WoW* community's practices of racialization is less relevant than the fact that its members discursively exert and promulgate a discourse of racialization at all. From the perspective of a seasoned *WoW* denizen, Pandaria literally—whether virtually or actually—becomes the New World; except that, unlike Columbus, *WoW* players actually discover the Orient and its Asian panda bear natives.

In intentional contrast to the landscape of evergreen forests, castles, and Western European villages found in the core *WoW* game, the gameworld of Pandaria contains resplendent pagodas, temples, ornate jade dragons, bamboo glades, and rice paddies (see Figure 17.1). As Earth's continents are racialized,[7] so too is the continent of Pandaria racialized. Yet, it is not just Oriental in this case, but also non-human. In describing the rice paddy farms, Cory Stockton states:

Figure 17.1 Pandaria's landscape. Image from Blizzard's official website battle.net.

> When we were trying to think about what Pandaren farmland would be, *we didn't want it to seem like any of the farmland you've seen in WoW*, like you see in Westfall or you see in other zones, *in Human farmlands*. We wanted it be different, to have that vibe. So *we've got those tiered rice paddies*.[8]

The rice paddy contrasts with the "Human" farmlands, which conflates the "Human" with White European normativity. The equation of rice with non-White otherness and exoticism within a U.S. racial context is as old as Samuel Gompers and Herman Gutstadt's infamous 1902 essay "Meat vs. Rice: American Manhood against Asiatic Coolieism" (Gompers and Gutstadt 1999: 436–438). They locate the Oriental/Occidental binary in the opposition of meat and bread against rice, all in the service of justifying Chinese exclusion from the United States and from U.S. organized labor.

But above all, the addition of the new China-inflected continent represents *WoW*'s own incorporation of China into its biopolitical optic. The ostensibly cosmopolitan addition of Pandaria to a preexisting collection of racialized (predominantly Horde) fantasy territories not only does the work of distancing the Chinese racial form further from the normatively human; it also produces an idyllic Orient that is subject to a range of apparatuses of knowledge, especially in terms of discovery and targetability. Pandaria is only relevant insofar as it adds complexity to a preexisting, unending war in *WoW*'s Azeroth, which is literally a world defined by the craft of war. It is a virtual landscape that is, while not a bombing target, nevertheless explorable and systematically mappable. Consequently, Pandaria is a target for both military and epistemological mastery. It transforms the Orient into a digestible reduction that can be regulated by the rationality of its lore. After all, Orientalism has long been critiqued as a technology for not only legibility, but also colonial mastery (Said 1978). *Mists of Pandaria* simply literalizes the "technology" of that relationship. The techno-oriental conversion of China into Pandaria-as-New-World, aesthetically and logically compatible with the pre-existing setting of Azeroth, renders Orientalized landscapes (and its people therein) subject to the schema of biopower already endemic to *WoW*. Regardless of who "controls" the virtual world of Pandaria (the answer, of course, ultimately being Blizzard Entertainment), the very existence of Pandaria is itself a form of epistemic control over Asia.

But *Mists of Pandaria*'s territory is a minor facet of its racialization compared with the expansion's biopolitical presentation of its populations and bodies. In panel discussions, the (White) lead game developers insist on the "rich culture" of the Pandaren, who, they claim, are portrayed "honorably" and "nobly." The promotional media of *Mists of Pandaria* present a comparatively benevolent Orientalism—a romanticized, exotic projection of a mystical, spiritual East. The official trailer for *Mists of Pandaria* portrays a brutish orc and a White human naval officer who have been shipwrecked on Pandaria and locked in mortal combat suddenly interrupted by an acrobatically superior native Pandaren. The Pandaren humiliates both of the Occidentalized hulks with his fast-paced wushu choreography, all to Chinese flute melodies reminiscent of a Hong Kong martial arts film. Every aspect, from the fast zoom-ins and portrayal of swift and controlled strikes, to the Pandaren's attire of conical coolie hat and silk monk robes, pays homage to the Hong Kong martial arts film aesthetic, and in turn exhibits the widespread transnational indexicality of the genre. The trailer ends with the deep, slightly accented voice of the presumably Pandaren narrator stating, to a rousing orchestral soundtrack: "Why do we fight? To protect home, and family. To preserve balance, and bring harmony. For my kind, the true question is: What is worth fighting for?" The camera pans over the colorful landscape of nature, pagodas, and cherry blossoms fluttering in the wind, while a contingent of Pandaren martial arts students practice katas in perfect unison in the distance.

We can see that the Pandaren is a clear embodiment of the Oriental monk (quite literally, since the default "class" of the Pandaren in-game is the Monk), whose presence in American cinema and other media has been well documented by Jane Iwamura (2011). According to Iwamura, the Oriental monk is a source of "Oriental wisdom" with "unparalleled insight into a situation" (18). Crucially, Iwamura invokes the "virtual" to describe the visually based Orientalism applied to the Oriental monk:

> [Visual] forms train the consumer to prefer visual representations, and the visual nature of the image lends the representation an immediacy and ontological gravity that words cannot. Thus, the Asian sage is not simply someone we imagine, but his presence materializes in the photograph or moving picture before us.
>
> (Iwamura 2011: 7)

Iwamura extends the "virtual" beyond the "virtual world" into photography and cinema, but the Pandaren represent the "virtual Orientalism" that Iwamura articulates, except that they are actually in a virtual world.

Mists of Pandaria does not simply create a virtual Orient, but a virtual Orient populated principally by panda bears rather than Chinese humans. The Pandaren are quite possibly the most unambiguously, analogously racialized group in *WoW* ("pandas chinese obviously"), given not only their cultural markers but also the fact that giant pandas have become such iconic symbols of China. However, in the aesthetic anthropomorphizing of the Pandaren, grotesquely Orientalized features are mapped onto the panda's body itself. This is especially blatant in the character creation screen, in which the player may choose various head and

Figure 17.2 Pandaren character creation screen, including facial hair choices. ©2012 Blizzard Entertainment, Inc. All rights reserved. Mists of Pandaria, World of Warcraft, Warcraft and Blizzard Entertainment are trademarks or registered trademarks of Blizzard Entertainment, Inc. in the United States and/or other countries

facial hair options for the Pandaren warrior (Figure 17.2). The player can browse an extensive array of Orientalist hairstyles from samurai ponytails to Fu Manchu mustaches and goatees, particularly for the male Pandaren. Meanwhile, the female Pandaren is not only racialized but gendered, as she is slimmer than the male (and thus less representative of the frame of the "actual" panda). Further, she possesses buxom breasts and can choose from various eroticized "China doll" hairstyle options such as up-dos with chopsticks and long pigtails. The Pandaren thus stand as the virtual representation of Chineseness and Asianness, in both their Oriental otherness and their sexualization and exploitability. However, the Pandaren serve not simply to make the panda bear more Asian, but to make the Asian more panda bear, or more bestial. The Orientalized hairstyles are not found on the human character, after all—only on the panda. The Pandaren's existence exacerbates the apparent impossibility for the Asian to occupy the space of human that the phenotypically White *WoW* humans inhabit so comfortably. Additionally, the romanticized space of Pandaria and the culture of its panda-people suggest a pleasure from gaining mastery of this Oriental New World—not just through the exploration of the gameworld, but from its simplification and essentialism. Pandaria and the Pandaren are pleasurable insofar as they are decipherable and legible to the player, and reducible to their pornographically cartoonish "essences."

A Warlock and Not a Druid?: Fan Cultural Investment in Racial Logic

The irony of the reductive romanticism of Pandaria is that within the *WoW* community, "actual" China and Chinese people have been historically vilified in *World of Warcraft* fan culture, due to the practice of "gold farming." In her examination of the practice, Nakamura (2009) explains that laborers ("gold farmers") are paid by East Asian companies to play the game and enable leisure players to advance in the game dramatically by trading in-game currency for real money. Nakamura explains the racial politics of the practice:

> Gold farming is especially disliked. Leisure players have been joined by worker players from poorer nations such as China and Korea who are often subject to oppression as both a racio-linguistic minority, and as undesirable underclassed social bodies in the context of game play and game culture.
>
> (Nakamura 2009: 129–130)

She further deconstructs a racist fan-made video entitled *Ni Hao (A Gold Farmer's Story)*. It features a song that disparages "China-men" for cheapening the game and approximates Chinese coolies using *WoW* humans bearing pickaxes with their heads obscured by conical hats so their European features are hidden. Digital labor becomes racialized, with all Asian players laughingly associated with gold farming.

The Ni Hao video emerged three years before *Mists of Pandaria*'s release, which in turn introduces a hyperreal juxtaposition of gold farmer and Pandaren. This irony is on full display in the online gaming blog following Blizzard's announcement of the release of *Mists on Pandaria* in China. Senior Editor "Rob" on *Flesh Eating Zipper* wrote: "So there you have it kids! The gold farmers aren't going to be lacking for resources any time soon. You're safe!"[9] Whereas the externalized, avatarial Pandaren reinforces and augments the racial system of *World of Warcraft*, the closeted "actual" Chinese gold farmer represents a threat to it—a capacity for "actual" Asians to subvert codes of "justice and honor" in leisure *WoW* playing. In terms of biopower, the Pandaren are made to live, while the gold farmers die a social death, and the Asian body itself is annihilated altogether.

Considered alongside the sinophobia embedded in preexisting *WoW* discourse, *Mists of Pandaria* enacts a peculiar epistemic violence. *WoW*'s grid of intelligibility allows the Asiatic racial form only in terms of its fantasyscape, preferring virtual non-human Chinese to actual human ones. While gold farming, to quote Dyer-Witheford and de Peuter (2009), "is not a revolutionary repudiation of ludocapitalism but itself a capitalist venture," it is nevertheless a "criminal revolt against the futuristic accumulation of digital capital, reappropriating the value-creating capacity that publishers privatize and fence around with intellectual property rights" (145). In contrast, the Pandaren, unlike the Chinese gold farmer, is an already-subjectified figure bounded by the rules and terms of *WoW*'s literally codified governmentality. The Pandaren becomes racially bounded within its innate strengths and weaknesses, monopolizing the visual vocabulary by which Chineseness exists in the virtual setting.

Yet, we cannot neglect that the participatory biopolitical nature of *WoW* lends the game a kind of pleasure, or at least affective investment from its players. Such investment was blatantly on display in the Lore Question and Answer period at BlizzCon 2011, where a panel of Blizzard developers expounded upon the lore and mythology of the not-yet-released *Mists of Pandaria* to the *WoW*-playing community. A young woman, donning a comical hat approximating the head of a tauren (a massive cow-like race of the Horde), approached the microphone and asked passionately and earnestly: "I have a really important question.... The panel—this panel—has said that Pandarians [sic] 'have no sense of hatred.' That Pandaria is one in a sense of *chi* and positive energy. So how does it make more sense for a Pandaren to be Warlock and not a Druid?" One person in the audience audibly shouts a "Yeah!" and cheers and applause commence. A dialogue then transpires between the developers and the fan; it is clarified that Pandarens cannot be evil spellcaster Warlocks after all, and cannot be nature-worshipping Druids because a primary Druid ability is to transform into a bear, which is a paradox if the character is already a bear. The fan rejects the latter excuse, saying that it is possible for the Pandaren to transform into some form of über-bear with augmented powers, but one of the developers counters that the Pandaren would not be able to become Druids because according to *WoW* lore, the founder of the Druids, a specific Euro-pagan spiritual order in *WoW*, had never discovered Pandaria; the fan concedes after the "historical" argument.[10]

The exchange demonstrates both the romanticized portrait of the Orientalized Pandaren as purported by the developers, and the insistence among the fan base that there must be consistent, essentialized logics that determine what a race can and cannot do or be. Those parameters are always matters of contention that are intensely argued about by the players who may choose to don their (essentialized) identities. Furthermore, the Druid paradox reveals a rupture in the entire racial logic of *WoW*: the Druid is a class that can "become" a bear, and a bear cannot become a bear. After all, the Pandaren demonstrates that rather, a bear can become Chinese. And the Chinese can only become bears, and never themselves.

Later in the Q&A, in responding to an audience question that accuses *Mists of Pandaria* of not being "serious enough," lead quest designer Dave Kosak counters ardently, arguing that the Pandaren are not "a joke race." He states:

> There's quite a bit to them. I think they're pretty badass. I think they're really awesome fighters. The Pandaren are just really fun to play with. I mean, they love life, they—they work hard, they play hard, they eat hard, they drink hard, they sleep hard. Uh, they do everything, they really live life to the fullest.

While the Pandaren lives contentedly off liquor and bamboo, waiting to be discovered in the New World Orient, the Asian body is buried ever deeper in the digital technologies of epistemic violence. As the *WoW* fan culture demonstrates, there is a kind of participatory essentialism that circulates among all actors—gamers, fans, and developers—demonstrating the circuitous flow of biopower and the collective investment projected from all sectors. It is an essentialism that insists on consistency and rules, a gameic sensibility that demands that the subject not exceed the boundaries of its original definition. And as a consequence, the Pandaren—like the troll and the tauren before it—must develop in accordance with its predetermined class and attribute limitations (ideally as a monk, its default), embodying the procedural rhetorics of a racial system premised precisely on the mismeasure of humanity.[11]

WoW remains massively popular with players in Asian countries, who often account for nearly half of online subscribers.[12] The world of *WoW* has been and remains a robust laboratory not only for identity tourism, but for the biopolitical mastery of otherness, inhabited even by those who are othered by it. As I have explored in previous work (Rivera 2014), the Asian/American gamer can have a wide range of responses to Orientalist material in the game, ranging from the disidentificatory (Muñoz 1999) to the pleasurably masochistic, and the content of *Mists of Pandaria* should be no different. Despite the White supremacist logic informing *WoW*'s construction of humanity, the racialized player may find empowerment in the figure of the essentialist fantasy race, and may even become invested in furthering its logics. For some, the Pandaren may be squarely descriptive rather than prescriptive; perhaps, the figure of the Pandaren can serve as an avatar of vengeance for the Other's exclusion from humanity. Still, such disidentificatory tactics are possible *despite* the participatory racialization of *WoW* rather than *because of* it. The racial system of *WoW* and *Mists of Pandaria* invites us to ethically problematize the pleasures of biopower and racialization that haunt the entire fantasy genre. Or, perhaps it inadvertently challenges us to imagine other possibilities: fantasyscapes that do not depend on procedural essentialism to produce their immersive pleasures.

Author's Note: The author would like to thank Prof. Lok Siu, Miyoko Conley, Terry Park, Joshua Williams, and Diana Rivera for their assistance in providing resources and feedback about various aspects of this chapter.

Notes

1 Asian American youth aged 8–18 have the highest rate of video game and computer game play compared with youth in other racial demographics, spending 73 percent more time on video games and 83 percent more time on computer games per day on average compared with White children, according to the Northwestern University Center on Media and Human Development's 2011 report "Children, Media, and Race."

2 Activision Blizzard. *Number of World of Warcraft subscribers from 1st quarter 2005 to 1st quarter 2015 (in millions).* www.statista.com/statistics/276601/number-of-world-of-warcraft-subscribers-by-quarter/.

3 "Human – Game Guide – World of Warcraft." http://us.battle.net/wow/en/game/race/human.

4 "Human (playable)." http://wowwiki.wikia.com/Human_(playable).

5 The notion of Whiteness assuming the place of "humanity" in fantasy and science fiction is a long tradition that goes back to Tolkien, of fair-skinned humanity juxtaposed against the dark-skinned orcs. As Anderson Rearick (2004) notes, in the Tolkienesque paradigm, elves additionally occupy the space of hyper-Whiteness, being visually extremely pale and blonde, all of which makes them more appealing rather than fear-inducing. Furthermore, we can find the tradition of humanity-as-Whiteness in the Star Trek franchise, as described thoroughly by Allen Kwan (2007).

6 "BlizzCon 2011 – World of Warcraft: Mists of Pandaria Preview Panel (Full)" YouTube Video, uploaded October 22, 2011, www.youtube.com/watch?v=iVSiFXI0FH0.

7 A concept strongly articulated by Walter Mignolo in *The Idea of Latin America* (Malden: Blackwell Publishing, 2005).

8 Mists of Pandaria Preview Panel YouTube, my emphasis.

9 Rob, "Mists of Pandaria to Release in China on October 2nd," *Flesh Eating Zipper*, September 18, 2012, blog entry, www.flesheatingzipper.com/gaming/2012/09/mists-of-pandaria-to-release-in-china-on-october-2nd/.

10 "BlizzCon 2011 – World of Warcraft: Mists of Pandaria Preview Panel (Full)," YouTube Video, uploaded October 22, 2011, www.youtube.com/watch?v=iVSiFXI0FH0.

11 I nod here to Stephen Jay Gould's canonical 1981 classic, *Mismeasure of Man.*

12 Although the rates of Asian American and Asian diasporic *WoW* players are unclear, players in East Asia accounted for at least 41 percent of *WoW* subscribers in 2011. That said, Blizzard Entertainment has remarked that Asian subscriber numbers fluctuate wildly according to season.

References

Bogost, Ian. 2007. *Persuasive Games: The Expressive Power of Videogames.* Cambridge: MIT Press.

Corneliussen, Hilde and Jill Walker Rettbergh (eds). 2008. *Digital Culture, Play, and Identity: A Critical Anthology of World of Warcraft Research.* Cambridge, MA: The MIT Press.

Chow, Rey. 2006. *The Age of the World Target: Self-Referentiality in War, Theory, and Comparative Work.* Durham: Duke University Press.

Deleuze, Gilles and Claire Parnet. 2007. *Dialogues II.* New York: Columbia University Press.

Dyer-Witheford, Nick and Greig de Peuter. 2009. *Games of Empire: Global Capitalism and Video Games.* Minneapolis: University of Minnesota Press.

Fanon, Frantz. 2008. *Black Skin, White Masks.* Translated by Richard Philcox. New York: Grove Press.

Fickle, Tara. 2014. "No No Boy's Dilemma: Game Theory and Japanese American Internment Literature." *Modern Fiction Studies* 60(4): 740–766.

Foucault, Michel. 1972. *Power/Knowledge: Selected Interviews and Other Writings, 1972–1977.* New York: Pantheon Books.

Foucault, Michel. 1978. *The History of Sexuality Volume 1: An Introduction.* New York: Random House.

Foucault, Michel. 2003. *Society Must Be Defended: Lectures at the Collège de France, 1975–1976.* New York: Picador.

Galloway, Alexander. 2006. *Gaming: Essays on Algorithmic Culture.* Minneapolis: University of Minneapolis Press.

Gompers, Samuel, and Herman Gutstadt. 1999. "Meat vs. Rice: American Manhood against Asiatic Coolieism." In *Documents of American Prejudice: An Anthology of Writings on Race from Thomas Jefferson to David Duke*, S.T. Joshi (ed.), 436–438. New York: Basic Books.

Gould, Stephen Jay. 1981. *Mismeasure of Man.* New York: W.W. Norton.

Higgin, Tanner. 2009. "Blackless Fantasy: The Disappearance of Race in Massively Multiplayer Online Role-Playing Games." *Games and Culture* 4(1): 3–26.

"Human – Game Guide – World of Warcraft." n.d. *WorldofWarcraft.com*. http://us.battle.net/wow/en/game/race/human.

"Human (playable)." n.d. *WorldofWarcraft.com*. http://wowwiki.wikia.com/Human_(playable).

Iwamura, Jane Naomi. 2011. *Virtual Orientalism: Asian Religious and American Popular Culture*. Oxford: Oxford University Press.

Krzywinska, Tanya. 2006. "Blood Scythes, Festivals, Quests, and Backstories: World Creation and Rhetorics of Myth in World of Warcraft." *Games and Culture* 1(4): 383.

Kwan, Allen. 2007. "Seeking New Civilizations: Race Normativity in the *Star Trek* Franchise." *Bulletin of Science, Technology, and Society* 27(1): 59–70.

Langer, Jessica. 2008. "The Familiar and the Foreign: Playing (Post)Colonialism in *World of Warcraft*. " In *Digital Culture, Play, and Identity: A Critical Anthology of World of Warcraft Research*, Hilde Corneliussen and Jill Walker Rettbergh (eds). Cambridge: The MIT Press.

Mignolo, Walter. 2005. *The Idea of Latin America*. Malden: Blackwell Publishing.

Monson, Melissa. 2012. "Race-Based Fantasy Realm: Essentialism in the *World of Warcraft*." *Games and Culture* 1(1): 48–71.

Muñoz, José Estéban. 1999. *Disidentifications: Queers of Color and the Performance of Politics*. Minneapolis: University of Minnesota Press.

Murray, Janet. 1997. *Hamlet on the Holodeck: The Future of Narrative in Cyberspace*. Cambridge: The MIT Press.

Nakamura, Lisa. 2002. *Cybertypes: Race, Ethnicity, and Identity on the Internet*. New York: Routledge.

Nakamura, Lisa. 2009. "Don't Hate the Player, Hate the Game: The Racialization of Labor in World of Warcraft." *Critical Studies in Media Communication* 26(2): 1295130.

Packer, Joseph. 2014. "What Makes an Orc? Racial Cosmos and Emergent Narrative in *World of Warcraft*." *Games and Culture* 9(2): 83–101.

Rearick, Anderson. 2004. "Why is the Only Good Orc a Dead Orc? The Dark Face of Racism Examined in Tolkien's World." *Modern Fiction Studies* 50(4): 861–864.

Rideout, Vicky; Alexis Lauricella and Ellen Wartella. 2011. "Children, Media, and Race: Media Use among White, Black, Hispanic, and Asian American Children." Report for the Center on Media and Human Development School of Communication Northwestern University. Evanston, IL: Center on Human Media and Development.

Rivera, Takeo. 2014. "Do Asians Dream of Electric Shrieks?: Techno-Orientalism and Erotohistoriographic Masochism in Eidos Montreal's *Deus Ex Human Revolution*. " *Amerasia Journal* 40(2): 67–86.

Rob. 2012. "Mists of Pandaria to Release in China on October 2nd," *Flesh Eating Zipper*, September 18. http://www.flesheatingzipper.com/gaming/2012/09/mists-of-pandaria-to-release-in-china-on-october-2nd/.

Said, Edward. 1978. *Orientalism*. New York: Vintage Books.

SoMuchMass. 2011. "BlizzCon 2011 – World of Warcraft: Mists of Pandaria Preview Panel (Full)." October 22. https://www.youtube.com/watch?v=iVSiFXI0FH0.

(SoMuchMass, 2011) instead of Mists of Pandaria Preview Panel YouTube, my emphasis.

The Statistics Portal. 2016. "Number of World of Warcraft subscribers from 1st quarter 2005 to 1st quarter 2015 (in millions)." http://www.statista.com/statistics/276601/number-of-world-of-warcraft-subscribers-by-quarter/.

Part V

EXPANDING THE BORDERS OF ASIAN AMERICA

DIASPORA AND TRANSNATIONALISM

18

VIETNAMESE DIASPORIC FILMS AND THE CONSTRUCTION OF DYSFUNCTIONAL TRANSNATIONAL FAMILIES

The Rebel and *Owl and the Sparrow*

Tony Tran

In an overview of contemporary Vietnamese films, film critic Thùy Linh (2013) contends that the majority of "Vietnamese" films made by the Vietnamese diaspora were unable to capture the true spirit of Vietnam. Besides being essentialist in its search for an authentic Vietnam, Linh's article is unable to recognize that the framing or comparing of films through a single nation is insufficient to fully understand the complexities of films produced by the Vietnamese and the Vietnamese diaspora.[1] This filtering of films with diasporic involvement through general notions of "Vietnamese cinema" ignores not just the transnational aspects of their production and distribution, but also the multifaceted and multisited histories of the Vietnamese and Vietnamese diaspora, which include war, loss, exile, and semi-reconciliation across multiple geographical and national borders. If films made by diasporic Vietnamese are, as Vo Hong Chuong-Dai (2011) argues, sites of the "intersection of national identity, diasporic identity, and post-war reconciliation," it is, then, unreasonable to judge these films only as Vietnamese (74).

In recognizing this intersection of identities, histories, and nations, this chapter argues that media produced by diasporic Vietnamese Americans within Vietnam's media industries create transnational sites of meaning where these producers, media texts, and audiences are simultaneously Vietnamese and Việt Kiều ("overseas Vietnamese"), political traitors and economic allies, local and foreign, and familiar and other.[2] With the growth of mass migration and global economic practices and technological networks, the concept of transnationalism is useful in theorizing cultural meanings and identities as they flow across national borders. For Bhabha (1994), the increasingly transnational contexts of globalization create a "Third Space" of hybridity, a theoretical liminal or in-between space where multiple subjectivities, positionalities, and cultural practices that span across boundaries of nation-states come together in irregular manners to produce overlapping, ambivalent, and possibly new meanings. In the stacking of these various positions and practices—such as Vietnamese American filmmakers negotiating on set with Vietnamese censors, or audiences decoding a Việt Kiều actor playing a Vietnamese character—the transnational and hybrid aspects of these filmmakers and films raise questions and meanings that destabilize static definitions of Vietnam and Vietnamese cultures and identities. As with most forms of hybridity and diaspora, the films and people discussed below are able to exist within and navigate multiple geographies, but often never exist fully in one space without question.

It is within these convoluted and frequently paradoxical transnational processes that I wish to position my analysis of two Vietnamese/Vietnamese diasporic films, *Owl and the Sparrow* (*Cú và Chim Se Sẻ*) (2007) and *The Rebel* (*Dòng Máu Anh Hùng*) (2007), and the discourses of their directors, writers, and lead actors. These films have many commonalities: both were filmed in Vietnam and financed by the private Vietnam-based Chánh Phương Phim company; both were directed, written, and produced by an interconnected wave of returning 1.5-generation Vietnamese Americans (with crew from both films assisting each other); and both had the goal of exhibiting these films to domestic and diasporic Vietnamese audiences. The settings and aesthetics of the films, however, drastically differ—*Owl and the Sparrow* is a low-budget "indie" romantic drama set in contemporary Hồ Chí Minh City (Saigon), while *The Rebel* is a relatively "big"-budget (1.6 million USD) martial-arts action film set in a 1922 French-colonial Vietnam. Nevertheless, these differences (as well as their commonalties) help illustrate how transnational aspects operate within different cinematic contexts and genres.

This chapter argues that if these films are framed as simply "Vietnamese," both *Owl and the Sparrow* and *The Rebel* could be read as suggesting that the solution to constructing and maintaining an authentic Vietnam in the modern age of globalization is the bringing together of a heterosexual Vietnamese family within the socialist state. These films, which were reviewed, approved, and internationally claimed as "Vietnamese films" by the Vietnamese government, could be seen as an official tool of the state, one that posits a vision of the perfect contemporary Vietnamese family, as well as offering a critique of uncontrolled capitalism and modernity.

These films, however, are hybrid at almost every structural level, including production (directors, actors, editors, etc.), distribution, and exhibition/audiences. Therefore, because these films are not meant to be *just* Vietnamese but, in fact, are both Vietnamese *and* Việt Kiều/American, I argue that this transnational hybridity creates additional layers of complex subtext that destabilize meanings that have been assembled through only a nationalistic framework, possibly producing clashing yet coexisting readings of the films within both local and diasporic Vietnamese audiences. While I am hesitant to assert a claim that an act of political resistance is occurring, I do suggest that the hybridity of these films and their cast and crew creates ambiguous readings that potentially highlight the conflicting histories of Vietnam and its past, current, and future relationships with its diasporic population(s).[3]

Thus, although these films still do desire and reunite a modern Vietnamese family under the current state, this family of Vietnamese and Việt Kiều is also one that is inherently transnational, ambivalent, contradictory, and, much like all families in reality, dysfunctional. Broadly, dysfunctional family dynamics generally involve bad communication skills, the uncritical blaming of each other, and histories of violence, trauma, and mistrust. As the works of Nguyen (2009), Duong (2012), Valverde (2012), and several others have illustrated in different contexts, the historical and current relationships between Việt Kiều and Vietnam are rife with censorship, historical revision, protest, suspicion, and the passing of trauma across generations. This should not be surprising in Southeast Asian diasporas, as Um (2012) notes that when "home and history evoke the imagery not only of familial warmth and belonging but also of reeducation camps and killing fields, memory itself is fraught with contestation and contradictions" (832).

In using the term "dysfunctional," I do not imply that there exists a correct version of a functional or authentic Vietnamese family. Rather, I use the term to highlight and push against the constructed normalization of "Vietnamese" families by the Vietnamese state, one that on its surface does not critically confront or acknowledge the core issues and divisions that exist within these families. The use of the term is not meant to pass judgment; as noted above, "home" and the family within it still evoke feelings of warmth and belonging. Ultimately, the use of "dysfunctional family" is an acknowledgment that bridges of reconnection are beginning to be built across populations of Vietnam and Vietnamese diasporas, but more work is needed, as they are built on unstable foundations of contested histories, identities, and power.

This chapter will first provide a brief historical, cultural, and industrial overview of the establishment of a Vietnamese film industry in which members of the Vietnamese diaspora are able to produce films with transnational dimensions and meanings. In exploring these films and interviews, I will then provide a surface "Vietnamese" reading to illustrate how these films can be seen to express a vision of the Vietnamese family in line with the politics of the state, allowing them to pass censorship within Vietnam. I will then explore how these films as transnational texts can also become convoluted and contradictory sites of meaning, allowing positionalities to simultaneously exist for both Vietnamese and Vietnamese American audiences.

Creating a New Wave of Vietnamese/Việt Kiều Filmmakers

Shortly before the withdrawal of U.S. forces and the fall of Saigon in 1975, the United States began massive evacuations of South Vietnamese who were closely involved with the U.S. government due to fears that their associations with the United States would put them at great risk in the new communist state. The majority of this first wave of immigrants—numbering around 130,000—eventually settled down in the United States, as well as Australia, France, and Canada (Valverde 2012: 7). Those who were left behind often faced harsh punitive measures established by the new government; in addition to this treatment, the failures of the Vietnamese economy further encouraged hundreds of thousands of Vietnamese to flee the country via boat in the early 1980s. It is estimated that over half of those who attempted to escape were killed, most likely by the Vietnamese Armed Forces, various pirates from all over Southeast Asia, and/or starvation and dehydration (9).

In the mid-1980s and following the economic footsteps of the USSR's *Perestroika*, the Communist Party approved *Đổi Mới* (renovation), which was a succession of steps that would transition the currently isolated country and centralized socialist economic system to a "socialist-oriented" open-market economic system that lifted the restrictions on private investment and ownership (Kokko 2004; SarDesai 2005). With the rise of globalizing economic forces, the rules of neoliberal capitalism quickly superseded—but did not eradicate—most of the political ideologies that the Vietnamese state held regarding its former enemies, including those in the diaspora. Thus, what had been a derogatory term after 1975 and was usually associated with traitors and individuals who had abandoned the motherland, "Việt Kiều" ("overseas" Vietnamese) now *also* represented a new and growing source of economic investment, opportunity, and profit. As such, collaborations between Vietnam and Việt Kiều have been growing for the past two decades and "in this new century are more economically tinted than politically tainted" (Duong 2012: 55).

As part of this paradoxical ideological compromise with the increasing forces of global capitalism came the opening of the cultural front of Vietnam, especially within the realm of cinema. Like other sectors in the economy, the Vietnamese state had initially funded all phases of the motion picture industry, but in 1989 the state begin promoting transnational productions, along with encouraging Việt Kiều investors and filmmakers to come and produce films in Vietnam (Vo 2012: 77). As Duong (2012) notes, Ngo Phuong Lan, the head of the national cinema department, expressed in 2005 the importance of "maintaining 'favorable conditions' for Việt Kiều to return and advance the development of Vietnamese cinema," recognizing the skilled artistic labor and the economic and cultural capital that possibly come with Western-trained Việt Kiều filmmakers (55).[4]

On the other side of this equation were over half a million people in the Vietnamese diaspora in the United States by 1990, who were experiencing the hardships that come with any immigrant population, such as poverty, culture shock, and overt racism. While the first wave of immigrants were often better adjusted due to their experiences with the U.S. government, those who came in boats had widely diverse socioeconomic backgrounds, and thus had a harder time adapting. For all Vietnamese Americans, these issues and hardships were compounded due to their adopted homeland's extensive, bloody, and failed military engagement with Vietnam, which still haunts the minds of many within the United States (Valverde 2012).

Within the Vietnamese American population, many considered themselves as either political exiles or, at least, relatives to exiles. As Hamid Naficy (2001) describes, exile is an even more painful form of diasporic movement, one that "often begins with trauma, rupture, and coercion" (14). However, as Naficy (1999) also notes, "exile is inexorably tied to homeland and to the possibility of return," and with the opening of borders, return was becoming a fairly realistic goal in the mid-1990s for some Vietnamese Americans (3). For many "newer" and more recent diaspora groups, this ability to connect back to the homeland was largely linked to and mediated by the rise of electronic media and advancements in technologies such as transportation, which were all major factors in the increased movement of people and culture in the age of globalization (Appadurai 1996; Naficy 1999). The ideological shift of the Vietnamese government also opened previously closed doors; as seen in the shifting meaning of the term "Việt Kiều," Vietnam in the late 1990s was now beginning to be seen as not just a tourist attraction, but a way for several of the then-coming-of-age 1.5-generation Vietnamese Americans to uncover their roots and origins. As Michele Janette (2006) explains, while many older Vietnamese Americans continued to perform a sense of self-exile by seeing Vietnam as a forever lost land whose painful memories prevented their immediate return,

> this [1.5] generation of Vietnamese Americans, so named for having immigrated as children and grown up in American culture, has tended to view Vietnam not with their parents' sense of exile, but rather through the lens of diaspora. Within this generation's discussion of Vietnam, curiosity vies with nostalgia, and reconciliation often overcomes resentment.
>
> Janette 2006: (254)

Especially intrigued and curious about these new openings in Vietnam's economic system were Vietnamese Americans in the U.S. entertainment industry. In their adopted homeland, Vietnamese American actors and actresses, like all Asian Americans, were limited to stereotypical or secondary roles, while Asian American directors and producers rarely received funding opportunities for their projects. Those who did break through barriers were often then tokenized as part of the contemporary politics of multiculturalism and color-blind casting (Ono and Pham 2008).

According to an interview on *The Rebel's* DVD, Dustin Nguyen, the film's villain, stated that the roles offered to him after *21 Jump Street* (1987–1990) ended were "abysmal." Additionally, the only paying role in which he could speak his "mother tongue" and explore his identity was to be "a VC [Viet Cong] in the bushes and get shot after two lines" (*The Dark Destroyer* 2007).[5] Similarly, Johnny Tri Nguyen—co-writer (with director/brother Charlie Nguyen) and star of *The Rebel*—was a relatively successful stunt double doing work in the *Spider-Man* franchise (2002–2007), but had to travel to Hong Kong and Southeast Asia for speaking roles (*The Dark Destroyer* 2007). Before her appearance in *Owl and the Sparrow*, Cat Ly was a successful singer and dancer within the U.S. Vietnamese diaspora. Although there is a growing Vietnamese population, her performing options were constrained in scope, scale, and location; similarly to Dustin and Johnny, there were also no viable long-term options outside the Vietnamese diaspora in the entertainment business.

During the late 1990s, the influx of forces of nostalgia, curiosity, identity, and global economics were producing an attractive and sustainable transnational environment for mutual gain between Vietnamese and Việt Kiều populations in terms of entertainment productions. For Vietnam, this meant not just box office returns, but the development of a cultural industry that could begin to compete with the rest of Asia and showcase a more polished national identity to foreign investors. For Việt Kiều actors and filmmakers, this meant a space where they could more easily explore their artistic and racial identities, as well as expand their potential audiences and careers—if it had not been for *The Rebel*, Dustin has stated he would have quit the entertainment industry (*The Dark Destroyer* 2007). For many Việt Kiều entertainers, Vietnam since the late 1990s has now become a desired destination, as it has allowed unprecedented opportunities that were practically non-existent in their adopted homelands.

This arrangement between the Vietnamese state and Việt Kiều entertainers, however, is not problem-free. Even with its yielding of oversight in the name of neoliberal economics, the government still holds much power over censorship, and anxieties still exist on both sides. As Miriam Lam (2012) documents, the Vietnamese state is involved to some degree in all film productions, including funding and enforcing censorship. While Việt Kiều (and Vietnamese) filmmakers often "circumvent channels" to create films, it is extremely difficult to cleanly disentangle the influence of the Vietnamese state. Films produced in Vietnam need to follow the rhetoric of state, at least in some capacity.

As Lee Ngo (2010) has argued, some of Vietnam's rhetoric and views of film can be inferred from Ngo Phuong Lan's *Modernity and Nationality in Vietnamese Cinema* (2007), which was published when she was the head of the Vietnamese national cinema department. In her overview of the current state and future of Vietnamese cinema, Ngo (2007) creates a clear link between cinema and nation, proclaiming that the "building [of] a modern Vietnamese Cinema is of practical significance to the nation" (15). Expanding on cinema's role in relation to nationality and culture, Ngo writes that the features and core attributes of the Vietnamese people in cinema should be positive and progressive, and should try to aim for the following elements: "love for the country and willingness to die for the homeland and national independence"; "the traditional fine virtues of the people are always highly appreciated"; "the family theme is extensively worked on"; and "happy endings, [where] protagonists and antagonists are clearly distinguished" (44).

While vague, and not the only guideline for all contemporary Vietnamese films, Ngo's list helps to illustrate some of the implications for filmmakers and frame their interactions with the state (via censorship officials). Although Vietnam is considered by many to be in a post-socialist phase, Ngo's mentioning of national independence invokes the importance of Vietnam's socialist political origins. Likewise, "traditional fine virtues" also emphasizes and conjures a link to a nostalgic past, as well as conservative notions of family and culture. Lastly, the desire for happy endings, positive viewpoints, and clear-cut morals illustrates a very specific image of culture, family, and the nation, where no gray zones exist.

The Construction of the Perfect Vietnamese Family in *Owl and the Sparrow* and *The Rebel*

In this section, I analyze *Owl and the Sparrow* (henceforth *Owl*) and *The Rebel* through a strictly Vietnamese nationalistic lens and illustrate how these films present a state-approved paradigm for the perfect family, while offering critiques of unhindered capitalism and modernism. Originally self-financed and filmed on a micro-budget, *Owl* is written and directed by Stephane Gauger, a biracial Vietnamese American born in Saigon and raised in California. Stephane said he wanted to tell a contemporary story that would feature the "bustling streets of Saigon and capture the energy of the city," as well as make a "statement about the modernization of a country usually associated with war films" (Elias 2007). The film follows the intertwined story of three different people in Saigon: Lan, a newly single and lonely Vietnam Air flight attendant (Vietnamese American singer/actress Cat Ly); Hải, a newly single keeper in a waning zoo (Vietnamese actor Lê Thế Lữ); and Thủy, a runaway ten-year-old girl who sells flowers in the street (Vietnamese actress Phạm Thị Hân). With Thủy as the common thread, Lan and Hải come together to help Thủy escape her life as a child street vendor, and they become a family at the conclusion of the film.

In terms of budget, style, and genre, *The Rebel* could be considered the opposite of *Owl and the Sparrow*. Taking place in 1922 in French-controlled Indochina (Vietnam), *The Rebel* is a quasi-historical action film loosely based on the filmmakers' grandfather, who was part of the revolution to expel the French during this time. Written by Vietnamese American brothers Charlie and Johnny Tri Nguyen and directed by the former, the film stars Johnny as Cường, an elite, French-educated Vietnamese operative working for the French to quell a rebellion. His partner and eventual nemesis is Sỹ (Vietnamese American Dustin Nguyen), a ruthless assassin who practices "Iron Jacket" kung fu and thirsts for power. After the pair captures Thúy (Vietnamese Norwegian Veronica Ngo/Ngô Thanh Vân), the daughter of the leader of the rebellion, Cường slowly recognizes that Thúy and her cause represent a better future for the nation and helps her escape the city to be reunited with her father in the countryside.[6] After several action scenes and chases, Cường and Thúy come together to defeat and kill Sỹ and his French associates. Despite their differences, both of these films employ similar themes to construct their family: technologies of modernity (such as industry, communication, and transportation) and their rejection; the imagery of nature; the lack of a family structure as a source of conflict; and the construction and costumes of the Vietnamese body.

Owl opens with an establishing shot of a water buffalo in a lush, green field, far away from the bustling city of Saigon. Following Stephane's desire not to exoticize Vietnam with "lingering shots of the landscape, [or] a girl in a traditional dress standing behind a tree," the film quickly cuts to a shot of a loud, industrial-sized machine processing bamboo (Gauger 2007). The viewer is introduced to Thủy, who, after making a mistake, is berated by her uncle. After this incident, Thủy packs her backpack and takes her "savings" (roughly 5 USD) and a boat to Saigon. Instantly, the film provides a harsh critique of the industrialized process. While the "countryside" was once a symbolic representation of the natural beauty of Vietnam—illustrated by the Vietnamese classic film *Nostalgia for the Countryside* (*Thương Nhớ Đồng Quê*) (1984) by Đặng Nhật Minh—the countryside is now another site of soulless modern machinery that destroys nature and the people within it.

The Rebel also uses the juxtaposition of nature and industrialization to make a similar argument. To escape the city, Cường and Thúy end up on a truck that takes them far out into the jungle to a French labor camp. Similarly to the opening scene of *Owl*, *The Rebel* sequence begins with shots of the lush, green vegetation. However, once at the labor camp, the camera (which is positioned as Cường's gaze) pans across the camp as he sees the destruction of nature in the name of capitalism and colonialism; what once was what beautiful is now a polluted site of industry and slave labor.

Another key element of industrialization featured is technologies of transportation, which are portrayed as having negative effects on characters. During the opening of *The Rebel*, Sỹ expresses his awe and respect for the new metal battleships that have recently arrived to aid the French military. Immediately, there is a clear connection from modernity and technologies of transportation to the ruthless Sỹ, France, and to an extent, Cường, who just nods along with Sỹ's comments. When a Frenchman drives a car through the street in front of them—furthering the links between modernity and transportation—an assassination attempt takes place, led by Thúy. After she mortally wounds the Frenchman, Thúy and Sỹ face off in battle; Thúy attempts to stab Sỹ, but does no harm. It is later revealed that through a combination of chi, black magic, and "Iron Jacket" techniques, Sỹ is able to withstand large amounts of damage, recalling the ironclad ships he admires and advancing the image of Sỹ as the Vietnamese man corrupted by technology and foreign powers.

Similarly, Lan's occupation in *Owl* as a flight attendant is hinted at as a limiting factor in her life. According to Stephane, Lan represents "a new upwardly post-war Vietnam" (Stone 2009). In addition to recalling the upward motion of both airplanes and the Vietnamese economy, Lan's job situates her within the technologies of travel, which has allowed the easy movement of culture, capital, and people and, as a result, the collapse of time and space in globalized economies (Appadurai 1996; Naficy 1999). This upward mobility, both physically and economically, however, does not guarantee happiness; as Stephane elaborates, "you see a lot of single Vietnamese women are climbing up the ladder socially, but they're still a little empty sometimes [and] it's hard to find the right guy" (Gauger 2007). Although this statement is highly problematic, *Owl* demonstrates this emptiness in Lan by showing her in a loveless relationship with a married pilot. Her situation reveals the lack of passion and humanity between two people closely associated with technologies of travel and modernity.

Framed as the foil to Lan's lifestyle, *Owl*'s Hải is the perfect Vietnamese man: resilient, humble, and ideologically strong. Facing funding cuts, Hải still fights the owner to keep the zoo open even as he receives little money for his labor. Living his ideology, Hải resides in an impoverished shack on the zoo's grounds and shares the living space with his animal friends, including an elephant and an orangutan. As Gauger (2007) describes the real-life zoo,

> I fell in love with the zoo because it was the few places in the city that it was quiet. Everywhere else, it's just like a million of motorbikes, screaming and honking. And you enter the zoo grounds, and all you hear are birds and animals.

Posited as a sanctuary, the Saigon Zoo is reminiscent of wilderness and the natural world, which Naficy (2001) considers to "be the sacred space-time of uncontaminated spirituality, contrasting it with the profane space-time of culture and civilization" (156). For both Gauger and Hải, the zoo is a peaceful space isolated from the noise of modernity, recalling the opening shot before the intrusion of the bamboo factory. This sanctuary, however, is once again threatened by globalization; the owner reveals he has sold Hải's favorite animal, a baby elephant, to a zoo in India, evoking the global movement and outsourcing of labor and capital.

This invasion of technology has also impacted Hải's personal life; his fiancée had just left him. In several attempts to win her back, the viewer learns that Hải's ex-fiancée sells mobile phones, which is ironic considering Hải is unable to directly speak with her. Like transportation, technologies of communication are often seen as symbols of modernity; Hải—who later reveals that his home has no phone—is incompatible with modern technology, and as a result, he and his ex-fiancée cannot exist together in harmony.

Like Hải in *Owl*, Thúy's unnamed father in *The Rebel* needs no modern technologies. Cường and Thúy leave the city to find her father, who is hiding in a small village. As the leader of the revolution against France, Thúy's father is clearly a protagonist with love for country and the nation's freedom, and the film makes a direct association between him and the natural environment outside the bounds of the French-influenced urban city. This plot point of reuniting the traditional family of Thúy and her father coincides with Cường's evolution in fully becoming the title character. Before meeting Thúy's father, Cường visits an opium den to say goodbye to his own father. As a harsh and direct symbol of the cruelties of both capitalism and colonialism, Cường bids farewell, and comments that he will never forget what his father did to his mother. Although this is never fully explained, it gives reason for Cường's troubled past and his relationship with the French—the lack of a traditional family.

This lack also drives the plot in *Owl*. Thủy's dire situation at the factory, which encourages her to run away, involves only her abusive uncle, and there seem to be no signs of a mother figure. Similarly, any discussion or mention of Lan's family is also absent; although she is free to move around the world, she is shown to have no physical or long-term home or family (besides a hotel and its workers) until the end of the film with Hải and Thủy.

For both *Owl*'s Lan and *The Rebel*'s Cường, to fulfill their happy ending of forming a family requires a movement away from modernity. After Lan reads a note written by Thủy, she abruptly leaves the airport in search of Hải and Thủy. As the music swells, Lan finds them and runs for an embrace, and the traditional heterosexual couple is reunited; Thủy now has both a mother and a father figure. In this scene, it is important to note that Lan is wearing the traditional Vietnamese dress, the *áo dài*. Lan is rarely seen in an *áo dài* throughout the film, and her costume and her departure from her job symbolize a shift to more traditional imagery of Vietnamese family. While it is never fully explained whether Lan has quit her job, been fired for her actions, or just taken a day off, the film suggests that in order for the family to be reunited, the Vietnamese body needs to reject the technologies of modernism; because she is upwardly mobile and economically successful (more so than Hải), Lan's movement needs to be grounded before the family can live happily ever after.

Costuming choices are similarly laden with meaning in *The Rebel*. Both Cường and Sỹ wear French-style clothing in the opening, which establishes their relation to the colonizing power—the clothing covers and hides their Vietnamese bodies. During the assassination attempt, Cường is forced to kill a young male Vietnamese rebel. Instantly after Cường shoots him, his white clothes are covered in blood. With this scene, Cường's clothes begin to evolve throughout the film—his first physical change is to shed one layer of his now tainted French-style clothes. As Cường escapes with Thúy, and throughout the film, his French clothes are slowly removed and he begins wearing the clothes of a Vietnamese commoner, signifying his increased devotion to Vietnam.

After Sỹ kidnaps Thúy's father, Cường and Thúy set up an ambush on Sỹ's train by destroying the tracks. In doing so, Cường and Thúy are able to stop the movement of Sỹ's train, thus rebuilding the time and space that had collapsed under the technologies of travel. It is only when they are able to force Sỹ off the train and into more natural surroundings that they are really able to hurt him. After Sỹ's chi has been depleted, Cường attempts to stab him, but is unable to do so alone. Thúy appears in the screen, and together, hand in hand, Thúy and Cường proceed to thrust a blade into Sỹ's eye, killing him and his associations with the French, technology, and modernity. With this, Cường and Thúy save her father—whom Sỹ jokingly called Cường's "father-in-law" earlier in the film—and the traditional Vietnamese family has become restored.

Disjuncture and Difference via the Dysfunctional Family

People unfamiliar with the history of Vietnamese diaspora, or those without the contextual knowledge that these films are made by and starring Việt Kiều, would most likely see these films as *just* Vietnamese. As established in the introduction, however, these films are hybrid at their very core and cannot be contained or processed through the view of one single nation-state. *Owl* and *The Rebel* were widely screened within both Vietnam and the Vietnamese American community.

Many in Vietnam and its diaspora are very aware of the image of Việt Kiều because it is a loaded marker of identification that establishes relational powers through its historical complexity. The Vietnamese government has struggled with this term. While the state has often claimed Việt Kiều and their works (like films) as solely Vietnamese, it has also applied different and specific legal statuses and policies toward them. Việt Kiều often see themselves, and are seen as, foreigners or different on some level in Vietnam, and it is not uncommon to be socially labeled as Việt Kiều in everyday life (Koh 2015; Nguyen-Akbar 2014). This labeling also occurs within the film industry, as press coverage often describes films, actors, and directors as Việt Kiều (Phan 2013; Trâm 2006).

So, while these films are unproblematically presented and judged as "Vietnamese" by the state cinema board and film critics, the recognition of both Vietnamese and Việt Kiều can possibly disrupt the state-approved presentations of model families to create ambivalent meanings, whereby Việt Kiều bodies create dysfunctional family dynamics that conjure histories of violence and distrust, but only indirectly communicated through subtext. These texts create liminal transnational spaces of interpretation where alternative meanings and critiques against both the state and Việt Kiều can occur for local and diasporic Vietnamese audiences (and those who are familiar with their histories) that threaten the coherency of these films' meanings and the families they create. In describing these families as dysfunctional, we can highlight the limits of presenting representations through an ahistorical single-nation-state viewpoint as normal or ideal.

For the family in *The Rebel*, Thúy represents the motherland, as she is fierce and powerful and physically embodies familial piety (in her refusal to give up her father) and national loyalty (in her bodily acts of rebellion and acceptance of torture). After Cường helps Thúy escape, she asks Cường why he helped her, to which he replies that he is "tired of all the bloodshed" and only wants to "live in peace and order." Recognizing Johnny Trí Nguyễn as Vietnamese American brings a strong subtext to this film, as it parallels the contemporary relationship between Vietnam and some of its diaspora. As Johnny, who also co-wrote the film, stated, the character of Cường was "close to [my own] state of mind." Cường's discovery of Vietnam corresponded with Johnny's own exploration of his identity and desire for reunification as a Vietnamese American (*The Dark Destroyer* 2007).

Here, both statements have dual meanings. The "bloodshed" is both actual blood and representative of emotional wounds that have not yet healed, but it could easily be read as a reference to the blood of the fallen South Vietnamese government and the diaspora that emerged from it. While relations have improved—as illustrated by the film's production—many bitter memories still exist, with many Việt Kiều refusing to reenter the borders of a communist nation. Cường/Johnny hopes to "live in peace and order" when he forms a familial relationship with Thúy, but this statement also becomes a contested site of meaning: whose version of order is being invoked? It is interesting, though, that while Johnny's grandfather (on whom the film is loosely based) fought against the French, it is later revealed in an interview that he also fought *with* the United States. Johnny's position/history as Việt Kiều labels him as someone who is related to South Vietnam; thus, the Vietnamese family formed during this film will not last, as the hero of this story (Johnny/Cường) and the generations after will become a future enemy of the Motherland/Thúy.

Similarly, having one Việt Kiều (Cường/Johnny) kill another Việt Kiều (Sỹ/Dustin) is also a multilayered and disruptive action. In this case, the reunion of one Việt Kiều with his motherland required the killing of another Việt Kiều. For Dustin, Sỹ was patriotic due to his desire to see Vietnam get better; although he took a different approach in working with the French, Sỹ's goal was always to take power away from them, and in the end, Sỹ was also a victim of the French (*The Dark Destroyer* 2007). Just like the parallels in Cường's and Johnny's narratives, Dustin's formulation of Sỹ is very similar to those who worked with the United States during the Vietnam War, as well as the notion that the United States abandoned several of its allies with its withdrawal. By having Cường/Johnny and Thúy/Vietnam kill Sỹ/Dustin as a team, the family needs to problematically kill and remove the history of those who worked with foreign forces. In doing so, the film ambivalently suggests that for Vietnamese Americans to rejoin the homeland, a symbolic cleansing of their hybrid American identity and history may need to occur. Instead of accepting and processing this history of difference, Cường and Sỹ's narrative arc advocates for Việt Kiều bodies to be conformed back to the defined boundaries of Vietnam.

As discussed above, these defined boundaries include elements such as the rejection of technology or the use of "traditional" costumes. But recognizing transnationalism also disrupts what is traditional or authentic. In the conclusion of *Owl*, Lan is shown in a red *áo dài* running to embrace her new family. Although this could be read as Lan/Cat's rejection of technology (the United States) and a re-embracing of traditional Vietnamese culture, Cat's position as Việt Kiều destabilizes the meaning of the *áo dài*. While the *áo dài* has long been held as the ultimate symbol of Vietnamese femininity, the Vietnamese government actually banned it in 1975 as, according to the government, the dress represented material excess; in response, diasporic Vietnamese emphasized the dress even more by establishing *áo dài* pageants (Lieu 2011: 60–61).

Within the United States (and even Vietnam), the *áo dài* is not considered normal dress; they are reserved for special occasions (such as weddings) or for pageants and cultural shows. Consequently, having a Việt Kiều wear the *áo dài* could be read as not being traditional or normal, but as a staged performance, highlighting the constructed nature of cultural dress, motherhood, and gender. Much like Thúy's use of a schoolgirl outfit as a masquerade for her position as an illegal child worker, the only time the viewers see Lan in an *áo dài* is for her job in the airline business. Thus, the viewer may see that this ideal presentation of a uniform, traditional, and feminine Vietnamese body results more from Vietnam's tourism board than from any authentic Vietnamese tradition or notion of motherhood. While this family is presented as a happy family on the surface, there are levels of misrepresentation and ambivalence that leave its future in question.

Conclusion

Describing both families as dysfunctional does not deny that love exists between the family members, but, rather, points to the love-hate relationship many Vietnamese and Việt Kiều have with each other. The dysfunction in these films occurs because they pretend that Việt Kiều/ Vietnamese American bodies can be easily integrated into a joyful Vietnamese family reunion without considering how the hybrid histories and identities that come along with the Việt Kiều may not easily fit within the defined definitions of "Vietnamese." While it is important to consider the limits of confining these texts within the impenetrable containers of the nation-state, this is not to argue that transnationalism means the end of the nation-state. As this chapter illustrates, the nation-state still has power to control and create meaning. Thus, it becomes critical to analyze *when* and *by whom* transnational hybridity is obscured or highlighted, and the resulting implications. Understanding these films, filmmakers, and actors as transnational and hybrid allows us to expand our conceptualization of the meanings created in both a culturally specific and globalizing context, those that exist within and across the borders of Vietnam.

Notes

1 Lam (2013) notes this is a common critique among several Vietnamese cultural critics. It is also common for non-Vietnamese critics and scholars to conflate diasporic Vietnamese films, such as *The Scent of the Green Papaya* (1993), *Cyclo* (1995), and *Three Seasons* (1999), as part of Vietnamese cinema.

2 Unless specified, for this chapter, I will use "Vietnamese diaspora" and "Việt Kiều" (overseas Vietnamese) to refer to Vietnamese Americans. Although this runs the risk of becoming U.S.-centric, most of the major players in the selected films are from the United States.

3 Bhabha (1994) has contended that "Third Space" and hybridity are inherently subversive and counter-hegemonic, and emancipate the colonial subject through the collapse of the idea of the colonial nation-state. This has been critiqued by Mitchell (1997) for its erasure of physical space and realities, and San Juan (1999) noted that a post-colonial discourse such as hybridity "generated in the 'first world' academies turns out to be one more product of flexible, post-Fordist capitalism, not its antithesis" (8). In this case, it could be seen as the Vietnamese diaspora seeking an untapped economic market in Vietnamese entertainment, rather than any form of revolution. While I do argue that these films are hybrid and potentially resistant, they are not completely emancipatory, and I still recognize the power and influence of the nation-state.

4 For a more detailed history of Vietnamese cinema, see Ngo (2007) and Lam (2013).

5 To avoid confusion, first names for all actors and directors will be used.

6 Veronica Ngo was born in Vietnam and at the age of 10 moved to Norway for schooling. She returned to Vietnam at the age of 18 to start a career in modeling. Although she provides a fascinating case, I will not focus on her due to the complexity of her hybridity. Judging from her biography, it seems that her family was able to send her to study aboard, so her diasporic movements are not considered to be those of "exile," which is the focus of this chapter.

References

Appadurai, Arjun. 1996. *Modernity at Large: Cultural Dimensions of Globalization*. Minneapolis: University of Minnesota Press.

Bhabha, Homi. 1994. *The Location of Culture*. New York: Routledge.

Bui, Tony (director). 1999. *Three Seasons*.

Duong, Lan P. 2012. *Treacherous Subjects: Gender, Culture, and Trans-Vietnamese Feminism*. Philadelphia: Temple University Press.

Elias, Debbie Lynn. 2007. "1:1 with Stephane Gauger." *Movie Shark Deblore*, http://moviesharkdeblore.com/site/interviews/stephane-gauger/.

Gauger, Stephane, interview by A. Tseng. 2007. "Anticipation of Flight: An Interview with Stephane Gauger," *UCLA International Institute: Asia Pacific Arts*, March 20.

Hung, Tran Anh (director). 1993. *The Scent of the Green Papaya*.

— (director). 1995 *Cyclo*.

Janette, Michelle. 2006. "*Three Seasons* Refocuses American Sights of Vietnam." *Journal of Vietnamese Studies* 1(1–2): 253–276. doi:10.1525/vs.2006.1.1-2.253.

Koh, Priscilla. 2015. "You Can Come Home Again: Narratives of Home and Belonging among Second-Generation Việt Kiều in Vietnam." *SOJOURN: Journal of Social Issues in Southeast Asia* 30(1): 173–214.

Kokko, Ari. 2004. "Growth and Reform since the 8th Party Congress." In *Rethinking Vietnam*, Duncan McCargo (ed.), 69–90. London: Routledge.

Lam, Miriam. 2012. "Circumventing Channels: Indie Filmmaking in Post-Socialist Vietnam and Beyond." In *Glimpses of Freedom: Independent Cinema in Southeast Asia*, May Adadol Ingawanij and Benjamin McKay (eds), 87–106. Ithaca: Southeast Asia Program Publications.

— 2013 "Viet Nam's Growing Pains; Postsocialist Cinema Development and Transnational Politics." In *Four Decades On: Vietnam, the* United States, *and the Legacies of the Second Indochina War*, Scott Laderman and Edwin Martini (eds), 155–182. Durham: Duke University Press.

Lieu, Nhi T. 2011. *The American Dream in Vietnamese*. Minneapolis: University of Minnesota Press.

Linh, Thùy. 2013. "Rose Tinted Lenses: Vietnam's Pretty, Empty Movies." *Diacritics*, April 1, http://diacritics.org/?p=17544.

Mitchell, Katharyne. 1997. "Different Diasporas and the Hype of Hybridity." *Environment and Planning D: Society and Space* 15: 533–553.

Naficy, Hamid. 1999. *Home, Exile, Homeland: Film, Media, and the Politics of Place*. New York: Routledge.

—. 2001. *An Accented Cinema: Exilic and Diasporic Filmmaking*. Princeton: Princeton University Press.

Ngo, Lee. 2010. "Book Review: Le cinéma vietnamien; Modernity and Nationality in Vietnamese Cinema." *Journal of Vietnamese Studies* 5(2) (Summer): 251–255.

Ngo, Phuong Lan. 2007. *Modernity and Nationality in Vietnamese Cinema*. Translated by Dang Viet Vinh and Nguyen Xuan Hong. Yogyakarta: JAFF Press.

Nguyen-Akbar, Mytoan. 2014. "The Tensions of Diasporic 'Return' Migration: How Class and Money Create Distance in the Vietnamese Transnational Family." *Journal of Contemporary Ethnography* 43(2): 176–201.

Nguyen, Charlie (director). 2007. *The Dark Destroyer: An Exclusive Interview*.

Nguyen, Charlie (director). 2007. *The Rebel*.

Nguyen, Marguerite. 2009. "Situating Vietnamese transnationalism and diaspora." *Diaspora* 18(3): 382–391.

Ono, Kent and Vincent Pham. 2008. *Asian Americans and the Media*. Malden: Polity Press.

Owl and the Sparrow. 2007. *Directed by* Stephane Gauger. Chatsworth, CA: Image Entertainment, 2007. *DVD*.

Phan, Cao Tùng. 2013. "Nở rộ phim của đạo diễn Việt kiều." *Thanh Niên*, September 22. http://thanhnien.vn/van-hoa/no-ro-phim-cua-dao-dien-viet-kieu-363016.html.

San Juan, E. 1999. *Beyond Postcolonial Theory*. New York: Palgrave Macmillan.

SarDesai, D. R. 2005. *Vietnamese: Past and Present*. Boulder: Westview Press.

Stone, J. 2009. "Stephane Gauger on Owl and the Sparrow." *San Francisco Film Society*, February 9. http://www.sf360.org/Articles/Reviews/?pageid=11819.

Trâm Anh. 2006. "Dòng máu anh hùng—phim dã sử VN của đạo diễn Việt kiều." Việt Báo, January 12. http://vietbao.vn/Van-hoa/Dong-mau-anh-hung-phim-da-su-VN-cua-dao-dien-Viet-kieu/45181198/181/.

Um, Khatharya. 2012. "Exiled memory: History, identity, and remembering in Southeast Asia and Southeast Asian diaspora." *positions* 20 (3): 831–850.

Valverde, Kieu-Linh Caroline. 2012. *Transnationalizing Viet Nam: Community, Culture, and Politics in the Diaspora*. Philadelphia: Temple University Press.

Vo, Hong Chuong-Dai. 2011. "When Memories Collide: Revisiting War in Vietnam and the Diaspora." In *Film in Contemporary Southeast Asia:* Cultural Interpretation and *Social Intervention*, David C. L. Lim and Hiroyuki Yamamoto (eds), 73–92. New York: Routledge.

19

CONSTRUCTING KOREAN AMERICA

KoreAm Journal and the Construction of Second-Generation Korean American Diasporic Identifications

David C. Oh

> We were founded 25 years ago to be the representative voice for Korean Americans, and as years have passed, we've certainly evolved in terms of the kinds of stories we cover in the issues and so forth … I think our purpose is to inform, enlighten, educate, entertain readers to reflect some aspect of Korean America that they may not have known or understood before and to touch on the stories that mainstream media may have missed.
>
> Suevon Lee, former editor-in-chief of *KoreAm Journal*

According to its official website, *KoreAm Journal* (hereafter *KoreAm*) is dedicated to covering "the news of Korean America." The English-language bi-monthly magazine was primarily distributed as a mail-order magazine with very limited physical distribution in Korean markets, and later included an official website as well (iamkoream.com).[1] The magazine's location in Korean homes and public spaces helped shape a diaspora mutually constituted by the transnational meanings of the immigrant generation and the lived perspectives of multiple-generation Korean Americans. It is a rare text, as there are few other Asian American ethnic media intended for multiple-generation, primarily English-speaking members of a diaspora. Instead, most English-language media in the United States that are targeted to multiple-generation Asian Americans (e.g. *Mochi Magazine*, *Hyphen Magazine*) construct their readers racially, pointing to similar political goals and experiences in the United States and drawing upon transnational symbols and texts from multiple Asian nations. *KoreAm*'s project is largely counter-hegemonic, as its publisher and writers seek to rectify perceived gaps and distortions in dominant U.S. media coverage. Acting as a hybrid representational space, it builds Korean American belonging that exists outside the gaze of dominant media. The magazine provides discursive resources that allow readers to articulate themselves into culture in ways that build pride and identification (Hall 1996a).

Given that media texts have power to construct "imagined communities" (Anderson 1983), ethnic media such as *KoreAm* do this for immigrant communities from the space of dislocation—constructing belonging in their adopted homes, while also connecting transnationally to their ethnic homelands. This chapter assesses *KoreAm* using what I call a *hybrid diasporic approach* because it recognizes that ethnic media produced in the diaspora's local context (the United States in this case) have what Moorti (2003) calls a diasporic optic, or "a way of seeing that underscores the interstices, the spaces that are and fall between the cracks of the national and the transnational as well as other social formations" (359). The texts of diaspora construct "third spaces" for their readers that are situated at the nexus of transnationally received symbols and locally produced meanings (Bailey 2007). In the case of Korean Americans, they are a visibly different ethnic minority racialized as Asian. A hybrid diasporic approach recognizes that this local condition as a racialized ethnic minority shapes Korean Americans' new ethnicities. It is premised on an understanding that ethnic media produce discursive symbols that construct what it means to be an ethnically specific racialized minority and how that ethnic specificity is shaped by transnationalism. Ethnic media texts, at least those that are produced in the national/cultural context of the diaspora, help make sense of local experiences by gazing at multiple homes and through multiple, simultaneous identifications.

In order to discover the hybrid diasporic meanings of *KoreAm*, I examine three print issues and the stories published online through its iamkoream.com official website between January and May 2015. The printed magazines include content not found on the website, such as special features and editor's notes. The year 2015 marks *KoreAm*'s 25th anniversary, which prompted a special issue that self-reflexively gives insight into its position as an ethnic magazine. Each issue featured roughly 30 stories and included about 75 pages, with roughly two-thirds for original content and one-third for full-page advertising. I also received official weekday emails from the journal that encouraged readers to view four to six stories per day, and I reviewed all stories linked in the emails from January 13 to April 30, 2015. Occasionally, online stories overlapped with print content, and in those cases, the story was only analyzed once. This resulted in 388 articles. The stories were coded using discourse analysis as situated in a cultural studies tradition (Barker and Galasinski 2001) with a focus on understanding how Korean America is constructed, including its boundaries and its meanings. As Georgiou (2006) notes, the media of a diaspora shape everyday negotiations about who belongs, what it means to belong, what the boundaries of the group are, and which symbols are used to maintain group coherence. In addition to this analysis of the texts, I also triangulated the findings by conducting a phone interview in July 2015 with Suevon Lee, the editor-in-chief of *KoreAm* at the time, to explore the magazine's representational strategies in the discursive construction of Korean America.

Together, this chapter examines the ways in which *KoreAm* constructs Korean America as a hybrid diaspora with meanings rooted in local experiences in the United States but that also draw on transnational symbols and connections from South Korea (hereafter Korea). These transnational connections contest and reify hegemonic practices, construct boundaries of inclusion, and define Korean Americanness through disidentification and identification with transnational symbols. I argue that *KoreAm* uses transnational symbols as resources to define Korean Americanness through identification and disidentification. In addition, it constructs Korean America in relationship to dominant culture through representations that simultaneously promote counter-hegemonic resistance and hegemonic integration.

Rethinking Ethnic Media in the Diaspora

The approach I take in this chapter's examination of *KoreAm* differs from much of the ethnic media research that has recycled Park's (1922) assimilation-pluralism model of the ethnic press. His argument rested on the faulty and reductive assumption that assimilation and pluralism are opposite ends of a mutually exclusive pole (Cheng 2005). To add complexity to the understanding of ethnic group membership, work on diasporas provides promising theoretical direction. The conceptualization of diasporas as scattered ethnic group members who construct themselves into "imagined community" through the use of communication technologies (Georgiou 2006) emphasizes transnationalism with symbols, discourses, and materials brought from the "homeland" and used for purposes specific to the experiences of a diaspora in their locally experienced "homes" (Gillespie 2000; Oh 2012b; Sreberny 2000). As such, diasporas are multiply identified with the local and the transnational.

Although they are often associated with the immigrant generation, diasporas can include multiple generations. Diasporas like Han Chinese in Malaysia and Jews in the United States point to generations-old diasporas that still construct themselves as multiply identified. For Asian Americans, their historically restricted immigration to the United States has led to a relatively recent maturing of its non-White diasporic communities. A useful framework for understanding these diasporas is Hall's (1996b) concept of "new ethnicities." In a foundational article, he points out that the experience of diaspora is located at the cultural margins in a space betwixt dominant and ethnic homeland cultures. Being fully acculturated does not remove affective and symbolic connections for many multiple-generation Asian Americans, particularly as it becomes a way of resisting racial marginalization in dominant culture (Kibria 2002). In this way, multiple-generation Asian Americans often articulate themselves into complex diasporic belongings. Particularly in this conjuncture in which digital media have collapsed spatial and temporal boundaries (Georgiou 2006) and in which Asian immigrants make up the largest percentage of new immigrants (Escobar 2015), multiple-generation Asian Americans can engage transnational symbols and meanings in unprecedented ways.

Just as multiple-generation Asian Americans construct diasporic meanings, English-language ethnic media construct "new ethnicities" that are located in the geographical and everyday experience of the local "home" while connecting with the transnational symbols and affective longing for the "homeland." Regrettably, there is little ethnic media research that focuses on a diaspora's English-language media; the vast majority of scholarship is centered on foreign-language ethnic media or on films (see Moorti 2003; Sharma 2011; Smets et al. 2013). In the context of the United States, English-language media matter because they are accessible resources for multiple-generation diasporas, particularly for those who do not have the ability to read proficiently in their ethnic languages. Through the remainder of the chapter, I examine *KoreAm*'s construction of "new ethnicities" for multiple-generation Korean Americans.

Ethnicity, Diaspora, and the Homeland

Most of *KoreAm*'s representational work as the "voice" of Korean America is to construct what it means to belong to the interstitial space of diaspora as an ethnic formation. Although this includes its relationship to dominant culture and its racial identification as Asian American, many articles studied were specific to ethnicity, that is, Korean America, transnational Korean news, and the intersection of Korea and the United States. It is in these stories that definitions of Korean Americanness are constructed, shifting the diasporic optic in multiple directions, at itself in the United States and abroad to Korea. The space is marked by hybridity, as it is about reconciling ethnic similarity with a different lived experience and social context from those in the homeland (Georgiou 2006). As scholars of diaspora have noted in studies of audience reception, texts are used to construct interstitial spaces in which "new ethnicities" are articulated and constructed

(Durham 2004; Gillespie 1995). In *KoreAm*'s construction of new ethnicities, Korean America inclusively is based on "fundamental essence," the notion that ethnicity is defined by ancestral heritage alone, with cultural knowledge as unnecessary to definitions of ethnic belonging (Kibria 2002). Thus, transnational symbols are used as resources for ethnic pride and meaning but are not necessary to claims of belonging.

KoreAm can also be seen to intentionally include difference within the diaspora in its construction of diasporic belonging. In an interview, editor-in-chief Suevon Lee said:

> The definition of being Korean American is changing. It's in flux, and as we have a greater mixing of cultures, for instance, or as we see or identify adoptees who have come forward and shared their story even, we tend to find that what being Korean American means is going to be is different for everybody.

Because of its shifting and multiple construction of Korean America, *KoreAm* positions fundamental essence as the ideological underpinning of belonging; that is, anyone with a heritage connection to Korea is given representational inclusion. Indeed, in the 25th anniversary issue, it included images of its most notable covers, including Korean Americans with immigrant parents such as Michelle Rhee and John Cho, biracial Korean Americans such as Karen O. (White/Korean) and Hines Ward (Black/Korean), and queer Korean Americans such as Margaret Cho and Lt Dan Choi. It also included a cover on queer issues in 1993 and adoptees in 2013. Although multiple-generation Korean Americans sometimes use cultural knowledge and linguistic fluency as markers of authenticity (Oh 2015), *KoreAm* constructs Korean America more broadly.

One way *KoreAm* demonstrates this inclusivity is through its code-switching practices. By using Korean words on its pages, the magazine reinforces a shared cultural identity marked by language and practices of code-switching that build cultural awareness. For example, in an article about a homeland tour for biracial adoptees, it states: "The school served snacks like *hotteok*, the sweet Korean pancake, and lunch items such as *ddeokbokgi*, rice cakes smothered in spicy chili sauce." In an article titled "Learn How to Make Traditional Korean Dishes from a Rapper," the author writes: "As a cute and hilarious bonus, Lyricks also includes a few tips he learned from his *halmeoni*, or grandma." Both quotes code-switch to reinforce ethnic belonging through shared everyday language, yet they also translate the terms for readers who may be unfamiliar with Korean. Notably, the articles mark Korean language with the use of italics, connoting the foreignness of the words. So while there is connection to the homeland, the homeland culture is marked as different. This reflects an understanding of multiple-generation Korean diasporas as connected to and a part of the home culture in the United States, but distinct from their heritage culture.

Despite the relative inclusivity of "fundamental essence" as the boundary for ethnic inclusion, *KoreAm* valorizes a specific articulation of Korean America: those who are wholly committed to life in the United States but who have transnational ties to their heritage culture, regardless of the strength or quality of the connection. This is most clear in stories of transnational Korean adoptees. In a feature article titled "Family Portrait" about Nathan Nowack, a 38-year-old transnational adoptee, the author points out that Nowack was content without knowing his birth family because of his loving appreciation for his adoptive parents. The story eventually notes that life circumstances led him to search for his birth family, leading to validation and transnational belonging, ending the article with Nowack quoted as saying: "I just want everyone to know, don't be afraid of it. There could be a happy outcome … [Knowing] that a family back in Korea might be wondering, wishing and hoping to find out how their adopted baby is doing, it's worth it." As with all stories about transnational adoptees during the time frame of the study, the adoptive family is represented as loving and valued while transnational connections are also portrayed as fulfilling.

This connection is valorized even when discoveries unearth psychic traumas, as in "A Clear Sky after the Rain," a story about a homeland tour for biracial Korean American adoptees. The article points out that biracial adoptees are doubly marginalized because they are physically neither "fully Korean nor fully Western," and because they are "a minority among more than 200,000 Korean adoptees worldwide." Despite uncovering pains during the trip, the article states that learning about the homeland is vital for healing. It concludes by stating: "We realized that a homeland tour for adoptees isn't really about coming home—home, we know, is where our loved ones are. Rather, a homeland tour is an opportunity to uncover parts of our past, to visit old wounds and to try to make peace with them." This marks the standpoint from which *KoreAm* situates its readership into diasporic identification. Through stories such as this, it argues that for members of the diaspora, local home cultures are what matters most, and transnational ties and symbols are meant to transform Korean Americans in the local space. Thus, *KoreAm* valorizes hybridity as an interstitial space anchored in the United States while reaching out to Korea.

Hybridity as a state of being for Korean Americans is expressed most strongly in the "I Am KoreAm" features, which profile ordinary Korean Americans. For example, profiles about Amy Shin and Jenny Kong Cha both emphasize their bicultural belonging. Amy is quoted as responding: "Korean American first generation immigrant (immigrated at age 9) – ethnically 100 percent Korean but very bicultural." Jenny Kong Cha writes:

> I am KoreAm and proud because being Korean American, I know about two cultures together ... Being KoreAm, another thing is I can teach my child about two cultures from the start and she'll have a head start in opening minds to other cultures too! Hopefully leading the way to more open minds!

Hybridity is not only constructed as the normative experience of Korean America, but it is constructed as normative because of the belief in the moral good that hybridity brings, differentiating Korean Americans from both monocultural U.S. Americans and Koreans. The "I Am KoreAm" features also include Korean Americans who represent a wider diversity of experiences, such as Marika Medrano, a Korean American adoptee who married a Mexican American man and has a biracial child. She said: "I was raised in a white family, but it's important to me to embrace my Korean culture & introduce Korean things to my son."

The most common portrayals of hybridity are stories about Korean Americans raised by immigrant Korean parents. This articulation of Korean America focuses on the hybridity of local and transnational identities, but also hybridity of generation as doubly understood—between young/old and first-generation/second-generation American. The cover story for the February/March issue with Benson Lee, the director of *Seoul Searching*, includes profiles of all major leads, who discuss their work on the film and also the meaning of Korean American identity. Writing about Lee's personal experiences, he is quoted as saying the following.

> When I walked outside of my house, I was in America, but when I walked into my house, it was Korea ... That was very hard for me in a lot of ways because, sometimes, these two cultures can be quite polarized, and they are very different from each other. But when I went to Korea and realized that everybody else was going through the same thing, that helped me to understand it wasn't just about my parents, it was

> about this duality I was living in ... We, at a very young age, realized that, wow, we're never going to be really Korean, nor are we going to be really fully American. So being Korean American or Korean German or Korean Spanish is who we are. We have to embrace the best of both worlds and grapple with the worst of both.

As Gillespie (1995) notes, members of diaspora construct "new ethnicities" that result in identifications and rejections of the local home culture and the transnational homeland culture. By highlighting stories such as Lee's, *KoreAm* endorses the view that Korean America is about a hybrid identity that is rooted in the local home, connecting to and rejecting aspects of ethnic heritage culture.

This understanding of diaspora is further reinforced in the online edition's spotlight on the film's lead actors. One article highlights Justin Chon's understanding of his experience of diaspora as marked by generational difference, disconnection with family, and hybridity. Chon is quoted as saying: "I grew up in the US. We have such different experiences [Korean diaspora in other nations], but it's so interesting that our experiences are very similar in terms of the main struggles we go through as second-generation *gyopo*." The use of the Korean word *gyopo*, which is untranslated for readers and means "overseas Korean," is assumed to be understood by readers as a state of being. Though it is used by the actor, the magazine itself does not use the term, perhaps because *gyopo* implies that Koreanness matters as an immutable identity marked by a state of dislocation rather than a different identification altogether. Finally, Esteban Ahn, a Korean Spaniard, highlights his connectedness to ethnicity despite his feelings of marginalization in both home and homeland, saying: "Even though I'm Korean, in Korea, people treat me like a foreigner, and in Spain, they also treat me like a foreigner. I don't have a proper identity. Those kinds of themes really touched me a lot in the movie because as you can see in the movie, we are all Koreans." Ahn's quote reinforces the representational work of the magazine, which shows that connections to heritage culture matter even as readers disidentify, or are made to disidentify, with it.

Transnational Symbols

Although the magazine's content is predominantly tied to experiences in the diaspora, most of the online articles and some of the print articles were transnational in nature, focusing on connections to Korea. Roughly three-quarters of the articles analyzed featured what I saw as transnational news. Korean culture in these articles is not represented as a place for dual, multiple belongings; rather, it is a symbolic universe to be drawn from in order to empower Korean *American* readers. For instance, an online story titled "South Korean Special Forces Train Shirtless in the Snow" featured multiple images of muscular soldiers training in preparation for a possible conflict in the frigid mountains of North Korea. Despite the seriousness of the subject matter, the first image connotes playfulness, as it features three shirtless soldiers kneeling, throwing a mist of snow in the air while appearing to laugh. The men's delight and lean, muscular bodies are exposed to the camera's gaze. The images work to intervene in the cultural terrain of Korean America by pointing out and celebrating Korean masculinity, which is frequently racialized in dominant media as asexual and feminized (Espiritu 2004; Oh 2012a).

Likewise, stories of sports success work to build pride in (ethno)nationalism and masculinity, as the two are linked in the United States cultural imagination (Butterworth 2012). Stories of Western recognition of Korean successes in other venues like the arts, popular culture, education, and fashion are also covered frequently. These stories are meant to generate greater pride and desire to identify, asserting a Korean American understanding of its heritage culture as articulated within U.S. politics of representation. For instance, articles highlighted Korea's relative value in the world by pointing to innovative industries and technologies that disrupt racist notions of Asians as robotic and uncreative (see Fong 2008), that assert the importance of Korea by emphasizing the "strength" of its passport, and that counter Orientalist views of Asian patriarchal domination (Said 1978) by pointing to progressive change, such as Korea's acceptance of its first female Reserve Officers' Training Corps (ROTC) cadet and Koreans' increasing LGBT acceptance.

In addition to transnational connections, diasporic media also construct disidentification with the homeland. As Bailey (2007) writes, media of the diaspora can disrupt idealized notions of the homeland. Indeed, to define Korean America, *KoreAm* must define what it is not and with which it might be most confused—Korea. As Hall (1996) notes, identities are frequently constructed through difference. To do this, there are multiple stories that openly highlight points of disidentification. This differs from representations of U.S. culture and society, which, when critiqued, are resisted obliquely and through inference. This may be because Korean Americans are conflated in dominant culture as Koreans and rarely as Americans, so there could be an implicit need to protect the community by defining Korean America as very much American. On the other hand, Asian and Asian American are often confounded in the dominant cultural imagination, as encapsulated in Palumbo-Liu's (1999) construction of the term Asian/American. Perhaps because of a desire to define difference from Korea, *KoreAm* also disidentifies with aspects of Korean cultural life.

One indication of disidentification is with moral failure in Korean culture. For instance, in the article "Protecting Youth from 'Culture of Drinking,'" blame is placed on Korean culture. The author states:

> My early exposure to drinking alcohol is probably familiar to many Korean Americans, who, starting at a young age, often witness how much alcohol is valued, celebrated and considered a key part of socializing and enjoyment with friends and family—or even bonding with one's dad. For an ethnic community known to stigmatize issues ranging from mental health to cancer, there seems to be a remarkably casual attitude and permissiveness toward exposing young people to this culture of drinking, even excessive drinking.

Although the story is not about Korea per se, it is centered on a harm that is thought to be transmitted transnationally through *Korean* parents. Later in the article, the author claims that "parents, who should be the messengers and disciplinarians on this issue, are often part of the problem." Thus, fault is located in the first generation, and multiple-generation Korean American binge drinkers are constructed as less blameworthy. The argument is premised on the idea that Korean Americans do not accept deviations from the norm (in mental health or physical health), yet excessive drinking is presented as problematically normalized in the diaspora. Particularly because the author's argument is a non sequitur, the purpose was most likely to assert an ideological belief about *Korean* culture. Importantly, while the article cites statistics on binge drinking in the United States, the data are used to point to a problem among Korean Americans, ignoring the interaction of U.S. cultural shifts toward binge drinking with ethnically specific attitudes and practices of alcohol consumption. Thus, Korean culture, in particular, is drawn in relief against the stated normative ideal of responsible drinking, which is legitimized as a U.S. value through UCLA professor Kyeyoung Park, who is quoted toward the article's conclusion as saying: "In the US, there's justified bias against drinking … Heavy drinkers or underage drinkers are perceived as near-criminals in the American culture. It goes against

American sensibilities. We should acknowledge that drinking isn't [stigmatized] enough in the Korean culture."

An online story titled "Korean Parents Shell Out $640 for Japanese Backpacks," focusing on Korean materialism and social appearances, is also a point of disidentification. The article notes: "Following the footsteps of North Face jackets, *randoseru* is the latest financial backbreaker for parents. Parents from even low-income households are purchasing these premium backpacks, afraid that their child might be ostracized or bullied in school." The desire for *randoseru* is explained as rooted in a culture in which not having expensive material possessions is enough justification for peers to bully classmates. Purchasing the backpack, then, is implied as necessary because of misaligned cultural values. Indeed, another article lampoons Koreans for their conformity. Replicating techno-Orientalist discourses about a lack of individuality and robotic personalities (Morley and Robins 1995), the article titled "Fashion Doppelgangers in South Korea" uses humor to present multiple images of similar Korean street fashion. The implicit point is that Koreans suffer from a lack of individuality, particularly as the argument about fashion similarity did not extend to the United States, a part of the hybrid space of Korean America. The exclusion denotes that Korean Americans as part of the United States are individualistic and creative, unlike their homeland counterparts. *KoreAm* ambivalently represents Korea as a site from which to draw transnational symbols that allow symbolic empowerment and disidentification. Whether it is for empowerment or disidentification, transnational symbols are used for locally meaningful esteem building by multiple-generation Korean Americans in the diaspora.

Racializing Korean America

The other lens of the diasporic optic is set on social formations in the local and national context in which Korean Americans live. In *KoreAm*, diasporic identity construction is further complicated by adopting racialized resistance to dominant culture articulated as pan-Asian belonging (Min 2002). It positions multiple-generation Korean Americans as both ethnically specific and racially identified. Racial meanings, especially, are expressed as political identities in a larger politics of representation and activism (Espiritu 1992). As Ono and Sloop (1995) point out, vernacular discourse, which is the language and representations of the marginalized, is able to resist dominant culture and to construct community. In *KoreAm*, racial discrimination is treated as a taken-for-granted reality that requires the marshaling of pan-Asian connections while avoiding the open contestation of White supremacy. In other words, it calls for racial equality without referencing racism. Anxieties around naming racism construct it as a concern on the periphery. This non-speaking functions as alternative pedagogy to teach readers that discussions of race and racism are sensitive and generally avoided. By avoiding race and racism, it furthers postracism, even if unintentionally.

Counter-hegemonic resistance is most frequently focused on self- and counter-representation in media that subjectify Korean Americanness and Asian Americanness. Stories of self-representation focus on alternative media and spaces that generate visibility, complexity, and opportunity. As mentioned before, the magazine featured a film titled *Seoul Searching*, an independent film about teens in the Korean diaspora in multiple parts of the world who go to Korea for a summer at a heritage camp in the 1980s. Featuring the film as its cover story and dedicating several pages to the perspectives of the director and several of the main leads, as discussed earlier, the magazine gave space to ethnically affirming alternative texts, but even as it did so, it relegated the need for alternative representation to a need to resist stereotyping. In an article titled "Benson Lee Gets Personal," it quotes the director as saying: "We live in a very diverse country, but quite often the studio system doesn't really reflect that in the types of movies they show." This signals to readers a commonsense understanding that racial stereotyping and underrepresentation exist.

However, *KoreAm* operates less by directly challenging racism than by affirming alternative expression itself. It assumes a shared understanding of the politics of representation, skipping past reflexive racialization and calls to action, and instead highlighting successes. Affirmations of symbolic representation were most evident in pan-Asian celebration of *Fresh Off the Boat*, a televised situation comedy featuring the first Asian American family on television in 20 years. Like most of the coverage of counter-representation within dominant popular culture, *KoreAm* praised the possibilities for greater Asian American complexity on screen. In the "Editor's Note" for the December/January issue, editor-in-chief Suevon Lee wrote:

> All around, it's been an exciting 2015 so far for Asian Americans in entertainment and pop culture. Raise your hand if, like me, you're in front of a TV at 8 p.m. on Tuesday night to catch *Fresh Off the Boat*, the new ABC sitcom starring Randall Park, Hudson Yang and Constance Wu ... Here's to its continuing success.

Further, in an article titled "For Viewers, a Fresh Start," *KoreAm* featured a watch party for the show, in which it observed: "And high up in the seats, a young man in a black sweatshirt took the microphone and, bellowing just a little at first, remarked on the sea of billboards plastered around LA promoting *Fresh Off the Boat*—prominently featuring the Asian American faces of Randall Park and co-star, Constance Wu, and how powerful a symbol that has served." The articles reflect the relief and excitement Asian Americans felt with on-screen visibility, but reduce the complexity of Asian American readings to celebration.

Indeed, the same article also states: "Asked by an audience member why a 20-year stretch must separate the appearance of an Asian American family on network television, Oliver Wang, an associate professor of sociology at California State University, joked, 'White supremacy.'" It is revealing that the article describes Wang's response as a *joke*, pointing to uneasiness over naming Whiteness as the cause of Asian American symbolic annihilation. This is reinforced in an article titled "The Line of Liberation" in a later issue. A contributor writes: "Sure, certain stereotypes, like 'ching-chong' accents or tiger moms, do matter and they can certainly be perpetuated. But we're talking mainstream network television here: it's doomed to compromise, and to obsess over those details is to miss the opportunity for other kinds of conversations." Unlike postracism, which denies racism altogether, the article acknowledges racism as a lived reality but minimizes it by stating that to actively challenge it is to miss "other" conversations, which are connoted as more important. In other words, celebrating its success in U.S. dominant culture (minus an understanding of racism) is considered most productive. The locally focused diasporic lens of *KoreAm* recognizes the harms of racism, particularly in the realm of symbolic representation, but it minimizes the harms of racism by reifying dominant culture as a space in which Korean Americans can achieve the "American Dream." Its desire for optimistic coverage has the consequence of minimizing racism and hiding its causes.

This is true in other "American Dream" narratives that work to reify U.S. dominant culture (Cloud 1996). Especially because the representations are not coupled with a critique of systemic racism, the multiple stories of individual successes prevail. Korean Americans in many different professional sectors—government, the arts, popular culture, sports, and business—are celebrated as ethnic role models to the exclusion of serious considerations of White oppression. In a story titled "L.A.'s Korean American Candidates Wage Uphill Battle" about David Ryu, the eventual winner of a city council seat in Los Angeles, the article states: "Part of Ryu's message has focused on his background growing up poor in Los Angeles in an immigrant Korean family, and overcoming those odds, thanks to public education and government assistance." The focus on Ryu's message of hardship reinforces the "American Dream" narrative, and though the story avoids neoliberal ideologies of "rugged individualism" embedded in the narrative (Butterworth 2007), it, nonetheless, advances the color-blind ideal that with enough hard work, racism is no longer a barrier to success. As a follow-up article titled "Candidate in Overdrove" states, "Ask him about his status as a Korean American running to join a historically non-diverse City Council, though, and expect no extended rumination on the relevance of his ethnic identity." Because the article only provides an implicit critique of his unwillingness to address political representation, it tacitly endorses his color-blind point of view. This is common in racial discourses of the "American Dream" that are coupled with an unwillingness to acknowledge the limits of systemic racism (Sun et al. 2002). The articulation of color-blindness is one part of the postracial discourses of dominant culture. Like postracism, *KoreAm* refuses to acknowledge the role of racism (Ono 2010), but, unlike postracism, it acknowledges ethnic and racial group membership. Thus, *KoreAm* negotiates the role of the diaspora in its local context as a racialized ethnic minority by affirming ethnic belonging, but it also advocates for dominant culture integration by reifying the "American Dream."

"Robert Refsnyder Making the Plays" is a rare example of an article that dealt explicitly with anti-Asian racism. Refsnyder, an adopted Korean American baseball player and minor league prospect for the New York Yankees, is described as defending his family against "racist taunts" in the College World Series against the University of South Carolina. However, Refsnyder is also described as apologizing after being drafted by the New York Yankees and placed on its class-A team, the Charleston RiverDogs. He is reported as saying: "I apologize for generalizing a whole state, that's so stupid and immature on my part." Although the story recognizes anti-Asian racism, it valorizes Refsnyder's apology as appropriate, despite his being the target of racism, thus accommodating postracial sanctions against discussing race and racism. Indeed, of the 388 articles, no article criticizes aspects of U.S. culture or systems as the central focus of the article, even in ones that highlight Asian American activism. Thus, the magazine's relationship with dominant culture is filled with contradiction. On the one hand, the need for Korean American representation is an a priori recognition of racial marginalization, but, on the other, *KoreAm* advances a negotiated form of postracism, a feature of dominant culture. Thus, its hybrid positioning is articulated within dominant culture—condoning resistance but also fitting in.

Conclusion

Shi (2005) writes that "ethnic media constitute a liminal space where ambivalent and unstable points of personal, national, and ethnic identifications are negotiated" (66). I extend her theoretical contribution by arguing that *KoreAm* constructs Korean America as a hybrid diasporic identity, shaped by the transnational experience of diasporic belonging, that is useful for the local experience as a racialized ethnic minority. In response to diasporic life in the United States, the magazine includes representations of Korean American success that are meant to celebrate and symbolically empower but that also construct a postracial "American Dream" narrative. It also includes transnationally drawn Korean symbols meant to generate ethnic esteem and disidentification—both necessary to construct "new ethnicities." Within the diaspora, it constructs Korean America as an inclusive, hybrid space that is represented by diversity of membership but fits a normative logic that values rootedness in the United States and transnational interests in Korea. Finally, it extends community in stories of resistance that connect to broader pan-Asian alliances that challenge White racism. However, the challenges are limited, as they do not name White supremacy directly, fitting in with postracial sanctions against discussing race and especially racism.

The conclusions of this research are important, not so much because of what they uncover about *KoreAm* as a specific text. Indeed, James Ryu, the publisher, reportedly sold *KoreAm* to London Trust Media, which proceeded to stop presses and terminate its staff (Kim 2015). The journal's 25-year run has concluded, so this case study examines *KoreAm* not for its own sake but, rather, to make broader theoretical arguments relevant to existing and new host-language ethnic media. Most importantly, I argue that the assimilation-pluralism model has limited utility because it does not capture the complexity of ethnic media (Cheng 2005). Using that model, I would only have been able to conclude that *KoreAm* is pluralistic because of its coverage of Korean Americans and inclusion of ethnically specific transnational news, but that it is assimilationist in its integrationist messages, use of dominant culture language, and dominant-culture journalistic norms. Instead, as the conclusions of this study find, it is necessary to understand how ethnic media construct diasporic belonging, that is, about how local experiences of diaspora are constructed as "new ethnicities," identities in the interstices that draw upon and disidentify with both dominant and ethnic culture within the particular conjuncture in which they are published. By reconceptualizing the work of ethnic media as multiple rather than singular, and by sidestepping the question of whether assimilation or pluralism is a desired end goal, it leads to conclusions that have more complexity. All representations matter to diasporic identification as it is projected onto the text's imagined audience. Moreover, *KoreAm* possesses a negotiated relationship with dominant and ethnic cultures that creates a third in-between space, new ethnicities, for its readership.

Researchers must continue to take ethnic media seriously as a site of inquiry. Although individual ethnic media texts have limited circulation, together they are used by roughly one-quarter of U.S. Americans (Shi 2009). This is due to increasing ethnoracial plurality in the United States and many racialized ethnic minorities' sense of marginalization by dominant culture media (Johnson 2010). Yet, the study of ethnic media is important not only because of the size of the audience, but because of its meaningfulness in the everyday lives of U.S. Americans who identify and are identified as ethnically and racially different. Studying ethnic media builds awareness of how identities and meanings of diasporas are constructed through vernacular discourse (Ono and Sloop 1995). A diasporic approach does not ask whether "their texts" are causing ethnic "others" to assimilate or whether ethnic media are promoting pluralism through authentic and pure difference; rather, it assumes hybridity as a logical condition, and it seeks to understand the nature of the hybridity within local and global contexts. Thus, it understands diasporic experience as fluid and multiple. In this way, understanding the meanings of ethnic media as diasporic texts can create openings for improved multicultural understanding, and it can create the potential to generate reflexivity in ethnic media newsrooms, which could lead to deliberative discussions that productively shape work that contributes to diasporic belongings.

Note

1 The circulation figures and click-through rates were unavailable because the publisher, James Ryu, sold the publication in August 2015.

References

Anderson, Benedict. 1983. *Imagined Communities: Reflections on the Origin and Spread of Nationalism.* Revised ed. New York, NY: Verso Books.

Bailey, Olga Guedes. 2007. "Transnational Identities and the Media." In *Transnational Lives and the Media: Re-imagining Diaspora,* Olga Guedes Bailey, Myria Georgiou, and Ramaswami Harindranath (eds), 212–230. New York, NY: Palgrave Macmillan.

Barker, Chris, and Dariusz Galasinski. 2001. *Cultural Studies and Discourse Analysis: A Dialogue on Language and Identity.* Thousand Oaks, CA: Sage.

Butterworth, Michael L. 2007. "Race in 'the Race': Mark McGwire, Sammy Sosa, and the Heroic Constructions of Whiteness." *Critical Studies in Media Communication* 24(3): 228–244. doi:10.1080/07393180701520926.

Butterworth, Michael L. 2012. "Militarism and Memorializing at the Pro Football Hall of Fame." *Communication and Critical/Cultural Studies* 9(3): 241–258. doi:10.1080/14791420.2012.675438.

Cheng, Hau Ling. 2005. "Constructing a Transnational, Multilocal Sense of Belonging: An Analysis of *Ming Pao (West Canadian Edition).* " *Journal of Communication Inquiry* 29(2): 141–159. doi:10.1177/0196859904273194.

Cloud, Dana L. 1996. "Hegemony or Concordance?: The Rhetoric of Tokenism in 'Oprah' Winfrey's Rags-to-Riches Biography." *Critical Studies in Mass Communication* 13(2): 115–137. doi:10.1080/15295039609366967.

Durham, Meenakshi Gigi. 2004. "Constructing the 'New Ethnicities': Media, Sexuality, and Diaspora Identity in the Lives of South Asian Immigrant Girls." *Critical Studies in Media Communication* 21(2): 140–161. doi:10.1080/07393180410001688047.

Escobar, Allyson. 2015. "Asian Immigrants Likely to Overtake Hispanics in US Population." *Asian Journal,* last modified November 29, 2015. http://asianjournal.com/news/asian-immigrants-likely-to-overtake-hispanics-in-us-population/.

Espiritu, Yen Le. 1992. "Asian American Panethnicity: Bridging Institutions and Identities." In *Asian American History and Culture,* Sucheng Chan, David Palumbo-Liu, Michael Omi, Scott Wong and Liinda Trinh Vo (eds). Philadelphia, PA: Temple University Press.

Espiritu, Yen Le. 2004. "Ideological Racism and Cultural Resistance: Constructing Our Own Images." In *Race, Class, and Gender: An Anthology,* Margaret L. Andersen and Patricia Hill Collins (eds), 175–184. Belmont, CA: Wadsworth.

Fong, Timothy P. 2008. *The Contemporary Asian American Experience: Beyond the Model Minority.* 3rd ed. Upper Saddle River, NJ: Pearson Prentice Hall.

Georgiou, Myria. 2006. *Diaspora, Identity, and the Media: Diasporic Transnationalism and Mediated Spatialities.* In *Urban Communication,* Gary Gumpert (ed). Cresskill, NJ: Hampton Press, Inc.

Gillespie, Marie. 1995. "Television, Ethnicity, and Cultural Change." In *Comedia Series,* David Morley (ed). New York, NY: Routledge.

Gillespie, Marie. 2000. "Transnational Communications and Diaspora Communities." In *Ethnic Minorities and the Media: Changing Cultural Boundaries,* Simon Cottle (ed), 164–179. Philadelphia, PA: Open University Press.

Hall, Stuart. 1996a. "Introduction: Who Needs 'Identity'?" In *Questions of Cultural Identity,* Stuart Hall and Paul Du Gay (eds), 1–17. Thousand Oaks, CA: Sage Publications.

Hall, Stuart. 1996b. "New Ethnicities." In *Stuart Hall: Critical Dialogues in Cultural Studies,* David Morley and Kuan-Hsing Chen (eds), 443–451. New York, NY: Routledge.

Johnson, Melissa. 2010. "Incorporating Self-Categorization Concepts into Ethnic Media Research." *Communication Theory* 20(1): 106–125. doi:10.1111/j.1468-2885.2009.01356.x.

Kibria, Nazli. 2002. *Becoming Asian American: Second-generation Chinese and Korean American Identities.* Baltimore, MD: The John Hopkins University Press.

Kim, Victoria. 2015. "Archivist to the Korean American Experience Says Goodbye to Print." *Los Angeles Times,* December 27. http://www.latimes.com/local/california/la-me-korean-magazine-20151227-story.html.

Min, Pyong Gap. 2002. "Introduction." In *The Second Generation: Ethnic Identity among Asian Americans,* Pyong Gap Min (ed), 1–17. New York, NY: AltaMira Press.

Moorti, Sujata. 2003. "Desperately Seeking an Identity: Diasporic Cinema and the Articulation of Transnational Kinship." *International Journal of Cultural Studies* 6(3): 355–376. doi:10.1177/13678779030063007.

Morley, David and Kevin Robins. 1995. *Spaces of Identity: Global Media, Electronic Landscapes and Cultural Boundaries.* New York, NY: Routledge.

Oh, David C. 2012a. "Black-Yellow Fences: Multicultural Boundaries and Whiteness in the *Rush Hour* Franchise." *Critical Studies in Media Communication* 29(5): 349–366. doi:10.1080/15295036.2012.697634.

Oh, David C. 2012b. "Mediating the Boundaries: Second-Generation Korean American Adolescents' Use of Transnational Korean Media as Markers of Social Boundaries." *International Communication Gazette* 74(3): 258–276. doi:10.1177/1748048511432607.

Oh, David C. 2015. *Second-Generation Korean Americans and Transnational Media: Diasporic Identifications.* Lanham, MD: Lexington Books.

Ono, Kent A. 2010. "Postracism: A Theory of the 'Post'—as Political Strategy." *Journal of Communication Inquiry* 34(3): 227–233. doi:10.1177/0196859910371375.

Ono, Kent A. and Sloop, John M. (1995). "The Critique of Vernacular Discourse." *Communication Monographs* 62(1): 19–46. doi:10.1080/03637759509376346.

Palumbo-Liu, David. 1999. *Asian/American: Historical Crossings of a Racial Frontier.* Palo Alto, CA: Stanford University Press.

Park, Robert Ezra. 1922. *The Immigrant Press and Its Control.* New York: Harper & Brothers.

Said, Edward W. 1978. *Orientalism.* New York, NY: Vintage Books.

Sharma, Rekha. 2011. "Desi Films: Articulating Images of South Asian Identity in a Global Communication Environment." *Global Media Journal—Canadian Edition* 4(1): 127–143, www.gmj.uottawa.ca/index_e.html.

Shi, Yu. 2005. "Identity Construction of the Chinese Diaspora, Ethnic Media Use, Community Formation, and the Possibility of Social Activism." *Journal of Media & Cultural Studies* 19(1): 55–72. doi:10.1080/1030431052000336298.

Shi, Yu. 2009. "Re-evaluating the 'Alternative' Role of Ethnic Media in the US: The Case of Chinese-language Press and Working-class Women Readers." *Media, Culture & Society* 31(4): 597–616. doi:10.1177/0163443709335219.

Smets, Kevin, Iris Vandevelde, Philippe Meers, Roel Vande Winkel, and Sofie Van Bauwel. 2013. "Diasporic Film Cultures from a Multi-level Perspective: Moroccan and Indian Cinematic Flows in and towards Antwerp (Belgium)." *Critical Studies in Media Communication* 30(4): 257–274. doi:10.1080/15295036.2012.672758.

Sreberny, Annabelle. 2000. "Media and Diasporic Consciousness: An exploration among Iranians in London." In *Ethnic Minorities and the Media: Changing Cultural Boundaries*, Simon Cottle (eds), 179–196. Philadelphia, PA: Open University Press.

Sun, Chyng Feng, Leda Cooks, Corey Rinehart, and Stacy A. S. Williams. 2002. "DMX, Cosby, and Two Sides of the American Dream." In *Saying It Loud!: African-American Audiences, Media, and Identity*, Robin R. Means Coleman (ed), 115–145. New York: Routledge.

20

SOUTH ASIANS AND THE CALL CENTER NARRATIVE

Accents and Cross-Cultural Communication in TV's *Outsourced*

Shilpa Davé

In 2010, NBC announced the premiere of a situation comedy called *Outsourced* to anchor their successful Thursday night back-to-back lineup of *Community* (2009–2015), *30 Rock* (2006–2013), and *The Office* (2005–2013). South Asian communities often referred to the Thursday night comedy lineup (which included *Parks and Recreation* the previous year) as "must see *desi* TV" because each of the comedies featured a South Asian American actor playing a South Asian American character. Featured actors included Daniel Pudi, Malik Pancholy, Aziz Ansari, and Mindy Kaling. The series *Outsourced* (2010–2011), however, departed from the previous programs because almost all the roles (as opposed to one role) were South Asian characters, and they were played by South Asian actors from Canada, Great Britain, and the United States. In addition, for the first time on American television, the show was set in the offices of an American corporate customer service call center in Mumbai, India.[1] The series debuted to a 3.6 rating in the 18–49 demographic and attracted 7.49 million viewers, making it NBC's second highest-rated scripted show. However, the first few episodes had mixed reviews from critics, fans, and the South Asian American community, and subsequent episodes did not match the ratings of the premiere.[2] In mid-season the series was moved to the 10:30 pm Eastern time slot after *30 Rock*, and ratings reached a low of 1.4 in the 18–49 demographic, with just 2.97 million viewers. Although the show continued to be one of the most DVR'd programs and a vigorous grassroots campaign was launched (including a Facebook site entitled SAVE OUTSOURCED) to renew the series, *Outsourced* was cancelled after one season.[3]

Despite its short duration, *Outsourced* remains noteworthy as one of the only narratives on television to tackle the complex issues of racial performance and national identity by focusing on the social, economic, and cultural ramifications of vocal accents. Specifically, the show speaks to the idea of accent normalization and accent performance in American and global contexts. The discussion of the role of language, speech, and accent in Critical Race Studies, Media Studies, and American and Asian American Studies has often been overlooked in favor of visual performance and representation. As cultural and social debates proliferate about language and word usage, communication and political correctness, and racial, gendered, and class rhetoric, the study of the relationship between race, language, and accent offers a lens through which to discuss the complex and variable nature of racial dialogue, as well as local and global hierarchies as presented in the media. Moreover, in its depiction of the cultural work of call centers, *Outsourced* demonstrates the complexities of American attitudes toward globalization. Broadly, the setting of the call center becomes a microcosm of globalization and its attendant anxieties. The show highlights the relationship of speaking American English to corporate labor practices, and Indian and American national and racial identities on American television. We see how the global world is portrayed in American contexts, where Indian accents are simultaneously deemed "foreign" and familiar; in this scenario, the spoken language is English, but it is English with a different phonetic signature and syntax emphasis. Hence, Indian accents are represented as integral to the multinational and transnational business practices that serve to support as well as critique and challenge the dominance of American cultural hierarchies.

South Asians and U.S. Racial Categories

In U.S. history, South Asians have been racially categorized at different points as Caucasian, non-White, other, and an Asian American minority group. In the nineteenth and early twentieth centuries, South Asians or "Hindoos," as the group was designated at the time, were initially categorized as White and allowed to become naturalized citizens. However, in a series of court cases that established citizenship, definitions of Whiteness, and naturalization rights for Chinese and Japanese immigrants and other groups, Indians were eventually denied the right to citizenship (Haney López 1997). In the 1923 *United States vs. Bhagwat Singh Thind* case, the U.S. Supreme Court case ruled that Hindoos were not recognized as "popularly white" and were designated as "non-white" and stripped of naturalization and immigration rights until 1947. In 1965, they were more formally granted rights to citizenship with the passage of the Hart–Celler Immigration and Naturalization Act (Ngai 2004). In the interim period prior to the 1980 Census, there was no category for South Asian or Indian immigrants to the United States, who often checked "other, white," or nothing at all. In the 1980 Census, some South Asian groups lobbied and successfully changed the status of South Asian to a minority group under the Asian American label. Since that time, the racial category of Asian American on the U.S. Census and other official documents has incorporated the phrase "including the Indian subcontinent." Despite this phrase, many Indians and South Asians do not identify with the legal or racial term of Asian American and continue to check "other." These multiple designations have led to a racial identity not easily explained or understood by dominant culture, American racial and ethnic minorities, or even Indian Americans and South Asian Americans.

The ambiguous nature of South Asian American identity challenges American paradigms of racial categorization, especially in the wake of twenty-first-century emphases on a postracial narrative for the United States. One of the main critiques of a postracial era, according to Eduardo Bonilla-Silva (2003), is that racial difference and racial language are relegated to the past as if they were no longer present. Racial difference remains, but it is gestured to in alternative ways. The representation of South Asian Americans as foreign immigrants with distinctive cultural practices and characteristics is an example of how race is discussed in a supposedly postracial world—in this case, cultural difference is stressed over racial difference. Another key way that difference is emphasized is through the discussion and use of language and accents. As I have previously argued, representations of Indians and South Asians have been racialized by their accents in American TV and film (Davé 2013). "Brown voice" is the act of speaking in an accented English associated with Indian nationals and immigrants: a combination of linguistic and phonetic markers that include stress points on particular words, cultural references, and words out of order (Davé 2005). More significantly, "brown voice" operates as a racializing characteristic among South Asians that suggests both foreignness and familiarity in a U.S. context. While "brown voice" most readily registers as a linguistic marker, *accent* goes beyond a phonetic signature and also operates to highlight the distinction between what is perceived as the norm or the mainstream and the cultural or exotic other. The call center (and stories that feature call centers) relies on vocal intercultural and interracial relations between individuals that depend upon hearing and registering meaning without visual cues and emerges as a critical site to examine how brown voice and accent are utilized as a similar American racializing trope outside of U.S. national borders.

Films such as *Looking for Comedy in the Muslim World* (2006), *Outsourced* (2006), and *Slumdog Millionaire* (2008) all feature Indian-based call centers in their stories. Increasingly, South Asians are racialized in the American media by vocal accents and, in the case of the television show *Outsourced*, the characters' work hinges on their ability to mimic American accents as customer service agents for American products and American companies. The important development here is that being a successful call center worker is not only about speaking English (pronunciation), but also hinges on sounding more American (cultural knowledge). The TV show *Outsourced* follows Todd, a young White male American manager who moves from Kansas to India (where his company's business has been outsourced) to train the Indian employees to sell American novelties such as celebrity bobble-head dolls and yellow foam Cheeseheads. While Indian American characters appear as the lone racial sidekick on several TV situation comedies, *Outsourced* makes *all* the sidekicks Indian. They have foreign customs and alternative cultural referents, but they are also presented as individuals who have universal problems, such as worrying about romantic relationships and living up to parents' expectations. The Indians in *Outsourced* can be culturally translated as similar and familiar to Americans because they are English-speaking and share recognizable experiences in the American workplace. However, underneath these similarities that elide racial, ethnic, and cultural difference, the title of the show also reminds us that South Asians represent economic competition to U.S. national employment because they can replace Americans (or take away American jobs) when U.S.-based global corporations retain their services.

Accent and the Indian Call Center

Since the late 1990s, many transnational corporations or third-party subsidiaries (international companies or Indian companies with global clientele) have opened customer service call centers in South Asia and the Philippines, primarily due to the ready availability of the native English-speaking populations and the reduced cost of operations. In his article on Pakistani call centers, Tariq Rahman (2009) makes it clear that it is the American accent (not just fluency in English) that is a commodity for Pakistani workers. American English is the language and the dialect to know and master in relation to global capital and trade. In Rahman's interviews of Pakistani call center employees, they admit to him that in the business world it is the American accent that they will most likely hear, and although Pakistanis (and Indians) do speak English, they are aware that they do not have an American accent. The better they can mimic an American accent, the better will be their employment rating. To them, the performance of an American accent is a means of class and economic advancement and perhaps a job opportunity in America. Accents do not only operate as phonetic markers, but also require cultural fluency. The ability to present a successful American accent is not just about correct grammar, but also being versed in topical issues such as local weather, national songs, sports teams, and the latest trends (from presidential elections to the latest films and TV shows).

Across all forms of media, American accents evoke popular knowledge of U.S. culture that combines vocal performance with cultural literacy.

While TV representations might generalize all Indian accents as a brown voice that sounds the same with similar phonetic tones, in fact accents are much more complicated because an accent is a combination of cultural fluency and phonetic markers. In the call center industry, there is a hierarchy of accents, whereby prestige accents afford the worker higher pay and better jobs. Winifred Poster (2007) has documented that companies hire "cultural" consultants to help train their workers for both their U.S. and British accents and for their experiences of living in the United Kingdom. While the corporate companies Poster looked at hired Asian Americans (including Indian Americans), in representations from films such as *The Best Exotic Marigold Hotel* (2012) and *Slumdog Millionaire* (2007), cultural consultants also included White British citizens (Judi Dench) and White Americans. In her analysis of the call center training handbooks, Claire Cowie (2007) finds that there are different standards of Indian English proficiency, but ultimately workers were asked to develop a "neutral" accent—one that is not necessarily associated with American, British, or Indian English. When Cowie asked some of her interviewees to identify the accent they were attempting to emulate, "they frequently mentioned BBC Asia newsreaders ... Some, however, also pointed towards newsreaders on Indian channels, probably the best representatives of Type A/Educated Indian English" (323). Training is not necessarily about mimicking the American accent, but instead achieving a "neutral" accent that is dependent on pronunciation and phonetic issues but does not aspire to authenticity, only familiarity.

The deployment of these accents has been seen to cater to and bolster the supremacy of British and American English in the world of business. Mary Grace Anthony (2013) sees this at work in the show *Outsourced*, arguing that the Indian actors performing brown voice mirror accent-neutralizing practices in Indian call centers and "[reinforce] inferiority and incompetence in post-colonial states" (210). While I would agree that this power dynamic exists within call centers, I would also allow for a more nuanced reading of the television show whereby accent performance holds up a mirror to American cultural bias. Audience complaints about actors using the wrong accent or business concerns about authenticity speak more to the idea of reinforcing regional, national, and racial categories rather than recognizing the influence of culture, language, and even labor history on accents and communications. Consider, for example, the development of Pidgin English in Hawai'i or hybrid languages such as Hinglish (Hindi and English), Taglish (Tagalog and English), and Spanglish (Spanish and English). The inequities and hierarchical power of English are still present, but "foreign" words (such as *pagoda* or *a capella* or *adios*), cultural references (from Homer Simpson's "doh" to "oy"), and regional accents have also become a part of the American English language.

Racialization of South Asian Americans on Television

These readings of accent must also be connected back to U.S. racial narratives, whereby Asian Americans are often seen as perpetual foreigners and model minority immigrants who can also be interpreted as "honorary whites" (Tuan 1999). American television tends to forefront a binary or Black/White racial narrative within the United States that only includes yellow and brown people as foreigners or immigrants, rather than as part of American national history. Additionally, South Asian Americans and Indian Americans are part of an immigration history known as the South Asian diaspora. This immigration history is not only U.S.-centric, but also comprised of multiple migration patterns, influenced by India's history as a former British colony, that include destinations in England, the United Kingdom, Australia, Canada, the Caribbean island nations, the Middle East, Hong Kong, and South African nations. More recently, Indians have been involved in a reverse migration process whereby immigrants and second-generation Indian Americans are returning to work in India. South Asian Americans disrupt the national borders and boundaries of geography and the nation-state because they represent linguistic variation in both global and local settings.

NBC's *Outsourced* offers an alternative or more nuanced example of the interaction of global and local flows of capitalism. Because the series is set outside of the United States, the story privileges cultural identity over a more potentially divisive racial narrative that might be present if the series were set in the United States. Cultural identity is predicated on knowledge and consumption of American products and values. Inderpal Grewal (2005) argues that in the 1990s, the narrative of American national identity crossed territorial boundaries and "America was important to so many across the world because its power enabled the American nation-state to disseminate the promise of democratic citizenship and belonging through consumer practices as well as disciplinary technologies" (2). Grewal emphasizes that the discourse of globalization was another means to promote American capitalism and thus served as an extension of American imperialism in foreign markets. The series complicates how American businesses teach American English and commodify American customs, and shows the inconsistencies of American cultural norms when placed in an Indian workplace. Instead of India and strange Indian customs being the sole source of humor in the show, the program pokes fun at foibles and strange practices in American culture.

In some ways this can be seen as putting forward a postracial narrative, as it homogenizes all the storylines into ones that negate or eliminate race as a subject. Instead of recognizing South Asian characters who have specific histories in the United States or as foreign immigrants with distinct cultural practices, representations of South Asian Americans as sidekicks to American White characters are an example of how race is discussed in a supposedly postracial world—cultural or sexual difference is emphasized over racial difference. In the case of South Asians, race becomes about cultural difference that can be added on to a character or scene, such as an exotic or foreign setting, a colorful piece of clothing, or a vocal accent. This is indicative of a surface understanding of race rather than recognition of the complex genealogy of racial representations in the United States. The setting of a call center provides a rich environment to show the complexities of racial interactions.

The "brown ensemble" cast gathered for *Outsourced* is possible for an American TV show not only because it is set outside of the United States, but also because the premise of the show presents a believable site of contact between Americans and Indians based on commerce and American consumerism—a call center. In business, overseas call centers are designed to cater to U.K. and U.S. customers and rely on "erasing" the ethnic, racial, and national identities of their workers, replacing those identities with someone who is familiar with the cultural details and regional knowledge of the customer (Cowie 2007). Although the call center is physically located in India, the work associated with the call center—the personal contact and conversations on the phone—represents how the changing global economic markets intersect with the postracial narrative, because international businesses are aiming to supply their U.S. and U.K. customers with the fantasy that they are talking to someone who knows them and their culture.

This study of the television show *Outsourced* gestures to a larger narrative about the cultural translations and global flows in television studies. TV scholars such as Michael Curtin (2004) have discussed the transitory nature of the medium in the twenty-first century, which includes new production, distribution, and narrative frameworks derived from the international licensing of television formats to global consumers. Call center stories, I would argue, reflect how global exchanges and technologies flow from what Curtin identifies as "particular cities that have become centers for the finance, production, and distribution of television programs: cities like Bombay, Hong Kong, and Cairo" (272). Curtin points out that these global centers of media have specific logics of their own and "don't correspond to the geography, interests, or policies, of a particular nation state" (273). These media capitals are more than just a site of capitalism or extension of the nation-state; they constitute sites that break out of national boundaries. Historically, U.S. and British television scholarship (Spiegel 1992) has emphasized how the production and consumption of television are connected to trends and patterns related to the nation-state, and specifically how producers in the United States have focused on developing shows that focus on national audiences. This analysis of *Outsourced* exposes the relation of the call center setting to American narratives of race, ethnicity, and labor but also reveals these global flows that transcend the boundaries of previous office and workplace narratives.

Rewriting *Outsourced* as Global/Universal Television

The television series *Outsourced* is based on the small independent film *Outsourced* (2006). The film's plot shapes the basic template for the television series, but also deviates in some interesting ways. In the film, Todd Anderson's office closes and his colleagues are laid off in the United States when executive officers outsource or relocate their customer service business center to the small town of Gharampuri, India. Todd's promotion to top-level executive administration is contingent on him moving to India to train his replacement at the Indian call center. His introduction to India is one of "a stranger in a strange land" who learns to appreciate Indian culture, falls in love with an Indian woman at the call center, and settles permanently in India when his company closes the call center and moves its operations to China. Located in a windowless cement building that is isolated from the town, the call center is depicted as a lonely outpost with no ties to the community. Todd works with his Indian assistant manager and socializes with Indians in Gharampuri, but the plot of the film largely focuses on Todd's alienation from Indian culture and how he comes to cherish the Indian people around him.

This differs from the television show, which sets the call center in Mumbai (formerly Bombay), the financial capital and one of the most populous cities in India, with over 12 million people. While the film's U.S. corporate headquarters is located in Seattle, in the television show, Todd (now Todd Dempsy) is based in St Louis, Missouri, and the company is called Midwestern American Novelties. Although both companies sell patriotic American cultural knickknacks such as bald eagles, renaming the business Midwestern Novelties rather than Western Novelties suggests a more insular and landlocked Midwestern population, less exposed to racial diversity compared with the high tech and cosmopolitan diversity of the coastal city of Seattle. Thus, the America represented in the TV show is even more provincial and depicted as even more strange to the global-savvy population of Mumbai. The setting of the show's Mumbai call center is one of several call centers in a multi-level building that feature employees and business from multiple economic classes and countries. Todd's social circle includes expatriates from other Western countries such as Australia and Britain, and features multiple call centers operating in concert and competition with each other, as well as employing other Indians. The competing international call centers evoke a colonial narrative wherein imperial powers compete over the best natives and try to make the largest profit with the available resources.

The television show, with its more expansive space for storytelling, also opens up additional opportunities to nuance and humanize both its Indian and White characters. The protagonist is at first a stranger to Indian customs, but as the season progresses, the series abandons some of the film's storylines to introduce more complex portrayals of expatriate life for the White American characters, the call center industry, and individual Indian characters. The regular cast members include Todd (Ben Rappaport), the assistant manager, Rajiv Gidwani (Rizwan Manji), and call center workers Manmeet (Sachan Dhawan), Gupta (Parveesh Cheena), Asha (Rebecca Hazelwood), and Madhuri (Anisha Nagarajan). The cast is largely comprised of accomplished actors from Britain, Canada, and the United States. Supporting characters include the obnoxious White American call center manager from the company All American Hunting, Charlie Davis (Diedrich Bader), and the White female Australian call center manager of Koala Airlines and one of Todd's potential love interests, Tonya (Pippa Black). The White characters are all expatriates and are all in managerial positions, and the Indians are Todd's employees or residents who provide services for the call center staff. Their interactions in and around the workplace drive each episode's plot.

When the show *Outsourced* premiered, many criticized the show for depicting two-dimensional characters, but the show evolved throughout the season from relying on American stereotypes of India to featuring a more nuanced portrayal that individualizes many of the Indian characters into distinct personalities rather than stereotypes. We might attribute this to the fact that the series featured several Indian American writers and directors, and was one of the first times a U.S. television program became an opportunity for multiple South Asian Americans to work both in front of and behind the camera for a U.S. show. Series writer Geetika Lizardi based the stories and scripts she submitted on her personal observations and experiences as a former call center manager in Mumbai. She was interested in creating and telling stories about characters who had not previously been seen on American TV rather than rehashing recognizable stereotypes. And yet, as she points out, stereotypes are complex in terms of representation. In some cases, they can be based on universalizing principles of behavior that can open up opportunities rather than limit characters:

> And as for stereotypes: Simple, recognizable characters are the building blocks of all comedies. The templates we build on are universal ones: the shy wallflower, the ruthless boss, and the guy with no social skills. We don't use what I consider to be Indian stereotypes: doctors, engineers, spelling bee champs, Kwik-E-Mart owners. (And for the record, I'm a huge fan of Apu on *The Simpsons*.)
>
> (Lizardi 2011)

She distinguishes between conventional Indian character stereotypes such as professionals and behavioral types such as the "shy wallflower," arguing that the latter are not racialized, but universal. Her explanation appeals to a universal characterization whereby Indians are just like other Americans.

Yet, these desires for "universal" representations do not necessarily shift the power dynamics that are at play within the racial and gendered hierarchies of office politics, or larger global venues. In fact, the tagline on the poster (see Figure 20.1) proclaims that the show is an "all-American comedy in India"—a brand that does not distinguish between cultures but instead emphasizes that the show is an American import that can thrive and achieve prominence in any geographical space. As Richard Dyer and others have pointed out, universalization can serve to reaffirm the status quo, whereby Whiteness and the accompanying power and privilege associated with normalcy dictate the terms. According to Dyer, Whiteness can claim normalcy only because of its proximity to difference (Dyer 1997). Rather than focusing on universalizing features, it would be more radical to create believable back stories for plots and characters that truly address ethnic and racial difference.

Figure 20.1 An advertisement for the NBC show *Outsourced*

Americanizing the Indian Worker

This emphasis on "universal" storylines that actually mirror the predominant norms of White middle-class America can be seen in many of the characters and plotlines on *Outsourced*. In the episode "Take This Punjab and Shove It," Todd is elated to hire Kamik (Andy Gala), an Indian American who was born in India and raised in Corpus Christi, Texas before returning to India. From their first interview, Todd relates to Kamik because although he is Indian, he has the voice, manners, and cultural knowledge of an American.[4] Todd tells Kamik: "It's so great that we don't have to work on your accent." Kamik speaks American English because he was taught as a child growing up in the United States, but it is not only his phonetic intonation that makes him a success. He is also fluent in American cultural norms such the branding slogan of the Slinky toy ("fun for a girl and a boy") and the importance of the *Sports Illustrated* Swimsuit Edition. As an Indian American, he knows American culture and American practices and doesn't have to be taught about customer relations. He outperforms everyone else in the office in terms of sales and experiences because he can fit into the American business culture. (See Figure 20.2.)

Yet, Kamik's story also serves to connect the performance of accent to success. Todd brags to the other managers, Charlie and Tonya: "I'm telling you he's amazing—no accent and a born salesman." In Kamik, Todd sees a version of himself that he can relate to as a White

Figure 20.2 Todd (Ben Rappaport) and his new hire and protégé, Kamik (Andy Gala) in *Take This Punjab and Shove It*

American—in terms of both accent and how to relate to the American materials he is selling. Yet, Kamik's easy relationship with Todd also magnifies Todd's struggles to relate to workers who are culturally different. Thus, this episode emphasizes that accent is less dependent on phonetic signature, and instead more related to national and cultural affinity. The appeal of Kamik's American accent (phonetics and cultural fluency) is juxtaposed in this episode with Manmeet's adoption of a clipped James Bond British accent. Manmeet's obsession with romance and women is a staple of his character in the show, and he poses as "Spencer, a British sports car driver" to get a date with a girl. While Kamik has a natural fluency with American culture, Manmeet is an example of how an inauthentic accent can lead to failure. Even with perfect intonation, Manmeet's British accent only works at the most superficial level because he only can mimic words about cars and women in British English that he has learned from James Bond movies. His accent makes him "exotic" to the woman on the bus, but once she discovers his deception (that he's not actually British), she is not interested. Manmeet can still be successful at his job by picking up new accents, but the story seems to be saying that to be truly exceptional requires that you are "born" or "raised" American. This type of narrative can be problematic, because it suggests that Todd's ideal and how he measures the success of his employees are always in comparison to his American norms.

Beyond highlighting the desirability of the "not quite White American" Indian, Kamik's presence also exposes the internal hierarchies among call center workers as being based on American values. The seating arrangement in the call center cafeteria reveals that the best seats are for the workers who are culturally more American. At the top of the labor chain are the Indians in the business suits, followed by the Australians who work for Koala Airlines, then the American worker Charlie's hunting gear company, and finally Mid American Novelties—where the product and the pay attract the last-chance employees whom we come to know in the series. While they may be positioned as the least American in their professional skill level, they become recognizable to American audiences in their rendering as classic sitcom characters. Rajiv is the conniving assistant manager who wants Todd's job, Asha is the smart single girl who is the object of our hero's unfulfilled desire, Manmeet is a young man who is obsessed with dating and sexual practices, Gupta is the socially challenged worker, Madhuri is the soft-spoken single girl, and Pinky is the chubby and reliable girl. As Bonnie Dow (1996) asserts in her work on television culture, "Television implicitly supports a view of the world that discounts the ways in which cultural norms and values affect people's lives. The medium's individualistic view of the world implies that most problems can be solved by hard work, good will, and a supportive family" (xxi). *Outsourced* creates a "family" community that replicates the sitcom format, and ultimately, despite some of its nuances about cultural exchanges, it becomes a show about Americans, albeit one with a slightly exotic flavor.

The assistant manager Rajiv, for example, aspires to become the office manager because he is a capable worker, but also so that his future in-laws can see him as an eligible candidate for marriage. However, as assistant manager, he maintains a rigid separation between himself and the other call center workers because of class, position, and education. The only people he can talk to about his goals are the White managers, which further isolates him from other Indians. What humanizes his character in the show and allows him to present a different side of his character to his employees and co-workers are his courtship, proposal, and marriage to an Indian woman, Vimi. The TV show often introduces the differences between Eastern/Indian practices and American practices, such as in romance and marriage, as the underlying premise of the narrative to show Todd's difficulty and subsequent attempts to understand and accept that while he and the employees he works with may have different approaches and cultural backgrounds, he does care about the success and lives of his employees.

Cultural Humor and Critiquing the American Accent

While the world of *Outsourced* is clearly portrayed as one in which American voices, cultures, and norms are powerful in comparison to the strangeness of India and Indian voices, the series also offers alternative messages about American culture. One way that the show attempts to create sympathy for the call center employees is to call attention to the everyday racism that the workers can encounter in their job. The show often demonstrates the fact that dealing with Americans can be difficult and annoying, and that Americans and American values are not universally good. In the episode "The Todd Couple," Todd presents a training video developed for Mid American Novelties employees to help them manage their anger and other emotions when dealing with difficult American customers. When the training video uses yoga as a relaxation technique for dispelling anger, he realizes that it projects a racist message about Asian and Indian culture. For example, the narrator reveals that yoga "was invented by a [Indian] people who had nothing but a dirt floor," while the Indians who watch the video are in an air-conditioned building with computers in an urban center. The tape reveals the way that the American commercialization of yoga into an industry might be construed as simply experiencing another culture, but it also shows us that what is sold as Indian in America does not accurately reflect the realities of the characters and personalities we see on the show. (See Figure 20.3.)

Instead of Indians being the target of the joke here, it is American appropriation of yoga and commodity culture that are pointedly laughed at and made fun of. Writer Geethika Lizardi comments that the show in general makes fun of both Indian and American culture, but that there are more jokes that satirize American culture.[5] In this episode, as the viewing audience, we are aligned with the Indian employees as they watch the tape. We also see their point of view (perplexity and even offense) because the narrative has shown us that these characters are not, as the video describes them, "spiritual magical people living in a magical land," but are individual and distinct characters. Todd affirms this point of view in the narrative by stopping the tape and saying he now realizes the tape is offensive. He has come to realize that media images do not match the reality of the people he works with and decides to train them himself.

The show also levels a satirical critique of American cultural norms by taking on American assumptions about Indians and call center workers. In this episode, Todd role-plays an array of

Figure 20.3 Watching the American training video in *The Todd Couple*

disgruntled American customers in order to train his employees how to respond to different situations. He pretends to be an angry customer with a heavy Boston accent who sneers at worker Manmeet for having such a heavy accent that he cannot understand him: "What, what are you saying … number? Your damn accent is so thick!" says Todd in his caricatured Boston accent. Yet, this exchange points out the paradoxical nature of accents. Viewers may often associate accents with foreigners, immigrants, and aliens, but in this case, American accents are depicted as equally strange and confusing and humorous as the Indian accents we have been hearing throughout the series. Todd also performs a Midwestern accent in which he vocalizes his thoughts on "burds" (as opposed to birds) and then challenges Gupta by adopting a Southern accent, in which he mis-names him and threatens him: "You listen to me M. Night, if I don't get my refund, the twist to my movie will be my foot up your ass." This is not only a phonetic accent that slowly draws out vowels, but also a cultural accent that depicts Southerners as the perpetrators of vulgar violence. Todd pulls out a further performance of the angry and ugly American when he says: "You are a moron and a monkey could do your job." This crossing of territorial boundaries using accents, a common critique of call center workers, questions the humor of the situation and also what we find humorous. In one case, audiences may laugh at American misunderstandings of Indian culture, but how does the humor of the situation change as Todd's performances of the ugly American escalate? Regional rivalries such as the Boston Red Sox versus the New York Yankees can be quite perplexing to many Americans as well as to foreigners, but they can also be a lovable quirk of Americans. Regional racism, bias, and violence, while more easily identifiable, are not something we usually see parodied in American comedies. This critique of American culture and American behavior though Todd's performance is ultimately explained away as a training exercise that depicts Gupta as a winner, because he does not respond emotionally to the "caller." This type of critique does not appear again in the series after this episode, but each subsequent show begins to comment on different aspects of the economic, racial, and social hierarchies of the call center.

One way in which this is accomplished is through positioning the workers at Mid American Novelties as sympathetic underdogs, rather than simply laughably unskilled workers. As we have seen here, it is often their failed American accents and lack of American cultural fluency that may make them "bad workers," but not bad people. This helps the audience to continue to root for them. Todd affectionately calls the team "The Bad News Bears," while their competitors on the so-called "A" team are positioned as arrogant and unlikeable. Such portrayals make the audience allies of the characters at Mid American Novelties. This is particularly evident in the episode "Todd's Holi War," when he defends his company's workers and products against the derision, pranks, and unequal treatment by the workers of the information technology call center located in the same building. The Mid American Novelties employees are a scrappy and resourceful team who band together in the face of an outside company threat, and that loyalty to each other is endearing. By the end of the series, the shows start to address a variety of social and cultural assumptions, and we can also see the ways *Outsourced* uses to criticize different hierarchies of power and remind us that although the power positions may be an unfortunate global reality, there are ways to challenge and confront these inequities.

Conclusion

Outsourced provides a cast of Indian sidekicks to one central White American male character and thereby repositions the call center narrative as one filled with individuals, rather than a group who are a faceless threat to American workers. The creation of multiple individual Indian characters with names and specific back stories can create empathy and affinities that are lost in a group generalization. While this might deflect the societal and cultural impact of call centers on the American economy, the narrative also gives us a variety of Indian individuals to disrupt and challenge previous racialized stereotypes of Indians and Indian Americans as outsiders and immigrants. In this case, Indians are foreign to the American audience, but because the series is set in India, they are not the foreigners—it is Todd, the American manager, who is the stranger and learns to see Indians as lovable and relatable even though they are not White and not American. Thus, the utilization of accent outside of the United States continues to homogenize South Asians and Indians as an acceptable form of difference that privileges American culture overseas. In this situation, the constructed nature of "brown voice" or an American accent becomes visible, so that accent is not so much about correct pronunciation but, instead, is more identified with dialogues that include American cultural referents. The narrative presented in *Outsourced* allows an examination of the way that racial hierarchies are not necessarily based simply on physical characteristics, but also through the cultural communication and deployment of accent that are so vital to the creation of American hierarchies of power and privilege.

Notes

1 The last successful situation comedy on network television set outside the United States was the CBS show *MASH* (1972–1983) set in the historical past of the Korean War. Asian characters and writers were absent from the show.

2 The *New York Times* liked it and *Entertainment Weekly* thought it was inoffensive. The comments on both online columns show how the discussion focused on whether or not the show was funny or racist. On *Sepia Mutiny*, the South Asian community complained about the "inauthentic" Indian customs or accents, which has been an ongoing criticism. See www.nytimes.com/2010/09/23/arts/television/23outsourced.html, http://watching-tv.ew.com/2010/09/23/outsourced-nbc-episode-1/, and www.sepiamutiny.com/sepia/archives/006330.html.

3 Fans wrote petitions on Facebook for the cable channel WTBS to show reruns of the show.

4 This is similar to Thomas Macaulay's description of British-educated Indians during the time of the British Raj.

5 In a radio interview with the South Asian Journalists Association, Lizardi and other cast members talked about the show. See www.blogtalkradio.com/saja/2011/03/17/tv-nbcs-outsourced. Accessed April 17, 2011.

References

Anthony, Mary Grace. 2013. "'Thank You for Calling': Accents and Authenticity on NBC's Outsourced." *Journal of Intercultural Communication Research* 42(2): 192–213.

Bonilla-Silva, Eduardo. 2003. *Racism without Racists: Color-Blind Racism and the Persistence of Racial Inequality in the US.* Lanham, MD: Rowan and Littlefield Publishers.

Cowie, Claire. 2007. "The Accents of Outsourcing: The Meanings of 'Neutral' in the Indian Call Center Industry." *World English* 26(3): 316–330.

Curtin, Michael. 2004. "Media Capitals: Cultural Geographies of Global TV." In *Television after* TV: Essays *on a Medium in Transition*, Lynn Spiegel and Jan Olsson (eds), 70–302. Durham, NC: Duke University Press.

Davé, Shilpa. 2005. "Apu's Brown Voice: Cultural Inflection and South Asian Accents." In *East Main Street: Asian American Popular Culture*. Shilpa Davé, Leilani Nishime, and Tasha Oren (eds), 313–336. New York: New York University Press.

Davé, Shilpa. 2013. *Indian Accents: Brown Voice and Racial Performance in American Television and Film*. Champaign, IL: University of Illinois Press.

Dow, Bonnie. 1996. *Prime Time Feminism: Television, Media Culture, and the Women's Movement since 1970*. Philadelphia: University of Pennsylvania Press.

Dyer, Richard. 1997. *White: Essays on Race and Culture*. New York: Routledge.

Entertainment Weekly. http://www.ew.com/.

Gelbart, Larry (director). 1972-1983. *MASH*. 20th Century Fox Television.

Grewal, Inderpal. 2005. *Transnational America: Feminisms, Diasporas, and Neo-Liberalisms*. Durham, NC: Duke University Press.

Haney López, Ian. 1997. *White by Law*. New York: New York University Press.

Jeffcoat, John (director). 2006. *Outsourced*.

—. "The Todd Couple" (Episode 14). Directed by Reginald Hudlin. Written by Robert Borden and Amit Bhalla. NBC. February 10, 2011.

—. "Take This Punjab and Shove It" (Episode 16). Directed by Dennie Gordon. Written by Robert Borden. NBC (February 24, 2011).

—. "Todd's Holi War" (Episode 17). Directed by Victor Nelli Jr. Written by Robert Borden and Michael Pennie. NBC, March 24, 2011.

Lizardi, Geetika Tandon. 2011. "Don't Hate *Outsourced*." *Los Angeles Times*, March 21.

New York Times. http://www.nytimes.com.

Ngai, Mae. 2004. *Impossible Subjects: Illegal Aliens and the Making of Modern America*. Princeton, NJ: Princeton University Press.

Poster, Winifred. 2007. "Who's on the Line? Indian Call Centers Agents Pose as Americans for US Outsourced Firms." *Industrial Relations* 46(2): 271–304.

Rahman, Tariq. 2009. "Language Ideology, Identity, and the Commodification of Language in the Call Centers of Pakistan." *Language in Society* 38: 233–258.

Sepia Mutiny. http://sepiamutiny.com/blog/.

Spigel, Lynn. 1992. *Make Room for TV: Television and the Family Ideal in Postwar America*. Chicago: University of Chicago Press.

Tuan, Mia. 1999. *Forever Foreigners or Honorary Whites: The Asian Ethnic Experience Today*. New Brunswick, NJ: Rutgers University Press.

21

TRANSNATIONAL TIES

Elite Filipino Migrants and Polymedia Environments

Cecilia S. Uy-Tioco

Just as she gets off the Washington DC metro train at the end of a workday, Rose's mobile phone starts beeping—halfway across the globe, her parents in the Philippines have just woken and want to video chat with their grandchild. When he wakes, Larry logs onto Facebook Messenger to receive updates from his cousin, who is running his business back home in the Philippines. For Nelia, part of her morning routine is to check social media and click on her friends' shared links to keep up with events in the Philippines. While early migrants were constrained by the limits of communication and transportation technologies in maintaining transnational ties, contemporary migrants are not limited by technological capability. Developments in new media and information communication technologies (ICTs) in the 1990s paved the way for cheap and affordable real-time communication that reordered time and space, allowing immediate interaction and communication across the globe instead of the previous "exchanges of amateur videos" via visual images, voice cassette tapes, and written letters (Moores 2000: 121). From text messaging to Facebook, transnational Filipino migrants use various new media and ICTs to maintain relationships between physically distant families and friends, and the homeland.

In this study, I explore the role of these communication platforms in how migrants navigate their relationship between their country of origin and their chosen home. While recent research on Filipino migrants has focused on the plight of overseas workers and undocumented Filipinos, I examine the media use of the largely ignored group of highly educated, professional Filipino migrants who have chosen to permanently reside in the United States. I draw on the theory of polymedia to examine the use of new media technologies such as mobile phones and social networking sites to maintain ties with the homeland. A polymedia approach places an emphasis on the various ways users navigate media environments, drawing attention to integration of the user's emotions and relationships with their choice of media technologies. These become a key way for highly educated Filipino migrants to maintain familial relationships, friendships, and a sense of belonging with the Filipino homeland while they live and work abroad.

After providing background information on new media technologies and Filipino migrants, I focus on the experiences of Filipinos in the metropolitan Washington DC area. My analysis is based on 12 interviews I conducted with Filipino migrants who are members of the alumni associations of what are considered the top three Philippine universities.[1] As media is integrated into the everyday lives of transnational migrants (Madianou and Miller 2013), I also conducted participant observation (on- and offline) as modes of ethnographic data gathering with interviewees who granted me permission to observe and quote from their social media (i.e. Facebook) accounts. I assert that theorizations of polymedia can illuminate how transnational migrants navigate and negotiate the contradictory processes of connection with and separation from distant others and the homeland. In doing so, I argue that "elite" Filipino migrants engage with a nationalism-from-afar that can be seen as weak and ambivalent, but still illustrates an affiliation and identification with their nation of origin while building lives in the United States.

Transnationalism and New Media Technologies

Through their extensive ethnographic research on migration and media, Madianou and Miller (2013) developed a theory of polymedia: "an emerging environment of communicative opportunities that functions as an 'integrated structure' within which each individual medium is defined in relational terms in the context of all other media" (170). Whereas Williams (1974) saw technologies as created for certain purposes and adopted by society based on pre-existing conditions and traditions in a culture, polymedia resocializes technology; it "shifts from an emphasis on the constraints imposed by each medium (often cost-related, but also shaped by specific qualities) to an emphasis upon the social and emotional consequences of choosing between those different media" (Madianou and Miller 2013: 170). Users thus choose technologies according to their affordances, marshaling them for their own purposes. With the variety of media technologies available to users, the choice among which is no longer about cost or convenience, the focus can now shift to the emotional intent of users and how people use technology to manage their relationships (Madianou and Miller 2013).

New media technologies have many complex effects in maintaining ties with the homeland. Much scholarship focuses on familial ties, demonstrating that impacts vary for different members of the family (Cabañes and Acedera 2012; Madianou 2016; Madianou and Miller 2011, 2012; Paragas 2005; Uy-Tioco 2007). Migrant mothers often experience a sense of empowerment in keeping regular contact with their far-away children (Madianou and Miller 2011, 2012; Uy-Tioco 2007), all while overcoming great distances and becoming the family breadwinner. Yet, migrant mothers are often seen to use media in ways that thrust them back into traditional mothering roles (Soriano et al., 2015; Uy-Tioco 2007), resulting in left-behind children feeling ambivalent (Madianou and Miller 2011) and resentful (Parreñas 2005). Similarly, for left-behind fathers/husbands, technology further complicates the already complex relationships between these long-distance spouses even as it mitigates some of the effects of migration and transnational relationships (Cabañes and Acedera 2012). With regard to ties to the nation, Ong and Cabañes (2011) find that elite Filipino migrants (scholars and students) maintain a strong interest in Philippine politics even though they are detached from other Filipinos in the diaspora, revealing that their connection to events in the Philippines is ambiguous and ambivalent even as they reinforce the Philippine class divides.

The "Elite" Filipino Migrant

Filipino migrants in the United States have a unique history that informs their current presence. Because the Philippines was a colony of the United States, Filipinos were historically considered "wards" of the state and were called "nationals"; thus, they were neither aliens nor citizens

(Lowe 1996). In 1934, the Tydings–McDuffie Act limited Filipino immigration to a quota of 50 persons per year, reclassifying all Filipinos in the United States as "aliens" despite the colonial relationship (Lowe 1996). This Act followed the pattern of several immigration laws excluding Asians from becoming naturalized citizens. It was not until 1965 that "national origins" was removed as a basis for immigration, opening the doors to immigrants from Asia. Although earlier Filipino migrants came to work as agricultural laborers, post-1965 Filipino immigrants were largely affluent (Espiritu 2003). By 1990, "more than half joined the ranks of managers and professionals; their median household income exceeded that of all Americans and even that of whites; and their percentage of college graduates was twice that of all Americans" (Espiritu 2003: 7). Filipinos comprise the fifth largest Asian group in the Metropolitan DC area (Hoeffel et al. 2012: 21), working in all sectors, including health and medicine, business, law, banking, education, hospitality, technology, and international non-profit organizations (i.e. the World Bank and the International Monetary Fund (IMF)).

In 2012, there were over ten million Filipinos living abroad, 47 percent of whom were permanent (immigrants, dual citizens, legal permanent citizens), 41 percent were temporary (overseas workers, students, receiving short-term work training, etc.), and 12 percent were irregular (undocumented workers, overstaying visas) (Commission on Filipinos Overseas 2014). Of the 4.9 million Permanent Overseas Filipinos, slightly over three million are in the United States (Hoeffel et al. 2012). Generally, there are two broad categories to describe Filipino migrant workers: *balikbayan*, or immigrant Filipinos, primarily from North America, who periodically visit the homeland, and overseas contract workers (OCWs)—now called Overseas Filipino Workers or OFWs—who are employed on a contractual basis around the world (Rafael 1990). OFWs are lauded by the Philippine government as *bagong bayani* or "new heroes" for the remittances that they send home, contributing 10 percent of the gross national product (World Bank 2015). On the other hand, and despite their efforts to maintain strong personal ties to the homeland, *balikbayans* are seen by some scholars as less concerned with Philippine politics. In addition, Filipino nationalists tend to mock *balikbayans* for their criticisms of the Philippines and preference for the United States, noting: "they do nothing else but point out what it is the Philippines lacks as compared to the United States, thereby appearing shameless and arrogant" (Rafael 1990: 272). For Ong and Cabañes (2011), a third category, "elite" migrants, refers to highly skilled professionals who, while abroad temporarily (i.e. on student visas), "have a chance to attain a life of comfort and security in their host country, to become *balikbayans*" (205). Although their legal status in the host country is temporary and fixed and thus similar to that of the OFW, Ong and Cabañes recognize that as students, they hold social and economic capital akin to that of the *balikbayans*.

While much research on Filipino migrants and new media technologies has been on OFWs and low-income, undocumented, blue-collar laborers in the United States, I turn my attention to this "elite" class of migrants for two reasons: to provide a more nuanced view of the diversity of Filipino migrants' experiences (Ong and Cabañes 2011: 202) and to point the researcher's ethnographic eye *up*, to people who wield power (Nader 1972). I use the term "elite" to refer to overseas Filipinos who have permanently settled in the United States (as citizens, dual citizens, or permanent residents) or hold a G visa and are employed long term in an international organization (such as the World Bank or IMF), work in white-collar jobs, and came to the United States as graduate students, through work placements, or because of family members. Generally, they did not leave the Philippines because of poverty or to escape economic or political situations. In fact, a number of the Filipinos in this study have higher cultural, social, and even economic capital in the homeland due to their family backgrounds and to being graduates of the top three universities in the country. Thus, the term "elite" here is related to a kind of cosmopolitanism, whereby individuals are "prone to articulate complex affiliations, meaningful attachments and multiple allegiances to issues, people, places, and traditions that lie beyond the boundaries of their resident nation-state" (Vertovec and Cohen 2002: 2). Cosmopolitan identities are fluid and premised on having "the ability to stand outside a singular location (the location of one's birth, land, upbringing, conversion) and to mediate traditions that lies at its core" (Held 2003: 58).

Polymediated Relationships across Time and Space

Elite Filipino migrants exist in rich and robust polymedia environments due to a number of factors. First, they have access to an array of new media technologies. The respondents for this study tended to use social media sites (i.e. Facebook and Instagram), digital apps (i.e. Viber, WhatsApp, Facetime, Skype), and VoIP (voice over internet protocol) devices (i.e. Vonage, Ooma, MagicJack). Social media and digital apps require the use of computers, tablets, smartphones, or feature phones (mobile phones with some internet capabilities) as well as internet or wireless data service, meaning that some kind of technological savvy and media literacy is necessary. Second, as highly educated professionals, they are not hindered by the cost of technology, nor are they technologically illiterate. Unlike overseas workers, they are on the "right side" of the digital divide and are able to maximize the environments polymedia provides to maintain ties with family and friends. They must navigate "home" as being in two places—the Washington DC area, where they work and live, and the Philippines, where loved ones remain. One respondent, Ronna, is a widow in her fifties with three children and moved to the United States in 1990 after marrying her husband. She describes her media use:

> Before, it was the phone, 60 cents a minute, so I did not keep in touch as much because I had to save up. Then it got better, then, with the social media, I can talk to [my parents and siblings] every single minute. Viber, Skype, Facebook, it's instantaneous! So from once every few weeks or once a month, now multiple times a day.

Similarly, Emma, also in her fifties with two college-aged children, points out: "[When I first came] in 1988, we kept in touch through phone. Because of technology, I call my mom everyday through Vonage. It's not limited to major news, it's everyday news, it's easier to be closer, to remain close, not like before it was a luxury to communicate." In both Ronna's and Emma's cases, the notions of time, of the everyday and the instantaneous, inform their choice of media usage.

We can see that Filipino migrant experiences of polymedia illustrate Giddens' concept of time-space distanciation, "a process in which social relations are lifted out of immediate interactional settings and stretched over potentially vast spans of global time-space" (Moores 2000: 106). In the statements above, we see the desire on both Ronna's and Emma's part to maintain familial relationships despite the physical distance, especially their role as daughters to aging parents. Importantly, these family dynamics are shaped by media technology usage and vice versa (Lister et al. 2003). Although far away, Ronna and Emma are able to continue their prescribed roles as caring daughters.

With the use of new media technologies, relationships are not limited to the place-based locale, but stretch far beyond it. Cecille, a mother of two teenagers, is part of a group chat on the mobile phone app Viber that includes her extended family—her mother, siblings and their spouses, nephews and nieces. She belongs to a similar group chat with her husband's extended family as well. Cecille delightedly exclaims: "You hit send, everyone gets it ... it makes you feel involved in everyday life of the extended family." Thus, where we physically are no longer determines who we are or who we are "with," because communication technologies can transform the situations we are in and the interactions we have, as well as how we identify ourselves (Moores 2000: 109).

More than being able to communicate from afar with ease, migrants' experiences with technologies form a "connected presence" in which continuous and "irregular interaction" are ever-present and easily activated to provide a "feeling of a permanent connection" (Licoppe 2004: 141). This "connected presence" is enabled by polymedia, whether synchronous (through video-chat apps like Skype, Viber, or Facetime) or asynchronous (such as a Facebook post that can be viewed at a later time). Through new media technologies, migrants are able to participate in the everyday, the mundane, with family and friends across the globe. Among the various ICTs available to her, Sheila, a single woman in her early fifties, says she uses the social media site Facebook and the mobile phone app Viber the most. She notes: "My high school friends and I have a chat group on Viber. Instead of using email, we use Viber, except there are those who still are not connected … There is always some useless clamor, we use it for everything, looking for help, prayer, suggestions where to buy something, etc. Anything, any topic, is discussed." On the other hand, Rose, who came to the United States as a graduate student, says: "The reason I opened the [Facebook] account in the first place was because of my friends in the Philippines. I use Facebook to keep up with people who I used to hang out with. I get to see milestones of friends like babies, marriages, work promotions." For both Sheila and Rose, asynchronous social media updates and synchronous chat messages make them feel that they are participating in the everyday lives of their friends despite the physical distance.

Larry, however, prefers using Facebook Messages to communicate with his cousin, who is running their old family ancestral home, which has since been turned into a bed and breakfast, saying: "I seldom use the phone. Facebook is easier." Criselda agrees: "Chatting through Facebook is so convenient. It's right there." For Cecille, the medium or app she uses depends on whom she is communicating with. She says: "Viber [group chat] is instant, and everybody gets to read it … the people who matter [read it]. Filipinos use the cellphone more … it's the easiest way to contact anyone in Manila." However, Cecille emphasizes that one-on-one voice conversations are more personal and thus uses a VoIP device, MagicJack, to communicate with her mother, despite the Viber group chat. She points out that "there is something about phone calls that make our conversation more focused, unlike when we are texting back-and-forth, sometimes I am doing other things at the same time." Similarly, Sheila keeps ties with her mother using older phone technology facilitated by new media technology. Her mother, who is in her eighties, doesn't use the internet or text messaging; thus, "My mom refuses to learn cellphone apps, doesn't want to text. She's more comfortable with the phone, so my cousin set up [the VoIP service] Ooma for her." Rose, on the other hand, has younger, technologically savvy parents, and thus uses mobile phone VoIP apps like Viber: "I'm in DC, my sister is in Toronto, so it's a good thing my parents know how to use smartphones." Ronna and Emma also have siblings in the Philippines who teach their parents to use Facetime or Skype.

As we have seen above, the respondents of this study credit new media and ICTs for making these relationships possible. However, instead of a technological determinist view, a polymedia perspective asserts that the choice of media technologies is very much tied to how interpersonal relationships are enacted and experienced (Madianou and Miller 2013). In other words, the kind of relationships and emotions being cultivated motivates the choice of a technology or app instead of the technology being the driver. For Sheila, Rose, and Larry, keeping tabs on friends' lives is important; thus, asynchronous social media sites such as

Facebook are useful. But as Sheila has pointed out, being part of a chat group on Viber keeps the connection frequent. Similarly, Rose keeps in touch with her closest girlfriends through group chats on Viber and Whatsapp. Cecille, who is a sporadic Facebook user, notes that it is much easier to contact friends and family through Viber's chat function because the act is similar to text messaging. In this case, Viber's use is facilitated by text messaging's ease and popularity as well as the ubiquity of mobile phones in the Philippines. However, for more intimate conversations with her mother, Cecille prefers to make voice calls, in which emotions can be conveyed through voice intonation. Thus, the choice of a particular medium is a social act, not simply because there is a proliferation of technologies but, rather, because of their affordances (Madianou and Miller 2013).

For Madianou and Miller (2013), three preconditions are necessary for polymedia to emerge: (1) access and availability, (2) affordability, and (3) media literacy. As illustrated above, overseas Filipinos are able to pick and choose among an array of media and communication technologies, both in the United States and in the Philippines. Cost is less of an issue and linked more to infrastructure (i.e. purchasing VoIP systems like MagicJack or Vonage) rather than each act of communication (i.e. the 60 cents a minute long-distance phone calls of the 1990s). As "elite" migrants, the respondents of this study have been able to furnish their family in the Philippines with the necessary technologies, as seen by Sheila's cousin setting up her mother's Ooma VoIP phone and Cecille paying for her mother's and her in-laws' MagicJack accounts, establishing "U.S. phone numbers" in the Philippines though VoIP systems. Both the overseas Filipino and the family back home can purchase smartphones that are used to access VoIP apps such as Viber or Whatsapp, as well as internet connections to Facebook, email, and other ways of communicating. The availability of media technologies gives users a diversity of choice and thus accommodates the varied preferences and levels of media literacy. As conditions of cost move to the background, and recognizing existing structures of capital, "both the choice and the legitimation of medium is transparently that of the user, and them alone, which means that they can be held responsible for choosing one medium as opposed to another" (Madianou and Miller 2012: 126).

A key aspect of polymedia is that the choice of which technology or app to use at a given time to deliver a certain message or engage in a specific communicative act is based on "how users exploit these affordances in order to manage their emotions and their relationships" (Madianou and Miller 2013: 172). For example, for her fiftieth birthday, Cecille's sister compiled a list of 50 things people liked about her as a PDF, and sent it as an email attachment. Similarly, when business matters regarding banking or property in the Philippines need to be discussed with her mother or siblings, Cecille says that email is the preferred medium, despite the daily text messaging through Viber or phone conversations through the MagicJack. Ronna points out that while texting through Viber is great and she uses it constantly, voice calls with aging parents are preferred, especially to check up on them and see how they are doing. She says: "[W]hen you hear their voices, you can really tell how they are." After a series of text messages over the family Viber chat group seemed to be resulting in misunderstandings, Rose shared, she eventually decided to call her siblings to ensure they were on the same page. Similarly, when her mother-in-law sent a present for their son, Rose and her husband said thank you via voice call instead of simply sending a text message, saying it was more appropriate and conveyed their gratitude more. While a message can be transmitted through a variety of media, overseas Filipinos "exploit the contrasts between media as an integrated environment in order to meet their relationship and emotional needs" (Madianou and Miller 2013: 128). Furthermore, the uses of these various media technologies become "embedded in everyday life and its domestic and urban environments ... permeating all the mundane activities" (Lister et al. 2003: 219–220). Filipino migrants no longer set aside a special time to call or write family in the homeland. Instead, keeping in touch with those far away is seamlessly woven into daily life via polymedia environments.

Polymedia and National Identity

Beyond the role of emotion and relationships in shaping the technologies used to connect overseas, we can also ask how technologies shape the emotional connection and relationship that immigrants possess with the homeland. Although migrants live in specific locales, they simultaneously live in national and transnational spaces where "traditional ideas of home, homeland, and nation have been destabilized, both by new patterns of physical mobility and migration and by new communication technologies" (Morley 2000: 3). Both the nation-state of origin and the nation-state of settlement require loyalty and commitment (Georgiou 2010), and polymedia provides the environment for migrants to navigate these spaces at the same time. What I found is that through their engagements with ICTs, elite Filipino migrants are able to demonstrate a continued, albeit somewhat ambiguous, allegiance to the homeland.

Coined by Anderson in 1992, "long-distance nationalism" describes the implications of continued allegiance to a country or place where one no longer lives, or in some cases, where one has never lived. It is often recognized as a form of nationalism in which migrants, after settling in their new country, "practice a kind of 'dream-politics' via long-distance participation such as funding and otherwise attempting to influence homeland politics" (Wong 2010: 8). Whether it is simply joining political parties in the homeland or monitoring homeland politics through media and internet, these acts of participation signal an effort toward maintaining a relationship with the homeland. Oftentimes, such nationalism is born from the migration experience of alienation, informed and shaped by life in the new place of settlement. Because migrants feel they do not fully belong in the new country and, thanks to new media technologies, the "mediated imagery of 'home' is always with them" (Anderson 1992: 8), they continue to identify with their nation of origin. At the same time, migrants are also influenced by the culture, values, and practices in the country of settlement, which, in turn, also shape how the homeland is imagined. Wong (2010) extends Anderson's concept, coining the term "cultural long-distance nationalism" to refer to "practices of culture in the diaspora that … derive their sense of legitimacy, their standard of authenticity, and often their content from the perceived source of culture" (9). These practices of culture can be shared by the community, such as celebrations of cultural holidays, or performed in daily practices, such as cooking food from the homeland or consuming diasporic media. The everyday, mundane practices that constantly and unconsciously define and confirm national identities cultivate what Billig (1995) calls "banal nationalism" (Beck 2003).

Just as early Filipino migrants consumed Philippine periodicals to keep up with events in the homeland, the internet and social media systems provide easy access to news from afar. Nelia points out that because she enjoys reading the news and learning about what is going on in the world, she "would have kept in touch with what's happening in the Philippines one way or another, but Facebook is more convenient." While she subscribes to several news sites and blogs on both the Philippines and the United States, Nelia values social networking sites such as Facebook because "it makes me more aware of what's going on in the Philippines in a more granular level compared to [simply reading] the news, [I get news] from the point of view of my friends, so I understand what's going on better." Thus, the commentary on Philippine news by trusted friends on social media sites helps her engagement in events and issues going on in the Philippines, putting a different value on Philippine news shared via Facebook compared with news read through online news sites and blogs.

When asked whether she used social media sites to post or share stories about the Philippines, Rose replied that she shares posts that place the Philippines in a positive light, such as "about lauding volunteers [during natural disasters], achievements of other people like the OFW who won a scholarship to NYU, the lady who won in *The Voice* in Israel. Things like that … individual achievements, group effort things …" Indeed, when events showcase the triumphs and achievements of Filipinos, particularly in the global sphere, overseas Filipinos turn to social media to join in celebrating Philippine pride. Posts and commentary from the diaspora during fights by renowned boxer Manny Pacquiao, performances by prominent singer and actress Lea Salonga, and Filipino Americans on shows like *The Voice* or *American Idol* are plentiful. A perusal of the Facebook timelines of my respondents also reveals postings on the Philippines of the past and recipes for Philippine food that express and elicit nostalgia for the homeland. Pride in the homeland and its cultural products demonstrates national identity that is "found in the embodied habits of social life" (Billig 1995: 8).

Associations with the homeland and nation of origin are also revealed during times of disaster, particularly during the catastrophic super-typhoons that have been plaguing the Philippines these past ten years. As Marie says, "[I share things about] catastrophes or natural disasters—to warn folks or remind them to keep safe." Similarly, Rose notes, "when disasters happen—updates on the areas that got struck, and ways you can help, how the government failed. How you can help from afar." In looking over Facebook timelines of the respondents of this study during times of natural disasters such as Super-typhoon Haiyan in 2013, postings on how to help or to inform others of what was going on were plentiful. Social media was utilized to mobilize Filipinos abroad to fundraise and send assistance to their countrymen. By tapping into the social media network of friends, whether Filipino or not, Filipino migrants organized fundraisers, collected goods to be shipped, and kept people informed. While Twitter was a good source of information and updates on disasters, Rose says, "through our [alumni association] Facebook page and our alumni listserv we were able to organize our group so that donations could be centralized." In addition, her husband sent an email to his office listserv to solicit donations, clearly identifying himself as Filipino. Here, we see that that using Facebook or listservs affords an avenue for fundraising and mobilizing disaster relief efforts, and thus factors into choosing which medium to use.

In contrast to the widespread interest in disasters, all respondents insisted that they do not use social media for political purposes. This is somewhat surprising, given that politics are a central way of maintaining ties to the Philippines. Sheila says: "I don't want to offend any of my political friends, so I don't post anything. Social media—it's social, it's not about putting my views. It's about keeping in touch with people." Emma echoes this sentiment: "No politics, social media is really more personal for me, not for conversation on politics or social issues, just personal." Ronna, on the other hand, notes: "I stay away from politics, but I read what other people post." Similarly, Rose says she doesn't share anything controversial or political. The semi-public nature of social networking sites such as Facebook and the varying levels of connections and relationships it affords factor into what is shared and posted by users. Rose notes that she texts messages or forwards interesting or controversial topics through a private message to friends who share the same political views.

Despite their avoidance of publicly engaging in political issues, both Ronna and Rose changed their profile pictures to the rainbow when the U.S. Supreme Court declared same-sex marriage as a constitutional right in June 2015. The legalization of same-sex marriage in the United States was widely covered and discussed in the Philippine (traditional and social) media, despite the Philippines being a largely Catholic country where marriage is defined by the constitution as a union of a man and a woman, and divorce (and the dissolution of marriage) does not exist. Thus, while the proliferation of rainbow profile photos on Facebook can be read as a depoliticized act, for migrant Filipinos, it can also be read as taking a stand against the dominance of traditional Catholic beliefs in the Philippines and influenced by more secular living in America. In doing so, posters risked ridicule, chastisements, and admonishment from friends and family in the homeland. They can be judged as becoming "more" American and "less" Filipino. Conversely, the act of activating the rainbow filter in solidarity with millions worldwide can be read as a political act with less risk versus posting a status update or forwarding an article or essay in celebration of same-sex marriage. Thus, we see the emotional consequences of the choice of which aspects of a medium or app to make in polymedia environments.

When asked about sharing political content on Facebook, Rose observes: "It seems my *Pinoy* (Filipino) friends here [in the United States] always post something negative about the Philippine government and compare to the way they live here; even though they don't post stuff on American politics." Critiques of the Philippine government are thus measured against the experience of a "better" life in the United States. While there is a longing for and continuous attachment to the homeland, it is also judged vis-à-vis life in the place of settlement. Ronna, while saying she stays away from politics, says:

> I support certain things like I don't like Binay to be president [referring to the vice-president whose family is being investigated for corruption, and a onetime front runner in the 2016 presidential elections], the 44 soldiers who were killed [in a botched anti-terrorism raid], and Amal Clooney saying the Philippines needs to apologize to GMA [referring to the previous president, Gloria Macapagal Arroyo, who was detained at a government hospital for committing plunder], seriously?

Both Rose and Sheila note that while they don't post political content on their Facebook timelines, they do read the posts of their friends and contacts, saying that it is a way to keep tabs on Philippine politics, affirming Ong and Cabañes' (2011) findings, that while they are engaged in the political goings-on in the Philippines, elite migrants are not immersed. They may "like" a post or make a comment, but don't share the articles on their own timelines. Emma agrees: "I read it [political posts] if it catches my eye." Here, we see how expressions of personal views on politics in public or semi-public spaces (i.e. Facebook) are enacted in ways that protect social relationships and reputations (Miller et al. 2016).

However, Ronna points out, "Philippine elections are coming up. I'll probably be more active." Indeed, in the months immediately preceding the May 2016 presidential elections, there was an increase in Facebook commentary regarding politics, including from those who said they didn't engage in it on social media. Rose, for example, posted a photograph of her overseas ballot on Facebook, exclaiming how she knew very little about the senatorial candidates. Marie shared photographs of family members campaigning in the Philippines and publicly declared her support for certain candidates on social media sites. Similarly, Nelia wrote a strong post on Facebook proclaiming her support for a specific presidential candidate, whom many found despicable, challenging others to contradict her. For Rose and Cecille, however, more substantial conversations about Philippine elections were conducted through voice calls or text messages with family members; they preferred to engage with the issues in private rather than on social media sites. Rose points out: "I don't want to get into arguments on social media. It's bad enough that my family was disagreeing," emphasizing the emotional consequences of choosing one medium over another. Clearly, it is evident that the ways social media are used during politically charged moments and places differ from the "ordinary" day-to-day lives of people (Miller et al. 2016). Once the Philippine elections were over and the winners declared, visible political engagement on social media ceased.

This ability to make comments, criticize the Philippines, and keep up to date reveals a "politics without accountability" (Anderson 1992: 12). It is a "safe" kind of nationalism whereby political participation occurs from a position "in which he does not intend to live, where he pays no taxes, where he cannot be arrested, where he will not be brought before the courts—and where he does not vote" (Anderson 1992: 11). Although the Philippines allows dual citizenship and overseas absentee voting, for elite overseas Filipinos, the outcomes have little bearing on their lives in their nation of settlement. Elite migrants do not have to live with the consequences of their political engagement. However, these links to the Philippines reveal that a form of nationalism or identification with the nation of origin based on political commitment continues to exist due to the continued growth in numbers of immigrants and the increased capacity for instantaneous communication (Eriksen 2014). While overseas Filipinos' engagement with politics in the homeland barely has any impact on their daily lives, a kind of Filipino-ness is enacted, strengthening ties to the Philippines, as well as maintaining their identity as Filipino or Filipino American. Regardless of place of birth, citizenship, dual citizenship, or visa status, a kind of belonging and identification with the Philippines is demonstrated through and facilitated by polymedia environments.

Conclusion

Without doubt, new media and ICTs have facilitated transnational ties to the homeland for Filipino migrants. Relationships with family, friends, and the nation of origin are maintained through an array of media technologies. Although they may remain far away, Filipino migrants are able to enrich familial relationships, rekindle old friendships, and keep abreast of what is going on in the Philippines through the internet, mobile phones and text messaging, and VoIP applications and devices such as Viber and MagicJack. Such technologies have, indeed, made physical presence less necessary for keeping these transnational ties.

Although migrant Filipinos credit the developments in new media technologies for allowing these relationships to flourish, this study pushes us to examine their use with regard to environment and circumstances. Analyzing new media use of overseas Filipinos via polymedia, we are able to better understand the interplay between new media platforms and the messages and emotions being conveyed. The presence of reasonably priced and easily accessible media technologies means that instantaneous communication across time and space is no longer a luxury, but an everyday routine that migrants engage in. Because cost and accessibility are not issues for these elite migrants, the choice of a specific medium is dependent on the needs and goals of the communicative act. Overseas Filipinos choose a specific medium based on social and emotional consequences. Thus, we see here a reclaiming of control over technology, because users have alternatives, albeit in the shadow of capital that provides these choices.

Similarly, in maintaining ties with the homeland, the media Filipino migrants choose is tied to the degree to which they want to express identification, affinity, and loyalty to the Philippines. This continued allegiance is influenced by both the sense of alienation and the experience of a "better" life that migrants perceive in the United States. Although somewhat weak and ambiguous, a kind of nationalism and loyalty to the nation of origin are being enacted through new media technologies and platforms. Glick Schiller (2005) carefully reminds us that, as with any form of nationalism, "identification with a homeland is polysemous, carrying simultaneously multiple and conflicting meanings" (579). Such polysemous identifications are manifested in the different media used by migrants to demonstrate their affiliation with the nation of origin. Indeed, it is a "safe" nationalism with little risk. But it nonetheless reveals an attachment to the homeland, whether through keeping abreast of what is going on, or mobilizing identification with the Philippines during times of crisis (i.e. natural disasters), or pride (i.e. Manny Pacquiao fights). For elite transnational Filipino migrants, negotiating the contradictory processes of connection with and separation from distant others and the homeland is made possible through the affordances of polymedia environments.

Acknowledgments

I would like to thank Fan Yang, Michael Lecker, and Jason Cabañes for conversations, feedback, and support. An earlier version of this chapter was presented at the Cultural Studies Association conference in 2015 thanks to travel funds from CSUSM's Faculty Center Professional Development Grant.

Note

1 Although the Philippines does not rank its universities, the University of the Philippines, the Ateneo de Manila University, and De La Salle University are considered to be the top universities in the Philippines and are regularly listed in international rankings. They are arguably the most difficult to get into, and in addition to educating some of the brightest minds in the nation, they also educate the elite. Their alumni associations in the Metropolitan Washington DC area are robust and active with large memberships. The names of the interviewees have been changed to protect their privacy.

References

Anderson, Benedict. 1992. *Long-Distance Nationalism: World Capitalism and the Rise of Identity Politics.* Amsterdam: Center for Asian Studies.

Beck, Ulrich. 2003. "Rooted Cosmopolitanism: Emerging from a Rivalry of Distinctions." In *Global America? The Cultural Consequences of Globalization*, Ulrich Beck, Natan Sznaider, and Rainer Winter (eds), 15–29. Liverpool: Liverpool University Press.

Beck, Ulrich, Natan Sznaider, and Rainer Winter (eds). 2003. *Global America? The Cultural Consequences of Globalization.* Liverpool: Liverpool University Press.

Billig, Michael. 1995. *Banal Nationalism.* London: Routledge.

Cabañes, Jason V. and Kristel Acedera. 2012. "Of Mobile Phones and Mother-Fathers: Calls, Text Messages, and Conjugal Power Relations in Mother-Away Filipino Families." *New Media & Society* 14(6): 916–930.

Commission on Filipinos Overseas. 2014. *CFO Primer: Responding to the Challenges of Migration and Development.* Manila, Philippines: Commission on Filipinos Overseas.

Eriksen, Thomas H. 2014. *Globalization: The Key Concepts.* 2nd ed. London: Bloomsbury.

Espiritu, Yen Le. 2003. *Homebound: Filipino American Lives across Cultures, Communities, and Countries.* Oakland, CA: University of California Press.

Georgiou, Myria. 2010. "Identity, Space and the Media: Thinking through Diaspora." *Revue Européenne des Migrations Internationals* 26(1): 17–35.

Glick Schiller, Nina. 2005. "Long Distance Nationalism." In *Encyclopedia of Diasporas: Immigrant and Refugee Cultures Around The World Volume I.* Skoggard (eds), 570–580. NY: Springer.

Held, David. 2002. "Culture and Political Community: National, Global, and Cosmopolitan." In S. Vertovec and R. Cohen (eds), 48–58, *Conceiving Cosmopolitanism: Theory, Context, and Practice.* Oxford: Oxford University Press.

Hoeffel, Elizabeth S. Rastogi, Myoung O. Kim, and Hasan Shahid. 2012. *The Asian Population. 2010 Census Briefs.* Washington, DC: United States Census Bureau.

Licoppe, Christian. 2004. "'Connected' Presence: The Emergence of a New Repertoire for Managing Social Relationships in a Changing Communication Technoscape." *Environment and Planning D: Society and Space* 22(1): 135–156.

Lister, Martin, Jon Dovey, Seth Giddings, Iain Grant, and Kieran Kelly. 2003. *New Media: A Critical Introduction.* London and New York: Routledge.

Lowe, Lisa. 1996. *Immigrant Acts: On Asian American Cultural Politics*. Durham, NC: Duke University Press.

Madianou, Mirca. 2016. "Ambient Co-Presence: Transnational Family Practices in Polymedia Environments." *Global Networks*, 4 January. http://onlinelibrary.wiley.com/doi/10.1111/glob.12105/epdf, doi:10.1111/glob.12105.

Madianou, Mirca and Daniel Miller. 2011. "Mobile Phone Parenting: Reconfiguring Relationships between Filipina Migrant Mothers and Their Left-Behind Children." *New Media & Society* 13(3): 457–470.

Madianou, Mirca and Daniel Miller. 2012. *Migration and New Media: Transnational Families and Polymedia*. London and NY: Routledge.

Madianou, Mirca and Daniel Miller. 2013. "Polymedia: Towards a New Theory of Digital Media in Interpersonal Communication." *International Journal of Cultural Studies* 16(2): 169–187.

Miller, Daniel, Elisabeth Costa, Nell Haynes, Tom McDonald, Razvan Nicolescu, Jolynna Sinanan, Juliano Spyer, Shriram Venkatraman, and Xinyuan Wang. 2016. *How the World Changed Social Media*. London: UCL Press.

Moores, Shaun. 2000. *Media and Everyday Life in Modern Society*. Edinburgh: Edinburgh University Press.

Morley, David. 2000. *Home Territories: Media, Mobility, and Identity*. London and New York: Routledge.

Nader, Laura. 1972. "Up the Anthropologist: Perspectives Gained from Studying Up." In *Reinventing Anthropology*, D. Hymes (ed.), 284–311. New York: Pantheon.

Ong, Jonathan and Jason Cabañes. 2011. "Engaged, But Not Immersed: Tracking the Mediated Public Connection of Filipino Elite Migrants in London." *South East Asia Research* 19(2): 197–224.

Paragas, Fernando. 2005. "Migrant Mobiles: Cellular Telephony, Transnational Spaces, and the Filipino Diaspora." In The Global *and the Local in Mobile Communication: Places*, Images, *People, Connections*, N. Kristof (ed), 241–250. Vienna: Passagen-Verlag.

Parreñas, Rhacel S. 2005. *Children of Global Migration: Transnational Families and Gendered Woes*. Stanford: Stanford University Press.

Rafael, Vicente. 1990. "Nationalism, Imagery, and the Filipino Intelligentsia in the Nineteenth Century." *Critical Inquiry* 16(3): 591–611.

Soriano, Cheryll R. R., Sun Sun Lim, and Milagros Rivera-Sanchez. 2015. "The Virgin Mary With a Mobile Phone: Ideologies of Mothering and Technology Consumption in Philippine Television Advertisements." *Communication, Culture & Critique* 8: 1–19.

Uy-Tioco, Cecilia S. 2007. "Overseas Filipino Workers and Text Messaging: Reinventing Transnational Mothering." *Continuum: Journal of Media and Cultural Studies* 21(2): 253–265.

Vertovec, Steven and Robin Cohen (eds). 2002. *Conceiving Cosmopolitanism: Theory, Context, and Practice*. Oxford: Oxford University Press.

Williams, Raymond. 1974. *Television: Technology and Cultural Form*, reprinted 1992. Hanover, NH: Wesleyan University Press.

Wong, Sau-Ling C. 2010. "Dancing in the Diaspora: Cultural Long-Distance Nationalism and the Staging of Chineseness by San Francisco's Chinese Folk Dance Association." *Journal of Transnational American Studies* 2(1): 1–35.

World Bank. 2015. *Open Data*. Washington, DC: World Bank. http://data.worldbank.org.

INDEX